D0996749

THE EAGLE Handbook of BIBLE PRAYERS

THE EAGLE Handbook of BIBLE PRAYERS

compiled by

MARTIN MANSER

and

MIKE BEAUMONT

Eagle Publishing
Trowbridge, Wiltshire

To Rosalind and Liz

British Library Cataloguing in Publication Data. A catalogue record for this book is available from the British Library.

Published by Eagle Publishing Ltd, 6 Kestrel House, Mill Street, Trowbridge BA14 8BE.

Designed and typeset by Eagle Publishing/David McLean

Printed by CPD, Wales (Ebbw Vale)

ISBN 0 86347 442 X

Contents

Introduction

Can you remember your first prayer? Or when you prayed it? Perhaps it was a rhyme you learned as a child, or a cry of desperation in some crisis, or a whispered 'Yes!' before some wonder of creation, or a yearning cry beside a dying loved one. Perhaps you were young, or perhaps you were not so young. Perhaps it sprang spontaneously from your heart, or perhaps it was a duty to be done in school assembly or on army parade.

Mike still remembers his first ever prayer. It was taught to him while very young by his parents – good people, but lapsed churchgoers at the time – and it went like this:

Matthew, Mark, Luke and John,
Bless the bed that I lay on;
If I should die before I wake,
I pray the Lord my soul to take.

Hardly the most optimistic of prayers for a child, in hindsight! But nevertheless, it was heartfelt at the time.

Martin's first prayer was:

God bless Mummy and Daddy,
God bless Roger and Paul,
God bless the twins,
Make me a good boy,
Thank you for a nice day.
Amen

This prayer for Martin and his family (including his twin sister Rosalind) was also sincerely prayed in his early years.

Of course, we all grow up; and as many of us grow up, we often grow out of those first prayers. We become more 'mature', more 'thoughtful' about life, more 'open' to other ideas, more 'independent' in our thinking. Or, to put it another way, we drift from the God who made us; whereas prayer is about *knowing* the God who made us.

It is about conversation with him – on the way to work or at the kitchen sink – not some formulae reserved for a 'religious' setting. It is about telling God when we are grateful, and complaining to him when we are mad. It is about finding his rest in the midst of busyness, his peace in the midst of turmoil, his answers in the midst of questions, his comfort in the midst of darkness. It is about letting the living God be our friend. Prayer is about developing a relationship, not about drowning in religion.

But is it that easy? Well, to be honest, not always! If you have tried praying, then you will probably have asked questions like:

- If God is all-powerful, why do I need to pray anyway? What difference does it make?
- If God is all-loving, why should I need to ask him for things?
- If God is all-knowing, why do I need to tell him my needs?
- If God is all-hearing, why do my prayers feel like they hit the ceiling and bounce back empty?
- If God is all-caring, why doesn't he do something?
- If God is all-seeing, why didn't he warn me?

Ever asked questions like those? If so, this book is for you! Because this book is based on the book that asks – and answers – those sort of questions: the Bible. The Bible tells us what prayer is – and what prayer isn't. It tells us it *isn't* a sort of 'magic' to be used to force the divine arm up the divine back so we can get our own way; nor is it some sort of mystical exercise to make us feel 'relaxed' or somehow 'better'. The Bible tells us that prayer is friendship with God. And the Bible is full of ordinary people like you and us who learned how to become friends with God and how to share every part of their lives with him in prayer.

The Eagle Handbook of Bible Prayers is divided into six parts. We have used modern phrases rather than 'classic' prayer language for their titles, for we believe that prayer is for today, not just for yesterday. Like all good prayer, we start with God, and in particular with the way God tells us we can know him; so in Part One we look at prayers that say 'Father'. The more we get to know God as Father, the more we want to respond to him; so in Part Two we look at prayers that say 'Amazing!' (prayers of 'worship' for who God is) and in Part Three prayers that say 'Thanks!' (prayers of 'thanksgiving' for what God has done). The more we look at God, the more we become aware, inevitably, of our own shortcomings, so in Part Four we look at prayers that say 'Sorry!' ('confession'). There are often times when we simply don't understand what is going on in life or why God is, or isn't, answering prayer in a particular way; so in Part Five we explore prayers that ask 'Why?' Finally, the Bible encourages us to bring all our needs and circumstances before God, so in Part Six we examine prayers that say 'Please' ('supplication' and 'intercession', for ourselves and others).

As in the companion volume, *The Eagle Handbook of Bible Promises*, each section begins with a key thought and a key Bible verse to set the scene. The main study material is built around various passages and quotations from the Bible that deal with prayer or that are themselves prayers. The section then concludes with a prayer drawn from church liturgy or church history and a final Bible quotation and conclusion to help us retain the main emphases. In each section, we try to look for the relevance of the prayers for today.

A recent opinion poll on religious attitudes in Great Britain said that 62% of people still believe in God, 69% believe we have a soul, 79% believe a religious ceremony should be held at death and 35% pray frequently. What this says to us is that people still have a profound longing in their hearts to find their true self and to find the living God, though most do not know how to do so.

Even many Christians struggle in how to talk to their Father God naturally and easily in prayer. It is our hope that, in some small way, this book may help you, wherever you are in your journey, and that you may be spurred on even more in your praying to the living God, as you are encouraged by the successes – and the failures! – of those in the Bible who went before you.

Martin Manser, Mike Beaumont

Part One

Prayers that say 'Father'

Chapter One

'Teach us to pray . . .'

> The almighty God who created everything does not stand aloof and far off from us. He wants us to know him as Father, and through Jesus his Son we can learn how to relate to him.
>
> ***'Our Father in heaven . . .'***
> (Matthew 6:9)

When Mike was a Religious Studies' teacher, he taught a course called 'Looking for God'. He introduced it by saying, 'I want you to imagine that there is a God – whether you think there is or not doesn't matter for the moment. But if there were a God, what do you think he would be like?' He gave the pupils several minutes to write down their thoughts and then invited feedback. The amazing thing was this: what they felt God would or should be like was exactly what Jesus said he was like!

God would be loving, caring, honest, fair, a good friend, went the answers; he would 'stand up' for his kids and they would have fun together. But the answer that came up again and again – perhaps surprisingly in days of so many broken families – was that he would be like a perfect father. They couldn't have written Jesus' message better if they had tried!

All true prayer, Jesus said, starts with knowing God as your *Father*. Without this, prayer will be little more than a religious duty, a calming exercise, or an attempt to manipulate God in time of need. But with this, prayer is transformed into an exciting relationship and adventure.

'Teach us to pray . . .'

We are often encouraged by Jesus' disciples – especially by their mistakes and slowness to grasp things! And we can certainly identify with how they felt when they came to Jesus one day, having seen him earnestly praying, and said to him, '*Lord, teach us to pray, just as John taught his disciples*' (Luke 11:1). It wasn't that they hadn't prayed before or didn't know how to; as Jews they would often have prayed – before meals, in the synagogue, and at great festivals. But Jesus had a completely different way of praying. He made it look so easy, so desirable, so enjoyable!

And they wanted more of that for themselves.

Jesus' response has become one of the most famous prayers in history, commonly called The Lord's Prayer; and this is where our book on prayer begins.

The Lord's Prayer is found twice in the New Testament – in Matthew and Luke – in slightly different forms, perhaps reflecting different occasions when Jesus taught it. Matthew presents it as a model to be followed. ('*This, then, is* **how** *you should pray*', Matthew 6:9), whereas Luke presents it as more of a prayer to be repeated. (*He said to them, 'When you pray,* **say** . . .', Luke 11:2). If we do use it as a prayer in its own right, individually or with others, we need to take care that we do not recite it in such a way, or at such a speed, that it becomes little more than a 'mantra', especially since Jesus teaches it in the context of not falling into mindless repetition of prayers (Matthew 6:5–8)!

Matthew's version

Our Father in heaven,
hallowed be your name,
your kingdom come,
your will be done
on earth as it is in heaven.
Give us today our daily bread.
Forgive us our debts,
as we also have forgiven our debtors.
And lead us not into temptation,
but deliver us from the evil one.

(Matthew 6:9–13)

Luke's version

Father,
hallowed be your name,
your kingdom come.
Give us each day our daily bread.
Forgive us our sins,
for we also forgive everyone who sins against us.
And lead us not into temptation.

(Luke 11:2–4)

Other translations of The Lord's Prayer

Here are some other translations of the Lord's Prayer from Matthew's Gospel – ranging from the King James Version, with its traditional poetic language, to more modern translations.

Our Father which art in heaven,
Hallowed be thy name.
Thy kingdom come.
Thy will be done in earth, as it is in heaven.
Give us this day our daily bread.
And forgive us our debts, as we forgive our debtors.
And lead us not into temptation, but deliver us from evil:
For thine is the kingdom, and the power, and the glory, for ever. Amen. (KJV)

Our Father in heaven,
help us to honour your name.
Come and set up your kingdom,
So that everyone on earth will obey you,
As you are obeyed in heaven.
Give us our food for today.
Forgive us for doing wrong,
As we forgive others.
Keep us from being tempted
And protect us from evil. (CEV)

Our Father in heaven,
may your name always be kept holy.
May your kingdom come
and what you want to be done,
here on earth as it is in heaven.
Give us the food we need for each day.
Forgive us for our sins,
just as we have forgiven those who sinned against us.
And do not cause us to be tempted,
but save us from the Evil One. (NCV)

Perhaps you are wondering where the traditional ending is that is found in the Authorized Version (KJV) and in many church prayer books: '*For thine is the kingdom, and the power and the glory, for ever. Amen!*' (Matthew 6:13, KJV). These words are not found in the oldest Greek texts and were almost certainly added later in church history as an ending suitable for formal liturgical settings. Hence most modern Bible translations do not include them.

What our Father wants to hear

In the Lord's Prayer Jesus provides us with an insight into what his Father wants us to talk to him about. Clearly, then, this is an important place for us to begin. So, what does the prayer include?

Prayer about God

The first half of the prayer focuses on God. This is not because God is some kind of divine megalomaniac who constantly needs us telling him how great he is! Rather it is because when we remember what God is like, other things start to take on their proper perspective again.

Many prayers in the Bible begin by focusing on God before bringing needs to him:

And Hezekiah prayed to the LORD: 'O LORD, God of Israel, enthroned between the cherubim, you alone are God over all the kingdoms of the earth. You have made heaven and earth. Give ear, O LORD, and hear; open your eyes, O LORD, and see . . .'

(2 Kings 19:15–16)

[Solomon] said: 'O LORD, God of Israel, there is no God like you in heaven or on earth – you who keep your covenant of love with your servants who continue wholeheartedly in your way. You have kept your promise to your servant David my father; with your mouth you have promised and with your hand you have fulfilled it – as it is today. Now LORD, God of Israel . . .'

(2 Chronicles 6:14–16)

See also Exodus 15:1–18; Deuteronomy 32:1–4; 2 Samuel 7:18–26; 1 Kings 3:6–9; 18:36–37; 2 Chronicles 20:5–12; Nehemiah 1:5–11; Jeremiah 32:17–25; Daniel 9:4–19; Acts 4:24–31

In the Lord's Prayer, Jesus encourages us to pray about three things as we think about God:

The honouring of God's name

Our Father in heaven, hallowed be your name . . . (Matthew 6:9)

In Bible times, a name was not just how you distinguished a person from someone else; their name summed up their character or calling (e.g. Genesis 17:5; 21:2–6; 2 Samuel 12:24–25; Isaiah 8:3–4; Matthew 1:21; John 1:42). Likewise, God's name tells us about who he is: he is first and foremost, Jesus says, a Father (see Part One, Chapter 2). When you come to him, start off with that thought!

He will call out to me, 'You are my Father,
my God, the Rock my Saviour'.

(Psalm 89:26)

Praise be to the God and Father of our Lord Jesus Christ, the Father of compassion and the God of all comfort, who comforts us in all our troubles, so that we can comfort those in any trouble with the comfort we ourselves have received from God..

(2 Corinthians 1:3–4)

See also Malachi 2:10; Luke 10:21; John 17:1–5; Ephesians 1:3, 17; 3:14–15; 5:18–20

The coming of God's kingdom

. . . your kingdom come . . . (Matthew 6:10)

When we use the word 'kingdom' we

think of 'a place' (like the 'United Kingdom'); but the Hebrew and Greek words for 'kingdom' carry the sense of 'rule' or 'government'. 'The kingdom of God' was the burden of Jesus' message (e.g. Matthew 4:23; Mark 1:14–15), and he tells us here to pray for more of that kingly rule to come. Why? Because when it does, things change for the better! Isaiah, looking ahead to the Messiah's coming, spoke of 'the increase of his government *and* peace' (Isaiah 9:7). In other words, the more we let God's kingly rule (his government) come, the more peace there will be around.

We can pray for more of that kingly rule, and its consequent blessing and 'peace', to come into:

- our own life and needs
- our family and friends
- our church and leaders
- our work and workplace
- our society and nation
- our world and events

Therefore, since we are receiving a kingdom that cannot be shaken, let us be thankful, and so worship God acceptably with reverence and awe, for our 'God is a consuming fire'. (Hebrews 12:28–29)

See also Isaiah 32:1–8; Daniel 2:44; 7:13–14; Romans 14:17; 1 Corinthians 4:20; Revelation 12:10–12

The doing of God's will

. . . your will be done . . . (Matthew 6:10). This is not the 'resigned submission' to the Allah of Islam – whatever God wills, happens, and all I can do is to receive it, for good or for bad – though, sadly, this is the view of prayer that some Christians fall into. Nor is it an 'escape route' for avoiding prayer in challenging circumstances. The Bible sees prayer as some-thing far more interactive and dynamic than that.

Jesus is encouraging us here, out of a growing trust and confidence in our Father God, to pray for his will to be implemented on earth, despite all obstacles and opposition, and to learn how to yield to God's will ourselves as he shares his heart with us as we pray:

Going a little farther, he fell with his face to the ground and prayed, 'My Father, if it is possible, may this cup be taken from me. Yet not as I will, but as you will.' . . . He went away a second time and prayed, 'My Father, if it is not possible for this cup to be taken away unless I drink it, may your will be done'.

(Matthew 26:39, 42)

For this reason, since the day we heard about you, we have not stopped praying for you and asking God to fill you with the knowledge of his will through all spiritual wisdom and understanding.

(Colossians 1:9)

See also Matthew 12:49–50; Acts 21:13–14; Romans 1:9–10; 8:27; 12:2; 15:31–32; Hebrews 5:7–8; 10:9

Jesus then adds a phrase: ' . . . *on earth as it is in heaven'.* These words probably govern all three prayers already prayed: *may your name be hallowed on earth as it is in heaven; may your kingly rule come on earth as it is in heaven; may your will be done on earth as it is in heaven.* And how are these things done in heaven? Joyfully! Instantly! Powerfully! Focus on some of these things when you talk to God in prayer, Jesus says, and your perspective will change unbelievably!

Prayer about us

Once we have focused on God to get our perspective right, we can turn to our own needs, confident that our Father wants to hear about them and to answer us.

Prayer for present need

Give us today our daily bread (Matthew 6:11)

Bread is the most basic need for daily living. Jesus is saying that our relationship with the living God can be such that even the most basic needs of daily life can be brought before him.

Two things I ask of you, O LORD;
do not refuse me before I die:
Keep falsehood and lies far from me;
give me neither poverty nor riches,
but give me only my daily bread.

Otherwise, I may have too much and disown you
and say, 'Who is the LORD?'
Or I may become poor and steal,
and so dishonour the name of my God.

(Proverbs 30:7–9)

Do not be anxious about anything, but in everything, by prayer and petition, with thanksgiving, present your requests to God.

(Philippians 4:6)

See also Matthew 6:25–34; 7:9–11; John 16:23–24; Ephesians 6:18; Hebrews 5:7; James 5:13–16

Prayer for past sin

'Forgive us our debts, as we also have forgiven our debtors' (Matthew 6:12)

It is astonishing that this comes almost at the end! When we come to pray, we so often feel we need to tell God all our sins and shortcomings first, for how can he listen to us otherwise? (Ever felt like that yourself?) Jesus teaches here that there is a very real place for 'coming clean' and confessing the wrong that we have thought, said, or done (see Part Four); but we don't start there! Start with God, Jesus says! Once you've seen how big and gracious he is, then you'll know that he wants to forgive you!

Then David said to Nathan, 'I have sinned against the LORD.' Nathan replied, 'The LORD has taken away your sin. You are not going to die.'

(2 Samuel 12:13)

If we say that we have not sinned, we are fooling ourselves, and the truth isn't in our hearts. But if we confess our sins to God, he can always be trusted to forgive us and take our sins away.

(1 John 1:8–9, CEV)

See also Psalm 41:4; Matthew 6:14–15; 18:23–35; Mark 11:25: Luke 15:11–32; 23:34; Colossians 3:13

Prayer for future welfare

'And lead us not into temptation, but deliver us from the evil one' (Matthew 6:13).

This sinful world can be a dangerous place! Accidents, sickness, unforeseen events, natural disasters – let alone the more direct attacks of the devil. So, pray for protection, Jesus says. (See Part Five for more on 'Spiritual warfare'.) God is your Father, and he wants to keep a 'fatherly eye' upon you.

'Simon, Simon, Satan has asked to sift you as wheat. But I [Jesus] have prayed for you, Simon, that your faith may not fail.'

(Luke 22:31)

'Holy Father, protect them by the power of your name – the name you gave me – so that they may be one as we are one . . . My prayer is not that you take them out of the world but that you protect them from the evil one."

(John 17:11, 15)

See also Psalm 35:10; 2 Corinthians 1:10–11; Ephesians 6:10–18; 1 Peter 5:8–9; Jude 24–25; Revelation 3:10

Too busy for relationship?

The essence of the Lord's Prayer is *relationship* rather than *religion*: it is coming to Almighty God who wants to be known as Father. The trouble is, 'relationship' is increasingly 'going by the board' in our busy world. Some are just 'too busy' in their workplace, too goal-orientated, to be bothered with people and relationships. That takes time – and time is money! Others are just too afraid of relationships or fatherhood, perhaps because of how it has been abused in their life.

But the Lord's Prayer is thoroughly relational from start to finish. It is prayer – honest, heart-to-heart sharing – between children and their father – and a perfect, heavenly Father at that, who knows no limits and who would never abuse us or trick us (e.g. Matthew 7:9–11).

If we are to discover prayer as 'happy company with God' (as Clement of Alexandria described it), then we need to learn how to develop the relationship; and that means learning how to slow down and stop, how to 'close the door' to the busyness all around us:

But when you pray, go into your room, close the door and pray to your Father, who is unseen.

(Matthew 6:6)

See also Psalm 46:10; 2 Kings 4:32–33; Job 37:14

The story of Martha and Mary brings home an important insight into this for busy people.

As Jesus and his disciples were on their way, he came to a village where a woman named Martha opened her home to him. She had a sister called Mary, who sat at the Lord's feet listening to what he said. But Martha was distracted by all the preparations that had to be made. She came to him and asked, 'Lord, don't you care that my sister has left me to do the work by myself? Tell her to help me.'

'Martha, Martha,' the Lord answered, 'you are worried and upset about many things, but only one thing is needed. Mary has chosen what is better, and it will not be taken away from her.'

(Luke 10:38–42)

Relationship takes time, and that means learning how to stop. As we stop (even for a few moments in the midst of a busy day), we are giving God an opportunity to refocus our hearts on him as our Father who cares and provides.

A FINAL PRAYER

O thou by whom we come to God,
The Life, the Truth, the Way!
The path of prayer
thyself hast trod;
Lord, teach us how to pray!

James Montgomery (1771–1854)

CONCLUSION

Prayer is about relationship with God; and, like all relationships, it can grow.

You have said, 'I know you by name and you have found favour with me.' If you are pleased with me, teach me your ways so I may know you and continue to find favour with you.

(Exodus 33:12–13)

Relevance for today

God wants relationship, not religion

For I desire mercy, not sacrifice, and acknowledgment of God rather than burnt offerings.

(Hosea 6:6)

'Jerusalem, Jerusalem, you who kill the prophets and stone those sent to you, how often I have longed to gather your children together, as a hen gathers her chicks under her wings, but you were not willing.'

(Matthew 23:37)

God still wants to be known as 'Father'

Do I see God as 'out there'? Or do I know him 'down here', as my loving Father?

'I thought you would call me "Father"
and not turn away from following me.'

(Jeremiah 3:19)

Praise be to the God and Father of our Lord Jesus Christ, who has blessed us in the heavenly realms with every spiritual blessing in Christ.

(Ephesians 1:3)

God wants us to grow in prayer

We can still say, 'Lord, teach us to pray" (Luke 11:1).

So one of the priests who had been exiled from Samaria came to live in Bethel and taught them how to worship the LORD.

(2 Kings 17:28)

Busy people need to slow down!

Am I like Mary who '*sat at the Lord's feet listening to what [Jesus] said'* or Martha who was '*distracted by all the preparations that had to be made*' (Luke 10:39–40)? What is the 'one thing' (v 42) that governs my life?

My heart is not proud, O LORD,
my eyes are not haughty;
I do not concern myself with great matters
or things too wonderful for me.
But I have stilled and quietened my soul;
like a weaned child with its mother,
like a weaned child is my soul within me.

(Psalm 131:1–2)

Chapter Two

I Can Call Him Father!

In contrast to the fatherlessness that is so characteristic of modern life, Jesus tells us that God is not only *his* Father, but that he can be *our* Father too!

For you did not receive a spirit that makes you a slave again to fear, but you received the Spirit of sonship. And by him we cry, 'Abba, Father.' (Romans 8:15)

Across the world, millions of children are growing up without fathers. Some have lost their fathers through war, or through AIDS, or through a broken marriage. Others have their fathers in the house, but not in the home. Their fathers leave for work early and come home late, wearied at the end of the day; and so their children get little of their time – or at least, little quality time. Other fathers were themselves not fathered properly and so have little concept of fathering their own children.

In such a world of 'fatherlessness', Jesus' message that there is a God we can know and talk to as 'Father' comes as a breath of fresh air.

Just a big picture of us?

But is seeing God as 'Father' simply a 'human projection' (our making God in our own image) or a 'personification' (our likening God to a human father)? Not at all, the Bible says; in fact, it is the other way round! The human race has fatherhood because God himself is a father. One of Paul's prayers sums it up like this:

For this reason I kneel before the Father, from whom his whole family in heaven and on earth derives its name. I pray that out of his glorious riches he may strengthen you with power through his Spirit in your inner being, so that Christ may dwell in your hearts through faith. And I pray that you, being rooted and established in love, may have power, together with all the saints, to grasp how wide and long and high and deep is the love of Christ, and to know this love that surpasses knowledge – that you may be filled to the measure of all the fullness of God.

(Ephesians 3:14–19)

This is a big prayer! But it came out of a conviction that he could ask such things because God really was his Father and theirs too. There is, in fact, a play on words in the Greek of verses 14 and 15. The word for Father is '*pater*' and the word for family is '*patria*'. Paul's argument is that '*patria*' flows out of a '*pater*', not the other way round. If there is no *pater* (father) there can be no *patria* (family); if there is no 'Fatherhood' in God, there would never have been fatherhood (and family) in human society.

This understanding of God as 'Father' is, then, not simply a reflection of a patriarchal society nor a human projection, but is a description of what God is essentially like and therefore of how we may approach him.

Is God 'male'?

Some people struggle with calling God 'Father' because they think this somehow makes him 'male'. Not at all! God may be a creator, but he is not a procreator; he may be a father, but he is not a man. In fact, he is neither male nor female – he is God! And when he created us, it needed both male and female to even begin to make the human race in his image (see Genesis 1:27).

When it comes to describing *God's care* of us, the Bible is happy to use both male and female imagery, as the following verses show:

Can a mother forget the baby at her breast and have no compassion on the child she has borne? Though she may forget, I will not forget you!

(Isaiah 49:15)

As a father has compassion on his children, so the LORD *has compassion on those who fear him; for he knows how we are formed, he remembers that we are dust.*

(Psalm 103:13–14)

But when it comes to describing *God's nature*, the Bible unhesitatingly sees him as a Father, to bring home, not his 'maleness', but his fatherly care and loving authority.

Is God a big version of my earthly father?

Some people are locked into a view of God as a big version of their own earthly father. You may have had a very good father; but he wasn't good enough in comparison to God! You may have had a very bad father and may still have unhappy memories of how he fathered (or failed to father) you; but God certainly isn't like that. The true picture of God's Fatherhood is that given to us by Jesus (see later in this chapter). So we need to look not at the 'god of our fathers' but 'the God and Father of our Lord Jesus Christ' (e.g. Romans 15:6; 2 Corinthians 1:3; Ephesians 1:3; 1 Peter 1:3).

God as Father in the Old Testament

While God was known as Father in the Old Testament, it was not in the highly personal way that we find in the New Testament. This may have been because surrounding pagan religions often saw their gods as 'fathers', with human beings as their 'offspring', and the Old Testament would certainly avoid any such concept. Nevertheless, at times he is described as a Father.

Father of Israel

God was seen first and foremost as Father of the nation of Israel, who was sometimes described as his 'son' (e.g. Exodus 4:22–23; Deuteronomy 1:31; Hosea 11:1) and who therefore could pray to him as 'Father'.

Look down from heaven and see from your lofty throne, holy and glorious. Where are your zeal and your might? Your tenderness and compassion are withheld from us. But you are our Father, though Abraham does not know us or Israel acknowledge us; you, O LORD, are our Father, our Redeemer from of old is your name.

(Isaiah 63:15–16)

Since ancient times no-one has heard, no ear has perceived, no eye has seen any God besides you, who acts on behalf of those who wait for him. You come to the help of those who gladly do right, who remember your ways. But when we continued to sin against them, you were angry. How then can we be saved? All of us have become like one who is unclean, and all our righteous acts are like filthy rags; we all shrivel up like a leaf, and like the wind our sins sweep us away. No-one calls on your name or strives to lay hold of you; for you have hidden your face from us and made us waste away because of our sins. Yet, O LORD, you are our Father. We are the clay, you are the potter; we are all the work of your hand. Do not be angry beyond measure, O LORD; do not remember our sins for ever. Oh, look upon us we pray, for we are all your people.

(Isaiah 64:4–9)

See also Psalm 103:8–14; Malachi 2:10

Because he was the Father of their nation, they saw that his fatherly care reached out to needy individuals within it:

Sing to God, sing praise to his name, extol him who rides on the clouds – his name is the LORD – and rejoice before him. A father to the fatherless, a defender of widows, is God in his holy dwelling. God sets the lonely in families, he leads forth the prisoners with singing; but the rebellious live in a sun-scorched land.

(Psalm 68:4–6)

As the 'figurehead' of the nation, Israel's king was often seen as God's 'son' in a special way:

He will call out to me, 'You are my Father, my God, the Rock my Saviour.'

(Psalm 89:26)

See also 2 Samuel 7:1–16; Psalm 2:6–7

The prophets' challenge

One responsibility of any good father is to discipline his children, and God does just that with his children (e.g. Deuteronomy 4:35–36; Job 5:17–18; Psalm 94:12; Proverbs 3:11–12; Jeremiah 46:28; Hebrews 12:5–11; Revelation 3:19–20). The prophets often brought God's challenges to Israel as his disobedient son:

'Have you not just called to me: "My Father, my friend from my youth, will you always be angry? Will your wrath continue for ever?" This how you talk, but you do all the evil you can.'

(Jeremiah 3:4–5)

'I myself said, "How gladly would I treat you like sons and give you a desirable land, the most beautiful inheritance of any nation." I thought you would call me "Father" and not turn away from following me. But like a woman unfaithful to her husband, so you have been unfaithful to me, O house of Israel.'

(Jeremiah 3:19–20)

See also Malachi 1:6; 2:10

The challenge still remains that if we are going to call God 'Father', then we need to listen to what he says and let our lives reflect his fatherhood of us.

God as Father in the life of Jesus

With the coming of Jesus, the picture is suddenly transformed – as we would expect with one who came as the Son of God incarnate. The New Testament is clear that God's Fatherhood of Jesus was of a kind never experienced before:

For to which of the angels did God ever say, 'You are my Son; today I have become your Father'? Or again, 'I will be his Father, and he will be my Son'?

(Hebrews 1:5)

Jesus called God 'Father'

Time and again, we find Jesus addressing God in prayer as 'Father', even at the most difficult points in his life, thereby reflecting his absolute trust in him.

Going a little farther, he fell with his face to the ground and prayed, 'My Father, if it is possible, may this cup be taken from me. Yet not as I will, but as you will.'

(Matthew 26:39)

At that time Jesus, full of joy through the Holy Spirit, said, 'I praise you, Father, Lord of heaven and earth, because you have hidden these things from the wise and learned, and revealed them to little children. Yes, Father, for this was your good pleasure. All things have been committed to me by my Father. No-one knows who the Son is except the Father, and no-one knows who the Father is except the Son and those to whom the Son chooses to reveal him.'

(Luke 10:21–22)

Jesus said, 'Father, forgive them, for they do not know what they are doing.'

(Luke 23:34)

Jesus called out with a loud voice, 'Father, into your hands I commit my spirit.' When he had said this, he breathed his last.

(Luke 23:46)

After Jesus said this, he looked towards heaven and prayed: 'Father, the time has come. Glorify your Son, that your Son may glorify you . . . And now, Father, glorify me in your presence with the glory I had with you before the world began.'

(John 17:1, 5)

See also Matthew 11:26; 26:53; Luke 2:41–50; John 5:17–18; 11:41–44; 12:28; 14:16–18; 17:20–26

The religious leaders of Jesus' day – caught up in their traditions – simply could not cope with someone speaking to God in such a personal and intimate way:

Jesus said, 'My Father has never stopped working, and that is why I keep on working.' Now the leaders wanted to kill Jesus for two reasons. First, he had broken the law of the Sabbath. But even worse, he had said that God was his Father, which made him equal with God.

(John 5:17–18, CEV)

How do you respond, we wonder, when you see others having a relationship with God that seems so personal?

Jesus taught his followers to call God 'Father'

Jesus encouraged his followers to call God 'Father' too and assured them that he heard their prayers:

'When you pray, go into your room, and when you have shut your door, pray to your Father who is in the secret place; and your Father who sees in secret will reward you openly.'

(Matthew 6:6, NKJV)

'Again, I tell you that if two of you on earth agree about anything you ask for, it will be done for you by my Father in heaven.'

(Matthew 18:19)

See also Matthew 6:9; 6:25–34

Jesus made clear that the title 'father' was not to be used to honour anyone except our heavenly Father:

'But you are not to be called "Rabbi", for you have only one Master and you are all brothers. And do not call anyone on earth "father", for you have one Father, and he is in heaven.

(Matthew 23:8–9)

Not just 'Father' but 'Abba'

But Jesus takes this one step further. Not only does he call God 'Father', he calls him '*Abba*' – the word in Aramaic (the everyday language that Jesus spoke) for 'daddy' – the word used by little children to their father. That this most intimate and trusting word should be found on his lips at the very moment when he could reasonably have cause for doubting his Father – in the Garden of Gethsemane before his arrest and crucifixion – is staggering indeed.

Going a little farther, he fell to the ground and prayed that if possible the hour might pass from him. 'Abba, Father,' he said, 'everything is possible for you. Take this cup from me. Yet not what I will, but what you will.'

(Mark 14:35–36)

This is the heart of prayer: knowing God in this personal and intimate way, and trusting in his fatherly care for us even when things don't look good. There is no example of '*Abba*' being used of God in any other Jewish prayer in history before or since. It comes, quite simply, out of Jesus' unique relationship with the Father.

The term 'Abba' in the early church

But Jesus was not content with keeping the word '*Abba*' to himself. Amazingly, he extends this privilege to us! The term clearly made a profound and life-changing impression on his disciples and the first Christians, for they cherished and preserved this Aramaic word even in the Greek world and it became part of their prayer language:

Those who are led by the Spirit of God are sons of God. For you did not receive a spirit that makes you a slave again to fear, but you received the Spirit of sonship. And by him we cry, 'Abba, Father.'

(Romans 8:14–15)

Because you are sons, God sent the Spirit of his Son into our hearts, the Spirit who calls out, 'Abba, Father.'

(Galatians 4:6)

The privilege of sonship and adoption

The early church understood that calling God 'Father' meant that all Christians were truly now his children – adopted into his family through our faith in Jesus. As children, rather than slaves, in the family, we have wonderful privileges, just like firstborn sons did in those days:

Praise be to the God and Father of our Lord Jesus Christ, who has blessed us in the heavenly realms with every spiritual blessing in Christ. For he chose us in him before the creation of the world to be holy and blameless in his sight. In love he predestined us to be adopted as his sons through Jesus Christ, in accordance with his pleasure and will – to the praise of his glorious grace, which he has freely given us in the One he loves.

(Ephesians 1:3–6)

See also Romans 8:14, 17, 23; 9:26; 2 Corinthians 6:18; Galatians 3:29; 4:6–7; Colossians 1:9–14; Titus 3:7; Hebrews 2:10–12; 1 Peter 1:3–4

Not just Father, but fatherly

The Bible makes clear that God is not a Father in a cold, formal way, like the fathers of Victorian times. The God to whom we pray is not just a Father, but he is fatherly in everything he does and in his intimate knowledge of us and care for us:

When you pray, don't babble on and on as people of other religions do. They think their prayers are answered only by repeating their words again and again. Don't be like them, because your Father knows exactly what you need even before you ask him!

(Matthew 6:7–8, NLT)

See also Psalm 8:3–4; Nahum 1:7; Matthew 6:25–34; 10:29–31; 1 Peter 5:7

A heavenly Father

We cannot conclude this chapter without commenting on an important phrase at the beginning of the Lord's Prayer:

'Our Father in heaven . . . '

(Matthew 6:9)

A Father without limits

This phrase brings home, not that God is 'out there' somewhere, but that his heavenly nature has no limitations. He is in heaven and the highest heavens – not trapped in one place like the territorial 'gods' of Israel's surrounding nations. When we come to God in prayer, we shouldn't think for one minute that there is a limit on what he can do!

I know that you can do all things; no plan of yours can be thwarted.

(Job 42:2)

Nothing is impossible with God.

(Luke 1:37)

See also Genesis 18:14; Jeremiah 32:17; Matthew 19:26; Luke 18:27

A Father without equal

There really is no one like him, the Bible says! Little wonder, then, that many of the Bible's prayers stand in amazement of him:

Praise be to the God and Father of our Lord Jesus Christ! In his great mercy he has given us new birth into a living hope through the resurrection of Jesus Christ from the dead, and into an inheritance that can never perish, spoil or fade – kept in heaven for you, who through faith are shielded by God's power until the coming of the salvation that is ready to be revealed in the last time.

(1 Peter 1:3–5)

See also Psalm 86:8–10; 89:5–8; Habakkuk 3:2; Hebrews 12:28–29

A FINAL PRAYER

O gracious and holy Father,
Give us wisdom to perceive thee,
intelligence to understand thee,
diligence to seek thee,
patience to wait for thee,
eyes to behold thee,
a heart to meditate upon thee,
and a life to proclaim thee;
through the power of the Spirit
of Jesus Christ our Lord.

(St Benedict, 480–543)

CONCLUSION

Through Jesus, everyone can now call God 'Father'.

'When you pray, say: "Father ..." '

(Luke 11:2)

Relevance for today

If God is our heavenly Father, then a number of things follow:

We can trust him

We need not fear that there is a 'nasty streak' in God or that he wants to 'catch us out' in some way. God isn't like that, said Jesus!

'Which of you, if his son asks for bread, will give him a stone? Or if he asks for a fish, will give him a snake? If you, then, though you are evil, know how to give good gifts to your children, how much more will your Father in heaven give good gifts to those who ask him!'

(Matthew 7:9–11)

We can know his love

See how very much our heavenly Father loves us, for he allows us to be called his children, and we really are!

(1 John 3:1, NLT)

We can be intimate with him

'When you pray, go into your room, close the door and pray to your Father, who is unseen. Then your Father, who sees what is done in secret, will reward you.'

(Matthew 6:6)

We can pray for others and ourselves

We always thank God for all of you, mentioning you in our prayers. We continually remember before our God and Father your work produced by faith, your labour prompted by love, and your endurance inspired by hope in our Lord Jesus Christ.

(1 Thessalonians 1:2–3)

Now may our God and Father himself and our Lord Jesus clear the way for us to come to you. May the Lord make your love increase and overflow for each other and for everyone else, just as ours does for you. May he strengthen your hearts so that you will be blameless and holy in the presence of our God and Father when our Lord Jesus comes with all his holy ones.

(1 Thessalonians 3:11–12)

Chapter Three

Can I Pray Too?

Prayer is not just for 'special' people or even 'religious' people. The Bible tells us that anyone can talk to God as Father.

Seek the LORD while he may be found; call on him while he is near. (Isaiah 55:6)

Mike will never forget the lady who just wouldn't set foot inside the church. A children's mission had been organized which was attracting hundreds of children each day. Parents would come at the end of the meeting to collect their children; but there was one lady who, even though it was pouring with rain, just wouldn't come inside the building, despite Mike's warmest invitations. She didn't seem angry with the church or with God (for her child wouldn't have been there if she had been); it seemed she just didn't think that church and God were for people like her. Perhaps she simply felt 'not good enough'. Some people feel like that about prayer too; but the Bible tells us that anyone can pray!

Not just for the 'religious'!

There were lots of 'religious experts' in Jesus' day who impressed themselves with their own praying; but they certainly didn't impress God, Jesus said!

'When you pray, don't be like the hypocrites who love to pray publicly on street corners and in the synagogues where everyone can see them. I assure you, that is all the reward they will ever get.'

(Matthew 6:5, NLT)

See also Isaiah 58:3–5; Matthew 6:16

In their desire 'to be seen by others', with the 'showy' and lengthy prayers that this involved, the Pharisees were a real obstacle to ordinary people praying, who were left feeling that prayer wasn't for 'people like them'. But it's exactly those sort of people that God loves to hear praying, said Jesus!

To some who were confident of their own righteousness and looked down on everybody else, Jesus told this parable:
'Two men went up to the temple to pray, one a Pharisee and the other a tax collector. The Pharisee stood up and prayed about himself: "God, I thank you that I am not like other men-robbers, evildoers, adulterers – or even like this tax collector. I fast twice a week and give a tenth of all I get." But the tax collector stood at a distance. He would not even look up to heaven, but beat his breast and

said, "God, have mercy on me, a sinner." I tell you that this man, rather than the other, went home justified before God. For everyone who exalts himself will be humbled, and he who humbles himself will be exalted.'

(Luke 18:9–14)

See also Luke 5:29–32; 16:15

The simple truth is: *anyone* can pray. You don't have to be 'religious' for God to hear your prayers. In fact, that can sometimes get in the way! You don't even have to be a Christian. Reaching out to God in time of need can often be the beginning of a real relationship with him.

Andrew was an amateur boxing champion, far from God. But when his young daughter was taken seriously ill, he cried out to God for the first time in his life – and God heard him. His daughter was miraculously healed, and he started on a journey that led him to find the friendship of God through Jesus for himself. He is now an active member of the church where Mike is pastor and loves praying – all because he dared to think that God would listen even to him.

Unbelievers who dared ask for help

The Bible contains a number of examples of unbelievers calling out to God in prayer who found that God listened to them:

The sailors on Jonah's ship

Then they cried to the LORD, 'O LORD, please do not let us die for taking this man's life. Do not hold us accountable for killing an innocent man, for you, O LORD, have done as you pleased.' Then they took Jonah and threw him overboard, and the raging sea grew calm. At this the men greatly feared the LORD, and they offered a sacrifice to the LORD and made vows to him. But the LORD provided a great fish to swallow Jonah, and Jonah was inside the fish three days and three nights.

(Jonah 1:14–17)

The citizens of Nineveh

Then [the king] issued a proclamation in Nineveh: 'By the decree of the king and his nobles: Do not let any man or beast, herd or flock, taste anything; do not let them eat or drink. But let man and beast be covered with sackcloth. Let everyone call urgently on God. Let them give up their evil ways and their violence. Who knows? God may yet relent and with compassion turn from his fierce anger so that we will not perish." When God saw what they did and how they turned from their evil ways, he had compassion and did not bring upon them the destruction he had threatened.

(Jonah 3:7–10)

The Syro-Phoenician woman

A woman whose little daughter was possessed by an evil spirit came and fell at [Jesus'] feet. The woman was a Greek, born in Syrian Phoenicia. She begged Jesus to drive the demon out of her daughter. 'First let the children eat all they want,' he told her, 'for it is not right to take the children's bread and toss it to their dogs.' 'Yes, Lord,' she replied, 'but even the dogs under the table eat the children's crumbs.' Then he told her, 'For such a reply, you may go; the demon has left your daughter.' She went home and found her child lying on the bed, and the demon gone.

(Mark 7:25–30)

The Roman centurion

Cornelius answered: 'Four days ago I was in my house praying at this hour, at three in the afternoon. Suddenly a man in shining clothes stood before me and said, "Cornelius, God has heard your prayer and remembered your gifts to the poor." '

(Acts 10:30–31)

See also Genesis 4:26; Daniel 4:34–37; Luke 7:1–10; 23:39–43

When people call out to God in their need and see him answering them, their response is often like that of Naaman, pagan commander of the Aramean army, who was healed when he reached out to God and (eventually!) obeyed Elisha's command to bathe in the River Jordan:

'Now I know that the God of Israel is the only God in the whole world.'

(2 Kings 5:15, CEV)

A vision of everyone praying

But it is not just one or two special people that God wants to come to him in prayer. He wants everybody to do it! In fact, the Old Testament prophets looked forward to the day when people of all backgrounds and all nations would come to him in prayer.

And foreigners who bind themselves to the LORD
to serve him,
to love the name of the LORD,
and to worship him,
all who keep the Sabbath without
desecrating it
and who hold fast to my covenant –
these I will bring to my holy mountain
and give them joy in my house of prayer.
Their burnt offerings and sacrifices
will be accepted on my altar;
for my house will be called
a house of prayer for all nations.

(Isaiah 56:6–7)

See also Matthew 21:13; Mark 11:17; Luke 19:46

In the last days the mountain of the LORD's temple will be established
as chief among the mountains;
it will be raised above the hills,
and peoples will stream to it.
Many nations will come and say,
'Come, let us go up to the mountain of the LORD,
to the house of the God of Jacob.
He will teach us his ways,
so that we may walk in his paths.'

(Micah 4:1–2)

This is what the LORD Almighty says: 'Many peoples and the inhabitants of many cities will yet come, and the inhabitants of one city will go to another and say, "Let us go at once to entreat the LORD and seek the LORD Almighty. I myself am going." And many peoples and powerful nations will come to Jerusalem to seek the LORD Almighty and to entreat him.'

(Zechariah 8:20–22)

If you have never prayed before, or feel that God couldn't possibly be interested in *your* prayers, our encouragement to you is to 'give it a go!' You will be surprised. The testimony of countless thousands through the ages is that God hears us when we call to him. Martin's own story is that he prayed a faltering prayer 'God, if you are real, show yourself to me' and soon afterwards God did just that!

The Father hears us when we call

The Bible is full of testimony to the fact that God really does hear people when they call out to him. In fact Abraham, originally from a pagan background, became so convinced that God hears us, that he called his first-born son 'Ishmael' ('God hears'), while Hagar, Ishmael's mother, called God by the name 'God sees' (Genesis 16:11,13). Here are the testimonies of some others:

You hear, O LORD, the desire of the afflicted;
you encourage them, and you listen to
their cry.

(Psalm 10:17)

I waited patiently for the LORD;
he turned to me and heard my cry.
He lifted me out of the slimy pit,
out of the mud and mire;
he set my feet on a rock
and gave me a firm place to stand.
He put a new song in my mouth,
a hymn of praise to our God.
Many will see and fear
and put their trust in the LORD.
Blessed is the man
who makes the LORD his trust.

(Psalm 40:1–4)

For he will deliver the needy who cry out,
the afflicted who have no-one to help.
He will take pity on the weak and the needy
and save the needy from death.
He will rescue them from oppression and violence,
for precious is their blood in his sight.

(Psalm 72:12–14)

How gracious he will be when you cry for help! As soon as he hears, he will answer you.

(Isaiah 30:19)

During the days of Jesus' life on earth, he offered up prayers and petitions with loud cries and tears to the one who could save him from death, and he was heard because of his reverent submission.

(Hebrews 5:7)

See also 1 Kings 8:30; Job 42:1–6; Psalm 6:9; 28:6; 31:21–22; 116:1–6

False gods and idols versus the God who speaks

In the Old Testament, 'not hearing' was always seen as characteristic of deaf and dumb idols and the false gods they represented, in contrast to the living God who always hears and speaks:

Then they called on the name of Baal from morning till noon. 'O Baal, answer us!' they shouted. But there was no response; no-one answered. And they danced around the altar they had made.

At noon Elijah began to taunt them. 'Shout louder!' he said. 'Surely he is a god! Perhaps he is deep in thought, or busy, or travelling. Maybe he is sleeping and must be awakened.' So they shouted louder and slashed themselves with swords and spears, as was their custom, until their blood flowed. Midday passed, and they continued their frantic prophesying until the time for the evening sacrifice. But there was no response, no-one answered, no-one paid attention.

(1 Kings 18:26–29)

See also Psalm 115:1–8; Isaiah 44:9–18; Jeremiah 10:1–5; Habakkuk 2:18–20

In contrast to this, the 'God of Abraham Isaac and Jacob' (e.g. Exodus 3:6) is the God who always sees and hears:

The Israelites groaned in their slavery and cried out, and their cry for help because of their slavery went up to God. God heard their groaning and he remembered his covenant with Abraham, with Isaac and with Jacob. So God looked on the Israelites and was concerned about them.

(Exodus 2:23–25)

The eyes of the LORD are everywhere,
keeping watch on the wicked and the good.

(Proverbs 15:3)

Hezekiah prayed to the LORD: 'O LORD, God of Israel, enthroned between the cherubim, you alone are God over all the kingdoms of the earth. You have made heaven and earth. Give ear, O LORD, and hear; open your eyes, O LORD, and see; listen . . . '

(2 Kings 19:15–16)

See also Genesis 21:17–18; 2 Chronicles 6:18–21; 16:9; 30:27; Psalm 6:8–9; 34:4–6; Lamentations 3:55–57; Daniel 9:17–19; Micah 7:7; John 11:41–42

Why God hears everyone's prayers

So, why is it that God listens to the prayers of anyone – even those who don't believe in him? If you were God, wouldn't you be tempted to say, 'Believe in me first – then I'll think about answering your prayers'? But God isn't like us! And that's certainly not how he operates.

There are two main reasons why God hears everyone's prayers:

Because he is near us

While God is beyond everything ('transcendent') in creation, he is nevertheless near to us all, both those who are his people and those who are not his people.

What other nation is so great as to have their gods near them the way the LORD our God is near us whenever we pray to him?

(Deuteronomy 4:7)

'What you worship as something unknown I am going to proclaim to you. The God who made the world and everything in it is the Lord of heaven and earth and does not live in temples built by hands. And he is not served by human hands, as if he needed anything, because he himself gives all men life and breath and everything else. From one man he made every nation of men, that they should inhabit the whole earth; and he determined the times set for them and the exact places where they should live. God did this so that men would seek him and perhaps reach out for him and find him, though he is not far from each one of us. "For in him we live and move and have our being." As some of your own poets have said, "We are his offspring." '

(Acts 17:23–28)

See also Psalm 75:1; 139:7–12; Jeremiah 23:23–24

Because he loves us

The amazing message of the Bible is that God loves us. That does not mean he is happy with everything in our lives or content to let us stay the same; but it does mean that his first response to us is always one of love, and not of judgment. When the religious leaders brought to Jesus a woman caught in adultery, he first loved her before he challenged her:

Jesus stood up and asked her, 'Where is everyone? Isn't there anyone left to accuse you?' 'No sir,' the woman answered. Then Jesus told her, 'I am not going to accuse you either. You may go now, but don't sin any more.'

(John 8:10–11, CEV)

God loves us, sinners though we are! (e.g., Exodus 34:6–7; Deuteronomy 7:7–9; Isaiah 43:1–4; Jeremiah 31:3; Matthew 5:45; John 3:16–17; Romans 5:7–8; 1 John 4:9–10). The more we get to know him, the more he will lovingly bring challenges to our lives, for he always wants the best for us. But we do not have to wait to get to know him before we can bring our needs to him, as many discovered during Jesus' ministry on earth. He hears us because he loves us!

A FINAL PRAYER

Lord, teach us to seek you, and reveal yourself to us when we seek you. For we cannot seek you unless you first teach us, nor find you except you reveal yourself to us. Let us seek you in longing, and long for you in seeking; let us find you in love, and love you in finding, O Jesus Christ our Lord. Amen.

St Ambrose of Milan (c. 339–397)

CONCLUSION

No one need ever say, 'Prayer couldn't work for me'. It is God's gift to all people.

Then you will call, and the LORD will answer; you will cry for help, and he will say: 'Here am I'.

(Isaiah 58:9)

Relevance for today

Some people don't pray, not because they wonder whether God is there or not, or whether he will hear their prayers or not, but because they fear the invitation to pray may not include them. Such fears are foundless!

I'm not a Christian

God loves to hear *everyone's* prayers, Christian or not!

Everyone will come to you because you answer prayer.

(Psalm 65:2 CEV)

It's a long time since I prayed

It was no doubt a long time since the robber who was crucified alongside Jesus had prayed; but Jesus still heard his cry for help, because it came from the heart:

He said, 'Jesus, remember me when you come into your kingdom.' Jesus answered him, 'I tell you the truth, today you will be with me in paradise.'

(Luke 23:42–43)

I don't feel good enough

None of us are good enough! But that's the heart of the good news: God comes to people who know they aren't good enough!

Out of the depths I cry to you, O LORD; O Lord, hear my voice. Let your ears be attentive to my cry for mercy. If you, O Lord, kept a record of sins, O LORD, who could stand? But with you there is forgiveness; therefore you are feared.

(Psalm 130:1–4)

I'm not sure if God is there

The Bible encourages us to 'try him out' and see!

Taste and see that the LORD is good; blessed is the man who takes refuge in him.

(Psalm 34:8)

I feel so 'flat'

Prayer doesn't depend on *our* feelings, but on *God's* faithfulness. Jeremiah, a prophet who often felt depressed, learned this lesson for himself:

I remember my affliction and my wandering, the bitterness and the gall. I well remember them, and my soul is downcast within me. Yet this I call to mind and therefore I have hope: Because of the LORD's great love we are not consumed, for his compassions never fail. They are new every morning; great is your faithfulness. I say to myself, 'The LORD is my portion; therefore I will wait for him.'

(Lamentations 3:19–24)

I've drifted away from God

Well, you won't be the first and you won't be the last. At such times, we need to know that God always leaves the door open to us!

Then Samson prayed to the LORD, 'O Sovereign LORD, remember me. O God, please strengthen me just once more . . .'

(Judges 16:28)

To all in this position, Jesus says:

'Listen! I am standing and knocking at your door. If you hear my voice and open the door, I will come in and we will eat together.'

Chapter Four

Any Place, Any Time, Any Words

Prayer is not about 'getting it right', but about a spontaneous relationship with Father God.

'I, the LORD, invite you to come and talk it over.' (Isaiah 1:18, CEV)

Young children have little sense of the 'right' or 'appropriate' moments to do, or not do, certain things. If they rush into your presence, then they will do it no matter how inconvenient it is to you; if they blurt out their questions, then they will do it no matter what 'important' visitor is there; if they 'tell things as they really are', then they will do it even if the whole world is listening. Why? Because you are their parent, and that's what parents are for. Young children do not 'stand on dignity'; they simply rush in.

And that, said Jesus, is how we can be with God – though everything within us reacts to such a thought!

People sometimes get in such a muddle when it comes to praying. 'Where should I do it? What words should I use? Should I stand or sit or kneel? What direction should I face? North, south, east or west? When should I do it? And how many times a day?' To all of these questions Jesus said: it simply doesn't matter! It is not about where or when or how you pray; what matters is the heart. This came out clearly in his conversation with the Samaritan woman for whom such things seemed so important:

Jesus replied, 'Believe me, the time is coming when it will no longer matter whether you worship the Father here or in Jerusalem. You Samaritans know so little about the one you worship, while we Jews know all about him, for salvation comes through the Jews. But the time is coming and is already here when true worshippers will worship the Father in spirit and in truth. The Father is looking for anyone who will worship him that way. For God is Spirit, so those who worship him must worship in spirit and in truth.'

(John 4:21–24, NLT)

It is not about doing it in the right place or at the right time or in the right way; as long as we pray sincerely, from the heart, God will hear us.

Where can we pray?

The Bible never restricts prayer to 'special places'. The role of local sanctuaries or the temple in Jerusalem was to provide a focal point for corporate worship or pilgrimage; but they were never intended to restrict prayer and worship to particular places.

Prayer could be offered anywhere. Why? Because God himself is everywhere and nowhere is big enough to contain him! Even Solomon, builder of the great temple in Jerusalem, recognized this:

'The temple I am going to build will be great, because our God is greater than all other gods. But who is able to build a temple for him, since the heavens, even the highest heavens, cannot contain him?'

(2 Chronicles 2:5–6)

See also 1 Kings 8:27; Isaiah 66:1; Jeremiah 23:23–24

There is no 'proper' place to pray and there is no 'better' place to pray. God is everywhere; so anywhere will do. In fact, the Bible shows us godly men and women praying in a tremendously wide variety of places and situations:

- at home (Daniel 6:10; Matthew 6:6; Acts 10:9)
- in the countryside (Mark 1:35; Luke 5:16)
- up a mountain (Exodus 34:1–9; 1 Kings 19:8–18; Matthew 14:23; Luke 9:28)
- at favourite spots (Matthew 26:36; Acts 16:13)
- at the temple or sanctuary (Exodus 33:7–11; 1 Kings 8:29–53; Luke 2:36–37; Acts 3:1)
- on a journey (1 Kings 19:3–4; Acts 9:3–6)
- on a ship in a storm (Jonah 1:11–16; Matthew 8:23–27; Acts 27:27–38)
- in jail or captivity (Judges 16:25–30; Acts 16:22–25)
- inside a fish (Jonah 2:1–10)
- with a group (Acts 1:14; 2:42; 4:31; 12:5)
- in private (Genesis 24:42–45; 2 Kings 4:32–33; Nehemiah 1:4; Matthew 6:6)
- in public (1 Kings 18:36–38; John 11:41–42; Acts 2:4–11)

From all of this it is obvious that the location of prayer is completely irrelevant to God. Thoughts that we can only pray 'properly' in a church building are completely alien to the Scriptures, therefore. What God is after is not our location but our heart.

When can we pray?

Unlike Islam, which prescribes prayer at five points in each day, the Bible makes no requirements about when or how often we should pray. In fact to answer the question 'When should we pray?' would be rather like answering the question 'How often should I talk to my husband or wife or children each day?' Prayer is not about rules; it is about a relationship with the living God; and relationship can never be put into a timetable.

We therefore find a whole variety of prayer patterns in the Bible.

Prayer in the morning

In the morning, O LORD, you hear my voice; in the morning I lay my requests before you and wait in expectation.

(Psalm 5:3)

See also Genesis 28:18–22; 1 Samuel 1:19; 2 Kings 6:15–17; Psalm 88:13; 92:1–2; Mark 1:35

Prayer in the evening

O LORD, I call to you; come quickly to me. Hear my voice when I call to you. May my prayer be set before you like incense; may the lifting up of my hands be like the evening sacrifice.

(Psalm 141:1–2)

See also Genesis 24:63; 2 Chronicles 7:11–12; Ezra 9:5–15; Psalm 42:8; Matthew 14:23; Luke 6:12

Prayer three times a day

Evening, morning and noon I cry out in distress, and he hears my voice.

(Psalm 55:17)

(In later Judaism – and hence by New Testament times – the three set times of prayer became 9 am, 3 pm and sunset.)

See also Daniel 6:10, 13; Acts 3:1

Prayer through the night

One of those days Jesus went out to a mountainside to pray, and spent the night praying to God.

(Luke 6:12)

See also Luke 2:36–37; Acts 16:25; 1 Thessalonians 3:10; 1 Timothy 5:5; 2 Timothy 1:3

Prayer over periods of days

When I heard these things, I sat down and wept. For some days I mourned and fasted and prayed before the God of heaven. Then I said: 'Lord, God of heaven, the great and awesome God, who keeps his covenant of love with those who love him and obey his commands, let your ear be attentive and your eyes open to hear the prayer your servant is praying before you day and night for your servants, the people of Israel.'

(Nehemiah 1:4–6)

See also 2 Samuel 1:11; 2 Chronicles 20:2–4; Zechariah 7:4–5; Matthew 4:1–2; Acts 13:1–3

Prayer in crisis moments

I call to the LORD, who is worthy of praise,
and I am saved from my enemies.
The cords of death entangled me;
the torrents of destruction overwhelmed me.
The cords of the grave coiled around me;
the snares of death confronted me.
In my distress I called to the LORD;
I cried to my God for help.
From his temple he heard my voice;
my cry came before him, into his ears.

(Psalm 18:3–6)

See also Genesis 32:7–12; Judges 3:7–9; 1 Kings 19:3–4; 2 Kings 19:14–9; 2 Chronicles 33:12–13; Psalm 31:9–24; 69:29; 107:6, 13, 19, 28; 120:1; Jonah 2:1–10; Matthew 26:39; Acts 7:59–60

Praying continually

Because prayer is about a relationship with God, the Bible often encourages God's people to 'pray continually' – that is, to maintain an ongoing intimacy and conversation with God, and not to confine our praying to just set times and places.

Be joyful always; pray continually; give thanks in all circumstances.

(1 Thessalonians 5:16–18)

See also Luke 18:1; Romans 1:9–10; Colossians 1:9–12; 4:12; 1 Thessalonians 3:10; 1 Timothy 5:5; 2 Timothy 1:3

How can we pray?

So, the place and the time are unimportant. But what about the words? Surely there must be a special language or vocabulary that is needed for prayer? But

Godly church leaders through the centuries have recognized the priority of the heart over words when it comes to prayer:

John Bunyan (1628–88), author of *Pilgrim's Progress:* 'When thou prayest, rather let thy heart be without words than thy words be without heart.'

St John of the Cross (1542–91): 'Great talent is a gift of God, but it is a gift which is by no means necessary in order to pray well. This gift is required in order to converse well with men; but it is not necessary in order to speak well with God.' For that, one needs good desires, and nothing more.'

Clement of Alexandria (c. 150–c. 215): 'Prayer is conversation with God.'

here once again is what is amazing. The God who has revealed himself as Father desires no special language at all!

The major terms used for 'prayer' in the Bible are all relational words drawn from everyday life, just like those used between family and friends. They are ordinary words, as men and women 'say', 'speak', 'cry', 'ask', 'request', 'enquire of' or 'call to' God. Unlike other religions, both ancient and modern, there is no 'technical vocabulary' to be mastered before prayer can be commenced or developed, no 'insider jargon' to be initiated into, no language that is different from the language of everyday life. Christian prayer is simply conversation with the God who has made us and who makes himself known as our Father, our 'Abba' (see Part One, Chapter 2). As our Father, he wants us to express what is in our heart to him – and we cannot do that if we have to constantly search for the right words, as though we might offend the dignity of his majesty if we were to get them wrong.

The heart is more important than words

'The LORD does not look at the things man looks at. Man looks at the outward appearance, but the LORD looks at the heart.'

(1 Samuel 16:7)

The Lord says:
'These people come near to me with their
mouth and honour me with their lips,
but their hearts are far from me.
Their worship of me
is made up only of rules taught by men.

(Isaiah 29:13)

Reality is more important than ritual

Sacrifice and offering you did not desire,
but my ears you have pierced;
burnt offerings and sin offerings
you did not require.
Then I said, 'Here I am, I have come –
it is written about me in the scroll.
To do your will, O my God, is my desire;
your law is within my heart.'

(Psalm 40:6–8)

With what shall I come before the LORD
and bow down before the exalted God?
Shall I come before him with burnt offerings,
with calves a year old?
Will the LORD be pleased with thousands of rams,
with ten thousand rivers of oil?
Shall I offer my firstborn for my transgression,
the fruit of my body for the sin of my soul?
He has showed you, O man, what is good.
And what does the LORD require of you?
To act justly and to love mercy
and to walk humbly with your God.

(Micah 6:6–8)

Sincere words are more important than many words

Guard your steps when you go to the house of God. Go near to listen rather than to offer the sacrifice of fools, who do not know that they do wrong. Do not be quick with your mouth, do not be hasty in your heart to utter anything before God. God is in heaven and you are on earth, so let your words be few.

(Ecclesiastes 5:1–2)

And when you pray, do not keep on babbling like pagans, for they think they will be heard because of their many words. Do not be like them, for your Father knows what you need before you ask him. This, then, is how you should pray: 'Our Father in heaven . . .'

(Matthew 6:7–8)

Words should express what is in the heart

It has been said by some that 'prayer is life'. In other words, we don't need to

The Bible's shortest prayers

Want to pray, but not sure how to begin? It is not the length of our prayers, or the correctness of our words that matters, but simply the sincerity of them. Here are some of the Bible's shortest – and most powerful! – prayers:

O my Lord, please send someone else.
(Exodus 4:13, NRSV)

Now show me your glory.
(Exodus 33:18)

O God, please heal her!
(Numbers 12:13)

Speak, for your servant is listening.
(1 Samuel 3:10)

O Lord*, open his eyes so that he may see.*
(2 Kings 6:17)

Remember me with favour, O my God.
(Nehemiah 13:31)

For how long, O Lord?
(Isaiah 6:11)

Lord, you can heal me if you will.
(Matthew 8:2, NCV)

Lord, save us! We're going to drown!
(Matthew 8:25)

Ephphatha! – Open up!
(Mark 7:34, The Message)

I believe; help my unbelief.
(Mark 9:24, NRSV)

Jesus, Master, have mercy on us!
(Luke 17:13, NKJV)

Sir, we would see Jesus.
(John 12:21, KJV)

Who are you Lord?
(Acts 9:5)

Come, O Lord!
(1 Corinthians 16:22)

'pray', we simply need to 'live', and that is sufficient for God. But the Bible constantly urges us to *express* what is in our hearts to our Father, and gives us countless examples of those who did so. Prayer that is not expressed (whether silently in the heart or spoken on the lips) would appear, from the Bible's point of view, not to be real prayer.

Hannah was praying in her heart, and her lips were moving but her voice was not heard . . . 'I was pouring out my soul to the Lord*.'*

(1 Samuel 1:13–15)

Trust in him at all times, O people;
pour out your hearts to him . . .

(Psalm 62:8)

What about 'Thee' and 'Thou'?

Some Christian traditions have been accustomed to speaking to God using 'Thee' and 'Thou', believing this to be more dignified and respectful. However, there is no such distinction in the original language of the Bible texts. Exactly the same words are used of speaking to God as to men and women. To add 'reverence' to our prayers by using 'Thee' and 'Thou', therefore, is to add something that the Bible never intended.

Also, this is not how those words 'thee' and 'thou' were originally used in the English language. In the period when versions such as The King James' (or, Authorized) Version were written, and some of the great Christian 'classics', 'thee' and 'thou' were common words of friendship and intimacy – between man and wife, and to their children and friends – in no way did the words carry a sense of 'respect' or 'esteem for someone higher'. Sadly, as English usage changed, this original meaning was lost, and we are now left with a tradition that thinks God needs special vocabulary if he is to be addressed 'properly'. Richness of language is no substitute for reality of relationship!

A FINAL PRAYER

Just as I am – without one plea,
But that Thy blood was
shed for me,
And that Thou bidd'st me
come to Thee,
O Lamb of God, I come.

Charlotte Elliott (1789–1871)

CONCLUSION

God is not bothered about the place or the time or the words of our prayers; our Father simply wants to hear the hearts of his children.

Neither here . . . nor there . . . It's who you are and the way you live that count before God. Your worship must engage your spirit in the pursuit of truth. That's the kind of people the Father is out looking for: those who are simply honestly themselves before him in their worship.

(John 4:21–23, The Message)

Relevance for today

We can still talk to God anwhere

From inside a fish to inside a jail; from the courts of the temple to the confines of the home; from the bath tub to the bus stop; there is nowhere where God cannot be found or where we cannot talk to him.

Where could I go to escape from your Spirit or from your sight? If I were to climb up to the highest heavens, you would be there. If I were to dig down to the world of the dead you would also be there. Suppose I had wings like the dawning day and flew across the ocean. Even then your powerful arm would guide and protect me. Or suppose I said, 'I'll hide in the dark until night comes to cover me over.' But you see in the dark because daylight and dark are all the same to you . . . . Everything you do is marvellous! Of this I have no doubt.

(Psalm 139:7–12,14, CEV)

We can still talk to God anytime

Morning or evening; midday or midnight; Sunday or weekday; in crisis or continually; there is no time when we cannot talk to God, for it is never inconvenient to him.

I lift up my eyes to the hills –
where does my help come from?
My help comes from the LORD,
the Maker of heaven and earth.
He will not let your foot slip –
he who watches over you will not slumber;
indeed, he who watches over Israel
will neither slumber nor sleep.
The LORD watches over you –
the LORD is your shade at your right hand;
the sun will not harm you by day,
nor the moon by night.
The LORD will keep you from all harm –
he will watch over your life;
the LORD will watch over your coming
and going
both now and for evermore.

(Psalm 121:1–8)

We can still talk to God anyhow

The right heart is more important than the right words; integrity is more important than impressiveness; reality is more important than ritual. God is our Father – so just talk to him!

O Lord, open my lips,
and my mouth will declare your praise.
You do not delight in sacrifice,
or I would bring it;
you do not take pleasure in burnt offerings.
The sacrifices of God are a broken spirit;
a broken and contrite heart,
O God, you will not despise.

(Psalm 51:15–17)

Chapter Five

Not Left Alone

We are not left alone to discover and develop a relationship with God; God himself comes to help us.

'I will ask the Father, and he will give you another Helper to be with you for ever.' (John 14:16, NCV)

There are times when it is wonderful to be left alone – ask any mother of toddlers or any busy executive! But equally, there are times when being left alone can feel so isolating – even so frightening. So what about being left alone with the Creator of the universe and having to explain yourself? As we saw in the previous chapter, any words will do; but sometimes we run out of words; sometimes we don't know what or how to pray. At such times we need to remember that our heavenly Father has not left us alone; he has sent someone to help us!

In other religions, prayer is a duty that you must perform, a technique that you must master. But that's not how it is in the Christian faith. Prayer is friendship with God; and, as our friend, God does not leave us to work things out on our own; he comes alongside to help us express our thoughts and longings to him. We are certainly not left alone!

The promise of God's presence

There are three key things we need to remember about God's presence when we come to pray:

God is with us

The Bible tells us again and again that God is always with us, always near:

When Jacob awoke from his sleep, he thought, 'Surely the LORD is in this place, and I was not aware of it.' He was afraid and said, 'How awesome is this place! This is none other than the house of God; this is the gate of heaven.'

(Genesis 28:16–17)

The LORD is near to all who call on him, to all who call on him in truth.

(Psalm 145:18)

The LORD your God is with you, he is mighty to save. He will take great delight in you, he will quiet you with his love, he will rejoice over you with singing.

(Zephaniah 3:17)

See also Deuteronomy 4:7; 1 Kings 8:56–57; Psalm 139:7–10; 119:151; Isaiah 55:6–7; 57:15; Zechariah 8:23; Matthew 1:23; Acts 17:27; Philippians 4:5

God wants to be found

Since God is a 'spirit' being, we could never discover him by our natural senses; but he himself comes and helps us. He does not play 'Hide and Seek' with us; rather he does everything possible to make himself known, even sending his own Son Jesus into the world.

But if from there you seek the LORD your God, you will find him if you look for him with all your heart and with all your soul.

(Deuteronomy 4:29)

'I revealed myself to those who did not ask for me; I was found by those who did not seek me. To a nation that did not call on my name, I said, "Here am I, here am I."'

(Isaiah 65:1)

'For I know the plans I have for you,' declares the LORD, 'plans to prosper you and not to harm you, plans to give you hope and a future. Then you will call upon me and come and pray to me, and I will listen to you. You will seek me and find me when you seek me with all your heart. I will be found by you,' declares the LORD.

(Jeremiah 29:11–14)

See also Genesis 35:7; Proverbs 2:1–5; 8:35–36; Isaiah 43:10–13; John 17:6; Acts 17:27; 1 Corinthians 2:6–10; 2 Timothy 1:8–10

Because God makes it plain that he wants to be found by us, this gives us confidence to approach him as Father, not with fear, but with boldness.

Therefore, since we have such a hope, we are very bold. We are not like Moses, who would put a veil over his face to keep the Israelites from gazing at it while the radiance was fading away. But their minds were made dull, for to this day the same veil remains when the old covenant is read. It has not been removed, because only in Christ is it taken away. Even to this day when Moses is read, a veil covers their hearts. But whenever anyone turns to the Lord, the veil is taken away. Now the Lord is the Spirit, and where the Spirit of the Lord is, there is freedom.

(2 Corinthians 3:12–17)

See also Genesis 18:31–32; Luke 11:5–10; Ephesians 3:12; Hebrews 4:14–16; 10:19–22; James 4:7–10

God wants to answer

The constant promise of the Bible is that God wants, not only to *hear* our prayers, but also to *answer* them.

Then Moses spoke and the voice of God answered him.

(Exodus 19:19)

I call on you, O God, for you will answer me; give ear to me and hear my prayer.

(Psalm 17:6)

'Have faith in God,' Jesus answered. 'I tell you the truth, if anyone says to this mountain, "Go, throw yourself into the sea," and does not doubt in his heart but believes that what he says will happen, it will be done for him. Therefore I tell you, whatever you ask for in prayer, believe that you have received it, and it will be yours.'

(Mark 11:22–24)

See also 1 Kings 18:36–39; 1 Chronicles 14:8–17; Ezra 8:21–23; Isaiah 41:17; Zechariah 10:6; John 14:13; 15:7, 16; Hebrews 4:16

The promise of God's Spirit

But simply making promises to be near

and to be found by us is not enough for God. He then takes steps to come and help us to respond to those promises through the gift of his Holy Spirit.

'I will give you a new heart and put a new spirit in you; I will remove from you your heart of stone and give you a heart of flesh. And I will put my Spirit in you and move you to follow my decrees and be careful to keep my laws.'

(Ezekiel 36:26–27)

'And afterwards, I will pour out my Spirit on all people. Your sons and daughters will prophesy, your old men will dream dreams, your young men will see visions. Even on my servants, both men and women, I will pour out my Spirit in those days.'

(Joel 2:28–29)

'Which one of you fathers would give your hungry child a snake if the child asked for a fish? Which one of you would give your child a scorpion if the child asked for an egg? As bad as you are, you still know how to give good gifts to your children. But your heavenly Father is even more ready to give the Holy Spirit to anyone who asks.'

(Luke 11:11–13, CEV)

'And I will ask the Father, and he will give you another Counsellor to be with you for ever – the Spirit of truth. The world cannot accept him, because it neither sees him nor knows him. But you know him, for he lives with you and will be in you. I will not leave you as orphans; I will come to you.'

(John 14:16–18)

See also Ezekiel 37:14; 39:29; Matthew 3:11; Luke 24:49; John 3:34; 7:37–39; Acts 1:4–5; 2:1–4, 38–39; 8:14–17; 10:44–47; 19:1–6

The Holy Spirit helps us know God as Father

Without the Holy Spirit, God remains, at best, a stranger who is present. But once we receive the Spirit into our lives, a new relationship begins. We become God's 'sons', God's children. From this basis, can we be confident about our prayers.

Those who are led by the Spirit of God are sons of God. For you did not receive a spirit that makes you a slave again to fear, but you received the Spirit of sonship. And by him we cry, 'Abba, Father' The Spirit himself testifies with our spirit that we are God's children.

(Romans 8:14–16)

Because you are sons, God sent the Spirit of his Son into our hearts, the Spirit who calls out, 'Abba, Father.' So you are no longer a slave, but a son; and since you are a son, God has made you also an heir.

(Galatians 4:6–7)

See also John 1:10–13; Romans 8:22–23; 1 John 3:1–2

The Holy Spirit helps us know God's heart, will and truth

Sometimes we can be unsure of what is right in life or what God wants; but as we pray, the Holy Spirit begins to makes it clear.

The original word in Greek for 'Counsellor', used of the Holy Spirit in John 14:16, is rich in meaning, as we see in the following different translations:

- Comforter (KJV)
- Helper (NASB, NKJV, NCV)
- Advocate (NRSV)
- Friend (The Message)
- Someone else to stand by you (J.B. Phillips)

Teach me to do your will,
for you are my God;
may your good Spirit
lead me on level ground.

(Psalm 143:10)

'But when he, the Spirit of truth, comes, he will guide you into all truth. He will not speak on his own; he will speak only what he hears, and he will tell you what is yet to come. He will bring glory to me by taking from what is mine and making it known to you.'

(John 16:13–14)

See also Psalm 25:4–5; Matthew 26:42; John 4:21–24; 14:17, 25–26; 1 John 5:6

The Holy Spirit helps us know when we've done wrong

None of us likes to be told that we've got it wrong! But the Holy Spirit is God's gift to us to point out things that are wrong so that we invite him to help us put them right.

The Spirit will come and show the people of this world the truth about sin and God's justice and the judgment.

(John 16:8, CEV)

See also Psalm 51:10–17; Acts 2:37–38; 24:25; Galatians 5:16–25; 1 Thessalonians 1:4–5

The Holy Spirit makes us more like Jesus

As we submit our lives to God in prayer, the Spirit works a miracle within us – he begins to make us more like Jesus!

Now the Lord is the Spirit, and where the Spirit of the Lord is, there is freedom. And we, who with unveiled faces all reflect the Lord's glory, are being transformed into his likeness with ever-increasing glory, which comes from the Lord, who is the Spirit.

(2 Corinthians 3:17–18)

See also Romans 8:9–14; 12:1–2; Galatians 5:16–25; 2 Thessalonians 2:13

The Holy Spirit helps us find the words

Ever felt lost for words? Most of us have felt like that when it comes to prayer. But the Holy Spirit is the one who helps us.

In the same way, the Spirit helps us in our weakness. We do not know what we ought to pray for, but the Spirit himself intercedes for us with groans that words cannot express. And he who searches our hearts knows the mind of the Spirit, because the Spirit intercedes for the saints in accordance with God's will.

(Romans 8:26–27)

And pray in the Spirit on all occasions with all kinds of prayers and requests.

(Ephesians 6:18)

But you, dear friends, build yourselves up in your most holy faith and pray in the Holy Spirit.

(Jude 20)

See also Romans 15:30; 1 Corinthians 14:14–15

The Holy Spirit helps us to praise God

When we run out of words to praise and thank God, the Holy Spirit again comes to help.

At that time Jesus, full of joy through the Holy Spirit, said, 'I praise you, Father, Lord of heaven and earth.'

(Luke 10:21)

While Peter was still speaking these words, the Holy Spirit came on all who heard the message. The circumcised believers who had come with Peter were astonished that the gift of the Holy Spirit had been poured out even on the Gentiles. For they heard them speaking in tongues and praising God.

(Acts 10:44–46)

Don't be drunk with wine, because that will ruin your life. Instead, let the Holy Spirit fill and control you. Then you will sing psalms and hymns and spiritual songs among yourselves, making music to the Lord in your hearts. And you will always give thanks for everything to God the Father in the name of our Lord Jesus Christ.

(Ephesians 5:18–20, NLT)

See also Isaiah 61:1–3; Acts 2:1–4; 19:6; 1 Corinthians 14:14–15; Philippians 3:3

The promise of God's encouragement

So, we have God's promise and we have God's Spirit. But the truth is – it can still be hard going at times! Prayer can sometimes be rather like a 'battle' – a 'spiritual warfare' (see Part Five, Chapter 7). The battle can be against circumstances that seem unyielding, or people who oppose God's purposes, or the devil's activity – or sometimes even against our own will! But our Father makes provision for this struggle and encourages us through it.

Encouragement to 'battle'

Paul, no doubt looking at the uniform of the Roman soldier who was guarding him at the time, summed up how to 'battle' like this:

Finally, be strong in the Lord and in his mighty power. Put on the full armour of God so that you can take your stand against the devil's schemes. For our struggle is not against flesh and blood, but against the rulers, against the authorities, against the powers of this dark world and against the spiritual forces of evil in the heavenly realms. Therefore put on the full armour of God, so that when the day of evil comes, you may be able to stand your ground, and after you have done everything, to stand. Stand firm then, with the belt of truth buckled round your waist, with the breastplate of righteousness in place, and with your feet fitted with the readiness that comes from the gospel of peace. In addition to all this, take up the shield of faith, with which you can extinguish all the flaming arrows of the evil one. Take the helmet of salvation and the sword of the Spirit, which is the word of God. And pray in the Spirit on all occasions with all kinds of prayers and requests. With this in mind, be alert and always keep on praying for all the saints.

(Ephesians 6:10–18)

See also Isaiah 26:1; Matthew 4:1–11; 1 Thessalonians 5:8; Hebrews 4:12

Encouragement to stand firm

Sometimes we simply need to 'stand our ground' and trust God.

'Do not be afraid or discouraged because of this vast army. For the battle is not yours, but God's. Tomorrow march down against them. They will be climbing up by the Pass of Ziz, and you will find them at the end of the gorge in the Desert of Jeruel. You will not have to fight this battle. Take up your positions; stand firm and see the deliverance the LORD will give you, O Judah and Jerusalem. Do not be afraid; do not be discouraged. Go out to face them tomorrow, and the LORD will be with you.'

(2 Chronicles 20:15–17)

See also Exodus 14:13; Psalm 62:5–8; Isaiah 7:4–9; 1 Corinthians 15:58; 16:13; Galatians 5:1; Ephesians 6:14; Colossians 4:12; James 5:7–8

Encouragement to 'stick at it'

When things don't happen straight away, don't give up, the Bible says!

Then Jesus told his disciples a parable to show them that they should always pray and not give up. He said: 'In a certain town there was a judge who neither feared God nor cared about men. And there was a widow in that town who kept coming to him with the plea, "Grant me justice against my adversary." For some time he refused. But finally he said to himself, "Even though I don't fear God or care about men, yet because this widow keeps bothering me, I will see that she gets justice, so that she won't eventually wear me out with her coming!"' And the Lord said, 'Listen to what the unjust judge says. And will not God bring about justice for his chosen ones, who cry out to him day and night? Will he keep putting them off? I tell you, he will see that they get justice, and quickly.'

(Luke 18:1–8)

See also Genesis 18:23–33; Deuteronomy 9:25–29; 1 Kings 18:41–46; Psalm 88:1–18; Isaiah 62:6–7; Luke 11:5–10; Acts 1:14; Romans 12:12; 1 Thessalonians 5:17

Encouragement to 'wrestle with God'

Sometimes prayer isn't answered immediately because God wants to 'wrestle' with us, seeing whether we will press on or give in the moment something doesn't happen. But this 'wrestling' with our Father is for our good, not our harm.

So Jacob was left alone, and a man wrestled with him till daybreak. When the man saw that he could not overpower him, he touched the socket of Jacob's hip so that his hip was wrenched as he wrestled with the man. Then the man said, 'Let me go, for it is daybreak.' But Jacob replied, 'I will not let you go unless you bless me.' The man asked him, 'What is your name?' 'Jacob,' he answered. Then the man said, 'Your name will no longer be Jacob, but Israel, because you have struggled with God and with men and have overcome.'

(Genesis 32:24–28)

See also Hosea 12:4–5; Colossians 2:1; 4:12

Encouragement to remember Jesus

Perhaps the greatest motivation to keep praying, even when things are hard, is to remember that Jesus himself is still praying for us.

Because Jesus lives for ever, he has a permanent priesthood. Therefore he is able to save completely those who come to God through him, because he always lives to intercede for them.

(Hebrews 7:24–25)

See also Luke 22:32; Romans 8:34; 2 Timothy 2:8–13; Hebrews 12:2–3

A FINAL PRAYER

Alone with none but thee,
my God,
I journey on the way.
What need I fear,
when thou art near
O king of night and day?
More safe am I within thy hand
Than if a host did
round me stand.

St Columba (c. 521–597)

CONCLUSION

God's presence, God's Spirit and God's encouragement assure us that the Father has not left us alone in the adventure of prayer.

'As I was with Moses, so I will be with you; I will never leave you nor forsake you.'

(Joshua 1:5)

Relevance for today

God's presence is always available to us

'The LORD himself goes before you and will be with you; he will never leave you nor forsake you. Do not be afraid; do not be discouraged.'

(Deuteronomy 31:8)

'So do not fear, for I am with you; do not be dismayed, for I am your God. I will strengthen you and help you; I will uphold you with my righteous right hand.'

(Isaiah 41:10)

'And surely I am with you always, to the very end of the age.'

(Matthew 28:20)

God's Spirit is always available to us

'My Spirit remains among you. Do not fear.'

(Haggai 2:5)

'Repent and be baptised, every one of you, in the name of Jesus Christ for the forgiveness of your sins. And you will receive the gift of the Holy Spirit. The promise is for you and your children and for all who are far off – for all whom the Lord our God will call.'

(Acts 2:38–39)

May the grace of the Lord Jesus Christ, and the love of God, and the fellowship of the Holy Spirit be with you all.

(2 Corinthians 13:14)

God's encouragement is always available to us

You hear, O LORD, The desire of the afflicted; you encourage them, and you listen to their cry,

(Psalm 10:17)

May the God who gives endurance and encouragement give you a spirit of unity among yourselves as you follow Christ Jesus, so that with one heart and mouth you may glorify the God and Father of our Lord Jesus Christ.

(Romans 15:5)

May our Lord Jesus Christ himself and God our Father, who loved us and by his grace gave us eternal encouragement and good hope, encourage your hearts and strengthen you in every good deed and word.

(2 Thessalonians 2:16–17)

Chapter Six

Listening to the Father

The more we listen to our Father, the more we learn about him.

I will listen to what God the LORD will say. (Psalm 85:8)

As inheritors of Greek thinking, we in the West tend to keep the 'spiritual' separate from the 'secular'. God and religion are in one box; 'real life' is in the other. Because of this, western Christianity has had little expectation of God reaching out of his 'box' into our ordinary, everyday life, and faith has often become entirely 'other worldly'. But this is far removed from the Bible, where God is fully involved in his world as a God who speaks and acts. The challenge to us today is: are we listening?

The God who speaks

In contrast to dumb idols, the living God loves to speak to his people.

God is eager to speak

'The LORD our God has shown us his glory and his majesty, and we have heard his voice from the fire. Today we have seen that a man can live even if God speaks with him.'

(Deuteronomy 5:24)

'Before they call I will answer; while they are still speaking I will hear.'

(Isaiah 65:24)

This is what the LORD says, he who made the earth, the LORD who formed it and established it – the LORD is his name: 'Call to me and I will answer you and tell you great and unsearchable things you do not know.'

(Jeremiah 33:2–3)

God is eager to reveal his will and purposes

Then the LORD said, 'Shall I hide from Abraham what I am about to do?'

(Genesis 18:17)

Surely the Sovereign LORD does nothing without revealing his plan to his servants the prophets.

(Amos 3:7)

After this I looked, and there before me was a door standing open in heaven. And the voice I had first heard speaking to me like a trumpet said, 'Come up here, and I will show you what must take place after this.'

(Revelation 4:1)

God stands in strong contrast to dumb idols

Our God is in heaven; he does whatever pleases him. But their idols are silver and gold, made by the hands of men. They have

God speaks in many different ways

Before he goes on to speak of the ultimate way that God has spoken to us in history – through sending his Son Jesus – the writer to the Hebrews begins his letter like this:

In the past God spoke to our forefathers through the prophets at many times and in various ways . . .

(Hebrews 1:1)

What were some of those ways that God used, and still uses, to speak to us?

- Audible voice (e.g. 1 Samuel 3:1–10; Matthew 3:16–17)
- God's word 'coming' (e.g. Genesis 15:4–5; 1 Kings 17:2–4)
  We are not told how this happened – perhaps audibly, perhaps through an inner sense or impression. The expression 'the word of the Lord came' occurs over 100 times in the Bible.
- Visions (e.g. Genesis 15:1; Acts 9:10–16)
- Dreams (e.g. Genesis 28:10–17; Matthew 2:19–23)
- Pictures (e.g. Jeremiah 1:11–17; Amos 8:1–2)
- Angels (e.g. Judges 6:11–22; Luke 1:26–38)
- Circumstances (e.g. 2 Chronicles 36:22–23; Acts 16:6–10
- Revelation (e.g. 2 Samuel 7:17; Revelation 1:1)

mouths, but cannot speak, eyes, but they cannot see; they have ears, but cannot hear, noses, but they cannot smell; they have hands, but cannot feel, feet, but they cannot walk; nor can they utter a sound with their throats. Those who make them will be like them, and so will all who trust in them.

(Psalm 115:3–8)

'Of what value is an idol, since a man has carved it? Or an image that teaches lies? For he who makes it trusts in his own creation; he makes idols that cannot speak. Woe to him who says to wood, "Come to life!" Or to lifeless stone, "Wake up!" Can it give guidance? It is covered with gold and silver; there is no breath in it. But the LORD is in his holy temple; let all the earth be silent before him.'

(Habakkuk 2:18–20)

See also Psalm 135:15–18; Isaiah 44:9–20; Jeremiah 10:1–5

The God who calls us to listen

God speaking is not enough – we need to listen too. Hence the Bible is full of exhortations to us to listen to God, and tells us that if we fail to listen it is to our loss.

Calls to listen to God

'Come, all you who are thirsty, come to the waters; and you who have no money, come, buy and eat! Come, buy wine and milk without money and without cost. Why spend money on what is not bread, and your labour on what does not satisfy? Listen, listen to me, and eat what is good, and your soul will delight in the richest of fare. Give ear and come to me; hear me, that your soul may live.'

(Isaiah 55:1–3)

See also Joshua 3:9; Psalm 81:8–16; Isaiah 51:1; Ezekiel 3:4–11; Micah 1:2; 6:1–5; Matthew 17:5

In Proverbs 8 God's 'wisdom' is personified – part of the preparation for the New Testament understanding of Jesus as the Word of God. This wisdom of God, of whom it is said, *'The LORD brought me forth as the first of his works, before his deeds of old; I was appointed from eternity, from the beginning, before the world began'*

(Proverbs 8:22–23), is synonymous with God himself. In the light of this, we hear God's pronouncement of blessing on the one who listens to him:

Blessed is the man who listens to me, watching daily at my doors, waiting at my doorway. For whoever finds me finds life and receives favour from the LORD.

(Proverbs 8:34–35)

Results of not listening to God

God speaks, but does not force us to listen. However, there are consequences of our not listening to him:

God is disappointed when we do not listen

God can expect unbelievers not to listen to him; but when his own people do not listen, that both breaks God's law and breaks God's heart.

Hear, O heavens! Listen, O earth! For the LORD has spoken: 'I reared children and brought them up, but they have rebelled against me. The ox knows his master, the donkey his owner's manger, but Israel does not know, my people do not understand.'

(Isaiah 1:2–3)

See also Genesis 6:6; 1 Samuel 15:10–35; Psalm 78:40–42; Isaiah 63:8–10

Not listening to God brings its own consequences

When we listen to God, we reap the consequent blessings:

'Now then, my sons, listen to me; blessed are those who keep my ways.'

(Proverbs 8:32)

But when we fail to listen to God, it will always be to our harm:

'If you fear the LORD and serve and obey him and do not rebel against his commands, and if both you and the king who reigns over you follow the LORD your God – good! But if you do not obey the LORD, and if you rebel against his commands, his hand will be against you, as it was against your fathers.'

(1 Samuel 12:14–15)

'If you do not listen, and if you do not set your heart to honour my name,' says the LORD Almighty, 'I will send a curse upon you, and I will curse your blessings.'

(Malachi 2:2)

See also Genesis 42:21–22; Exodus 7:14–18; Deuteronomy 1:42–45;

Prohibited ways of listening to God

While God eagerly wants us to listen to him, there are some things that he expressly forbids us to engage in, because of their link to occult powers. These include:

- **Astrology** (e.g. Deuteronomy 4:19; 17:2–5; Jeremiah 8:1–2)
- **Consulting mediums or spiritists** (e.g. Leviticus 19:31; 20:6; Deuteronomy 18:10–12; 1 Samuel 28:7–20; 2 Kings 21:6; 1 Chronicles 10:13–14; Isaiah 8:19–20)
- **Divination of any sort** (e.g. Leviticus 19:26; Deuteronomy 18:10–12; 1 Samuel 15:23; 2 Kings 21:6)
- **Magic and sorcery** (e.g. Ezekiel 13:18–20; Acts 8:9–13; 19:18–20; Revelation 21:8; 22:15)

Many 'New Age' practices fall within these sort of bounds and we need to beware of them. They may be 'spiritual' but they are certainly not of God.

28:15–18; 2 Chronicles 33:10–13; Isaiah 28:11–13; 65:11–16; Jeremiah 7:12–29; 12:17; 25:8–11

God stops speaking when we stop listening

While this may seem a scary thought, it is what the Bible says. Thankfully, God's nature is always to be patient and forgiving and to hold his arms out to us. But a point does come when he says, 'Enough!' and has nothing more to say to us.

'I spoke to you again and again, but you did not listen; I called you, but you did not answer. Therefore, what I did to Shiloh I will now do to the house that bears my Name, the temple you trust in, the place I gave to you and your fathers. I will thrust you from my presence, just as I did all your brothers, the people of Ephraim. So do not pray for this people nor offer any plea or petition for them; do not plead with me, for I will not listen to you.'

(Jeremiah 7:13–16)

'When I called, they did not listen; so when they called, I would not listen,' says the LORD Almighty.

(Zechariah 7:13)

See also 1 Samuel 14:36–37; 28:5–6; Jeremiah 6:16–19; Malachi 2:13–14

This is why the Bible urges us:

Today, if you hear his voice, do not harden your hearts . . .

(Psalm 95:7–8)

Prayer as interactive conversation

Listening means taking on board what we have heard and then responding to it. In fact, the Hebrew word for 'hear' carries within it the sense of 'hear and obey'. We are not just to listen to our Father; we are to do something about what we have listened to.

In the Bible, people's response is not always immediate, however. Sometimes the listener engages in conversation with God to 'talk things through' first. Such conversations reveal much to us about God's heart and purposes, and how ready he is to draw us in to all that he does.

One of the lengthiest prayer conversations is found in Exodus 3:1–4:17, where God calls Moses to lead his people out of slavery and where Moses finds lots of excuses for not being suitable for the job. Do read the whole passage – it's wonderful! But for the moment, just look at the excuses:

But Moses said to God, 'Who am I, that I should go to Pharaoh and bring the Israelites out of Egypt?' And God said, 'I will be with you . . .'

(3:11–12)

Moses said to God, 'Suppose I go to the Israelites and say to them, "The God of your fathers has sent me to you," and they ask me, "What is his name?" Then what shall I tell them?' God said to Moses, 'I AM WHO I AM. This is what you are to say to the Israelites: "I AM has sent me to you." '

(3:13–14)

Moses answered, 'What if they do not believe me or listen to me and say, "The LORD did not appear to you"?' Then the LORD said to him, 'What is that in your hand?'

(4:1–2)

Moses said to the LORD, 'O Lord, I have never been eloquent, neither in the past nor since you have spoken to your servant. I am slow of speech and tongue.' The LORD said to him, 'Who gave man his mouth? Who makes him deaf or mute? Who gives him sight or makes him blind? Is it not I, the

LORD? Now go; I will help you speak and will teach you what to say.'

(4:10–12)

But Moses said, 'O Lord, please send someone else to do it.' Then the LORD's anger burned against Moses and he said, 'What about your brother, Aaron the Levite? I know he can speak well . . .'

(4:13–14)

How our prayer life would be transformed if we were to see prayer more as this sort of interactive conversation with God – listening and responding, until the issue has been worked through.

See also Genesis 15:1–16; 18:17–33; Jonah 4:1–11; Acts 10:9–16; 2 Corinthians 12:7–9

Listening changes things

The story of Samuel is a remarkable story about how listening can change things. A 'miracle baby' born to a barren mother, Samuel had been dedicated to God's service even before his conception (1 Samuel 1:10–11). Around the age of three he was entrusted to the priest Eli at the central sanctuary in Shiloh (1:24–28), and there he began to 'minister before the LORD' (2:18). In contrast to Eli's wicked sons (2:12–17, 22–25), Samuel was a godly boy who *'continued to grow in stature and in favour with the LORD and with men'* (2:26). As yet, however, he had had no personal encounter with God (3:7); but all that was about to change.

At a time when '*the LORD hardly ever spoke directly to people, and he did not appear to them in dreams very often*' (3:1, CEV), Samuel suddenly found himself confronted with the voice of God, at the age (according to Jewish tradition) of just twelve. Hearing a voice calling him during the night, he naturally thought it was the old man Eli, in need of something. We can perhaps imagine Eli's irritation on being needlessly awakened! But by the third time it had happened, even the old man – as unspiritual as he had become – realized something was going on, and that it must have been God who was calling.

So Eli told Samuel, 'Go and lie down, and if he calls you, say, "Speak, LORD, for your servant is listening." So Samuel went and lay down in his place. The LORD came and stood there, calling as at the other times, 'Samuel! Samuel!' Then Samuel said, 'Speak, for your servant is listening.'

(1 Samuel 3:9–10)

And so began a long and distinguished career as the prophet of God whose '*word came to all Israel*' (4:1), who would steer Israel out of its dark days, and who would see Israel through the failure of the kingship of Saul and prepare the way for the success of the kingship of David. A wonderfully successful ministry – but it all began with listening.

Those who listened and whose lives were changed

The Bible tells of countless people whose lives were changed and who were then significantly used by God – and all because they stopped to listen what God had to say and then responded to it.

Abraham

The LORD had said to Abram, 'Leave your country, your people and your father's household and go to the land I will show you. I will make you into a great nation and I will bless you; I will make your name great, and you will be a blessing. I will bless those who bless you, and whoever curses you I will curse; and all peoples on earth will be blessed through you.' So Abram left, as the LORD had told him.

(Genesis 12:1–4)

Job

Then Job replied to the LORD: 'I know that you can do all things; no plan of yours can be thwarted. You asked, "Who is this that obscures my counsel without knowledge?" Surely I spoke of things I did not understand, things too wonderful for me to know. You said, "Listen now, and I will speak; I will question you, and you shall answer me." My ears had heard of you but now my eyes have seen you. Therefore I despise myself and repent in dust and ashes.'

(Job 42:1–6)

Paul

Meanwhile, Saul was still breathing out murderous threats against the Lord's disciples. He went to the high priest and asked him for letters to the synagogues in Damascus, so that if he found any there who belonged to the Way, whether men or women, he might take them as prisoners to Jerusalem. As he neared Damascus on his journey, suddenly a light from heaven flashed around him. He fell to the ground and heard a voice say to him, 'Saul, Saul, why do you persecute me?' 'Who are you, Lord?' Saul asked. 'I am Jesus, whom you are persecuting,' he replied. 'Now get up and go into the city, and you will be told what you must do.'

(Acts 9:1–6)

A FINAL PRAYER

Jesus, my strength, my hope,
On Thee I cast my care,
With humble confidence look up,
And know thou hear'st my prayer.
Give me on Thee to wait,
Till I can all things do,
On Thee, almighty to create,
Almighty to renew.

Charles Wesley (1707–1788)

CONCLUSION

There is no doubt that God wants to speak. The issue is: do we want to listen?

'Speak, LORD; for thy servant heareth.'

(1 Samuel 3:9, KJV)

Relevance for today

Because life is so busy these days, most of us find it hard to listen. So, what are some of the things that can help us?

Taking time to stop

Like Martha long ago, most of us find it hard to 'stop'; but stopping is a key to listening to God. 'Hurry is the death of prayer' (Samuel Chadwick).

'Martha, Martha, you are worried and bothered about so many things; but only one thing is necessary.'

(Luke 10:41–42, NASB)

Being alone

It is often hard to listen when distractions (of things or people) are around. Try getting alone at times.

'But when you pray, go into your room, close the door and pray to your Father, who is unseen.'

(Matthew 6:6)

Being convinced God wants to speak

We will never hear our Father if we are not convinced he wants to speak to us. But this is his promise:

The LORD will cause men to hear his majestic voice.

(Isaiah 30:30)

Meditation

Meditation is the practice of quietly, deeply and repeatedly reflecting on one main thing – perhaps an aspect of God's character or a Bible verse.

I will remember the deeds of the LORD; yes, I will remember your miracles of long ago. I will meditate on all your works and consider all your mighty deeds.

(Psalm 77:11–12)

Receiving spiritual gifts

God can speak to us through a 'spiritual gift' such as prophecy or a word of knowledge (e.g. 1 Corinthians 12:7–11; 14:1–33), especially when the person bringing it doesn't know our situation. But do we make room for such things?

Be eager to have the gifts that come from the Holy Spirit, especially the gift of prophecy.

(1 Corinthians 14:1, CEV)

Reading the word of God

If we can grasp that the Bible is God's inspired word, then we will have no difficulty in hearing him speak through it and bringing his guidance to us.

All Scripture is inspired by God and is useful to teach us what is true and to make us realize what is wrong in our lives. It straightens us out and teaches us to do what is right. It is God's way of preparing us in every way, fully equipped for every good thing God wants us to do.

(2 Timothy 3:16–17, NLT)

Chapter Seven

Like a Little Child

Jesus does not ask us to be childish; but he certainly asks us to be child-like, if we want to know more of the Father.

Jesus said, 'Let the little children come to me, and do not hinder them, for the kingdom of heaven belongs to such as these.' (Matthew 19:14)

As we look back to the time when our children were little, we never cease to be amazed at how they trusted us. They would leap from high walls into our arms, never for one moment thinking that we might miss! They would bring their broken toys to us, never for one moment doubting that we would be able to mend them. They would run to their mothers after a fall, never for one moment considering that a kiss on the knee might not 'make it better'!

There is something wonderfully trusting about young children – something that we lose as we grow up. Of course, we rationalize it: the world is a hard place; people trample on you if you trust them; things go wrong in life and you get hurt. Putting it another way, we get hardhearted. But, said Jesus, if you really want to know the Father's heart, then you will become like those little children again.

So, what are some of those childlike qualities that God is looking for in us?

Childlike trust

Trust is foundational to any good relationship. Without trust, there is no relationship; without trust, the relationship will never grow. So, the Bible encourages us to have childlike trust (or 'faith' to use another word) in our heavenly Father.

Psalms of trust

The book of Psalms – the prayer book of the Old Testament – is full of exhortations and testimonies about trusting God, especially in the face of trying or difficult circumstances. Psalm 9:10 sums up the essence of their testimony: '*Those who know your name will trust in you, for you, LORD, have never forsaken those who seek you.*'

Here are some well-known psalms of trusting:

Psalm 23

The LORD is my shepherd;
I shall not want.
He maketh me to lie down in green pastures:
he leadeth me beside the still waters.
He restoreth my soul: he leadeth me in the paths of righteousness for his name's sake.
Yea, though I walk through the valley of the shadow of death, I will fear no evil: for thou art with me; thy rod and thy staff they comfort me.
Thou preparest a table before me in the presence of mine enemies:
thou anointest my head with oil; my cup runneth over.
Surely goodness and mercy shall follow me all the days of my life: and I will dwell in the house of the LORD For ever.

(KJV)

Psalm 46

God is our refuge and strength,
an ever-present help in trouble.
Therefore we will not fear,
though the earth give way
and the mountains fall into the heart of the sea,
though its waters roar and foam
and the mountains quake with their surging. *Selah*
There is a river whose streams make glad the city of God,
the holy place where the Most High dwells.
God is within her, she will not fall;
God will help her at break of day.
Nations are in uproar, kingdoms fall;
he lifts his voice, the earth melts.
The LORD Almighty is with us;
the God of Jacob is our fortress. *Selah*
Come and see the works of the LORD,
the desolations he has brought on the earth.
He makes wars cease to the ends of the earth;
he breaks the bow and shatters the spear,
he burns the shields with fire.
'Be still, and know that I am God;
I will be exalted among the nations,
I will be exalted in the earth.'
The LORD Almighty is with us;
the God of Jacob is our fortress. *Selah*

Psalm 91

He who dwells in the shelter of the Most High
will rest in the shadow of the Almighty.
I will say of the LORD, 'He is my refuge and my fortress,
my God, in whom I trust.'
Surely he will save you from the fowler's snare
and from the deadly pestilence.
He will cover you with his feathers,
and under his wings you will find refuge;
his faithfulness will be your shield and rampart.
You will not fear the terror of night,
nor the arrow that flies by day,
nor the pestilence that stalks in the darkness,
nor the plague that destroys at midday.
A thousand may fall at your side,
ten thousand at your right hand,
but it will not come near you.
You will only observe with your eyes
and see the punishment of the wicked.
If you make the Most High your dwelling
even the LORD, who is my refuge –
then no harm will befall you,
no disaster will come near your tent.
For he will command his angels concerning you
to guard you in all your ways;
they will lift you up in their hands,
so that you will not strike your foot against a stone.
You will tread upon the lion and the cobra;
you will trample the great lion and the serpent.
'Because he loves me,' says the LORD, 'I will rescue him;
I will protect him, for he acknowledges my name.

He will call upon me, and I will answer him;
I will be with him in trouble,
I will deliver him and honour him.
With long life will I satisfy him
and show him my salvation.'

See also Psalm 16:1–11; 40:1–5; 52:1–9; 55:22–23; 56:1–4; 62:1–12; 112:1–8; 118:6–14; 125:1–2

Those who trusted

But it isn't just in the Psalms that we find encouragements to trust; many others experienced the blessing of God through trusting too. Such encouragements form a strong basis for our prayer life.

Trust in the LORD with all your heart
and lean not on your own understanding;
in all your ways acknowledge him,
and he will make your paths straight.

(Proverbs 3:5–6)

Fear of man will prove to be a snare,
but whoever trusts in the LORD is kept safe.

(Proverbs 29:25)

You will keep in perfect peace
him whose mind is steadfast,
because he trusts in you.
Trust in the LORD for ever,
for the LORD, the LORD, is the Rock eternal.

(Isaiah 26:3–4)

This is what the Sovereign LORD, the Holy One of Israel, says:
'In repentance and rest is your salvation,
in quietness and trust is your strength.'

(Isaiah 30:15)

'Blessed is the man who trusts in the LORD,
whose confidence is in him.
He will be like a tree planted by the water
that sends out its roots by the stream.
It does not fear when heat comes;
its leaves are always green.
It has no worries in a year of drought
and never fails to bear fruit.'

(Jeremiah 17:7–8)

May the God of hope fill you with all joy and peace as you trust in him, so that you may overflow with hope by the power of the Holy Spirit

(Romans 15:13)

See also 2 Samuel 7:27–29; 2 Kings 18:5–6; Proverbs 3:5–12; Isaiah 8:17; 12:1–3; 25:9; 50:10; John 14:1–3; Acts 14:23; Romans 10:5–11

Trust expressed in action

We wrote in the introduction to this chapter about how our children, when young, would leap from some great height into our arms. Real trust demands action! Sometimes, our trust in God needs to be demonstrated in outward action in some way, so that we 'nail our colours to the mast'. This is what King Hezekiah did when he spread out a threatening letter he had received before the Lord to demonstrate that he was trusting in God alone to deal with the situation.

Hezekiah received the letter from the messengers and read it. Then he went up to the temple of the LORD and spread it out before the LORD. And Hezekiah prayed to the LORD: 'O LORD Almighty, God of Israel, enthroned between the cherubim, you alone are God over all the kingdoms of the earth. You have made heaven and earth. Give ear, O LORD, and hear; open your eyes, O LORD, and see; listen to all the words Sennacherib has sent to insult the living God.

'It is true, O LORD, that the Assyrian kings have laid waste all these peoples and their lands. They have thrown their gods into the fire and destroyed them, for they were not gods but only wood and stone,

fashioned by human hands. Now, O LORD our God, deliver us from his hand, so that all kingdoms on earth may know that you alone, O LORD, are God.'

(Isaiah 37:14–20)

Esther, a young Jewish woman in exile who was commandeered into the harem of the king of Persia (Esther 2:8–9), was another who dared to express her trust in God through action.

When Esther's words were reported to Mordecai, he sent back this answer: 'Do not think that because you are in the king's house you alone of all the Jews will escape. For if you remain silent at this time, relief and deliverance for the Jews will arise from another place, but you and your father's family will perish. And who knows but that you have come to royal position for such a time as this?'

Then Esther sent this reply to Mordecai: 'Go, gather together all the Jews who are in Susa, and fast for me. Do not eat or drink for three days, night or day. I and my maids will fast as you do. When this is done, I will go to the king, even though it is against the law. And if I perish, I perish.'

(Esther 4:12–16)

See also Genesis 22:1–14; Nehemiah 2:1–8; 4:1–21; Daniel 3:1–30; 6:1–23; Acts 4:1–20

Trust expressed in acknowledging weakness

Few of us like to acknowledge that there are things we can't do on our own. But if we truly trust someone, we let them in to those areas where we are weak, and not just the areas where we are strong. True childlike trust says, 'This is me! – warts and all!' and invites God to come and help. It is a strong person who admits their own weaknesses.

To keep me from getting puffed up, I was given a thorn in my flesh, a messenger from Satan to torment me and keep me from getting proud. Three different times I begged the Lord to take it away. Each time he said, 'My gracious favour is all you need. My power works best in your weakness.' So now I am glad to boast about my weaknesses, so that the power of Christ may work through me . . . For when I am weak, then I am strong.

(2 Corinthians 12:7–10, NLT)

See also Psalm 31:9–10; Isaiah 38:9–20; Romans 8:26; 1 Corinthians 1:27–29; 2:1–5; 2 Corinthians 11:30

Childlike humility

True humility has nothing to do with the grovelling behaviour of Charles Dickens' character, Uriah Heap. True humility is about knowing who we really are, before God and before others. Paul summed it up like this:

Trust

Some Scriptures to use when we need to trust:

- **In times of confusion**
  Jeremiah 33:3; Haggai 2:3–5; John 14:25–27; Ephesians 1:18–19; Philippians 1:9–10; James 1:5
- **In face of difficulty or danger**
  2 Chronicles 20:12; Psalm 23:4; 46:1–7; Isaiah 43:1–7; Daniel 3:1–30; 6:1–23; Romans 8:31–39; 2 Corinthians 1:8–11; 1 John 4:4
- **In times of fear**
  Exodus 14:13–14; Joshua 1:6–9; 2 Kings 6:15–16; Isaiah 41:10; Matthew 10:26–31; Acts 18:9–10; Romans 8:15; 1 John 4:18
- **In times of uncertainty**
  Proverbs 3:5–6; Isaiah 30:21; Matthew 7:24–25; Romans 8:26; 1 Corinthians 15:58; 1 Peter 5:7–9

For by the grace given me I say to every one of you: Do not think of yourself more highly than you ought, but rather think of yourself with sober judgment, in accordance with the measure of faith God has given you.

(Romans 12:3)

In other words: get real! There is little that is 'unreal' about young children; what you see is what you get! So, Jesus says, be real about yourself, your circumstances, and your requests when you come to God in prayer.

True humility involves:

Knowing our limitations

We do not dare to classify or compare ourselves with some who commend themselves. When they measure themselves by themselves and compare themselves with themselves, they are not wise. We, however, will not boast beyond proper limits, but will confine our boasting to the field God has assigned to us, a field that reaches even to you. We are not going too far in our boasting, as would be the case if we had not come to you, for we did get as far as you with the gospel of Christ. Neither do we go beyond our limits by boasting of work done by others. Our hope is that, as your faith continues to grow, our area of activity among you will greatly expand, so that we can preach the gospel in the regions beyond you. For we do not want to boast about work already done in another man's territory. But, 'Let him who boasts boast in the Lord.'

For it is not the one who commends himself who is approved, but the one whom the Lord commends.

(2 Corinthians 10:12–18)

See also John 3:30; Romans 12:3

Asking for help

Now when Daniel learned that the decree had been published, he went home to his upstairs room where the windows opened towards Jerusalem. Three times a day he got down on his knees and prayed, giving thanks to his God, just as he had done before. Then these men went as a group and found Daniel praying and asking God for help.

(Daniel 6:10–11)

When Jesus had entered Capernaum, a centurion came to him, asking for help. 'Lord,' he said, 'my servant lies at home paralysed and in terrible suffering.' Jesus said to him, 'I will go and heal him.'

(Matthew 8:5–7)

See also 1 Samuel 12:8; 2 Chronicles 14:11; Psalm 18:6; Jonah 2:1–2; Luke 4:38–39; 1 Timothy 5:5

Taking advice

The way of a fool seems right to him,
but a wise man listens to advice.

(Proverbs 12:15)

Pride only breeds quarrels,
but wisdom is found in those who take advice.

(Proverbs 13:10)

Listen to advice and accept instruction,
and in the end you will be wise. Many are the plans in a man's heart,
but it is the LORD's purpose that prevails.

(Proverbs 19:20–21)

See also Exodus 18:13–27; 2 Samuel 16:23; 1 Kings 12:1–19; Acts 5:33–40; 27:9–25

Seeking wisdom

That night God appeared to Solomon and said to him, 'Ask for whatever you want me to give you.' Solomon answered God . . . 'Give me wisdom and knowledge, that I may lead this people, for who is able to govern this great people of yours?'

(2 Chronicles 1:7, 8, 10)

My son, if you accept my words
and store up my commands within you,
turning your ear to wisdom
and applying your heart to understanding,
and if you call out for insight
and cry aloud for understanding,
and if you look for it as for silver
and search for it as for hidden treasure,
then you will understand the fear of the LORD
and find the knowledge of God.
For the LORD gives wisdom,
and from his mouth come knowledge and understanding.
He holds victory in store for the upright,
he is a shield to those whose walk is blameless,
for he guards the course of the just
and protects the way of his faithful ones.
Then you will understand what is right and just
and fair – every good path.
For wisdom will enter your heart,
and knowledge will be pleasant to your soul.
Discretion will protect you,
and understanding will guard you.

(Proverbs 2:1–11)

See also 1 Kings 4:29–34; Psalm 111:10; Proverbs 1:1–7; 4:5–13; 24:3–4; Luke 2:52; Colossians 2:2–3; James 1:5

A FINAL PRAYER

'Tis a gift to be simple,
'tis a gift to be free,
'Tis a gift to come down
where we ought to be,
And when we find ourselves
in the place just right
'Twill be in the valley of love
and delight.
When true simplicity is gained
To bow and to bend
we shan't be ashamed,
To turn, turn, shall be our delight,
Till by turning, turning
we come round right.

The Shaker Community (1747)

CONCLUSION

Our Father is looking for child-like hearts where he can share his own heart. Will he find such a heart in us?

Search me, O God, and know my heart; test me and know my anxious thoughts. See if there is any offensive way in me, and lead me in the way everlasting.

(Psalm 139:23–24)

Relevance for today

Our Father wants us to learn simplicity

- Simplicity lets us be trained by Father's word (e.g. Psalm 19:7)
- Simplicity keeps us open to the gospel's power (e.g. 1 Corinthians 1:18–25)
- Simplicity focuses us on the 'one thing' that is important (e.g. Luke 10:40–42)
- Simplicity opens up the blessings of the kingdom to us (e.g. Mark 10:15–16)

Our Father wants us to learn trust

- Despite the hard knocks of life (e.g. Genesis 50:20)
- Despite those who have let us down (e.g. 2 Timothy 4:16)
- Despite prayers that seem to go unanswered (e.g. 2 Corinthians 12:8–10)
- Despite our not always understanding God's timing (e.g. 2 Peter 3:9)

Those who trust in the LORD are like Mount Zion, which cannot be shaken but endures for ever. As the mountains surround Jerusalem, so the LORD surrounds his people both now and for evermore.

(Psalm 125:1–2)

Our Father wants us to learn humility

- Humility before him (e.g. James 4:7–10)
- Humility before others (e.g. Ephesians 4:2)
- Humility that is ready to learn (e.g. Psalm 25:8–9)
- Humility like that of little children (e.g. Matthew 18:1–4)

Humble yourselves, therefore, under God's mighty hand, that he may lift you up in due time. Cast all your anxiety on him because he cares for you.

(1 Peter 5:6–7)

Part Two
Prayers that say 'Amazing!'

Chapter One

Called to Worship

> The things that make us say 'Wow!' in life are the things that truly amaze us. God invites us to look at him and say 'Wow!'
>
> ***How awesome is the LORD Most High, the great King over all the earth!*** (Psalm 47:2)

Amazing! Fantastic! Awesome! Wow! (Or, if you belong to a younger generation: Cool! Magic! – even 'Wicked'!) What words do you use when something is so good that it takes your breath away? Whatever your words, that's exactly how the writers of the Bible felt about God. For them, talking to God did not demand 'special' language, far removed from ordinary life; God was so amazing that he was worth telling so with words that came naturally and spontaneously! The football fan might shout; the play-goer might applaud; the nature-lover might sigh; but the worshipper who knows his God has real cause for getting excited. For worship is what we were made for, and worship is what God calls us to.

A call to worship

In some church traditions, worship services begin with a 'call to worship' – a scripture or anthem that focuses on God and helps us 'tune in'. The Bible is full of such 'calls to worship'. Here are some examples, all inviting us to 'come!'

Psalm 66

Shout with joy to God, all the earth!
Sing the glory of his name;
make his praise glorious!
Say to God, 'How awesome are your deeds!'
So great is your power
that your enemies cringe before you.
All the earth bows down to you;
they sing praise to you,
they sing praise to your name.' *Selah*
Come and see what God has done,
how awesome his works on man's behalf!
(Psalm 66:1–5)

Psalm 95

Come, let us sing for joy to the LORD;
let us shout aloud to the Rock of our salvation.
Let us come before him with thanksgiving
and extol him with music and song.
For the LORD is the great God,
the great King above all gods.
In his hand are the depths of the earth,
and the mountain peaks belong to him.
The sea is his, for he made it,
and his hands formed the dry land.

Come, let us bow down in worship,
let us kneel before the LORD our Maker;
for he is our God
and we are the people of his pasture,
the flock under his care.

(Psalm 95:1–7)

Psalm 100

Shout for joy to the LORD, all the earth.
Worship the LORD with gladness;
come before him with joyful songs.
Know that the LORD is God.
It is he who made us, and we are his;
we are his people, the sheep of his pasture.
Enter his gates with thanksgiving
and his courts with praise;
give thanks to him and praise his name.
For the LORD is good and his love endures for ever;
his faithfulness continues through all generations.

Going up the hill!

We don't know about you, but we confess that – despite God's invitation to come – we don't always find it easy to begin to worship God. We sometimes need to throw off thoughts that have occupied our minds and to 'prime the pump' of our hearts to 'get them going'. The Bible seems to recognize that this is how we will feel at times; and so it helps us to 'get up the hill' to worship God.

The temple in Jerusalem was built on top of a hill, so it could be seen from all around. But to get to that temple, you had to 'go up' the hill or 'ascend' – a phrase that often appears in worship contexts in the Old Testament:

Who may ascend the hill of the LORD?
Who may stand in his holy place?

(Psalm 24:3)

I rejoiced with those who said to me,
'Let us go to the house of the LORD.'
Our feet are standing
in your gates, O Jerusalem.
Jerusalem is built like a city
that is closely compacted together.
That is where the tribes go up,
the tribes of the LORD,
to praise the name of the LORD
according to the statute given to Israel.

(Psalm 122:1–4)

In the last days
the mountain of the LORD's temple will be established
as chief among the mountains;
it will be raised above the hills,
and all nations will stream to it.
Many peoples will come and say,

Selah!

Ever wondered about that strange word '*Selah*' that crops up in the Psalms at regular intervals? It occurs 71 times in Psalms and 3 times in Habakkuk. But what does it mean?

The honest answer is: scholars aren't completely sure. But it is generally agreed to be some sort of musical term – perhaps indicating a musical interlude or a change of key – in order to bring some emphasis to the words or allow some pause for thought.

In the light of this, perhaps a good translation of it might be, 'Just think about that for a moment!' Try reading some of the Psalms and replacing '*Selah*' with that expression – and then make sure you do just that!

Some examples: Psalm 3, 24, 32, 46, 62, 66, 89, 140; Habakkuk 3

'Come, let us go up to the mountain of the
LORD,
to the house of the God of Jacob.
He will teach us his ways,
so that we may walk in his paths.'

(Isaiah 2:2–3)

Helps to climbing

'Going up' a hill can be hard; we may need help and encouragement on the way. And that's how it can be in worship too. We sometimes need help to 'get going' or 'keep going'. The Bible has a simple pattern to help us in this, summed up in words from Psalm 100: come . . . know . . . thank . . . praise.

Come

'*Come before him . . .*' (v 2).

Ever received an invitation to something? The invitation is the assurance you are welcome; but the invitation in itself doesn't get us there. We have to make the decision and go. Likewise, God invites us to come; but this then demands our response. We have to decide; we have to choose not to stay in our present circumstances, but to 'go up the hill' to God; we have to choose to throw off the things that have filled our minds, captivated our hearts, and demanded our time. We will never worship if we never decide. Worship does not 'drop out of heaven'!

But I, by your great mercy,
will come into your house;
in reverence will I bow down
towards your holy temple.

(Psalm 5:7)

I will come to your temple with burnt
offerings
and fulfil my vows to you –
vows my lips promised and my mouth spoke
when I was in trouble.

(Psalm 66:13–14)

But as for me, I shall always have hope;
I will praise you more and more.
My mouth will tell of your righteousness,
of your salvation all day long,
though I know not its measure.
I will come and proclaim your mighty acts,
O Sovereign LORD;
I will proclaim your righteousness, yours
alone.
Since my youth, O God, you have taught
me,
and to this day I declare your marvellous
deeds.

(Psalm 71:14–17)

Know

'*Know that the LORD is God*' (v 3).

As we come, we need to start focusing consciously on God, thinking about *him* and not ourselves, remembering what he has done for us, remembering that there is no other God but him alone, and that he is *for* us.

You were shown these things so that you might know that the LORD is God; besides him there is no other . . .

Acknowledge and take to heart this day that the LORD is God in heaven above and on the earth below. There is no other.

(Deuteronomy 4:35, 39)

'Be still, and know that I am God.'

(Psalm 46:10)

Among the gods there is none like you,
O Lord;
no deeds can compare with yours.
All the nations you have made
will come and worship before you,
O Lord;
they will bring glory to your name.
For you are great and do marvellous deeds;
you alone are God.

(Psalm 86:8–10)

Do you not know?
Have you not heard?
The LORD *is the everlasting God,*
the Creator of the ends of the earth.

(Isaiah 40:28)

Thank

'*Enter his gates with thanksgiving . . .*' (v 4). As we will see in Part Three, thanksgiving has an important place in prayer. For now, let us simply note that the more grateful we become, the more 'praise-ful' we become. A grateful heart more easily becomes a praising heart.

One of Mike's early memories is of sitting with his grandparents in their local Salvation Army 'citadel' where his grandfather played the trombone and his grandmother sang with the 'Songsters'. A much-used chorus at that time (and one that Mike still remembers!) went like this:

Count your blessings, name them one by one.
Count your blessings, see what God has done.
Count your blessings, name them one by one,
And it will surprise you what the Lord has done.

The words may be old, and the tune might certainly now seem dated; but the truths are profound – and they work!

With praise and thanksgiving they sang to the LORD*:*
'He is good;
his love to Israel endures for ever.'
And all the people gave a great shout of praise to the LORD *. . .*

(Ezra 3:11)

Come, let us sing for joy to the LORD*;*
let us shout aloud to the Rock of our salvation.
Let us come before him with thanksgiving
and extol him with music and song.

(Psalm 95:1–2)

'Those who cling to worthless idols
forfeit the grace that could be theirs.
But I, with a song of thanksgiving,
will sacrifice to you.'

(Jonah 2:8–9)

Rejoice in the Lord always. Again I will say, rejoice! Let your gentleness be known to all men. The Lord is at hand. Be anxious for nothing, but in everything by prayer and supplication, with thanksgiving, let your requests be made known to God; and the peace of God, which surpasses all understanding, will guard your hearts and minds through Christ Jesus.

(Philippians 4:4–7, NKJV)

Praise

'*. . . and his courts with praise*' (v 4). Thanksgiving – thanking God for what he has *done* – can then begin to turn into praise – thanking God for what he *is* (faithful, true, dependable, etc.) – and ultimately into worship – thanking God for *who he is.* The English word 'worship' means literally 'worth-ship'; it is telling God how much he is worth to us. This is the climax of our journey up the hill, and it is to this that we turn in the following chapters of this Part of the book.

He is your praise; he is your God . . .

(Deuteronomy 10:21)

'Stand up and praise the LORD *your God, who is from everlasting to everlasting.*

'Blessed be your glorious name, and may it be exalted above all blessing and praise. You alone are the LORD*. You made the heavens, even the highest heavens, and all their starry host, the earth and all that is on it, the seas and all that is in them. You give life to everything, and the multitudes of heaven worship you.'*

(Nehemiah 9:5–6)

I will praise you, O LORD, with all my heart;
before the 'gods' I will sing your praise.
I will bow down towards your holy temple
and will praise your name
for your love and your faithfulness,
for you have exalted above all things
your name and your word.
When I called, you answered me;
you made me bold and stout-hearted.
May all the kings of the earth praise you, O LORD,
when they hear the words of your mouth.
May they sing of the ways of the LORD,
for the glory of the LORD is great.

(Psalm 138:1–5)

What about me?

Do I 'climb up the hill'? Or do I stop halfway up? Do I give in, or do I press through? This pattern of 'come . . . know . . . thank . . . praise' can still be helpful to us in our worship as individuals and as churches. Why not try it and see what it unlocks for you?

Let us know, let us press on to know the LORD.

(Hosea 6:3, NRSV)

Worship of God alone

When John, overcome by the amazing vision he had experienced, fell down at the angel's feet to worship, he was quickly stopped with the following words:

'Do not do it! . . . Worship God!'

(Revelation 22:9)

This is the constant theme of the Bible: God and God alone is to be worshipped. False gods and idols of all kinds are to be avoided at all costs.

'I am the LORD your God,
who brought you out of Egypt, out of the land of slavery.
You shall have no other gods before me. You shall not make for yourself an idol in the form of anything in heaven above or on the earth beneath or in the waters below. You shall not bow down to them or worship them; for I, the LORD your God, am a jealous God . . .'

(Exodus 20:2–5)

'Serve the LORD with all your heart. Do not turn away after useless idols. They can do you no good, nor can they rescue you, because they are useless.'

(1 Samuel 12:20–21)

God alone, then, is to be the one who receives the passion and worship of our hearts:

Hear, O Israel: The LORD our God, the LORD is one. Love the LORD your God with all your heart and with all your soul and with all your strength.

(Deuteronomy 6:4–5)

See also Deuteronomy 4:29; 5:7–8; 10:12–13; Joshua 22:1–5; Matthew 22:37–39

For most of us (certainly in the West) worshipping a stone or wooden carving is not an issue; but less obvious forms of idolatry certainly are. Whatever we give most of our energy and passion to is our idol. As Jesus put it, '*For where your treasure is, there your heart will be also*' (Luke 12:34). Our idols are often things like our job, our family, our car, our football team, our hobby; these are what so often have 'number one' place in our life – the place that God says belongs to him alone! When we recognize that such things have pushed God from that central place, this prayer might be appropriate to help us turn from them:

*O LORD, our God, other lords besides you
have ruled over us,
but your name alone do we honour.*
(Isaiah 26:13)

(For more on the Bible's view of idols, see Part One, Chapters 3 and 6.)

A FINAL PRAYER

My God, I love thee above all else and thee I desire as my last end. Always and in all things, with my whole heart, and strength I seek thee. If thou give not thyself to me, thou givest nothing; if I find thee not, I find nothing. Grant to me, therefore, most loving God, that I may ever love thee for thyself above all things, and seek thee in all things in this life present, so that at last I may find thee and keep thee for ever in the world to come.

Thomas Bradwardine (c.1290–1349), confessor to King Edward III

CONCLUSION

Amazing! Fantastic! Wow! God invites us to so get to know him that this is the spontaneous response of our hearts. He alone is our greatest treasure.

'No-one is like you, O LORD; you are great, and your name is mighty in power. Who should not revere you, O King of the nations? This is your due.'

(Jeremiah 10:6–7)

Relevance for today

What do we really worship?

If the English word 'worship' means literally 'worth-ship' – telling God how much he is worth to us – what does my worship tell God that he is worth to me? As much as my football team? Or that concert? Or my computer game? Or my job? Or my boyfriend or girlfriend? What I really get excited about is what I really worship.

'For where your treasure is, there your heart will be also.'

(Luke 12:34)

Why should we worship?

Let's be clear about one thing: God does not *need* our worship! God is not some sort of 'divine battery' that needs recharging through our prayers, nor some psychologically dependent being who needs propping up through our worship. God needs nothing – that's why he is God!

'The God who made the world and everything in it is the Lord of heaven and earth and does not live in temples built by hands. And he is not served by human hands, as if he needed anything, because he himself gives all men life and breath and everything else.'

(Acts 17:24–25)

So, then, what is the relevance of worship for today?

Worship is what we were made for

St Augustine summed it up like this: 'You have made us for yourself and our hearts are restless till they find their rest in you.'

But you are a chosen people, a royal priesthood, a holy nation, a people belonging to God, that you may declare the praises of him who called you out of darkness into his wonderful light.

(1 Peter 2:9)

Worship is what God commands

Jesus answered, 'It is written: "Worship the Lord your God and serve him only." '

(Luke 4:8)

Worship is the proper response to God's love

When all the Israelites saw the fire coming down and the glory of the LORD above the temple, they knelt on the pavement with their faces to the ground, and they worshipped and gave thanks to the LORD, saying, 'He is good; his love endures for ever.'

(2 Chronicles 7:3)

Worship releases God's blessing on our lives

'Worship the LORD your God, and his blessing will be on your food and water. I will take away sickness from among you, and none will miscarry or be barren in your land. I will give you a full life span.'

(Exodus 23:25–26)

Worship keep us in our proper place!

Worship reminds us that the universe does not revolve around us or our plans. It reminds us that there is someone greater; it reminds us that we are not God! David, great king as he was, prayed this:

'Praise be to you, O LORD,
God of our father Israel,
from everlasting to everlasting.
Yours, O LORD, is the greatness and the power
and the glory and the majesty and the splendour,
for everything in heaven and earth is yours.
Yours, O LORD, is the kingdom;
you are exalted as head over all.
Wealth and honour come from you;
you are the ruler of all things.
In your hands are strength and power
to exalt and give strength to all.
Now, our God, we give you thanks,
and praise your glorious name.'

(1 Chronicles 29:10–13)

Chapter Two

Praising God For Who He Is

God wants us so to get to know him that we learn how to praise him, not just for what he has done for us, but also because of who he is.

Who among the gods is like you, O LORD? Who is like you – majestic in holiness, awesome in glory, working wonders? (Exodus 15:11)

'*Who is the LORD, that I should obey him . . .*' (Exodus 5:2)? So asked the great Pharaoh of Egypt when Moses demanded, in God's name, that he should free the Israelite slaves. In many ways, Pharaoh's question was an excellent one. Egypt had many gods; why should Pharaoh obey this one, about whom he knew nothing?

But in contrast to Pharaoh, Moses had had a life-changing encounter with the Living God. He now knew him – The LORD, Yahweh, the great 'I AM' – and he would never be the same again. Moses' life would now be one of coming to know his God better and learning how different he was from the Egyptian gods with which he had grown up. And the more he got to know him, the more he knew there was no one like him and the more he wanted to praise him.

Moses' encounter with God, at a burning bush in a desert, was where he first learned about real prayer – talking and listening to God in two-way conversation. As his relationship with God developed, he learned more and more about this amazing God and his purposes.

A second key moment of revelation for Moses was at Mount Sinai, where he discovered what God was really like. Moses had asked (somewhat foolhardily!) to see God's glory (Exodus 33:18). He must have been staggered at what God showed him:

Then the LORD came down in the cloud and stood there with him and proclaimed his name, the LORD. And he passed in front of Moses, proclaiming, 'The LORD, the LORD, the compassionate and gracious God, slow to anger, abounding in love and faithfulness, maintaining love to thousands, and forgiving wickedness, rebellion and sin. Yet he does not leave the guilty unpunished; he punishes the children and their children for the sin of the fathers to the third and fourth generation.'

Moses bowed to the ground at once and worshipped.

(Exodus 34:5–8)

This passage is foundational to our understanding of what God is like, for it is God's revelation of himself. In this chapter, we will look at this revelation of his nature; in the following chapter, we will look at other aspects revealed elsewhere in the Bible.

The God who is 'LORD'

At the burning bush, God revealed his personal name – the LORD – to Moses.

God said to Moses, 'I am who I am. This is what you are to say to the Israelites: "I AM has sent me to you." '

God also said to Moses, 'Say to the Israelites, "The LORD [YAHWEH], the God of your fathers – the God of Abraham, the God of Isaac and the God of Jacob – has sent me to you." This is my name for ever, the name by which I am to be remembered from generation to generation.'

(Exodus 3:14–15)

The Hebrew for Lord can mean either 'He is' or 'He will be'. The word comes from the same verb translated 'I will be' in 3:12 and 'I am who I am' in 3:14. God is saying here, not simply 'I exist', but rather 'I am always, actively present – whether in the past, present or future.' God is always there; he always has been, and always will be. Nothing, therefore, is beyond his reach or power. Such a one is surely worthy of our praise!

Then Moses and the Israelites sang this song to the LORD:
'I will sing to the LORD,
for he is highly exalted.
The horse and its rider
he has hurled into the sea.
The LORD is my strength and my song;
he has become my salvation.
He is my God, and I will praise him,
my father's God, and I will exalt him.
The LORD is a warrior;
the LORD is his name.

(Exodus 15:1–3)

Sing to the LORD a new song;
sing to the LORD, all the earth.
Sing to the LORD, praise his name;
proclaim his salvation day after day.
Declare his glory among the nations,
his marvellous deeds among all peoples.
For great is the LORD and most worthy of praise;
he is to be feared above all gods.
For all the gods of the nations are idols,
but the LORD made the heavens.
Splendour and majesty are before him;
strength and glory are in his sanctuary.
Ascribe to the LORD, O families of nations,
ascribe to the LORD glory and strength.
Ascribe to the LORD the glory due to his name;
bring an offering and come into his courts.
Worship the LORD in the splendour of his holiness;
tremble before him, all the earth.
Say among the nations, 'The LORD reigns.'
The world is firmly established, it cannot be moved;
he will judge the peoples with equity.
Let the heavens rejoice, let the earth be glad;
let the sea resound, and all that is in it;
let the fields be jubilant, and everything in them.
Then all the trees of the forest will sing for joy;
they will sing before the LORD, for he comes,
he comes to judge the earth.
He will judge the world in righteousness
and the peoples in his truth.

(Psalm 96:1–13)

See also Numbers 10:35–36; 1 Chronicles 17:16–27; Psalm 3:1–8; 8:1–9; 18:1–3; 23:1–6; 35:1–10; 91:1–2; 103:1–22; Isaiah 12:1–6

A psalm that says it all

David captured so much of God's heart in his psalms. Here is one that picks up many of the things revealed on Mount Sinai to Moses which David had dis-covered for himself. It is a beautifully written acrostic psalm; that is, each stanza begins with successive letters of the Hebrew alphabet:

I will exalt you, my God the King;
I will praise your name for ever and ever.
Every day I will praise you
and extol your name for ever and ever.
Great is the LORD and most worthy of praise;
his greatness no-one can fathom.
One generation will commend your works to another;
they will tell of your mighty acts.
They will speak of the glorious splendour of your majesty,
and I will meditate on your wonderful works.
They will tell of the power of your awesome works,
and I will proclaim your great deeds.
They will celebrate your abundant goodness
and joyfully sing of your righteousness.
The LORD is gracious and compassionate,
slow to anger and rich in love.
The LORD is good to all;
he has compassion on all he has made.
All you have made will praise you, O LORD;
your saints will extol you.
They will tell of the glory of your kingdom
and speak of your might,
so that all men may know of your mighty acts
and the glorious splendour of your kingdom.
Your kingdom is an everlasting kingdom,
and your dominion endures through all generations.
The LORD is faithful to all his promises
and loving towards all he has made.
The LORD upholds all those who fall
and lifts up all who are bowed down.
The eyes of all look to you,
and you give them their food at the proper time.
You open your hand
and satisfy the desires of every living thing.
The LORD is righteous in all his ways
and loving towards all he has made.
The LORD is near to all who call on him,
to all who call on him in truth.
He fulfils the desires of those who fear him;
he hears their cry and saves them.
The LORD watches over all who love him,
but all the wicked he will destroy.
My mouth will speak in praise of the LORD.
Let every creature praise his holy name
for ever and ever.

(Psalm 145:1–21)

The God who is compassionate

Dictionaries define compassion as 'feeling pity for the suffering or distress of another'. But true compassion doesn't just *feel* like this; it *does* something about it. God's compassion – felt and demonstrated – is a good reason for worshipping him, and it provides a firm basis on which to bring our requests.

The LORD is compassionate and gracious,
slow to anger, abounding in love.
He will not always accuse,
nor will he harbour his anger for ever;
he does not treat us as our sins deserve
or repay us according to our iniquities.
For as high as the heavens are above the earth,
so great is his love for those who fear him;
as far as the east is from the west,

so far has he removed our transgressions from us.
As a father has compassion on his children,
so the LORD has compassion on those who fear him;
for he knows how we are formed,
he remembers that we are dust.

(Psalm 103:8–14)

'Even now,' declares the LORD,
'return to me with all your heart,
with fasting and weeping and mourning.'
Rend your heart
and not your garments.
Return to the LORD your God,
for he is gracious and compassionate,
slow to anger and abounding in love,
and he relents from sending calamity.
Who knows? He may turn and have pity
and leave behind a blessing . . .'

(Joel 2:12–14)

Praise be to the God and Father of our Lord Jesus Christ, the Father of compassion and the God of all comfort, who comforts us in all our troubles, so that we can comfort those in any trouble with the comfort we ourselves have received from God.

(2 Corinthians 1:3–5)

See also 2 Chronicles 30:6–9; Nehemiah 9:16–31; Psalm 51:1; 86:15–17; 111:1–9; 116:1–7; 145:8–9; Isaiah 54:1–8; Jonah 4:1–11; Micah 7:18–19; Romans 9:14–16; James 5:11

Martin ponders the words of Psalm 103 on the occasions that he is travelling by plane: at 35,000 feet, the words 'as high as the heavens are above the earth, so great is his love for those who fear him' and on a long-haul flight to Australia 'as far as the east is from the west, so far has he removed our transgressions from us' remind him how great is God's kindness and love!

The God who is gracious and merciful

Grace and mercy are two opposite sides of the coin: mercy is about our not being given what we deserve; grace is about our being given more than we deserve. What we deserve, because of sin, is God's judgment; but God doesn't give us that! As we trust in Jesus, God gives us more than we deserve or could ever hope for – his grace and forgiveness.

The LORD said to Moses, 'Tell Aaron and his sons, "This is how you are to bless the Israelites. Say to them: 'The LORD bless you and keep you; the LORD make his face shine upon you and be gracious to you; the LORD turn his face towards you and give you peace.' " So they will put my name on the Israelites, and I will bless them.'

(Numbers 6:22–27)

May God be gracious to us and bless us
and make his face to shine upon us, Selah
that your ways may be known on earth,
your salvation among all nations.

(Psalm 67:1)

Grace, mercy and peace from God the Father and from Jesus Christ, the Father's Son, will be with us in truth and love.

(2 John 3)

See also Ezra 9:5–9; Psalm 5:7; 6:1–4; 86:1–7, 15; Daniel 9:4–19; Jonah 4:1–11; Micah 7:18–20; Luke 1:67–75; Acts 20:32; 2 Corinthians 13:14; Ephesians 2:4–8

Mary was profoundly aware of the grace that had come to her through the amazing privilege of bearing God's Son within her womb and of how that grace and mercy would extend to others. Her prayer is often called 'The Magnificat' (from its first word in Latin):

'My soul glorifies the Lord
and my spirit rejoices in God my Saviour,
for he has been mindful of the humble state of his servant.
From now on all generations will call me blessed,
for the Mighty One has done great things for me –
holy is his name.
His mercy extends to those who fear him,
from generation to generation.
He has performed mighty deeds with his arm;
he has scattered those who are proud in their inmost thoughts.
He has brought down rulers from their thrones
but has lifted up the humble.
He has filled the hungry with good things
but has sent the rich away empty.
He has helped his servant Israel,
remembering to be merciful
to Abraham and his descendants for ever,
even as he said to our fathers.'

(Luke 1:46–55)

The God who abounds in love

God does not simply love; he abounds in love! He has so much love, it overflows richly and constantly from him.

'Now may the Lord's strength be displayed, just as you have declared: "The LORD is slow to anger, abounding in love and forgiving sin and rebellion. Yet he does not leave the guilty unpunished; he punishes the children for the sin of the fathers to the third and fourth generation." In accordance with your great love, forgive the sin of these people, just as you have pardoned them from the time they left Egypt until now.'

(Numbers 14:17–19)

Your love, O LORD, reaches to the heavens,
your faithfulness to the skies.
Your righteousness is like the mighty mountains,
your justice like the great deep.
O LORD, you preserve both man and beast.
How priceless is your unfailing love!
Both high and low among men
find refuge in the shadow of your wings.
They feast in the abundance of your house;
you give them drink from your river of delights.
For with you is the fountain of life;
in your light we see light.

(Psalm 36:5–9)

You are forgiving and good, O Lord,
abounding in love to all who call to you.
Hear my prayer, O LORD;
listen to my cry for mercy.
In the day of my trouble I will call to you,
for you will answer me.

(Psalm 86:5–7)

See also Deuteronomy 7:7–11; 1 Kings 8:22–24; 2 Chronicles 7:1–6; Nehemiah 9:16–17; Psalm 23:6; 86:15; 103:8–18; 109:21–31; 136:1–26; Joel 2:13; Jonah 4:1–2

The God who is faithful

God is faithful. What he means, he says; what he says, he does. Faithfulness, like love, is something that God 'abounds' in. Faithfulness means 'maintaining love to thousands' (Exodus 34:7), even when we don't deserve it.

I will proclaim the name of the LORD.
Oh, praise the greatness of our God!
He is the Rock, his works are perfect,
and all his ways are just.
A faithful God who does no wrong,
upright and just is he.

(Deuteronomy 32:3–4)

I will sing of the LORD's great love for ever;
with my mouth I will make your faithfulness known through all generations.
I will declare that your love stands firm for ever,

that you established your faithfulness in
heaven itself.
You said, 'I have made a covenant with my
chosen one,
I have sworn to David my servant,
"I will establish your line for ever
and make your throne firm through all
generations." ' Selah
The heavens praise your wonders, O LORD,
your faithfulness too, in the assembly of
the holy ones.
For who in the skies above can compare with
the LORD?
Who is like the LORD among the heavenly
beings?
In the council of the holy ones God is greatly
feared;
he is more awesome than all who
surround him.
O LORD God Almighty, who is like you?
You are mighty, O LORD, and your
faithfulness surrounds you.

(Psalm 89:1–8)

Because of the LORD's great love we are not
consumed,
for his compassions never fail.
They are new every morning;
great is your faithfulness.
I say to myself, 'The LORD is my portion;
therefore I will wait for him.'

(Lamentations 3:22–24)

See also Genesis 24:26–27; Nehemiah 1:4–11; Psalm 36:5; 91:1–16; 146:1–6; Isaiah 25:1; Daniel 9:4–19; 1 Corinthians 1:4–9; Philippians 1:3–6

The God who forgives

One aspect of God's love is his readiness to forgive 'wickedness, rebellion and sin' (Exodus 34:7). Note how God piles up the words – 'wickedness, rebellion and sin' – as though he would not have us fear that there is any sin that he cannot forgive.

"If my people, who are called by my name, will humble themselves and pray and seek my face and turn from their wicked ways, then will I hear from heaven and will forgive their sin and will heal their land."

(2 Chronicles 7:14)

Praise the LORD, O my soul;
all my inmost being, praise his holy name.
Praise the LORD, O my soul,
and forget not all his benefits–
who forgives all your sins
and heals all your diseases,
who redeems your life from the pit
and crowns you with love and compassion,
who satisfies your desires with good things
so that your youth is renewed like the
eagle's.

(Psalm 103:1–5)

Who is a God like you,
who pardons sin and forgives the
transgression
of the remnant of his inheritance?
You do not stay angry for ever
but delight to show mercy.
You will again have compassion on us;
you will tread our sins underfoot
and hurl all our iniquities into the depths
of the sea.

(Micah 7:18–19)

See also Numbers 14:17–20; Nehemiah 9:16–18; Psalm 32:1–5; 51:1–12; 103:10–13; Isaiah 55:6–7; Jeremiah 31:33–34; Mark 2:5–12; Hebrews 10:19–23; James 5:13–16; 1 John 1:8–10

The God who is righteous

Forgiveness is not about 'sweeping things under the carpet' however. Sin cannot be overlooked – but it can be dealt with! All God requires is that we trust in the sacrifice of his Son, Jesus, who died in our place (e.g. 1 Peter 2:24; 3:18). When we trust in him, God gives us his righteousness (e.g. Romans 3:21–24; 4:6–8)! But if we will not let our sin be dealt with, then

God, who is righteous and just, has no alternative but to judge it and to 'not leave the guilty unpunished' (Exodus 34:7).

Sing to the LORD a new song,
for he has done marvellous things;
his right hand and his holy arm
have worked salvation for him.
The LORD has made his salvation known
and revealed his righteousness to the nations.
He has remembered his love
and his faithfulness to the house of Israel;
all the ends of the earth have seen
the salvation of our God.
Shout for joy to the LORD, all the earth,
burst into jubilant song with music;
make music to the LORD with the harp,
with the harp and the sound of singing,
with trumpets and the blast of the ram's horn –
shout for joy before the LORD, the King.
Let the sea resound, and everything in it,
the world, and all who live in it.
Let the rivers clap their hands,
let the mountains sing together for joy;
let them sing before the LORD,
for he comes to judge the earth.
He will judge the world in righteousness
and the peoples with equity.

(Psalm 98:1–9)

O LORD, hear my prayer,
listen to my cry for mercy;
in your faithfulness and righteousness
come to my relief.
Do not bring your servant into judgment,
for no-one living is righteous before you.

(Psalm 143:1–2)

See also Genesis 18:16–33; Psalm 5:8; 7:17; 23:1–3; 33:1–5; 89:14–15; 97:1–6; Daniel 9:7–19; Zephaniah 3:5

A FINAL PRAYER

Worthy of praise from every mouth,
of confession from every tongue,
of worship from every creature,
is thy glorious name, O Father,
Son, and Holy Ghost:
who didst create the world
in thy grace
and by thy compassion
didst save the world.
To thy majesty, O God, ten thousand times ten thousand
bow down and adore, singing and
praising without ceasing
and saying,
Holy, holy, holy LORD
God of Hosts;
Heaven and earth are full
of thy praises;
Hosanna in the highest.

(Nestorian Liturgy, 5th Century)

CONCLUSION

Moses discovered that there really is no one like the Lord. God wants each one of us to make that discovery for ourselves.

My whole being will exclaim,
'Who is like you, O Lord?'

(Psalm 35:10)

Relevance for today

God is still the same

Because God is 'I AM', his revelation to Moses can be his revelation to us.

'I the LORD do not change.'

(Malachi 3:6)

God still brings his grace

God's first words to Moses were words of grace; we need not fear, in any situation, that his first words to us will be any different.

'The LORD the LORD, the compassionate and gracious God . . .'

(Exodus 34:6)

God can break the chain

People are sometimes troubled by the thought that God visits the consequences of sin 'to the third and fourth generation' (e.g. Exodus 20:5; Numbers 14:18; Deuteronomy 5:9). Does that mean there is no hope for me? That I must pay for my forebears' sins? Not at all!

The expression signifies not compulsion, but continuity. This is not divine arithmetic, but divine observation: those who break God's laws pass on their ways to their families, thereby affecting generations to come. But it doesn't have to be like that! Thankfully, the vicious cycle can be broken for any person at any time through Jesus Christ.

If anyone is in Christ, he is a new creation; the old has gone, the new has come!

(2 Corinthians 5:17)

God's revelation can stimulate our worship

Moses' response to God's revelation was that he 'bowed to the ground and worshipped' (Exodus 34:8). Try taking passages like Exodus 34:6–8 or others in this chapter – and using them as a framework for your own worship.

Chapter Three

Praising God For What He Is Like

Once we have seen God's revelation of himself,
it changes our lives for ever.

'Lord, now lettest thou thy servant depart in peace, according to thy word: For mine eyes have seen thy salvation . . .' (Luke 2:29–30, KJV)

Ever seen a young couple newly in love? They seem to be in a world of their own, with eyes for no one else. Their finding each other seemed to unlock something in their hearts – new smiles, new joy, new laughter, new ways of looking at things. It's as if life had started all over again!

This is how it can be with God and us. Once we have discovered who God is and have become his friend, life no longer looks the same. We have 'seen his salvation' – and we can never be the same again.

The God who is holy

Isaiah was a man whose life was transformed by an encounter with the holiness of God 'in the year that King Uzziah died' – 740 BC (Isaiah 6:1). Uzziah had led Judah through a long period of prosperity and blessing; but now he was dead, what would happen next? Well, the earthly king might no longer be on the throne; but God was still on his throne, as Isaiah was about to discover.

In the year that King Uzziah died, I saw the Lord seated on a throne, high and exalted, and the train of his robe filled the temple. Above him were seraphs, each with six wings: With two wings they covered their faces, with two they covered their feet, and with two they were flying. And they were calling to one another: 'Holy, holy, holy is the LORD Almighty; the whole earth is full of his glory.' At the sound of their voices the doorposts and thresholds shook and the temple was filled with smoke. 'Woe to me!' I cried. 'I am ruined. For I am a man of unclean lips, and I live among a people of unclean lips, and my eyes have seen the King, the LORD Almighty.' Then one of the seraphs flew to me with a live coal in his hand, which he had taken with tongs from the altar. With it he touched my mouth and said, 'See, this has touched your lips; your guilt is taken away and your sin atoned for.' Then I heard the voice of the Lord saying,

'Whom shall I send? And who will go for us?' And I said, 'Here am I. Send me.'

(Isaiah 6:1–8)

God's holiness shows us his uniqueness

Isaiah's vision clarified to him that this king was absolutely unique – he was 'the King, the LORD Almighty' (v 5). No one, not even good King Uzziah, is like him!

'Who among the gods is like you, O LORD?
Who is like you –
majestic in holiness,
awesome in glory,
working wonders?'

(Exodus 15:11)

'There is no-one holy like the LORD; there is no-one besides you; there is no Rock like our God.'

(1 Samuel 2:2)

God's holiness shows us our sinfulness

When we encounter God's holiness, it inevitably shows up what is wrong in our lives. Our first response, like that of Isaiah, is to want to withdraw:

'Woe to me!' I cried. 'I am ruined! For I am a man of unclean lips, and I live among a people of unclean lips, and my eyes have seen the King, the LORD Almighty.'

(Isaiah 6:5)

Others, too, experienced this when they encountered the holiness of God:

'My ears had heard of you but now my eyes have seen you. Therefore I despise myself and repent in dust and ashes.'

(Job 42:5–6)

'Lord, don't come near me! I am a sinner.'

(Luke 5:8, CEV)

See also Psalm 51:1–12

God's holiness shows us how to get clean

But Isaiah discovered that God's holiness does not 'stand at a distance', accusing us of our sin; it takes action to come and change us.

'See, this has touched your lips; your guilt is taken away and your sin atoned for.'

(Isaiah 6:7)

This key revelation – that it is *God himself* who deals with our sin! – is taught throughout the Scriptures.

'Consecrate yourselves and be holy, because I am the LORD your God. Keep my decrees and follow them. I am the LORD who makes you holy.'

(Leviticus 20:7–8)

I delight greatly in the LORD
my soul rejoices in my God.
For he has clothed me with garments of salvation
and arrayed me in a robe of righteousness,
as a bridegroom adorns his head like a priest,
and as a bride adorns herself with her jewels.
For as the soil makes the young plant come up
and a garden causes seeds to grow,
so the Sovereign LORD will make righteousness and praise
spring up before all nations.

(Isaiah 61:10–11)

See also Exodus 31:13; Ezekiel 37:27–28; Ephesians 5:25–27

God's holiness leads us to serve him

Having let God deal with his sin, Isaiah then discovered that he could be sent out to serve God:

Then I heard the voice of the LORD saying, 'Whom shall I send? And who will go for us?' And I said, 'Here am I. Send me!'
(Isaiah 6:8)

Moses, too, had made this discovery:

When the LORD saw that he had gone over to look, God called to him from within the bush, 'Moses! Moses!'
And Moses said, 'Here I am.'
'Do not come any closer,' God said. 'Take off your sandals, for the place where you are standing is holy ground.' Then he said, 'I am the God of your father, the God of Abraham, the God of Isaac and the God of Jacob.' At this, Moses hid his face, because he was afraid to look at God . . .
'So now, go.'
(Exodus 3:4–6, 10)

See also Luke 1:67–75

God's holiness stirs our worship

When Isaiah encountered God's holiness in his vision, he encountered the worship of heaven (Isaiah 6:2–4). Whenever we encounter holiness, it will lead to worship.

Ascribe to the LORD, O families of nations,
ascribe to the LORD glory and strength,
ascribe to the LORD the glory due to his name.
Bring an offering and come before him;
worship the LORD in the splendour of his holiness.
Tremble before him, all the earth!
The world is firmly established; it cannot be moved.
Let the heavens rejoice, let the earth be glad;
let them say among the nations, 'The LORD reigns!'
Let the sea resound, and all that is in it;
let the fields be jubilant, and everything in them!
Then the trees of the forest will sing,
they will sing for joy before the LORD
for he comes to judge the earth.
(1 Chronicles 16:28–33)

The LORD reigns,
let the nations tremble;
he sits enthroned between the cherubim,
let the earth shake.
Great is the LORD in Zion;
he is exalted over all the nations.
Let them praise your great and awesome name –
he is holy.
The King is mighty, he loves justice –
you have established equity;
in Jacob you have done
what is just and right.
Exalt the LORD our God
and worship at his footstool;
he is holy.
(Psalm 99:1–5)

See also 2 Chronicles 20:20–21; Psalm 29:1–2; 103:1; 145:21; Revelation 4:6–8

The God who is eternal

Most foodstuffs have a 'sell-by' date – the final date by which the product must be sold to ensure its freshness. But God has no 'sell-by' date! He is eternal – without beginning and without end – yet ever fresh and new! He is unchanging – yet never boring!

The eternal God is your refuge, and underneath are the everlasting arms.
(Deuteronomy 33:27)

'Stand up and praise the LORD your God, who is from everlasting to everlasting.'
(Nehemiah 9:5)

Do you not know?
Have you not heard?
The LORD is the everlasting God,
the Creator of the ends of the earth.
He will not grow tired or weary,

and his understanding no-one can fathom.
He gives strength to the weary
and increases the power of the weak.
Even youths grow tired and weary,
and young men stumble and fall;
but those who hope in the LORD
will renew their strength.
They will soar on wings like eagles;
they will run and not grow weary,
they will walk and not be faint.

(Isaiah 40:28–31)

Now to the King eternal, immortal, invisible, the only God, be honour and glory for ever and ever. Amen.

(1 Timothy 1:17)

See also 1 Chronicles 16:34–36; 29:10–13; Psalm 145:13; Daniel 4:3, 34–35; Hebrews 13:20–21

The God who is good

One of the basic affirmations of the Bible is that God is good. This is a constant feature of his nature, unlike pagan deities who were often vacillating in character and attitude and whom you had to take care not to upset.

Keep me safe, O God,
for in you I take refuge.
I said to the LORD, 'You are my Lord;
apart from you I have no good thing.'
As for the saints who are in the land,
they are the glorious ones in whom is all my delight.
The sorrows of those will increase
who run after other gods.
I will not pour out their libations of blood
or take up their names on my lips.
LORD, you have assigned me my portion and my cup;
you have made my lot secure.
The boundary lines have fallen for me in pleasant places;
surely I have a delightful inheritance.

(Psalm 16:1–6)

I am still confident of this:
I will see the goodness of the LORD
in the land of the living.
Wait for the LORD;
be strong and take heart
and wait for the LORD.

(Psalm 27:13)

How can I repay the LORD
for all his goodness to me?
I will lift up the cup of salvation
and call on the name of the LORD. I will
fulfil my vows to the LORD
in the presence of all his people.

(Psalm 116:12–14)

You are good, and what you do is good.

(Psalm 119:68)

The Lord is good, a refuge in times of trouble. He cares for those who trust in him.

(Nahum 1:7)

See also 1 Kings 8:65–66; 1 Chronicles 16:34–36; 2 Chronicles 30:18–20; Ezra 3:11; Psalm 23:6; 31:19–24; 116:7; 145:1–9

The God who is almighty

Not only is God good, he also has all the power he needs to bring about his good purposes. There are no limits to his power; there is no one and nothing that can resist him.

'O Sovereign LORD, you have begun to show to your servant your greatness and your strong hand. For what god is there in heaven or on earth who can do the deeds and mighty works you do?'

(Deuteronomy 3:24)

'O LORD, God of our fathers, are you not the God who is in heaven? You rule over all the kingdoms of the nations. Power and might are in your hand, and no-one can withstand you.'

(2 Chronicles 20:6)

Lift up your heads, O you gates;
be lifted up, you ancient doors,
that the King of glory may come in.
Who is this King of glory?
The LORD strong and mighty,
the LORD mighty in battle.
Lift up your heads, O you gates;
lift them up, you ancient doors,
that the King of glory may come in.
Who is he, this King of glory?
The LORD Almighty–
he is the King of glory.

(Psalm 24:7–10)

'Ah, Sovereign LORD, you have made the heavens and the earth by your great power and outstretched arm. Nothing is too hard for you . . . O great and powerful God, whose name is the LORD Almighty, great are your purposes and mighty are your deeds.' . . . Then the word of the LORD came to Jeremiah: 'I am the LORD, the God of all mankind. Is anything too hard for me?'

(Jeremiah 32:17–19, 26–27)

See also Job 36:5; Psalm 46:1–11; 84:1–4; 89:5–8; 93:1–4; 118:15–16; 145:8–13; Jeremiah 10:6–7; Daniel 4:1–3; Zephaniah 3:17; Luke 1:46–49

What is even more amazing, is that God wants to share his power with *us*!

I pray that out of his glorious riches he may strengthen you with power through his Spirit in your inner being, so that Christ may dwell in your hearts through faith. And I pray that you, being rooted and established in love, may have power, together with all the saints, to grasp how wide and long and high and deep is the love of Christ, and to know this love that surpasses knowledge – that you may be filled to the measure of all the fulness of God. Now to him who is able to do immeasurably more than all we ask or imagine, according to his power that is at work within us, to him be glory in the church and in Christ Jesus throughout all generations, for ever and ever! Amen.

(Ephesians 3:16–21)

See also Ephesians 1:15–21

The God who is awesome

The word 'awesome' is often used today to simply mean 'fantastic' or 'wonderful'; but this is not its original meaning. If something was awesome, it brought about 'awe' – that is, reverential fear, or healthy respect.

Sing to God, O kingdoms of the earth,
sing praise to the Lord,, Selah
to him who rides the ancient skies above,
who thunders with mighty voice.
Proclaim the power of God,
whose majesty is over Israel,
whose power is in the skies.
You are awesome, O God, in your sanctuary;
the God of Israel gives power and strength to his people.
Praise be to God!

(Psalm 68:32–35)

See also Exodus 15:11; Deuteronomy 28:58–63; Nehemiah 1:5–6; Psalm 47:1–2; 66:1–5; 99:1–5; Daniel 9:4

It is because God is awesome that we are called to 'fear' him. This does not mean 'being afraid of' him; indeed if we have trusted in Jesus, we have no need to fear any longer (e.g. Isaiah 41:13; Romans 8:1). But it does mean that we should have a proper respect of and reverence for God and his commandments. God wants us to be his friends, but we should not reduce that to the level of 'being pals' with no sense of 'healthy respect'.

And now, O Israel, what does the LORD your God ask of you but to fear the LORD your God, to walk in all his ways, to love him, to serve the LORD your God with all your heart and with all your soul, and to observe the LORD's commands and decrees that I am giving you today for your own good?

(Deuteronomy 10:12–13)

Serve the LORD with fear
and rejoice with trembling.
Kiss the Son, lest he be angry
and you be destroyed in your way,
for his wrath can flare up in a moment.
Blessed are all who take refuge in him.

(Psalm 2:11–12)

But the eyes of the LORD are on those who fear him,
on those whose hope is in his unfailing love.

(Psalm 33:18)

Teach me your way, O LORD,
and I will walk in your truth;
give me an undivided heart,
that I may fear your name.

(Psalm 86:11)

See also Joshua 24:14–15; Psalm 22:23; 34:8–10; 147:10–11; Luke 12:4–5; Acts 9:31; 10:35; Revelation 14:7; 15:3–5

A FINAL PRAYER

Therefore with Angels and Archangels, and with all the company of heaven, we laud and magnify thy glorious Name; evermore praising thee, and saying: Holy, holy, holy, Lord God of hosts, heaven and earth are full of thy glory: Glory be to thee, O Lord most High. Amen.

(The Book of Common Prayer)

CONCLUSION

The more we look at God, the more there is to see. The more we see, the more there is to praise.

For this reason, ever since I heard about your faith in the Lord Jesus and your love for all the saints, I have not stopped giving thanks for you, remembering you in my prayers. I keep asking that the God of our Lord Jesus Christ, the glorious Father, may give you the Spirit of wisdom and revelation, so that you may know him better. I pray also that the eyes of your heart may be enlightened in order that you may know the hope to which he has called you, the riches of his glorious inheritance in the saints, and his incomparably great power for us who believe.

(Ephesians 1:15–17)

Relevance for today

Reflecting on God's character

As we reflect on what God has revealed of his character and nature, it reminds us who he is and stimulates our worship. Try reflecting now on those aspects we have looked at in this and the previous chapter, and praise God that this is what he is really like.

God is –

- the LORD
- compassionate
- gracious
- merciful
- loving
- faithful
- forgiving
- righteous
- holy
- eternal
- good
- almighty
- awesome

Reflecting on God's names

Sometimes, using the very name of God can express our praise or confidence in him. The Hebrew word *el* ('God') is often combined with other words to show God's amazing nature and character. For example,

- El Shaddai – God Almighty (Genesis 17:1; 28:3; 35:11; Exodus 6:3; Ezekiel 10:5)
- El Elyon – God the Most High (Genesis 14:18–20)
- El Olam – Eternal God (Genesis 21:33)
- El Roi – God who sees (Genesis 16:13)

God's personal and covenant name, Yahweh (Jehovah in older books) – 'I AM' – is usually represented in most English translations as The LORD (in capital letters). This name too is often combined with other words.

- Jehovah-Jireh (the LORD will provide, Genesis 22:8, 14)
- Jehovah-Nissi (the LORD is my banner, Exodus 17:15)
- Jehovah-Shalom (the LORD is peace, Judges 6:24)
- Jehovah-Tsidkenu (the LORD our righteousness, Jeremiah 23:6; 33:16)
- Jehovah-Tsebaoth (Sabaoth) (the LORD Almighty, or, 'the LORD of hosts', 1 Samuel 17:45)
- Jehovah-Rophi (the LORD my healer, Exodus 15:26).
- Jehovah-Mekaddishkem (the LORD who makes holy, Exodus 31:13)
- Jehovah-Shammah (the LORD who is there, Ezekiel 48:35)

Focusing on these names can be a powerful aid in our worshipping, praying and meditating. Why not try it and see?

Chapter Four

Lost in Wonder, Love and Praise

Thanksgiving and praise should lead us to become 'lost' in God's presence and to be focused solely on him, and not on ourselves.

Pour out your heart like water in the presence of the Lord.
(Lamentations 2:19)

Ever tried talking to your children when they're watching their favourite TV programme? Or to your husband when his head is in the newspaper? Or to your wife when a friend brings their newborn baby? The chances are: you just won't get through! They're so caught up with what they are focused on that they are lost to the world. It's as if nothing else existed!

That's God's heart for us when we worship – to be so caught up with him that nothing else really matters, that everything else fades into insignificance, and that he alone becomes the focus of our attention as we pour out our hearts to him. When that happens, we have truly had a foretaste of heaven!

A foretaste of heaven!

The final verse of Charles Wesley's great hymn 'Love Divine, All Loves Excelling' ends like this:

Changed from glory into glory,
Till in heaven we take our place,
Till we cast our crowns before Thee,
Lost in wonder, love and praise.

'Lost in wonder, love, and praise'. That's how it's going to be in heaven! There will be nothing to distract us, worry us, or take our minds from God and his wonderful presence.

But it is a poor faith that waits until heaven to start enjoying God's blessings! Jesus' message was that the kingdom of God had come because he, the King, had come. That kingdom is breaking into lives right now; and that means we can begin to get a foretaste of heaven right now – including in worship.

The trumpeters and singers joined in unison, as with one voice, to give praise and thanks to the LORD. Accompanied by trumpets, cymbals and other instruments, they raised their voices in praise to the LORD and sang:
'He is good;
his love endures for ever.'
Then the temple of the LORD was filled with a cloud, and the priests could not

perform their service because of the cloud, for the glory of the LORD filled the temple of God.

(2 Chronicles 5:13–14)

After they prayed, the place where they were meeting was shaken. And they were all filled with the Holy Spirit and spoke the word of God boldly.

(Acts 4:31)

See also Genesis 28:16–22; Exodus 40:34–35; Leviticus 9:23–24; 1 Kings 8:10–11; 2 Chronicles 7:1–3; Acts 2:1–4; Revelation 1:10–18

Of course, to experience a foretaste of heaven we really have to want it. God forces nothing on us – least of all, the enjoyment of his presence!

Longing for God

Knowing God's intimate presence in our worship and daily lives begins as we start to long for it. The Psalms are a rich source of prayers to help us call out to God to know more of him.

As a deer longs for flowing streams,
so my soul longs for you, O God.
My soul thirsts for God,
for the living God.

(Psalm 42:1–2, NRSV)

God, you are my God. I search for you. I thirst for you like someone in a dry, empty land where there is no water.

(Psalm 63:1, NCV)

Whom have I in heaven but you?
And there is nothing on earth that I desire other than you.
My flesh and my heart may fail,
but God is the strength of my heart and my portion for ever.

(Psalm 73:25–26, NRSV)

How lovely is your dwelling-place,
O LORD Almighty!
My soul yearns, even faints,
for the courts of the LORD;
my heart and my flesh cry out
for the living God.
Even the sparrow has found a home,
and the swallow a nest for herself,
where she may have her young –
a place near your altar,
O LORD Almighty, my King and my God.
Blessed are those who dwell in your house;
they are ever praising you. *Selah*

(Psalm 84:1–4)

See also Job 19:25–27; Psalm 27:7–8; 84:10–11; 119:20, 131; Isaiah 26:8–9; 33:2

Settling our priorities

Longing for God can only grow if we have settled our priorities. Of course there are

'Lord Jesus Christ, pierce my soul with thy love so that I may always long for thee alone, who art the bread of angels and the fulfilment of the soul's deepest desires. May my heart always hunger and feed upon thee, so that my soul may be filled with the sweetness of thy presence. May my soul thirst for thee, who art the source of life, wisdom, knowledge, light and all the riches of God our Father. May I always seek and find thee, think upon thee, speak to thee and do all things for the honour and glory of thy holy name. Be always my only hope, my peace, my refuge and my help in whom my heart is rooted so that I may never be separated from thee.'

Bonaventure (1217–74),
Franciscan theologian

other important things in life – family, work, friends; but the challenge to us is: what is the most important thing to me? Jesus promised this: *'Seek first God's kingdom and his righteousness, and all these things will be given you as well'* (Matthew 6:33). And what were 'all these things'? Why, the very things that take so much of our attention – life, food, drink, clothes. Life hasn't changed much really, has it?

The story of Jesus' visit to Mary and Martha underlines the importance of our prioritizing 'one thing' as the focus of our lives.

As Jesus and the disciples continued on their way to Jerusalem, they came to a village where a woman named Martha welcomed them into her home. Her sister, Mary, sat at the Lord's feet, listening to what he taught. But Martha was worrying over the big dinner she was preparing. She came to Jesus and said, 'Lord, doesn't it seem unfair to you that my sister just sits here while I do all the work? Tell her to come and help me!'

But the Lord said to her, 'My dear Martha, you are so upset over all these details! There is really only one thing worth being concerned about. Mary has discovered it – and I won't take it away from her.'

(Luke 10:38–42, NLT)

God is looking for us to abandon our lives to him, to come to the point where we say, 'You are the most important thing in my life! Everything else is insignificant in comparison to you.' This means letting go of things that have taken up the most precious places in our hearts, and becoming 'detached from other attachments, whether they are addictive, habitual, enslaving or just plain fascinating' (James Houston).

Searching for simplicity

This 'abandonment to one thing' is what spiritual writers over the centuries have sometimes called 'simplicity'. The Greek word for 'simplicity' is translated 'singleness of heart' in many English versions; but it also means 'sincerity', 'straightness', 'unaffectedness', or 'without hidden agendas'. If we are going to be 'lost in wonder, love and praise', then 'simplicity' is an important step towards it, where God alone becomes the 'one thing' that we desire more than anything – without any hidden agendas!

- 'Hold fast to simplicity of heart and innocence.' (Hermas, second century)
- 'Take from us, O God, the care of worldly vanities; make us content with necessaries.' (Edmund Grindal, Chaplain to Edward VI and Archbishop of Canterbury)
- 'Simplicity is the ordinary attendant of sincerity.' (Richard Baxter, Puritan, 1615–91)
- 'Simplicity is found in the unfettered joy of a brother who forsakes an obsession with his own progress or backslidings in order to fix his gaze on the light of Christ.' (The Taizé Rule)
- 'Hair-splitting can be left to theologians and legalists; simplicity is the aim of the life of prayer.' (Hubert van Zeller, monk and spiritual writer, born 1905)

Some helps to becoming 'lost' in worship

So, what are some of the things that can help us in our pursuit of being 'lost in wonder, love and praise'?

Resisting self-awareness

It's so easy to rush into God's presence thinking only of ourselves and our requests – and then wonder why we didn't 'break through' to God. In Part One, Chapter 1, we noted how the Lord's Prayer began, by focusing on 'Our Father in heaven'. This, not ourselves, is where we need to begin when we worship or pray.

Not to us, O LORD, not to us
but to your name be the glory,
because of your love and faithfulness.
(Psalm 115:1)

When our thoughts start wandering back to ourselves, we need to take hold of them, to '*take captive every thought to make it obedient to Christ*' (2 Corinthians 10:5). As we saw in the previous two chapters, focusing on God's character and nature (rather than on our own sin or needs) helps to 'prime the pump' of our hearts as we 'go up the hill' to the Lord.

Resting in God's presence

Like Martha, we need to learn how to 'stop' and how to be still in God's presence. Just being quiet gives God a chance to speak and to reveal himself.

Be still before the LORD, and wait patiently for him;
do not fret over those who prosper in their way,
over those who carry out evil devices.
Refrain from anger, and forsake wrath.
Do not fret – it leads only to evil.
For the wicked shall be cut off,
but those who wait for the LORD shall inherit the land.
(Psalm 37:7–9, NRSV)

This is what the Sovereign LORD, the Holy One of Israel, says:
'In repentance and rest is your salvation,
in quietness and trust is your strength.'
(Isaiah 30:15)

'Resting' sometimes means having to *wait* (a horrible thought for us busy Westerners!); but waiting brings its own blessing:

They that wait upon the LORD shall renew their strength; they shall mount up with wings as eagles; they shall run, and not be weary; and they shall walk, and not faint.
(Isaiah 40:31, KJV)

Since ancient times no-one has heard,
no ear has perceived,
no eye has seen any God besides you,
who acts on behalf of those who wait for him.
(Isaiah 64:4)

See also Psalm 40:1; 130:5–6; Isaiah 8:16–17; Lamentations 3:24–26; Micah 7:7

Reflecting through meditation

Meditation (or 'contemplation') is about reflecting on something deeply and at length. In it, we deliberately focus on 'one thing' in order to 'shut the door' to everything else that would crowd into our thoughts. It may involve focusing on just one verse of Scripture or one aspect of

Called to be still!

Perhaps one of the best-known Bible verses about 'being still' is Psalm 46:10:

'Be still, and know that I am God;
I will be exalted among the nations,
I will be exalted in the earth.'

Other English versions, bringing out different emphases of the Hebrew, translate the opening words like this:

'Calm down and learn that I am God!' (CEV)
'Be quiet and know that I am God.' (NCV)
'Pause a while and know that I am God.' (JB)

Which of these do you need to do at this moment?

God's nature or one object. Ignatius Loyola, the founder of the Jesuits, encouraged people to meditate by using all five human senses – in other words, to use 'godly imagination'.

Meditation is a skill lost to many of us because we cannot 'stop' from our busyness; but it was a key feature of life for many in the Bible and throughout church history. Meditation seeks to draw close to God to 'contemplate' on him and be drawn deeper into his love, understanding that prayer is not a 'technique' but a relationship, and that only in that relationship can our deepest longings be satisfied. Meditation sees God as a deep ocean to be explored rather than a divine Father Christmas to be used. Catherine of Siena, a fourteenth-century Dominican Sister, wrote this: 'O eternal Trinity! O Godhead! You are a deep sea, into which the deeper I enter the more I find, and the more I find the more I seek.'

Do not let this Book of the Law depart from your mouth; meditate on it day and night, so that you may be careful to do everything written in it. Then you will be prosperous and successful.

(Joshua 1:8)

May the words of my mouth and the
meditation of my heart
be pleasing in your sight,
O LORD, my Rock and my Redeemer.

(Psalm 19:14)

See also Genesis 24:63; Psalm 1:1–3; 39:3; 104:33–34; 119:15, 23, 27, 48, 78, 97–99, 148; 143:5–6; Luke 2:51; 2 Timothy 2:7

The Bible encourages us to meditate on –

- God's word (e.g. Psalm 1:1–3)
- God's love (e.g. Psalm 48:9)
- God's works (e.g. Psalm 77:10–12)

Receiving God's love

Never forget that the essence of the Christian faith is not about filling our heads with knowledge, but filling our hearts with love. When we come to worship, we should expect something to happen, to receive a fresh infilling of God's love that overflows into worship and then out into life.

May your unfailing love rest upon us, O LORD,
even as we put our hope in you.

(Psalm 33:22)

May the Lord direct your hearts into God's love and Christ's perseverance.

(2 Thessalonians 3:5)

One whole book of the Bible is given over to the intimacy of love – Song of Songs (or, Song of Solomon). At its most fundamental level, it is a collection of love songs between a man and a woman, depicting love in all its power and wonder. Over the centuries, however, many have seen in it parallels to the love between God and his people or Christ and his church. When seen in this way, there are some powerful passages that can express the intimacy of our hearts and open the way for God's love to flood in.

Let him kiss me with the kisses of his mouth
– for your love is more delightful than wine.

(Song of Songs 1:2)

Like an apple tree among the trees of the
forest
is my lover among the young men.
I delight to sit in his shade,
and his fruit is sweet to my taste.
He has taken me to the banquet hall,
and his banner over me is love.

(2:3–4)

My beloved is mine and I am his.

(2:16, KJV)

My lover is radiant and ruddy,
outstanding among ten thousand.

(5:10)

His mouth is sweetness itself;
he is altogether lovely.
This is my lover, this my friend,
O daughters of Jerusalem.

(5:16)

Church leaders throughout the centuries have stressed the importance of receiving God's love in worship and prayer. For example, St Francis of Assisi (1181/2–1226), wrote this:

May the power of your love, Lord Christ, fiery and sweet, so absorb our hearts as to withdraw them from all that is under heaven; grant that we may be ready to die for love of your love, as you died for love of our love. Amen.

Responding to the Spirit

Without the Holy Spirit, worship and prayer is a dry and dull affair. But Jesus promised that he would send his Spirit to help us.

On the last and greatest day of the Feast, Jesus stood and said in a loud voice, 'If anyone is thirsty, let him come to me and drink. Whoever believes in me, as the Scripture has said, streams of living water will flow from within him.' By this he meant the Spirit, whom those who believed in him were later to receive.

(John 7:37–39)

The feast in question was the Feast of Tabernacles, one of three occasions when all Jewish men had to worship at the temple in Jerusalem. The festival commemorated God's provision, both in the recent harvest, but also during Israel's wilderness wanderings. It was one of the favourite festivals in Jesus' day, full of joy and ceremony, which included priests taking a jug of water from the Pool of Siloam and going in grand procession to the altar in the temple where the water was poured out.

This ritual happened every day for a week; but on the last day of the festival ('the last and greatest day'), no water was collected or poured. It was, instead, 'a day of solemn assembly'. And it was on that day, when religion had run out, as it were, that Jesus invited men and women to come to him for an experience of the Spirit that would never run out and never run dry. Any worship, therefore, that now discounts the Spirit, or that merely pays lip-service to him, is going back into the old ways that Jesus brought us out of.

We should therefore expect the Spirit's life to 'flow from within' (v 38) when we worship and pray, including such things as:

- Allowing joy to be expressed (e.g. Isaiah 61:1–3; Luke 10:21; Acts 13:52)
- Responding to 'nudges' when we pray (e.g. Acts 8:2–29)
- Using the gift of tongues (e.g. Acts 2:4, 11; 1 Corinthians 14:4–5, 13–26)
- Receiving prophecy to bring words of encouragement or direction (e.g. Romans 12:4–6; 1 Corinthians 14:1–4, 26)
- Expecting to receive guidance (e.g. Acts 10:19–20; 13:1–3)

A FINAL PRAYER

Lord Jesus, come quickly; my heart is desirous of thy presence, and would entertain thee, not as a guest, but as an inhabitant, as the Lord of my faculties. Enter in and take possession, and dwell with me for ever, that I also may dwell in the heart of my dearest Lord, which was opened for me with a spear and love.

Jeremy Taylor (1613–1667), Chaplain to Charles I, Bishop of Down and Connor, and Vice-Chancellor of Dublin University

CONCLUSION

'Lost in wonder, love, and praise.' The real issue is not 'Is it possible?' but 'Do I want it?'

My heart says of you, 'Seek his face!'
Your face, LORD, I will seek.

(Psalm 27:8)

Relevance for today

What we long for is what we truly want

'Wherever your treasure is, there your heart and thoughts will also be.'

(Matthew 6:21, NLT)

What we focus on is what we truly worship

'You can't worship two gods at once. Loving one god, you'll end up hating the other. Adoration of one feeds contempt for the other. You can't worship God and Money both.'

(Matthew 6:24, The Message)

What our priorities are is what really matters to us

'Don't worry and say, "What will we eat?" or "What will we drink?" or "What will we wear?" The people who don't know God keep trying to get these things, and your Father in heaven knows you need them. The thing you should want most is God's kingdom and doing what God wants. Then all these other things you need will be given to you.'

(Matthew 6:31–33, NCV)

What we wait for is what is truly important

I say to myself, 'The LORD is my portion; therefore I will wait for him.'

(Lamentations 3:24)

What we meditate on is what fills our minds and hearts

'It is the thought-life that defiles you. For from within, out of a person's heart, come evil thoughts, sexual immorality, theft, murder, adultery, greed, wickedness, deceit, eagerness for lustful pleasure, envy, slander, pride, and foolishness. All these vile things come from within; they are what defile you and make you unacceptable to God.'

(Mark 7:21–23, NLT)

What we expect from the Spirit is what we will experience

While Apollos was at Corinth, Paul took the road through the interior and arrived at Ephesus. There he found some disciples and asked them, 'Did you receive the Holy Spirit when you believed?' They answered, 'No, we have not even heard that there is a Holy Spirit.' . . . When Paul placed his hands on them, the Holy Spirit came on them, and they spoke in tongues and prophesied.

(Acts 19:1–2, 6)

Chapter Five

Worship from the Heart

God wants our worship – but not at any price! 'Externals' without 'heart' are meaningless to him, no matter how fine the gestures or the words.

'These people come near to me with their mouth and honour me with their lips, but their hearts are far from me. Their worship of me is made up only of rules taught by men.' (Isaiah 29:13)

How much do externals matter to you? If your answer is, 'Not at all', then you're certainly an exception. Externals drive so much of life today and keep our economies going. Wearing 'designer label' clothes, having the latest fashions, updating the car to this year's model, being seen with 'the right people' or in 'the right places', 'looking good'; all of these are externals that most of us, from time to time, embrace. What a contrast to God's viewpoint! For God is quite disinterested in externals; what matters to God is the heart.

'Snake pit. Whitewashed graves. Blind guides. Hypocrites.' Not terms likely to help you win friends and influence people! But Jesus used these words a lot. Not about corrupt tax collectors, or prostitutes, or the irreligious; but about the crème de la crème of religious society of his day – the Pharisees. We might laugh at their behaviour; but tears, not laughter, are really what are called for. For the Pharisees are a classic example of what can happen to a revival movement gone wrong.

The Pharisees' roots go back to the time of the exile, when God's people were banished to the hostile evil nation of Babylon. While there for the seventy years that Jeremiah had prophesied (Jeremiah 25:8–14; 29:10–14), God's people began to ask the question, 'How on earth did we end up here?' And as they reflected on their history, the answer they came up with was: 'Because we disobeyed God's word.' And so it was that, as they eventually returned from exile, they began to give themselves to strictly living by God's word lest anything like that should ever happen again. And somewhere around that time, the precursors of the Pharisees arose.

So fearful were they now of breaking God's Law, even accidentally (and so ending up under judgment again), that they began to put 'a hedge' around it to ensure they wouldn't even get anywhere near breaking it. And so arose a whole body of 'by-laws', added alongside the Law, to help them keep that Law. The Scribes were those who worked these laws out, and the Pharisees those who lived them out. By the time of Jesus, there were hundreds of these 'by-laws'; but what had started out as a well-intentioned revival movement to ensure obedience to God's word had degenerated into a legalistic bunch of nit-picking bigots who would rather have the Son of God obey their regulations and interpretations than let him do wicked things like heal people on the Sabbath. The revivalists had gone backwards! And all because they lost the priority of the heart.

The priority of the heart

Throughout the Scriptures, God points us to the priority of the heart over everything else.

The LORD saw how great man's wickedness on the earth had become, and that every inclination of the thoughts of his heart was only evil all the time. The LORD was grieved that he had made man on the earth, and his heart was filled with pain.

(Genesis 6:5–6)

The LORD said to Samuel, 'Do not consider his appearance or his height, for I have rejected him. The LORD does not look at the things man looks at. Man looks at the outward appearance, but the LORD looks at the heart.'

(1 Samuel 16:7)

'Because your heart was responsive and you humbled yourself before God when you heard what he spoke against this place and its people, and because you humbled yourself before me and tore your robes and wept in my presence, I have heard you,' declares the LORD.

(2 Chronicles 34:27)

Above all else, guard your heart,
for it is the wellspring of life.

(Proverbs 4:23)

With what shall I come before the LORD
and bow down before the exalted God?
Shall I come before him with burnt offerings,
with calves a year old?
Will the LORD be pleased with thousands of rams,
with ten thousand rivers of oil?
Shall I offer my firstborn for my transgression,
the fruit of my body for the sin of my soul?
He has showed you, O man, what is good.
And what does the LORD require of you?
To act justly and to love mercy
and to walk humbly with your God.

(Micah 6:6–8)

See also Deuteronomy 5:29; 6:4–6; 10:16; 1 Kings 8:58; 2 Chronicles 17:3–6; Psalm 17:3; 26:2–3; 51:10–12; 95:6–11; Proverbs 28:14; Jeremiah 17:9–10; Ezekiel 36:26–27; Matthew 5:8; Hebrews 3:15–18

It is because of the priority that God attaches to the heart that David wrote:

Search me, O God, and know my heart;
test me and know my anxious thoughts.
See if there is any offensive way in me,
and lead me in the way everlasting.

(Psalm 139:23–24)

The priority of the heart in worship

Because the heart has such an important place, it should not surprise us to discover that God calls us to pay particular attention to its condition when we come to worship him; for without the heart being right – obedient, trusting and tender – worship is a meaningless ritual.

'Does the LORD delight in burnt offerings and sacrifices as much as in obeying the voice of the LORD? To obey is better than sacrifice, and to heed is better than the fat of rams. For rebellion is like the sin of divination, and arrogance like the evil of idolatry.'

(1 Samuel 15:22–23)

'These people come near to me with their mouth and honour me with their lips, but their hearts are far from me. Their worship of me is made up only of rules taught by men.'

(Isaiah 29:13)

'Even now,' declares the LORD, 'return to me with all your heart, with fasting and weeping and mourning. Rend your heart and not your garments.'

(Joel 2:12–13)

'I hate, I despise your religious feasts;
I cannot stand your assemblies.
Even though you bring me burnt offerings
and grain offerings,
I will not accept them.
Though you bring choice fellowship offerings,
I will have no regard for them.
Away with the noise of your songs!
I will not listen to the music of your harps.
But let justice roll on like a river,
righteousness like a never-failing stream.'

(Amos 5:21–24)

See also Exodus 25:1–2; Psalm 24:3–4; 27:8; Isaiah 1:10–17; Ezekiel 33:31; Hosea 6:6; Malachi 2:1–2; Mark 7:6–7; John 4:19–24

Worship and prayer can be hindered

So worship and prayer can be hindered by wrong relationships, motives and attitudes. The Christian faith is not like some magic cult where the act of worship itself brings benefit (though sadly some churches have sometimes fallen into that trap); worship derives its value from our heart.

Wrong relationships with God hinder prayer

If I had cherished sin in my heart,
the Lord would not have listened;
but God has surely listened
and heard my voice in prayer.
Praise be to God,
who has not rejected my prayer
or withheld his love from me!

(Psalm 66:18–20)

See also Deuteronomy 1:43–45; 1 Samuel 8:7–18; Proverbs 28:9

Wrong relationships with others hinder prayer

'So when you are offering your gift at the altar, if you remember that your brother or sister has something against you, leave your gift there before the altar and go; first be reconciled to your brother or sister, and then come and offer your gift.'

(Matthew 5:23–24, NRSV)

See also Genesis 4:3–16; Luke 18:9–14; 1 Peter 3:7

Wrong motives hinder our prayer

You want what you don't have, so you scheme and kill to get it. You are jealous for what others have, and you can't possess it, so you fight and quarrel to take it away from them. And yet the reason you don't have what you want is that you don't ask God for it. And even when you do ask, you don't get it because your whole motive is wrong – you want only what will give you pleasure.

(James 4:2–3, NLT)

See also 1 Samuel 15:12–23; Isaiah 1:10–17; 1 John 3:21–22

The practice of the Pharisees

Jesus had many confrontations with the Pharisees throughout his ministry, largely because of this matter of the heart. In Matthew 23 we find Jesus teaching at length about these religious men, warning his followers not to become like them. He highlights seven key features of Pharisaic religion – features that still challenge us today.

Seven key features of Pharisaism

1. A focus on words, not deeds (vv 1–4)
The Pharisees were quick to tell others what to do, but slow in doing it themselves or helping others to do it. Their speciality was fine words rather than fair deeds, for they felt that words made them seem so spiritual (e.g. Matthew 6:5). This is why Jesus could say, '*I tell you that unless your righteousness surpasses that of the Pharisees and the teachers of the law, you will certainly not enter the kingdom of heaven*' (Matthew 5:20). They had forgotten that '*the kingdom of God is not a matter of talk but of power*' (1 Corinthians 4:20).

2. A focus on externals, not internals (vv 5–7)
So much that the Pharisees did was rooted in Scripture, even down to their wearing of phylacteries (Deuteronomy 11:18) and tassels (Numbers 15:37–41); but they had lost the heart behind it. Rather than these serving as a reminder to *them* that they were God's people, they became a reminder to *others* – a cause for showing off. 'Look how long my tassels are – I must be very spiritual!' This majoring on the 'outside' led them to neglect the 'inside', and it inevitably led them to focus on others' faults rather than their own (e.g. Matthew 7:1–5; 9:9–11; 23:25–26).

3. A focus on self, not others (vv 6–12)
How the Pharisees loved the focus of attention to be on them! They liked the best seats in the synagogue (v 6), to be greeted with the right titles (v 7), to be seen as really zealous (v 15). But Jesus showed that what God is looking for in us is the heart of a servant, demonstrating this in his own life again and again (e.g. Matthew 20:20–28; John 13:1–17).

4. A focus on their cause, not God's kingdom (vv 13–15)
The Pharisees would do anything to promote their 'cause' – the continuance of Pharisaism. They would 'travel over land and sea' (v 15) – in other words, go to any lengths – to make converts to their cause. But they had little time for God's kingdom; if they had, they would have gladly welcomed Jesus. But not only did they reject his message themselves (e.g. John 8:48–59), they kept others from it too, shutting the door of the kingdom in their faces (v 13).

5. A focus on the letter, not the Spirit (vv 16–22)
The Pharisees were experts at knowing God's Law. They could tell you every one of the 613 laws that had been identified in the Old Testament (248 positive ones, 365 negative ones) and all the interpretations and by-laws that had been passed down by the rabbis. But with such a focus on the 'letter' of the Law, they missed the spirit of it; so much so that they happily engaged in 'casuistry' – the apparent keeping of the Law while finding ways to break it (vv 16–22)!

6. A focus on the minor, not the major (vv 23–28)
The Pharisees would assiduously tithe, even to the level of their tiny herb plants; but they neglected '*the more important*

matters of the law – justice, mercy and faithfulness' (v 23). Jesus didn't condemn practising the former, but he certainly condemned neglecting the latter. Little wonder he called them 'blind guides' (v 24) and used the hilarious picture of them straining out a gnat from their drinking water (lest it make them unclean) but failing to notice the camel in the cup that they had swallowed!

7. A focus on the past, not the present (vv 29–36)
The past (and a rather over-rosy view of the past, at that) was the constant focus of their attention (vv 29–31). And how different things would have been if they had been there (v 30). But their view contrasted strongly with that of Jesus, who saw that they were so locked up in the past that they couldn't see what was happening in the present, right before their very eyes (vv 33–36). In aligning themselves against him, they would choose their past over God's present and future.

But Pharisees can change!

All these characteristics led the Pharisees to become hard-hearted and unresponsive to God – the very people who had started their spiritual journey with a pledge to be the very opposite! And so they missed the new thing that God was doing in Jesus.

But, thankfully, Pharisees can change! Nicodemus (John 3:1–21; 19:38–42) and Paul (Philippians 3:4–9; Acts 9:1–19) both encountered Jesus and their lives were changed; and 'Pharisees' today can be changed too!

The principles of worship

From what we have seen so far, it should be clear that God's focus is on the heart, rather than on externals. This brings both challenge and opportunity. The challenge is to ensure that, whatever externals may characterize our worship and prayer, whether personally or corporately, the essential feature is the heart. The opportunity is that, because worship and prayer are matters of the heart and not externals, we have a tremendous breadth for expressing ourselves to God.

Methods of prayer and worship

The Bible presents us with a wide range of expressions of prayer and worship. In truth, most of us find this challenging, for we all become stuck in our patterns (or are they ruts?), whether privately or corporately, and we are quick to judge others who do things differently. But here are various methods that God deems acceptable to him:

- **Singing** (e.g. Exodus 15:1, 20–21; Judges 5:1–3; 2 Chronicles 20:20–22; Psalm 33:1–3; Acts 16:25; 1 Corinthians 14:15; Ephesians 5:18–20)
- **Speaking** (e.g. Genesis 32:9–12; 1 Samuel 1:10–17; 1 Kings 18:36–40; 2 Kings 20:1–6; Nehemiah 1:4–11; Daniel 9:4–19; Matthew 26:36–46; Acts 4:23–31)
- **Shouting** (e.g. Leviticus 9:23–24; Joshua 6:1–20; Ezra 3:10–13; Psalm 47:1–6; 71:23; 95:1; Isaiah 12:4–6; Mark 11:8–10; Revelation 19:1–8)
- **Being silent** (e.g. Psalm 4:4; Ecclesiastes 3:1–8; Isaiah 41:1; Lamentations 3:28–29; Habakkuk 2:20; Revelation 8:1)
- **Dancing** (e.g. Exodus 15:20; 2 Samuel 6:12–16; Psalm 30:11–12; 149:2–3; 150:4; Acts 3:8)
- **Playing musical instruments** (1 Chronicles 6:31–32; 25:6–8; Psalm 81:1–4; 98:4–6; 150:1–6; Ephesians 5:19)

Of course, God's focus on the heart does not mean that externals are irrelevant to him. Immoral behaviour (an aspect of fertility religions of Bible times) was completely taboo (e.g. Deuteronomy 12:29 –31), as was an utter disregard of cultural norms that could bring the gospel into disrepute (e.g. 1 Corinthians 11:2– 16).

Postures for prayer and worship

In this area, too, God allows a tremendous breadth of expression to us. Once again, we should take care not to get into a rut, but to use variety according to what it is we are seeking to express.

- **Sitting** (e.g. 1 Kings 19:3–4; 1 Chronicles 17:16; Nehemiah 1:4; Luke 10:13)
- **Standing** (e.g.1 Samuel 1:26; 1 Kings 8:22; Luke 18:11, 13; Mark 11:25)
- **Kneeling** (e.g. Ezra 9:5–6; Psalm 95:6; Daniel 6:10; Acts 9:40; Ephesians 3:14–19)
- **Bowing** (e.g. Genesis 24:26–27; Exodus 34:8–9; 2 Chronicles 29:27–30; Psalm 95:6; Matthew 2:11)
- **Prostrating oneself** (e.g. Genesis 17:3; Leviticus 9:23–24; Joshua 5:13–14; 2 Chronicles 7:1–3; Luke 17:15–16)
- **Lifting hands** (e.g. 1 Timothy 2:8; Exodus 17:15–16; Leviticus 9:22; Nehemiah 8:6; Psalm 28:2; 63:4; 134:2; Lamentations 3:41)

Public versus private

If worship and prayer are essentially heart matters, then is there a place for doing it publicly; or should all true worship and prayer be kept 'between me and God'?

Well, if public worship and prayer were removed from our Bibles, they would be an awful lot thinner! The issue is not about being alone to pray and worship (or being together), but praying and worshipping with the right heart, wherever we do it. It is perfectly possible to worship or pray privately and yet to have a proud heart, or to pray fervently aloud in public with the most humble of spirits. The issue is not *where* but *how*.

Never to worship or pray alone robs us of the opportunity to be intimate with God; but never to worship or pray with others robs us of the power that is released when God's people come together (e.g. Acts 4:31).

Examples of personal praise

The Bible is full of people who prayed or praised on their own. Here are just some examples:

- **Daniel** (Daniel 2:19–23)
- **Hannah** (1 Samuel 2:1–10)
- **Mary** (Luke 1:46–55)
- **Miriam** (Exodus 15:20–21)
- **Moses** (Deuteronomy 32:3–4)
- **Zechariah** (Luke 1:67–79)

Examples of corporate praise

Much Jewish worship was a corporate affair, bringing home the fact that together they were the redeemed people of God. So, for example, all men had to go to Jerusalem three times a year to celebrate the festivals of Passover, Pentecost and Tabernacles; and the very nature of the sacrificial system made it a corporate, rather than personal affair. In addition to this, we get many glimpses of people praising God along with his people. For example,

- **David** (1 Chronicles 29:10–13)
- **Deborah and Barak** (Judges 5:1–31)
- **Ezra** (Nehemiah 8:5–6)
- **Jehoshaphat** (2 Chronicles 20:20–22)
- **Moses** (Exodus 15:1–18)
- **Solomon** (2 Chronicles 6:1–7:6)

This corporate dimension of praise and prayer clearly continued in the life of the early church (e.g. Acts 1:14; 2:1–11, 42–47; 4:23–31; 6:1–6; 13:1–2).

A FINAL PRAYER

O Lord, you have mercy on all, take away from me my sins, and mercifully set me ablaze with the fire of your Holy Spirit. Take away from me the heart of stone, and give me a human heart, a heart to love and adore you, a heart to delight in you, to follow and enjoy you, for Christ's sake. Amen.

St Ambrose (c. 339–397)

CONCLUSION

God hates religion that has no heart. But wherever there is a good heart, God will receive its prayers and praise.

Who may ascend the hill of the LORD?
Who may stand in his holy place?
He who has clean hands and a pure heart,
who does not lift up his soul to an idol
or swear by what is false.
He will receive blessing from the LORD
and vindication from God his Saviour.

(Psalm 24:3–5)

Relevance for today

Modern day Pharisees?

Of course, Pharisaism could never rear its head among us, could it? None of us would ever so cling on to what God has given our church, denomination, or movement in the past that it closed us to what God is doing now in the present – would we? And while, admittedly, we have our personal preferences about prayer and worship, none of us would ever look down on other Christians who do it differently – would we?

Sadly the answer of history is – yes, we would! Catholics opposed the Anglicans; Anglicans opposed the Methodists; everyone opposed the Pentecostals; the Pentecostals opposed the Charismatics; the Charismatics opposed new moves of the Spirit. And all because we all wanted to hold on so much to the good things God had given us in the past and to do things our way – the best way!

So, to close this chapter, let's review prayerfully the seven characteristics of the Pharisees that we identified. Take a moment to pray and ask God whether any of these are found in you.

1. A focus on words, not deeds
2. A focus on externals, not internals
3. A focus on self, not others
4. A focus on their cause, not God's kingdom
5. A focus on the letter, not the Spirit
6. A focus on the minor, not the major
7. A focus on the past, not the present

Chapter Six

Praising in All Circumstances

Even unbelievers can thank God when things go well; but God wants us so to know him and trust him that we can praise him even in hard times; for praise unlocks things!

Rejoice in the Lord always. I will say it again: Rejoice! (Philippians 4:4)

It was one of the first occasions when Mike, as a young pastor, had witnessed anyone die. The lady had struggled with cancer for some time, and as her death drew closer, her husband asked Mike to come to their home. It was not long before the end came. As she breathed her last, her husband softly said, 'She's gone!' and dropped quietly to his knees by the bedside. He began to praise God, even through his tears, for the assurance that his wife was now with the Lord, free from pain, and that one day they would be together again.

His praise was not dependent on his circumstances; his praise was dependent on his God.

Praising 'in' or praising 'for'?

The apostle Paul certainly knew how to set his heart on praising God in difficult times. Yet one of his most famous passages encouraging people to do the same has sometimes been misunderstood.

Rejoice in the Lord always. I will say it again: Rejoice! Let your gentleness be evident to all. The Lord is near. Do not be anxious about anything, but in everything, by prayer and petition, with thanksgiving, present your requests to God. And the peace of God, which transcends all understanding, will guard your hearts and your minds in Christ Jesus.

(Philippians 4:4–7)

Some people have interpreted Paul as saying, 'Praise God for the bad things that happen in life!' But that is not what he says – indeed, to insist he does so is to turn God into some sort of monster, sending bad things our way and then expecting us to praise him for them. Paul's exhortation here is not to praise God 'for' everything, but 'in' everything (v 6) – a small, but very significant, difference. God does not expect us to praise him *for* everything; but he does want us to praise him *in* everything. For when our focus is on him, and not on our problems, things begin to happen.

Let's look at some individuals who learned this lesson of praising God in all circumstances.

Job: a case study

Ask most people what the story of Job is about, and they will answer, 'Suffering'. But while suffering is clearly a major theme, the real issue tackled is *righteousness* (e.g. Job 9:2; 12:4; 22:3; 32:1; 33:8–10; 40:7–8). Job had lived all his life as righteously as he could, and still things were going badly for him. Why?

In the midst of all his struggles and complaints, there are sudden glimpses of how, despite everything, he is holding on in faith. These are expressed in strong declarations of praise. Right at the beginning of the story, when he loses everything, his response is this:

He fell to the ground in worship and said:
'Naked I came from my mother's womb,
and naked I shall depart.
The LORD gave and the LORD has taken away;
may the name of the LORD be praised.'
In all this, Job did not sin by charging God with wrongdoing.

(Job 1:20–22)

Even when afflicted by painful sores and encouraged by his wife to 'curse God and die', he replies:

'You are talking like a foolish woman. Shall we accept good from God, and not trouble?'

(Job 2:10)

And then, throughout the story, we see ongoing glimpses of his praise to God, even in his darkest days:

'To God belong wisdom and power;
counsel and understanding are his.'

(12:13)

'Though he slay me, yet will I hope in him.'

(13:15)

'Even now my witness is in heaven;
my advocate is on high.
My intercessor is my friend
as my eyes pour out tears to God;
on behalf of a man he pleads with God
as a man pleads for his friend.'

(16:19–21)

'I know that my Redeemer lives,
and that in the end he will stand upon the earth.
And after my skin has been destroyed,
yet in my flesh I will see God;
I myself will see him
with my own eyes – I, and not another.'

(19:25–27)

'But he knows the way that I take;
when he has tested me, I shall come forth as gold.'

(23:10)

'He spreads out the northern skies over empty space;
he suspends the earth over nothing.
He wraps up the waters in his clouds,
yet the clouds do not burst under their weight.
He covers the face of the full moon,
spreading his clouds over it.
He marks out the horizon on the face of the waters
for a boundary between light and darkness.
The pillars of the heavens quake,
aghast at his rebuke.
By his power he churned up the sea;
by his wisdom he cut Rahab to pieces.
By his breath the skies became fair;
his hand pierced the gliding serpent.
And these are but the outer fringe of his works;
how faint the whisper we hear of him!

Who then can understand the thunder of
his power?'

(26:7–14)

We love that phrase: '*And these are but the outer fringe of his work*'. Job's God was big! And when the experience is over and Job has had a fresh encounter with God, this is his reply:

'I know that you can do all things;
no plan of yours can be thwarted.
You asked, "Who is this that obscures my
counsel without knowledge?"
Surely I spoke of things I did not
understand,
things too wonderful for me to know.
'You said, "Listen now, and I will speak;
I will question you,
and you shall answer me."
My ears had heard of you
but now my eyes have seen you.
Therefore I despise myself
and repent in dust and ashes.'

(42:1–6)

Here is a man who, despite all his struggles, held on in faith and praised God 'in' (though not 'for') the difficulties. This pleased God, for the story ends with how God's blessing came to him once again (Job 42:10–13, 16–17). The message of the book is clear: those who praise God in hard times keep their focus on him and, in so doing, on the one solution to their circumstances.

Others who praised in hard times

Let's look at three others who learned the secret of praise in hard times.

Jehoshaphat

Jehoshaphat, king of Judah between 872–848 BC, was essentially a godly king, who 'did what was right in the eyes of the LORD' (2 Chronicles 20:32). At some point in his reign, there was an invasion of Judah by neighbouring peoples. The pressure from this was clearly great; but Jehoshaphat's response was to keep focussed on God, as we see in his prayer of praise:

'O LORD, God of our fathers, are you not the God who is in heaven? You rule over all the kingdoms of the nations. Power and might are in your hand, and no-one can withstand you . . . We have no power to face this vast army that is attacking us. We do not know what to do, but our eyes are upon you.'

(2 Chronicles 20:6, 12)

Jehoshaphat understood the importance of praising God in difficult circumstances, as we see as the story unfolds.

After consulting the people, Jehoshaphat appointed men to sing to the LORD and to praise him for the splendour of his holiness as they went out at the head of the army, saying:

'Give thanks to the LORD,
for his love endures for ever.'

As they began to sing and praise, the LORD set ambushes against the men of Ammon and Moab and Mount Seir who were invading Judah, and they were defeated.

(2 Chronicles 20:21–22)

Praise kept them focused on God; and in keeping focused on him, they kept focused on the one thing that could change their situation.

Habakkuk

Habakkuk, a contemporary of Jeremiah, lived in the days leading up to the Babylonian invasion of Jerusalem. His short recorded writings express his inner struggles that, not only did God's ways seem unfathomable, they seemed down-right unjust. 'God, why aren't you answering our prayers? And why does evil prevail?' he cried (1:2). 'I'm about to do something you couldn't believe,' God answered, 'and I'm going to do it through the Babylonians!' (1:5–11). 'How can a holy God like you do that?' went back Habakkuk's reply (1:13–17). 'Come on, God; give me an answer; I'm waiting!' (2:1).

'You'll have to wait and see!' God answered (2:2–3). 'But it will happen (2:3); and Babylon will be destroyed (2:4–17); and '*the earth will be filled with the knowledge of the glory of the LORD, as the waters cover the sea*' (2:14); 'and you, Habakkuk, are just going to have to trust me!'

Habakkuk's response is one of praise to God in the face of difficulties (3:1–15). And then comes an amazing declaration of trust:

Though the fig-tree does not bud
and there are no grapes on the vines,
though the olive crop fails
and the fields produce no food,
though there are no sheep in the pen
and no cattle in the stalls,
yet I will rejoice in the LORD,
I will be joyful in God my Saviour.
(Habakkuk 3:17–18)

Here was a man who had not had all his questions answered; but he had met with God in prayer, and that had changed everything.

Paul

Trouble seemed to follow Paul wherever he went. Not that he went looking for it! He was simply so committed to sharing the good news of Jesus that it constantly got him into hot water. It was during his second missionary journey that a vision had led him to cross over into modern Europe (Acts 16:6–10). Arriving in Philippi, a largely Gentile city, Paul and Silas quickly got into trouble through delivering a slave girl possessed of an evil spirit of fortune-telling (Acts 16:16–18). While the girl was no doubt pleased to be rid of it, her owners were livid that their source of income had gone and soon stirred up a riot that ended with Paul and Silas being flogged, thrown into jail and put into the stocks (Acts 16:19–24). But rather than fall into self-pity, or waste endless hours asking 'Why?', they began to praise God! And then some amazing things happened.

About midnight Paul and Silas were praying and singing hymns to God, and the other prisoners were listening to them. Suddenly there was such a violent earthquake that the foundations of the prison were shaken. At once all the prison doors flew open, and everybody's chains came loose. The jailer woke up, and when he saw the prison doors open, he drew his sword and was about to kill himself because he thought the prisoners had escaped. But Paul shouted, 'Don't harm yourself! We are all here!'

The jailer called for lights, rushed in and fell trembling before Paul and Silas. He then brought them out and asked, 'Sirs, what must I do to be saved?' They replied, 'Believe in the Lord Jesus, and you will be saved – you and your household.' Then they spoke the word of the Lord to him and to all the others in his house. At that hour of the night the jailer took them and washed their wounds; then immediately he and all his family were baptised.

(Acts 16:25–33)

There are several results here of their praising God:

- It was a witness to the non-Christian prisoners who were listening (v 25)
- It released God's hand to act – in quite an amazing way! (v 26)

- It produced peace in them rather than panic (vv 27–28)
- It brought a whole family to faith in Jesus (vv 30–33)

It was through circumstances like this that Paul had learned to say, *'Rejoice in the Lord always'* (Philippians 4:4). And the reason he could say this was his absolute conviction that, no matter what happens, '*the Lord is near*' (Philippians 4:5).

A sacrifice of praise

'*Through Jesus, therefore, let us continually offer to God a sacrifice of praise*' (Hebrews 13:15).

Let's face it: praising God in hard times like the ones we have just looked at isn't always easy. The truth is, it involves a sacrifice; a sacrifice of our own feelings and emotions, of our own questions and answers. But those who chose to make this sacrifice found that God did not disappoint them, and that joy resulted, just as he promised.

Again there shall be heard in this place . . . the voice of joy, and the voice of gladness, the voice of the bridegroom, and the voice of the bride, the voice of them that shall say, Praise the LORD of hosts: for the LORD is good; for his mercy endureth for ever: and of them that shall bring the sacrifice of praise into the house of the LORD.

(Jeremiah 33:10–11, KJV)

Of course, our praise may not be as exuberant in the hard times as in the good times. But that is not the point. What matters is not the volume, but the sincerity.

Why can we praise in hard times?

It is certainly not because we are 'burying our head in the sand' or 'whistling in the dark'. It is because we can trust God, who is the sovereign LORD. Even when things seem to go wrong, he is still in control – working everything together into his plan – and we need to learn to trust him. When we moan rather than praise, we're saying, 'God, I don't think you know what you're doing!' But when we praise rather than moan, we're saying, 'God I may not understand you; but I will trust you!'

Paul summed up his absolute conviction that God is always working things out for good like this:

And we know that in all things God works for the good of those who love him, who have been called according to his purpose . . .

What, then, shall we say in response to this? If God is for us, who can be against us? He who did not spare his own Son, but gave him up for us all – how will he not also, along with him, graciously give us all things? . . . Who shall separate us from the love of Christ? Shall trouble or hardship or persecution or famine or nakedness or danger or sword? As it is written:

'For your sake we face death all day long;

The cry of 'Hallelujah!'

One of the simplest expressions of praise in the Bible is 'Hallelujah!' – Hebrew words (*Hallelu Yah*) meaning 'Praise the LORD'. Its presence is not always easy to recognize because many versions translate the phrase, rather than simply reproduce it. It is found frequently in the Psalms, often as an acclamation at the beginning (e.g. Psalms 111–113) or at the end (e.g. Psalms 115–117) of the psalm.

This expression brings home to us that sincere praise does not always need many words! Try using it more yourself and see!

we are considered as sheep to be slaughtered.'

No, in all these things we are more than conquerors through him who loved us. For I am convinced that neither death nor life, neither angels nor demons, neither the present nor the future, nor any powers, neither height nor depth, nor anything else in all creation, will be able to separate us from the love of God that is in Christ Jesus our Lord.

(Romans 8:28, 31–32, 35–39)

See also Genesis 50:19–20; Isaiah 8:10; Jeremiah 29:11; 1 Corinthians 15:57; Hebrews 13:6

A FINAL PRAYER

O give us patience and steadfastness in adversity, strengthen our weakness, comfort us in trouble and distress, help us to fight; grant unto us that in true obedience and contentation [contentment] of mind we may give over our own wills unto thee our Father in all things, according to the example of thy beloved Son: that in adversity we grudge not, but offer up ourselves unto thee without contradiction.

Miles Coverdale (1488–1568),
English Bible translator

CONCLUSION

We may not always be able to rejoice in the circumstance, but we can always rejoice in the Lord.

I will bless the LORD at all times: his praise shall continually be in my mouth.

(Psalm 34:1, NRSV)

Relevance for today

Who will we bless?

When we can pray '*Bless the LORD, O my soul*' (Psalm 104:1, KJV) rather than the self-centred 'Bless my soul, O the LORD', we are learning the secret of praise. Which will we choose to bless?

How will we fight?

Praise is God's 'shock troops' against his enemies – and ours. When Israel was about to enter the promised land, God chose the tribe of Judah (Judah means 'Praise') to go into battle first (Judges 1:1–2). Praise always leads the way and clears the way. Jehoshaphat would learn this lesson many years later (2 Chronicles 20). Have we – especially when practical problems arise?

How will we respond?

Despite the injustices that came his way – sold into slavery (Genesis 37:19–36), falsely accused of attempted rape (Genesis 39:1–23), left to languish in jail (Genesis 40:1–23) – Joseph kept his heart soft and focused on God.

'So then, it was not you who sent me here, but God.'

(Genesis 45:8)

'You intended to harm me, but God intended it for good to accomplish what is now being done, the saving of many lives"

(Genesis 50:20)

This is the attitude God wants to find in us when things go wrong. It releases his hand to work.

When will we do it?

Knowing praise should be our first response when faced with difficulties isn't enough. We need to do it! The fact of praise must become the act of praise. Will we begin to put that into practice – right now?

Chapter Seven

What Does Worship Do?

While the focus of praise and worship is God himself, the amazing thing is that, when we focus on him, we end up getting blessed!

He is your praise; he is your God. (Deuteronomy 10:21)

'But what will I get out of it?' We wonder how many times you have heard (or asked!) that question! It is a question that reflects the utilitarian society that we live in these days. Everything must have an immediate purpose or return; and that purpose or return should in some way benefit *me.*

Worship cuts across this utilitarian instinct, for it promises nothing for *me*; it is something that is given solely to *God.* And yet, here is the strange thing: when I give myself to praising and worshipping him, a whole host of things happen to me and for me! Such is the mystery of worship.

Worship and God

Let us never forget: God does not need our worship. He is not in some way 'lessened' if we do not bring it to him; and nor is he 'greatened' if we do! The fact that God does not need our worship is reflected in the way that, again and again, he says he will not accept worship at any price. If our heart is not right or our behaviour has been wrong, then our worship is quite meaningless to him.

'The multitude of your sacrifices –
what are they to me?' says the LORD.
'I have more than enough of burnt offerings,
of rams and the fat of fattened animals;
I have no pleasure
in the blood of bulls and lambs and goats.
When you come to appear before me,
who has asked this of you,
this trampling of my courts?
Stop bringing meaningless offerings!
Your incense is detestable to me.
New Moons, Sabbaths and convocations –
I cannot bear your evil assemblies.
Your New Moon festivals and your appointed feasts
my soul hates.
They have become a burden to me;
I am weary of bearing them.
When you spread out your hands in prayer,
I will hide my eyes from you;
even if you offer many prayers,
I will not listen.
Your hands are full of blood;
wash and make yourselves clean.

Take your evil deeds
out of my sight!
Stop doing wrong,
learn to do right!
Seek justice,
encourage the oppressed.
Defend the cause of the fatherless,
plead the case of the widow.'

(Isaiah 1:11–17)

See also Jeremiah 7:1–19; Amos 5:21–24; Micah 6:6–8; Mark 7:6–7

It is interesting to note that God says more in the Bible about unacceptable worship than he does about acceptable worship!

So God does not want our worship at any price. And yet, he makes clear that our worship is certainly something he desires.

Worship pleases God

God has revealed himself as our Father; and, as a Father, he loves to hear his children bring their expressions of delight to him. Worship really pleases him!

I will sing to the LORD all my life;
I will sing praise to my God as long as I live.
May my meditation be pleasing to him,
as I rejoice in the LORD.

(Psalm 104:33–34)

Therefore, I urge you, brothers, in view of God's mercy, to offer your bodies as living sacrifices, holy and pleasing to God – this is your spiritual act of worship.

(Romans 12:1)

See also Genesis 8:20–21; Leviticus 2:1–2; Psalm 19:14; 51:19; 147:11; Philippians 4:18

Worship honours God

Remember: our worship comes from an old English word, 'worth-ship'. When we worship, we are assigning to God his true worth, acknowledging his perfection in everything and thereby giving him the honour that is rightfully his.

You who fear the LORD, praise him!
All you descendants of Jacob, honour him!
Revere him, all you descendants of Israel!

(Psalm 22:23)

He who sacrifices thank-offerings honours me,
and he prepares the way
so that I may show him the salvation of God.

(Psalm 50:23)

See also Exodus 12:42; Jeremiah 33:9; Daniel 4:34; Revelation 4:9–11

Worship and us

As we said in the introduction to this chapter, while our worship is to be solely focused on God, the amazing thing is that it has so many 'spill-over' blessings to us! Just look at the following list of things and see!

Worship marks us out as God's true people

Anybody (even unbelievers) can pray; but worship is the language of those who know they are God's children.

We are the ones who are truly circumcised, because we worship by the power of God's Spirit and take pride in Christ Jesus.

(Philippians 3:3, CEV)

See also John 4:21–24

Worship 'opens the door'

Worship 'opens up the door' to heaven so that we may encounter God and hear his Spirit, as John discovered in his vision.

After this I looked, and there before me was a door standing open in heaven. And the voice I had first heard speaking to me like a trumpet said, 'Come up here, and I will show you what must take place after this.' At once I was in the Spirit, and there before me was a throne in heaven . . .

(Revelation 4:1–2)

See also Revelation 1:10–19

Worship brings God's presence

Whenever men and women turn to God in worship, he comes with his presence in a special way.

When Solomon finished praying, fire came down from heaven and consumed the burnt offering and the sacrifices, and the glory of the LORD filled the temple. The priests could not enter the temple of the LORD because the glory of the LORD filled it. When all the Israelites saw the fire coming down and the glory of the LORD above the temple, they knelt on the pavement with their faces to the ground, and they worshipped and gave thanks to the LORD, saying, 'He is good; his love endures for ever.'

(2 Chronicles 7:1–3)

See also 2 Chronicles 5:13–14

Worship changes us

If we have truly met with God in our worship (and if we haven't, then we haven't worshipped!), we will come out from his presence different.

When Moses came down from Mount Sinai with the two tablets of the Testimony in his hands, he was not aware that his face was radiant because he had spoken with the LORD. When Aaron and all the Israelites saw Moses, his face was radiant . . .

(Exodus 34:29–30)

See also 2 Corinthians 3:7–18

Worship brings blessing

God promises that if we will worship and serve only him, then that will lead to blessing flowing into our lives; but if we worship other gods or other things, we will bring a curse upon ourselves.

The LORD your God commands you to love him and to serve him with all your heart and soul. If you obey him, he will send rain at the right seasons, so you will have more than enough food, wine and olive oil, and there will be plenty of grass for your cattle. But watch out! You will be tempted to turn your backs on the LORD. And if you worship other gods, the LORD will become angry and keep the rain from falling. Nothing will grow in your fields, and you will die and disappear from the good land that the LORD is giving you.

(Deuteronomy 11:13–17, CEV)

See also Exodus 23:25–26

Worship brings boldness

We get afraid when we focus on ourselves and our own limitations. But when we focus on God through praise and worship, we become more aware of his power and less aware of our weakness.

When they heard this, they raised their voices together in prayer to God. 'Sovereign Lord,' they said, 'you made the heaven and the earth and the sea, and everything in them . . .'

'Now, Lord, consider their threats and enable your servants to speak your word with great boldness. Stretch out your hand to heal and perform miraculous signs and wonders through the name of your holy servant Jesus.'

After they prayed, the place where they were meeting was shaken. And they were all filled with the Holy Spirit and spoke the word of God boldly.

(Acts 4:24, 29–31)

See also Ezra 8:21–23

Doxologies

Scattered throughout the Scriptures are lots of doxologies – exclamations of praise that glorify God. Such prayers can be used in corporate worship; but perhaps more importantly they serve as models of how to call out to God in praise, briefly but powerfully, in all sorts of circumstances. Learning to use these, or our own, doxologies could transform our own life of praise and therefore the results we see!

'Praise be to the LORD, who this day has not left you without a kinsman-redeemer.'

(Ruth 4:14)

'Praise be to the Lord, the God of Israel, because he has come and has redeemed his people.'

(Luke 1:68)

Now to him who is able to do immeasurably more than all we ask or imagine, according to his power that is at work within us, to him be glory in the church and in Christ Jesus throughout all generations, for ever and ever! Amen.

(Ephesians 3:20–21)

Now to the King eternal, immortal, invisible, the only God, be honour and glory for ever and ever. Amen.

(1 Timothy 1:17)

Grow in the grace and knowledge of our Lord and Saviour Jesus Christ. To him be glory both now and for ever! Amen.

(2 Peter 3:18)

To him who is able to keep you from falling and to present you before his glorious presence without fault and with great joy – to the only God our Saviour be glory, majesty, power and authority, through Jesus Christ our Lord, before all ages, now and for evermore! Amen.

(Jude 24–25)

To him who loves us and has freed us from our sins by his blood, and has made us to be a kingdom and priests to serve his God and Father – to him be glory and power for ever and ever! Amen.

(Revelation 1:5–6)

See also 1 Chronicles 29:10–13; Romans 11:33–36; 16:25–27; 1 Corinthians 15:57; Galatians 1:4–5; Philippians 4:20; 1 Timothy 6:16; 2 Timothy 4:18; Hebrews 13:20–21; 1 Peter 4:11; 5:10–11; Revelation 5:13; 7:1

Worship increases faith

The more we focus on God through praise and worship, the more we see how big he is; and the more we see how big he is, the more we grasp how he is able to answer our prayers; and the more we see how he is able to answer our prayers, the more faith we have!

Jehoshaphat bowed with his face to the ground, and all the people of Judah and Jerusalem fell down in worship before the LORD. Then some Levites from the Kohathites and Korahites stood up and praised the LORD, the God of Israel, with a very loud voice. Early in the morning they left for the Desert of Tekoa. As they set out, Jehoshaphat stood and said, 'Listen to me, Judah and people of Jerusalem! Have faith in the LORD your God and you will be upheld; have faith in his prophets and you will be successful.'

(2 Chronicles 20:18–20)

See also Nehemiah 1:4–2:8

Worship brings deliverance

There is undoubtedly something of a mystery here; but God's Word shows that whenever when we focus on God in worship, there is a breakthrough in the spiritual dimension of life. Hindrances can be removed, difficulties overcome, problems resolved and enemies defeated.

I call to the LORD, who is worthy of praise,
and I am saved from my enemies.

(2 Samuel 22:4)

See also Psalm 50:14–15

Worship brings God's judgment

The God who is 'the compassionate and gracious God' (Exodus 34:6) is also, as we saw in Chapter 2 of this Part, a God who ultimately brings judgment on sin and on those who oppose him. Praise sometimes plays a part in this judgment being released.

Let the high praises of God be in their mouth, and a two-edged sword in their hand; to execute vengeance upon the heathen, and punishments upon the people; to bind their kings with chains, and their nobles with fetters of iron; to execute upon them the judgment written: this honour have all his saints. Praise ye the LORD.

(Psalm 149:6–9, KJV)

We deliberately chose this older rendering of this psalm to retain the phrase 'high praises'. There are times when 'ordinary praise' just won't do and when we really need to 'give it all we've got' – in volume, in passion, in faith, in the Spirit – and attain a 'higher level' of praise to God that breaks through spiritual barriers, as Daniel once had to do (see Daniel 10:2–14). Such praise engages things at a spiritual level – in the 'heavenly realms' (e.g. Ephesians 6:12), where we can't see unless our eyes are opened (e.g. 2 Kings 6:17).

In Psalm 149, the psalmist recognizes that such divine breakthroughs and judgments can as easily come through the mouth of praise as by the hand with a sword. For us today, of course, the only sword permitted to us to do battle on behalf of God is 'the sword of the Spirit, which is the word of God' (Ephesians 6:17; see also Hebrews 4:12).

We end this section on 'Prayers that say amazing!' with a well-known prayer of praise, called *Te Deum Laudamus.* It is taken from 'Morning Prayer' in *The Book of Common Prayer,* and has been used in many different sorts of churches. It sums up so much of what we have to praise God for and some of the blessings that are ours in Christ.

A FINAL PRAYER

We praise thee, O God:
we acknowledge thee to be the Lord.
All the earth doth worship thee:
the Father everlasting.
To thee all Angels cry aloud:
the Heavens and all the
Powers therein.
To thee Cherubin and Seraphin
continually do cry,
Holy, holy, holy: Lord God of
Sabaoth;
Heaven and earth are full
of the Majesty of thy glory.
The glorious company of the
Apostles praise thee;
The goodly fellowship of the
Prophets praise thee.
The noble army of martyrs
praise thee.
The holy church throughout
all the world
doth acknowledge thee,

The Father of an infinite majesty;
Thine honourable, true
and only Son;
Also the Holy Ghost the Comforter.
Thou art the King of glory
O Christ.
Thou art the everlasting
Son of the Father.
When thou tookest upon thee to
deliver man
thou didst not abhor the
Virgin's womb.
When thou hadst overcome the
sharpness of death
thou didst open the kingdom of
heaven to all believers.
Thou sittest at the right hand of
God in the glory of the Father.
We believe that thou shalt come to
be our Judge.
We therefore pray thee,
help thy servants
whom thou hast redeemed
with thy precious blood.
Make them to be numbered with
thy saints in glory everlasting.
O Lord, save thy people and bless
thine heritage.
Govern them and lift them up
for ever.
Day by day we magnify thee;
And we worship thy Name ever
world without end.
Vouchsafe O Lord to keep us this
day without sin.
O Lord, have mercy upon us: have
mercy upon us.
O Lord, let thy mercy lighten upon
us as our trust is in thee.
O Lord, in thee have I trusted, let
me never be confounded.

Te Deum Laudamus,
Book of Common Prayer

CONCLUSION

When we focus on blessing God, God is able to focus on blessing us!

What other nation is so great as to have their gods near them the way the LORD our God is near us whenever we pray to him?
(Deuteronomy 4:7)

Relevance for today

Let's end this chapter by looking again at the nine things that worship does for us, for these are still as true today as when the Bible was first written. As you read through them, reflect on how your own praise and worship matches up. Do these things happen when you worship? If not, God is eager to help bring about change!

- Worship marks us out as God's true people
- Worship 'opens the door'
- Worship brings God's presence
- Worship changes us
- Worship brings blessing
- Worship brings boldness
- Worship increases faith
- Worship brings deliverance
- Worship brings God's judgment

But remember: these things come to us, not because we search for them, but because we search for God. May God help us so to focus on him that all these things become part of our growing experience!

Part Three

Prayers that say 'Thanks!'

Chapter One

Thanksgiving for God's Creation

We only have to open our eyes and look! There before us, in creation, is ample evidence of God's existence and ample reason to thank him.

From the time the world was created, people have seen the earth and sky and all that God made. They can clearly see his invisible qualities – his eternal power and his divine nature. So they have no excuse whatsoever for not knowing God. (Romans 1:20, NLT)

Say, 'Thank you!' If you are a parent, you will no doubt (like us and our wives) have uttered those words many times to your children as they were growing up – and they will no doubt have failed to say them, generally at the most embarrassing moments! Trying to get our children to say 'Thank you!' is important to most of us, because we want the words, and the heart behind them, to become second nature as they grow up. People who are thankful not only appreciate in life what others fail to notice; they also are simply nicer people!

God too wants his children to learn to say 'Thank you!' – for all that he has done for us. And God says that we don't have far to look to see things we can be grateful for. Why, we only have to open our eyes and look at creation around us.

Perhaps one of the best known passages in the Old Testament celebrating God's creation is Psalm 8.

O LORD, our Lord,
how majestic is your name in all the earth!
You have set your glory
above the heavens.
From the lips of children and infants
you have ordained praise
because of your enemies,
to silence the foe and the avenger.
When I consider your heavens,
the work of your fingers,
the moon and the stars,
which you have set in place,
what is man that you are mindful of him,
the son of man that you care for him?
You made him a little lower than the heavenly beings
and crowned him with glory and honour.
You made him ruler over the works of your hands;

you put everything under his feet:
all flocks and herds,
and the beasts of the field,
the birds of the air,
and the fish of the sea,
all that swim the paths of the seas.
O LORD, our Lord,
how majestic is your name in all the earth!
(Psalm 8:1–8)

This psalm is not in praise of 'nature' (an unbiblical concept at the best of times!) but in praise of God, as we see in the way that it focuses on him at both the beginning and end. *He* is the one who brought everything into being. It didn't just 'happen'; *he* created it! And while we all may have different understandings of exactly how God did that, the end result should be the same: we, like the psalmist, should look on his works with breathless admiration and say 'Thanks!'

The psalm focuses on two main things for which we should be thankful: the creation of the universe and the creation of the human race.

Thankfulness for the creation of the universe

We can imagine the scenario, most of us having done it ourselves at some time or other. There was the psalmist, standing out in the open one evening, looking up at the stars. It was a perfectly clear night; and so, the more he looked, the more he saw! And the more he saw, the more gratitude arose in his heart towards God for his wonderful work of creation. And then, he went inside and wrote this psalm.

The psalm is headed 'According to gittith' – almost certainly a musical term. The Septuagint (the Greek translation of the Hebrew Old Testament) associates the word with the Hebrew for 'winepress'. It is 'A song of the winepress'. Was this a type of tune? Or was it sung in a certain way? Whichever, perhaps it arose from the overwhelming 'pressing down' that David felt within his heart as he stood, so small and insignificant, in God's universe. So small and insignificant; yet also so great and significant!

Creation reflects God's glory

The psalmist's wonder and amazement did not stop at the starlit night; he saw beyond the glory of the stars to the glory of the God who had made them (v 1). Such splendour is so obvious that even children can see it and praise God for it; and their instinctive awe and praise silences those adversaries who have lost the ability to wonder at anything (v 2).

The heavens declare the glory of God;
the skies proclaim the work of his hands.
Day after day they pour forth speech;
night after night they display knowledge.
There is no speech or language
where their voice is not heard.
Their voice goes out into all the earth,
their words to the ends of the world.
(Psalm 19:1–4)

Praise the LORD, O my soul.
O LORD my God, you are very great;
you are clothed with splendour and majesty.
He wraps himself in light as with a garment;
he stretches out the heavens like a tent
and lays the beams of his upper chambers on their waters.
He makes the clouds his chariot
and rides on the wings of the wind.
He makes winds his messengers,
flames of fire his servants.
(Psalm 104:1–4)

See also Psalm 72:18–19; Isaiah 6:3; Habakkuk 2:14

Creation is God's work

The Bible is clear that creation did not just 'happen'; it was planned and formed by God himself. So the psalmist could look at the sky and see it as 'the work of your fingers' and write of the moon and stars 'which you have set in place' (v 3). Creation is *God*'s work – which is why he is described as 'the Maker of heaven and earth' (e.g. Psalm 121:1–2) – and for that we should give him thanks!

The earth is the LORD's, and everything in it,
the world, and all who live in it;
for he founded it upon the seas
and established it upon the waters.

(Psalm 24:1–2)

In the beginning you laid the foundations of the earth,
and the heavens are the work of your hands.
They will perish, but you remain;
they will all wear out like a garment.
Like clothing you will change them
and they will be discarded.
But you remain the same,
and your years will never end.

(Psalm 102:25–27)

'Sovereign Lord,' they said, 'you made the heaven and the earth and the sea, and everything in them.'

(Acts 4:24)

See also Nehemiah 9:5–6; Psalm 33:6–9; 104:1–35; 136:1–9; Proverbs 8:22–31; Ecclesiastes 11:5; Isaiah 66:1–2; Jeremiah 32:17; Acts 14:15; 17:24–25; Hebrews 1:1–2, 10–12

Creation itself praises God

Because of all this, the writers of the Bible sometimes call on creation itself to praise God for his creative work. Jesus once said that if we didn't give praise to God, then something as simple as stones would do it (Luke 19:37–40) – which somehow puts us in our place!

Praise the LORD.
Praise the LORD from the heavens,
praise him in the heights above.
Praise him, all his angels,
praise him, all his heavenly hosts.
Praise him, sun and moon,
praise him, all you shining stars.
Praise him, you highest heavens
and you waters above the skies.
Let them praise the name of the LORD,
for he commanded and they were created.
He set them in place for ever and ever;
he gave a decree that will never pass away.
Praise the LORD from the earth,
you great sea creatures and all ocean depths,
lightning and hail, snow and clouds,
stormy winds that do his bidding,
you mountains and all hills,
fruit trees and all cedars,
wild animals and all cattle,
small creatures and flying birds,
kings of the earth and all nations,
you princes and all rulers on earth,
young men and maidens,
old men and children.
Let them praise the name of the LORD,
for his name alone is exalted;
his splendour is above the earth and the heavens.
He has raised up for his people a horn,
the praise of all his saints,
of Israel, the people close to his heart.
Praise the LORD.

(Psalm 148:1–14)

See also Job 12:7–10; Psalm 69:34; 145:10

God is still actively involved in creation

Sometimes God has been seen as an 'absent landlord'. In other words, he made creation and then withdrew, leaving it to get on with running itself through the mechanism he had put in place, rather like a watchmaker might make a clock, wind it up, set it on the mantelpiece and then leave it (an image used by some of the deists in the eighteenth century). This could not be further from the picture that the Bible gives us! In both Old and New Testaments God himself is shown to be still actively involved in the operation of the natural world. That is why, when we hear someone say, 'Isn't nature wonderful?' our cry should be, 'No! *God* is wonderful!' *God* maintains his world, not 'nature'!

He makes springs pour water into the ravines;
it flows between the mountains.
They give water to all the beasts of the field;
the wild donkeys quench their thirst.
The birds of the air nest by the waters;
they sing among the branches.
He waters the mountains from his upper chambers;
the earth is satisfied by the fruit of his work.
He makes grass grow for the cattle,
and plants for man to cultivate-
bringing forth food from the earth:
wine that gladdens the heart of man,
oil to make his face shine,
and bread that sustains his heart.

(Psalm 104:10–15)

You take care of the land and water it;
you make it very fertile.
The rivers of God are full of water.
Grain grows because you make it grow.
You send rain to the ploughed fields;
you fill the rows with water.
You soften the ground with rain,
and then you bless it with crops.
You give the year a good harvest,
and you load the wagons with many crops.
The desert is covered with grass
and the hills with happiness.
The pastures are full of flocks,
and the valleys are covered with grain.
Everything shouts and sings for joy.

(Psalm 65:9–13, NCV)

See also Psalm 135:5–7; 145:14–16; Isaiah 40:25–26; Daniel 2:19–23; Matthew 10:29–30; 1 Corinthians 8:6; Colossians 1:15–17; Hebrews 1:3; Revelation 3:14

Thankfulness for the creation of the human race

Let's return to Psalm 8. Having marvelled at God's vast creation, David then turns his thoughts to the place of the human race in all of this. He stands amazed that God should care about people (v4) – even more so that he should have made 'man' the crown of his creation (v 5), only a little lower than 'the heavenly beings' (NIV) or even than God himself (NRSV), and that he should have delegated his authority to men and women to rule over creation on his behalf (vv 6–8). And yet, despite this high calling, the tone throughout the psalm is one of humility, and not arrogance.

God created all humanity

Whatever we might (or might not!) understand about the 'how' of creation, the Bible is clear that men and women are no 'accident' but are the direct creation of God – indeed, the pinnacle of his creation.

Come, let us bow down in worship,
let us kneel before the LORD *our Maker;*
for he is our God
and we are the people of his pasture,
the flock under his care.

(Psalm 95:6–7)

Rich and poor have this in common:
The LORD is the Maker of them all.
(Proverbs 22:2)

See also Job 35:9–11; Isaiah 51:12–13; Acts 17:24–28

The Bible sees every human being as the result, not merely of human procreation, but of the direct creative action of God.

For you created my inmost being;
you knit me together in my mother's womb.
I praise you because I am fearfully and wonderfully made;
your works are wonderful,
I know that full well.
My frame was not hidden from you
when I was made in the secret place.
When I was woven together in the depths of the earth,
your eyes saw my unformed body.
All the days ordained for me
were written in your book
before one of them came to be.
(Psalm 139:13–16)

See also Job 10:8–12; Psalm 119:73; Isaiah 44:2; Jeremiah 1:5

God sustains all humanity

'The Spirit of God has made me;
the breath of the Almighty gives me life.'
(Job 33:4)

'In him we live and move and have our being.'
(Acts 17:28)

See also Psalm 36:6; Daniel 4:34–35; 5:22–23; James 4:13–15

God crowns all humanity

Because people are the special and crowning creation of God, they are honoured by him as such, and should therefore be honoured by us also.

What is man that you are mindful of him,
the son of man that you care for him?
You made him a little lower than the heavenly beings
and crowned him with glory and honour.
(Psalm 8:4–5)

See also Psalm 103:1–4

God is sovereign over all humanity

His dominion is an eternal dominion;
his kingdom endures from generation to generation.
All the peoples of the earth
are regarded as nothing.
He does as he pleases
with the powers of heaven
and the peoples of the earth.
No-one can hold back his hand
or say to him: 'What have you done?'
(Daniel 4:34–35)

See also Psalm 115:1–3; 135:5–6; Isaiah 29:15–16; 45:9–12; Romans 9:1–29

God determines the length of our days

While this may seem a strange thing to give thanks for, it nevertheless is true! God knows our days; and this means that we do not need to be anxious or fearful about life, or death.

Show me, O LORD, my life's end
and the number of my days;
let me know how fleeting is my life.
You have made my days a mere handbreadth;
the span of my years is as nothing before you.
Each man's life is but a breath. Selah
Man is a mere phantom as he goes to and fro:
He bustles about, but only in vain;
he heaps up wealth, not knowing who will get it.
But now, Lord, what do I look for?
My hope is in you.
(Psalm 39:4–7)

See also Genesis 27:2; Job 14:1–5; Psalm 90:10; Isaiah 38:10–20; James 4:13–14

God has set eternity in our hearts

As we reflect on God's creation, it quickly becomes apparent that it is just too vast for us to take in! And the more we explore the universe and all that lies beyond it, the more the vastness comes home to us. Yet the Bible tells us – and experience confirms it – that no matter how much of that vast creation we explore and discover, there is still a yearning for more – and that more, of course, is God himself. King Solomon summed it up like this:

He has made everything beautiful in its time. He has also set eternity in the hearts of men; yet they cannot fathom what God has done from beginning to end.

(Ecclesiastes 3:11)

A coming new creation

Beautiful as this earth is, it is not perfect – though it was perfect when God first created it; so much so he could look at it and pronounce it 'very good' (Genesis 1:31). But sin came into this world and spoiled it, finding expression nowadays, for example, in the ecological disasters that we experience.

However, the Bible looks forward to the day when Jesus will return and when creation will be freed from its 'struggles' (Romans 8:19–21) and a new creation will be brought into being – like this one, but without any of its imperfections.

'Behold, I will create
new heavens and a new earth.
The former things will not be remembered,
nor will they come to mind.
But be glad and rejoice for ever
in what I will create.'

(Isaiah 65:17–18)

See also Romans 8:18–21; 1 Corinthians 15:42–55; Ephesians 1:9–10; 2 Peter 3:8–13; Revelation 21:1–6; 22:1–6

A FINAL PRAYER

Now we must praise the ruler
of heaven,
The might of the Lord
and his purpose of mind,
The work of the glorious father;
for he, God eternal,
established each wonder,
He, holy creator, first fashioned
the heavens
As a roof for the children of earth.
And then our guardian, the
everlasting Lord,
Adorned this middle-earth
for men.
Praise the almighty king
of heaven.

Caedmon, English monk (d. c. 680)

CONCLUSION

'Wonders are many, and none is more wonderful than man.' (Sophocles, *Antigone*)

'Look at the birds of the air; they do not sow or reap or store away in barns, and yet your heavenly Father feeds them. Are you not much more valuable than they? . . . So do not worry . . .'

(Matthew 6:26, 31)

Relevance for today

Stop rushing – start looking

In a busy world we need to learn how to stop and look afresh at God's creation, so that we might marvel again at all he has made. When did you last really stop and look at a leaf, or a cloud, or your fingerprints, or a rainbow? 'Familiarity breeds contempt' goes the saying; but it is a foolish contempt that directs itself to God – even by neglect.

Think: **Do I take time to stop, marvel and thank?**

Stop thinking 'nature' – start thinking 'creation'

'Nature' is a common word in modern usage; but it is woefully inadequate. It speaks of a self-sufficient 'closed' system that has no need of God. The biblical term is not 'nature' but 'creation' – that which is created! By whom? By God!

Think: **Do I talk about 'nature' or 'creation'? What opportunities there might be to talk to others about God if I were to change this word in my conversation!**

Stop thinking 'equals' – start thinking 'crown'

Any theory of human development that fails to see men and women as a special creation of God, but rather as merely another animal, fails to do justice to God's Word. We are not the same as animals – we are special! It is we who are the crown of God's creation!

Think: **Do I see human beings as the crown of God's creation, distinct and special to him in a way that no other creature is? Or have I swallowed the lie that I am 'just another animal'? Thank God that you are special!**

Creation should challenge us!

In an age when we understand more and more of 'how' things operate, we have lost the ability to wonder at creation – to marvel at a sunset, or a rainbow, or a spider's web, or a snowflake, or breath on the cold morning air. Yet such wonders can put things in perspective and remind us of who God is and who we are, as Job learned in his prayerful encounter with God. The whole of Job 38–41 is a powerful challenge from creation (do read it!) to respond to God with thankfulness. Little wonder after such an experience Job turned to God and said,

'I know that you can do all things;
no plan of yours can be thwarted.
You asked, "Who is this that obscures my counsel without knowledge?"
Surely I spoke of things I did not understand,
things too wonderful for me to know.
You said, "Listen now, and I will speak;
I will question you,
and you shall answer me."
My ears had heard of you
but now my eyes have seen you.'

(Job 42:2–5)

Chapter Two

Thanksgiving for God's Salvation

God does not stand at a distance and watch us in our difficulties; he is a God who comes to save us.

Our God is a God who saves. (Psalm 68:20)

Mike and his wife were on a boating holiday with friends when they suddenly became aware of people on the opposite riverbank shouting and waving in their direction. Unable to hear what they were saying, they simply gave a cheery wave in return. But when the crowd started frantically pointing downwards, raising their voices still more, they looked over the side of the boat and there, being swept downstream with the strong current, was a young boy, unable to swim. Without a moment's hesitation, Mike's friend leapt into the river to get the youngster out, while Mike hung over the railing to pull him on board. The youngster was saved and was returned to his parents – shaken but safe.

Of course, we would all have done the same. So, why should it surprise us to discover that God, in whose image we are made, is a God who 'leaps in' to come and help us? For that is exactly what he does.

The word 'salvation' is not often used these days, even by Christians. Perhaps it sounds rather old-fashioned and carries connotations of miserable Christians with big black Bibles. But 'salvation' is a very common concept in the Bible, and God is constantly seen as our 'Saviour'.

In this chapter we will look at the idea of salvation in the Old Testament. In the next chapter we will look at how that salvation came to fulfilment through Jesus.

God as Saviour

Throughout the Old Testament God was acknowledged as the Saviour of his people, who saved them from a whole range of circumstances. Recollection of this was a strong basis for praise and thanksgiving, a strong motivation to prayer, and a strong encouragement to stand firm in the face of difficulties.

Show me your ways, O LORD,
teach me your paths;
guide me in your truth and teach me,
for you are God my Saviour,
and my hope is in you all day long.
(Psalm 25:4–5)

Why are you downcast, O my soul?
Why so disturbed within me?
Put your hope in God,
for I will yet praise him,
my Saviour and my God.

(Psalm 42:5–6)

Praise be to the Lord, to God our Saviour,
who daily bears our burdens.

(Psalm 68:19)

Although our sins testify against us,
O LORD, do something for the sake of your name.
For our backsliding is great;
we have sinned against you.
O Hope of Israel,
its Saviour in times of distress,
why are you like a stranger in the land,
like a traveller who stays only a night?
Why are you like a man taken by surprise,
like a warrior powerless to save?
You are among us, O LORD,
and we bear your name;
do not forsake us!

(Jeremiah 14:7–9)

See also 1 Chronicles 16:34–36; Psalm 79:9; 85:4–9; Micah 7:7; Habakkuk 3:17–18

This understanding that God himself is our Saviour continues in the New Testament.

We have put our hope in the living God, who is the Saviour of all men, and especially of those who believe.

(1 Timothy 4:10)

But when the kindness and love of God our Saviour appeared, he saved us, not because of righteous things we had done, but because of his mercy.

(Titus 3:4)

To him who is able to keep you from falling and to present you before his glorious presence without fault and with great joy – to the only God our Saviour be glory, majesty, power and authority, through Jesus Christ our Lord, before all ages, now and for evermore! Amen.

(Jude 24–27)

See also Luke 1:46–47; 1 Timothy 1:1; 2:3–4; Titus 1:1–3; 2:9–10

It would be because God is a 'Saviour God' that his Son, Jesus Christ, would come into the world as the Saviour, as we will see in the next chapter.

Knowing God as Saviour inspires confidence

When we know God is our Saviour, it produces tremendous confidence within us and removes our fears.

The LORD is my light and my salvation –
whom shall I fear?
The LORD is the stronghold of my life –
of whom shall I be afraid?
When evil men advance against me
to devour my flesh,
when my enemies and my foes attack me,
they will stumble and fall.
Though an army besiege me,
my heart will not fear;
though war break out against me,
even then will I be confident.
One thing I ask of the LORD,
this is what I seek:
that I may dwell in the house of the LORD
all the days of my life,
to gaze upon the beauty of the LORD
and to seek him in his temple.
For in the day of trouble
he will keep me safe in his dwelling;
he will hide me in the shelter of his tabernacle
and set me high upon a rock.
Then my head will be exalted

above the enemies who surround me;
at his tabernacle will I sacrifice with shouts of joy;
I will sing and make music to the LORD.
Hear my voice when I call, O LORD;
be merciful to me and answer me.
My heart says of you, 'Seek his face!'
Your face, LORD, I will seek.
Do not hide your face from me,
do not turn your servant away in anger;
you have been my helper.
Do not reject me or forsake me,
O God my Saviour.
Though my father and mother forsake me,
the LORD will receive me.
Teach me your way, O LORD;
lead me in a straight path
because of my oppressors.
Do not hand me over to the desire of my foes,
for false witnesses rise up against me,
breathing out violence.
I am still confident of this:
I will see the goodness of the LORD
in the land of the living.
Wait for the LORD;
be strong and take heart
and wait for the LORD.

(Psalm 27:1–14)

See also Exodus 15:1–18; 2 Chronicles 32:6–8; Psalm 3:1–8; 20:6–9

Psalm 3: A case study

While not one of the best-known psalms, Psalm 3 contains many features found in other psalms too.

O LORD, how many are my foes!
How many rise up against me!
Many are saying of me,
'God will not deliver him.' *Selah*
But you are a shield around me, O LORD;
you bestow glory on me and lift up my head.
To the LORD I cry aloud,
and he answers me from his holy hill. *Selah*
I lie down and sleep;
I wake again, because the LORD sustains me.
I will not fear the tens of thousands
drawn up against me on every side.
Arise, O LORD!
Deliver me, O my God!
Strike all my enemies on the jaw;
break the teeth of the wicked.

Images of salvation

A whole variety of imagery is used in the Old Testament when thinking of God as our Saviour. The opening lines of one of David's psalms, as recorded in 2 Samuel 22, piles up lots of these images.

The LORD is my rock, my fortress and my deliverer;
my God is my rock, in whom I take refuge,
my shield and the horn of my salvation.
He is my stronghold, my refuge and my saviour.

(2 Samuel 22:2–3)

- **Rock** (see also e.g. Deuteronomy 32:3–4; 1 Samuel 2:2; Psalm 18:31; 62:7–8)
- **Fortress** (see also e.g. Psalm 46:7; 48:1–3; 144:1–2; Isaiah 17:10)
- **Deliverer** (see also e.g. Psalm 40:17; 70:1–5; 140:6–7; 144:1–2)
- **Shield** (see also e.g. Genesis 15:1; Deuteronomy 33:29; Psalm 3:3; 18:30)
- **Horn** (see also e.g. 1 Samuel 2:1; Psalm 148:13–14; Ezekiel 29:21)
- **Stronghold** (see also e.g. Psalm 9:9–10; 27:1; 43:2; 144:2; Joel 3:16)
- **Refuge** (see also e.g. Deuteronomy 33:27; Psalm 46:1–7; 91:1–2, 9–16; Nahum 1:7)

From the L*ORD comes deliverance.*
May your blessing be on your people.
Selah
(Psalm 3:1–8)

From this psalm we can see how David laid out things before God when he prayed:

David's circumstances (vv 1–2)
The psalm's title gives us its historical setting. It was during the time that King David had to flee from his kingdom when his own son Absalom led a coup against him (see 2 Samuel 15:1–17:22). Not only were 'many foes' against David (v 1), they were also trying to discourage him by saying he could forget any ideas of God coming to help him (v 2). All of this David brought before God in prayer.

The Bible always encourages us to be bold in bringing our situations and circumstances to God in prayer, whatever they may be. Only as we do so will we see God's salvation and have cause for thanksgiving.

David's confidence (vv 3–6)
Despite the very real threats facing him, David turned to God and expressed his confidence in him. David knew that speaking out what God has shown us of himself is a key to our faith being strengthened, and here he speaks of who God is and what he does (v 3), how God answers (v 4), and what God brings (v 5), all of which help him to declare in faith that he will not be afraid (v 6).

Lifting our eyes from our circumstances to our God is always a key to seeing God's salvation.

David's cry (v 7)
Encouraged by his recounting of what God is like and had done for him in the past, David's boldness is now expressed as he commands God to action. Commands? Yes! For all these verbs are 'imperatives'. This, however, was not arrogance, but supreme confidence, based on his knowledge of God.

Calling out boldly to God is what God loves to hear from his children; and the more we take time to get to know him, the more bold we can be.

David's confession (v 8)
A common feature of the psalms is a final declaration of confidence in God. This alone is where things will get settled; for, at the end of the day, salvation is not a thing but a person.

'Break their teeth, O God!'
Ever been troubled by the language that the psalmists use at times, such as in Psalm 3:7? Surely calls for striking our enemies' jaws and breaking their teeth aren't very godly, are they? So how do such things come to be in the word of God?

Well, be honest; have you never felt like that? Of course you have! This is the Bible telling us that we can be utterly honest when we bring our feelings and prayers before God. God is not shocked – he knew the thoughts before we spoke them anyway!

But of course, just because this is what *the psalmist* felt doesn't at all mean that it is what *God* felt. But God says, 'Get it off your chest – and then we can talk about it.' And the Bible records just as much what they 'got off their chest' as God's reply to them. Only as our cries are honest will we see God's salvation truly coming to us – and that may change us as much as others!

When you are crying out to God for salvation in some situation, always let your thoughts end up with him, declaring along with Isaiah:

'Surely God is my salvation;
I will trust and not be afraid.
The LORD, the LORD, is my strength and my song;
he has become my salvation.'

(Isaiah 12:2)

Salvation from . . .

In the Old Testament, salvation was not a vague concept; rather it was always seen as something very specific: people were saved *from* something and *for* something. Let's look at some of the aspects of salvation that are mentioned in the Old Testament. We are saved from:

. . . our sin

Help us, O God our Saviour,
for the glory of your name;
deliver us and forgive our sins
for your name's sake.

(Psalm 79:9)

Israel, trust the LORD! He is always merciful,
and he has the power to save you.
Israel, the LORD will save you from all of your sins.

(Psalm 130:7–8, CEV)

See also Psalm 51:7–12; 103:8–12; Isaiah 6:5–7; 12:1–6; Jeremiah 4:14; Micah 7:18–19

. . . our sickness

Surely he took up our infirmities
and carried our sorrows,
yet we considered him stricken by God,
smitten by him, and afflicted.
But he was pierced for our transgressions,
he was crushed for our iniquities;
the punishment that brought us peace was upon him,
and by his wounds we are healed.

(Isaiah 53:4–5)

Heal me, O LORD, and I shall be healed;
save me and I shall be saved,
for you are the one I praise.

(Jeremiah 17:14)

See also Exodus 15:26; 2 Kings 20:1–11; Psalm 41:1–3; 103:1–3; Malachi 4:2

. . . our enemies

'My father's God was my helper; he saved me from the sword of Pharaoh.'

(Exodus 18:4)

You are enthroned as the Holy One;
you are the praise of Israel.
In you our fathers put their trust;
they trusted and you delivered them.
They cried to you and were saved;
in you they trusted and were not disappointed.

(Psalm 22:3–5)

See also Exodus 14:21–15:21; 18:8; Deuteronomy 33:29; Judges 2:18; 1 Samuel 17:45–47; 2 Chronicles 32:20–23; Psalm 18:1–3

. . . our circumstances

Glorify the LORD with me:
let us exalt his name together.
I sought the LORD, and he answered me;
he delivered me from all my fears.
Those who look to him are radiant;
their faces are never covered with shame.
This poor man called, and the LORD heard him;
he saved him out of all his troubles.
The angel of the LORD encamps around those who fear him,
and he delivers them.

(Psalm 34:3–7)

Then they cried to the LORD in their trouble,
and he saved them from their distress.
He sent forth his word and healed them;

he rescued them from the grave.
Let them give thanks to the LORD for his unfailing love
and his wonderful deeds for men.

(Psalm 107:19–21)

See also Exodus 14:13–14; Psalm 69:1–18; Isaiah 43:1–13; Daniel 6:26–27; Jonah 2:1–10

. . . despair

The LORD is close to the broken-hearted
and saves those who are crushed in spirit.

(Psalm 34:18)

Why are you downcast, O my soul?
Why so disturbed within me?
Put your hope in God,
for I will yet praise him,
my Saviour and my God.

(Psalm 42:11)

He heals the broken-hearted
and binds up their wounds.

(Psalm 147:3)

See also 1 Kings 19:1–18; Psalm 22:1–31; 30:1; Habakkuk 3:16–18

. . . death

I love the LORD, for he heard my voice;
he heard my cry for mercy.
Because he turned his ear to me,
I will call on him as long as I live.
The cords of death entangled me,
the anguish of the grave came upon me;
I was overcome by trouble and sorrow.
Then I called on the name of the LORD:
'O LORD, save me!'
The LORD is gracious and righteous;
our God is full of compassion.
The LORD protects the simple-hearted;
when I was in great need, he saved me.
Be at rest once more, O my soul,
for the LORD has been good to you.

(Psalm 116:1–7)

On this mountain the LORD Almighty will prepare
a feast of rich food for all peoples,
a banquet of aged wine –
the best of meats and the finest of wines.
On this mountain he will destroy
the shroud that enfolds all peoples,
the sheet that covers all nations;
he will swallow up death for ever.
The Sovereign LORD will wipe away the tears
from all faces;
he will remove the disgrace of his people
from all the earth.
The LORD has spoken.
In that day they will say,
Surely this is our God;
we trusted in him, and he saved us.
This is the LORD, we trusted in him;
let us rejoice and be glad in his salvation.'

(Isaiah 25:6–9)

See also Psalm 18:4–6; 23:4; 33:12–19; 68:20; Isaiah 38:1–21

God invites all to be saved!

'There is no God apart from me,
a righteous God and a Saviour;
there is none but me.
Turn to me and be saved,
all you ends of the earth;
for I am God, and there is no other.'

(Isaiah 45:21–22)

Everyone who calls on the name of the LORD will be saved.

(Joel 2:32)

See also Psalm 67:1–2; 98:1–3; Isaiah 49:5–6; Jeremiah 4:14

A FINAL PRAYER

May the strength of God pilot us,
May the power of God preserve us,
May the wisdom of God
instruct us,
May the hand of God protect us,
May the way of God direct us,
May the shield of God defend us,
May the host of God guard us
against the snares of evil
And the temptations of the world.

St Patrick (c.389–461)

CONCLUSION

God never stands at a distance, but happily comes to all who call to him to save them.

The LORD your God is with you, he is mighty to save.

(Zephaniah 3:17)

Relevance for today

Is God my Saviour in everything?

Do I really believe that God can save me from every circumstance and situation? Do I look to him to save me in situations at work, with my family, with my health, with my finances? Or is my faith for his salvation restricted solely to 'spiritual' things?

First Saviour – or last resort?

Do I look to myself and my own resources and abilities before I look to God, leaving him to be little more than a 'last resort'? Or is God the first one that I turn to in every circumstance?

Am I confident in God my Saviour?

Does knowing God as Saviour inspire confidence in me, as it did in David? If I have truly experienced God's salvation then it should inspire me to trust him for every situation that arises, confident that he is with me and for me.

Am I thankful to God my Saviour?

When God answers my cry and saves me from situations or difficulties, do I remember to thank God for his salvation, as the psalmist did? Or do I quickly forget what he has done for me as I rush on to the next thing in life?

Am I embarrassed by 'salvation"?

In the twenty-first century, 'salvation' is what a financier brings to a troubled business or a football manager brings to a troubled team. Am I embarrassed by reclaiming the word and putting it back where it rightfully belongs – in the realm of people's relationship with God? Am I embarrassed by the thought that people need to be 'saved' from something?

What about salvation today?

Are there any areas that we have looked at in this chapter where, right now, you need God's salvation?

- Sin?
- Sickness?
- Enemies?
- Circumstances?
- Despair?
- Death?

If there are, call out to God right now. He is ready to hear you!

Chapter Three

Thanksgiving for the Saviour

In the new covenant, God no longer intervenes by sending others, but comes himself in the person of his Son, Jesus, our Saviour.

'God has come to help his people.' (Luke 7:16)

Waiting, waiting, waiting. The years had ticked by so slowly. And still they were waiting. God had said the Messiah would come; but still they waited. Of course, many became weary and gave up – or adopted their own agendas. Some became revolutionaries (like the Zealots) and tried to bring God's kingdom by force. Others pursued legalistic implementation of the Law (like the Pharisees) to try to pave the way. But for the handful of truly faithful, the waiting was over. At last, 'the time had fully come' (Galatians 4:4); God's plan of salvation was about to burst onto the scene. Except the plan was not a plan; the plan was a person.

The Saviour's birth

It was almost too good to be true! The promised Messiah had arrived – but not how people expected. For him, no glorious palace and luxurious cradle, but rather, a humble (and no doubt somewhat smelly) stable with a feeding trough from which the animals had just been shooed away. And yet, through the Spirit, some knew who this was – the Saviour! Little wonder they burst out with thanksgiving!

Shepherds – working-class men of the time – were the first to hear of the Saviour's arrival and to participate in the joy and thanksgiving (Luke 2:8–20). At the other end of the social scale were the Persian astrologers, wealthy intellectuals of their day, who also came to acknowledge the arrival of the King of kings with their worship and their gifts (Matthew 2:1–11).

When Jesus was six weeks old, two others added their testimony about him when he was brought by his parents to the temple. Simeon, a man sensitive to God's Spirit (Luke 2:25–26), was stirred to go there just at the time they arrived. When he saw Jesus, he just knew this was 'the one'. He took him in his arms and prayed a prayer of thanksgiving, which has become known as the *Nunc Dimittis,* from its first words in Latin:

'Sovereign Lord, as you have promised,
you now dismiss your servant in peace.
For my eyes have seen your salvation,

which you have prepared in the sight of all people,
a light for revelation to the Gentiles and for glory to your people Israel.'
(Luke 2:29–32)

And then he prophesied of how the story would end:

'This child is destined to cause the falling and rising of many in Israel, and to be a sign that will be spoken against, so that the thoughts of many hearts will be revealed. And a sword will pierce your own soul too.'
(Luke 2:34–35)

A prophetess called Anna who 'never left the temple but worshipped night and day, fasting and praying' (Luke 2:37) then approached and 'gave thanks to God and spoke about the child to all who were looking forward to the redemption of Jerusalem' (Luke 2:38). At last, the Saviour was here!

The Saviour's death

But here is the strange thing: this Saviour came, not to live, but to die. True enough, his life and teaching powerfully demonstrated his ability to save people – from sin, from sickness, from circumstances, from the grip of the devil (see e.g. Mark 1:21–2:17); but the heart of the plan of salvation could take place only through his death, not his life.

The first Christians were absolutely clear that Jesus' death was the focal point of his ministry. But not just his death; his resurrection too. They were convinced that though Jesus had been cruelly executed by crucifixion and though a spear had been thrust into him to ensure he was dead (John 19:31–37), he walked out of his tomb three days later (though some of them just didn't believe it at first! – e.g. John 20:25), having gloriously conquered our last enemy, death. Indeed they were so convinced of this that they said they had no message to preach if the resurrection were not true (e.g. 1 Corinthians 15:14–19).

Their convictions, which follow, can be used as an excellent basis for thanksgiving to God.

Jesus the Saviour

Just as the Father had been seen as Saviour in the Old Testament, so the first Christians had no hesitation in applying this title to his Son.

Grace and peace from God the Father and Christ Jesus our Saviour.
(Titus 1:4)

But grow in the grace and knowledge of our Lord and Saviour Jesus Christ. To him be glory both now and for ever! Amen.
(2 Peter 3:18)

See also Luke 2:11; John 4:42; Acts 5:30–31; 13:23; Titus 3:6; 2 Peter 1:1; 3:2

Jesus the only Saviour

Jesus is not just one saviour among many, one path to God among many. The Bible is clear that Jesus is the *only* Saviour; there is no other way of coming to God except through his death and through trusting in him.

'Salvation is found in no-one else, for there is no other name under heaven given to men by which we must be saved.'
(Acts 4:12)

For there is only one God and one Mediator who can reconcile God and people. He is the man Christ Jesus.
(1 Timothy 2:5, NLT)

See also John 6:66–69; 10:9; 14:6; Acts 10:42–43

Jesus the dying Saviour

Even though Isaiah had prophesied it seven centuries earlier (Isaiah 53:1–12), the thought of a suffering Messiah was beyond people's ability to grasp. They were locked into thinking that the Messiah would be a military and political deliverer – and so they missed him. But the first Christians were clear that it was through his death that Jesus saved people.

'The God of our fathers raised Jesus from the dead – whom you had killed by hanging him on a tree. God exalted him to his own right hand as Prince and Saviour that he might give repentance and forgiveness of sins to Israel.'

(Acts 5:30–31)

We preach Christ crucified: a stumbling-block to Jews and foolishness to Gentiles, but to those whom God has called, both Jews and Greeks, Christ the power of God and the wisdom of God.

(1 Corinthians 1:23–24)

See also John 12:32–33; Acts 17:2–3; Ephesians 1:7–10; Hebrews 2:9–15

Jesus the risen Saviour

But if the early Christians were convinced that Jesus died on the cross to forgive their sins, they were just as convinced that he rose from the dead to prove that 'the deal was done'.

'Men of Israel, listen to this: Jesus of Nazareth was a man accredited by God to you by miracles, wonders and signs, which God did among you through him, as you yourselves know. This man was handed over to you by God's set purpose and fore-knowledge; and you, with the help of wicked men, put him to death by nailing him to the cross. But God raised him from the dead, freeing him from the agony of death, because it was impossible for death to keep its hold on him. David said about him:

"I saw the Lord always before me.
Because he is at my right hand,
I will not be shaken.

The Saviour's death – prophecies and fulfilment

- Sold for thirty pieces of silver (Zechariah 11:12; Matthew 26:14–16)
- Betrayed by a friend (Psalm 41:9; Matthew 26:23–25, 47–54)
- Deserted by his disciples (Zechariah 13:7; Matthew 26:31, 56)
- Suffered (Psalm 22:1–24; Matthew 16:21)
- Silent before his accusers (Isaiah 53:7; Matthew 26:62–63; 27:12–14)
- Abused by others (Isaiah 50:6; 52:14; Matthew 26:67–68)
- Nailed to the cross (Psalm 22:16; Matthew 27:35)
- Clothes divided up (Psalm 22:18; Matthew 27:35)
- Mocked (Psalm 22:6–8; Matthew 27:39–44)
- Abandoned by God (Psalm 22:1; Matthew 27:46)
- Wine vinegar offered (Psalm 69:21; Matthew 27:48)
- Prayed for his executioners (Isaiah 53:12; Luke 23:34)
- Death (Isaiah 53:12; Matthew 27:50; John 19:30)
- Bones not broken (Numbers 9:12; Psalm 34:20; John 19:32–36)
- Pierced (Zechariah 12:10; John 19:34–37)
- Buried (Isaiah 53:9; Matthew 27:57–60)

With so much specific prophecy fulfilled, little wonder people have seen Jesus as the promised Saviour!

Therefore my heart is glad and my tongue
rejoices;
my body also will live in hope,
because you will not abandon me to the
grave,
nor will you let your Holy One see decay.
You have made known to me the paths of
life;
you will fill me with joy in your presence."
'... God has raised this Jesus to life, and we are all witnesses of the fact. Exalted to the right hand of God, he has received from the Father the promised Holy Spirit and has poured out what you now see and hear. For David did not ascend to heaven, and yet he said,
"The Lord said to my Lord:
'Sit at my right hand
until I make your enemies
a footstool for your feet.' "
'Therefore let all Israel be assured of this: God has made this Jesus, whom you crucified, both Lord and Christ.'

(Acts 2:22–28, 32–36)

See also Acts 3:13–15; 4:1–20; 10:39–40; 17:18; 1 Corinthians 15:3–8, 12–20; 1 Peter 3:21–22

Jesus the waiting Saviour

However, this salvation is not automatically ours. We need to respond in repentance and faith. Jesus is ready to save us; have we asked him to do so?

"Whoever believes and is baptised will be saved, but whoever does not believe will be condemned."

(Mark 16:16)

'Repent and be baptised, every one of you, in the name of Jesus Christ for the forgiveness of your sins. And you will receive the gift of the Holy Spirit. The promise is for you and your children and for all who are far off – for all whom the Lord our God will call.'

(Acts 2:38–39)

See also John 3:16–18; 5:24; Acts 3:19–20; Romans 1:16–17; 5:1–2; 2 Corinthians 7:10; Revelation 3:20

Reflecting on the Saviour

As the apostles reflected on the cross and resurrection, and saw how it fitted in with Old Testament promises, they began to understand more of what Jesus the Saviour had done for them and recorded this in their letters. Such passages form an excellent basis for rich prayers of thanksgiving! Let's look at one passage from Paul and one from Peter.

How we praise God, the Father of our Lord Jesus Christ, who has blessed us with every spiritual blessing in the heavenly realms because we belong to Christ. Long ago, even before he made the world, God loved us and chose us in Christ to be holy and without fault in his eyes. His unchanging plan has always been to adopt us into his own family by bringing us to himself through Jesus Christ. And this gave him great pleasure.

So we praise God for the wonderful kindness he has poured out on us because we belong to his dearly loved Son. He is so rich in kindness that he purchased our freedom through the blood of his Son, and our sins are forgiven. He has showered his kindness on us, along with all wisdom and understanding.

God's secret plan has now been revealed to us; it is a plan centred on Christ, designed long ago according to his good pleasure. And this is his plan: At the right time he will bring everything together under the authority of Christ – everything in heaven and on earth. Furthermore, because of Christ, we have received an inheritance from God, for he chose us from the beginning, and all things happen just as he decided long ago. God's purpose was that we who were the first to trust in Christ should praise our

The blessings of salvation

Salvation now involves a complete change of relationship between us and God – all of it *his* doing! This change of relationship is expressed in a number of different ways:

- Access to God (e.g. Romans 5:1–2; Hebrews 4:16)
- Adoption into God's family (e.g. Romans 8:14–17, 23; Galatians 4:4–7)
- Becoming a new creation (e.g. 2 Corinthians 5:17; Galatians 6:14–15)
- Escape from condemnation (e.g. Romans 8:1–4, 31–39; Colossians 1:22)
- Forgiveness of sin (e.g. Acts 5:30–32; Ephesians 1:7–8)
- Heavenly citizenship (e.g. Philippians 3:20–21; Colossians 3:1–4)
- New birth (e.g. John 3:3–8; 1 Peter 1:23)
- New inheritance (e.g. Matthew 25:34; Ephesians 1:11–14)
- Peace with God (e.g. (Romans 5:1–2; Ephesians 2:13–18)
- Righteousness before God (e.g. Romans 1:17; 3:21–26)

glorious God. And now you also have heard the truth, the Good News that God saves you. And when you believed in Christ, he identified you as his own by giving you the Holy Spirit, whom he promised long ago. The Spirit is God's guarantee that he will give us everything he promised and that he has purchased us to be his own people. This is just one more reason for us to praise our glorious God.

(Ephesians 1:3–14, NLT)

Praise be to the God and Father of our Lord Jesus Christ! In his great mercy he has given us new birth into a living hope through the resurrection of Jesus Christ from the dead, and into an inheritance that can never perish, spoil or fade – kept in heaven for you, who through faith are shielded by God's power until the coming of the salvation that is ready to be revealed in the last time.

(1 Peter 1:3–5)

See also 2 Timothy 1:8–10; Titus 2:11; 3:4–7; 1 Peter 3:18

Rejoicing about the Saviour

Rejoicing about the Saviour is not just confined to earth; it's happening in heaven too! John caught a glimpse of this in his revelation:

And they sang a new song:
'You are worthy to take the scroll
and to open its seals,
because you were slain,
and with your blood you purchased men for God
from every tribe and language and people and nation.
You have made them to be a kingdom and priests to serve our God,
and they will reign on the earth.'
Then I looked and heard the voice of many angels, numbering thousands upon thousands, and ten thousand times ten thousand. They encircled the throne and the living creatures and the elders. In a loud voice they sang:
'Worthy is the Lamb, who was slain,
to receive power and wealth and wisdom and strength
and honour and glory and praise!'
Then I heard every creature in heaven and on earth and under the earth and on the sea, and all that is in them, singing:
'To him who sits on the throne and to the Lamb
be praise and honour and glory and power,
for ever and ever!'

(Revelation 5:9–13)

See also Revelation 7:9–12

Remembering the Saviour

Instituted by the Lord Jesus himself before his death (e.g. Matthew 26:17–30), the Lord's Supper (also called Communion, the Eucharist or Breaking of Bread) quickly became a central part of the meetings of the early church (e.g. Acts 2:42; 20:7). This was a wonderful opportunity to remember with thanksgiving what Jesus had done for them at the cross. When we break bread together today, our thoughts and prayers can focus on four different dimensions:

Looking back

We can look back and remember what Jesus did on the cross – giving up his life, for us! – and thank him for that with all our hearts.

For I received from the Lord what I also passed on to you: The Lord Jesus, on the night he was betrayed, took bread, and when he had given thanks, he broke it and said, 'This is my body, which is for you; do this in remembrance of me.' In the same way, after supper he took the cup, saying, 'This cup is the new covenant in my blood; do this, whenever you drink it, in remembrance of me.'

(1 Corinthians 11:23–25)

Looking in

We can look within ourselves and confess any sins we have committed, for how can we say, 'Thank you for saving me!' while still harbouring sin or wrong thoughts and plans in our heart?

Therefore, whoever eats the bread or drinks the cup of the Lord in an unworthy manner will be guilty of sinning against the body and blood of the Lord. A man ought to examine himself before he eats of the bread and drinks of the cup. For anyone who eats and drinks without recognising the body of the Lord eats and drinks judgment on himself. That is why many among you are weak and sick, and a number of you have fallen asleep. But if we judged ourselves, we would not come under judgment.

(1 Corinthians 11:27–31)

Looking round

We can look around at our brothers and sisters in the church and remember that Jesus died not just for *me* but for *us*, and that we are now his Body here on earth. We can thank God for the particular church that we are part of.

Is not the cup of thanksgiving for which we give thanks a participation in the blood of Christ? And is not the bread that we break a participation in the body of Christ? Because there is one loaf, we, who are many, are one body, for we all partake of the one loaf.

(1 Corinthians 10:16–17)

Looking forward

We can remember that we share this meal together only until Jesus comes again, just like he promised he would.

For whenever you eat this bread and drink this cup, you proclaim the Lord's death until he comes.

(1 Corinthians 11:26)

This 'memorial service' does not need to be solemn, however. Many churches become more 'religious' at this point than at any other point in their meetings! It is certainly serious, but that doesn't mean it has to be miserable! In fact, Paul's constant theme about the Lord's Supper in 1 Corinthians is 'thankfulness'.

A FINAL PRAYER

I bind this day to me for ever,
by power of faith,
Christ's incarnation,
his baptism in the Jordan river,
his death on cross for my salvation:
his bursting from the spiced tomb,
his riding up the heavenly way,
his coming at the day of doom,
I bind unto myself today . . .

I bind unto myself today
the power of God to hold and lead,
his eye to watch, his might to stay,
his ear to hearken to my need.
The wisdom of my God to teach,
his hand to guide,
his shield to ward,
the word of God to give me speech,
his heavenly host to be my guard . . .
Christ be with me,
Christ within me,
Christ behind me,
Christ before me,
Christ beside me, Christ to win me,
Christ to comfort and restore me,
Christ beneath me,
Christ above me,
Christ in quiet, Christ in danger,
Christ in hearts of all that love me,
Christ in mouth of friend
and stranger.
I bind unto myself the name,
The strong name of the Trinity,
By invocation of the same,
The three in one, and one in three,
Of whom all nature hath creation,
Eternal Father, Spirit, Word.
Praise to the Lord of my salvation:
Salvation is of Christ the Lord.

An eighth-century Celtic 'Breastplate'

CONCLUSION

A God who comes to die for us on a cross! This is the ultimate expression of salvation, and the ultimate assurance that, because it was God himself who did it, it will work!

Let us thank God for his priceless gift!
(2 Corinthians 9:15, GNB)

Relevance for today

Jesus is still the Saviour! Still today he can save us from all that spoils our lives. He can save us from –

- The power of sin (Romans 6:6–7; Galatians 1:4; 1 John 1:7–10)
- The curse of trying to keep the Law (Acts 13:38–39; Romans 8:1–4; Galatians 3:13)
- God's righteous anger (Romans 5:9–10; Ephesians 2:3–9; 1 Thessalonians 1:10; 5:9)
- The fear of death (1 Corinthians 15:50–57; Philippians 1:21–24; Hebrews 2:14–15)
- Satan's power (Acts 26:17–18; Colossians 1:13; 1 John 3:8)
- Physical dangers (e.g. Matthew 8:23–27; 2 Corinthians 1:8–11; 2 Timothy 4:16–18)
- Sickness (e.g. Acts 3:1–10; 5:12–16; 9:32–35; James 5:13–16)

In which of these do *you* need to see his salvation today?

Chapter Four

Thanksgiving for God's Intervention

We should be grateful that God does not stand back, but intervenes in human lives and history.

He saw that there was no-one, he was appalled that there was no-one to intervene; so his own arm worked salvation for him. (Isaiah 59:16)

'Don't get involved!' How many times have you heard those words? They certainly seem to be the watchword of many today. But God isn't like that. God loves to get involved! He isn't some 'remote creator' who stands far off; rather, he 'rolls his sleeves up' to intervene in his world.

This means that history is not meaningless – an endless cycle of events going nowhere in particular. God is the God of history, intervening in the lives of individuals and nations to bring about his end-time purpose of filling the earth with his glory (Habakkuk 2:14). Looking back upon his involvement should cause us to be thankful; looking forward in anticipation of his involvement should cause us to be encouraged.

The potter's hands

The Bible sometimes likens God to a potter, who carefully shapes his clay on the wheel. But the clay is us and our lives. Not only does this mean we are secure in his hands, it also means God can do with us as he pleases! Thankfully, he knows what he is doing and we can trust him!

Yet, O LORD, you are our Father.
We are the clay, you are the potter;
we are all the work of your hand.
(Isaiah 64:8)

I went down to the potter's house, and I saw him working at the wheel. But the pot he was shaping from the clay was marred in his hands; so the potter formed it into another pot, shaping it as seemed best to him. Then the word of the LORD came to me: 'O house of Israel, can I not do with you as this potter does?' declares the LORD. 'Like clay in the hand of the potter, so are you in my hand, O house of Israel.'
(Jeremiah 18:3–6)

See also Isaiah 29:16; 45:9–11

Martin's wife, Yusandra, is a potter, or

as we put it, a 'ceramic sculptor'. She makes decorative figures out of clay. Sometimes a piece doesn't work out properly and she has to start all over again; but eventually we see the beautiful sculptures that she has created out of ordinary clay. Jeremiah used the picture of a potter to show God's moulding of his people as he wants them to be: 'Like clay in the hand of the potter, so are you in my hand, O house of Israel' (Jeremiah 18:6).

When we feel 'the fingers of the potter' going into our lives, we need not fear! God is our Father and we can be confident that 'in all things God works for the good of those who love him' (Romans 8:28).

God's intervention for individuals

Just as the potter 'intervenes' in his clay, so God intervenes in our lives when we call out to him – and sometimes, even when we don't! The Bible is packed with examples of his intervention in people's lives. Here are just three of them.

Jacob

Jacob was, quite frankly, a rogue, even cheating his elder brother out of his birthright (Genesis 27:1–45). But God has ways of 'catching up with us'! He intervened in Jacob's life in two significant ways.

First, he gave Jacob a dream of how easy and close access to heaven and God's presence really is. He saw 'a stairway resting on the earth, with its top reaching to heaven, and the angels of God were ascending and descending on it. There above it stood the LORD . . .' (Genesis 28:12–13). As God spoke to Jacob, promising he would return home to see the promises to Abraham and Isaac fulfilled, he realized something significant was happening, and he responded to God's intervention:

When Jacob awoke from his sleep, he thought, 'Surely the LORD is in this place, and I was not aware of it.' He was afraid and said, 'How awesome is this place! This is none other than the house of God; this is the gate of heaven . . . If God will be with me and will watch over me on this journey I am taking and will give me food to eat and clothes to wear so that I return safely to my father's house, then the LORD will be my God and this stone that I have set up as a pillar will be God's house, and of all that you give me I will give you a tenth.'

(Genesis 28:16–17, 20–22)

But God hadn't finished with Jacob yet. Meeting God is only the first stage of the process; God then wants to change us! For Jacob, this involved an experience of wrestling with a man one night – and then discovering that 'the man' was God! He came out of the incident different, as a 'man with a limp', not just physically, but metaphorically: he would never be the same again after this intervention by God in his life.

So Jacob was left alone, and a man wrestled with him till daybreak. When the man saw that he could not overpower him, he touched the socket of Jacob's hip so that his hip was wrenched as he wrestled with the man. Then the man said, 'Let me go, for it is daybreak.'

But Jacob replied, 'I will not let you go unless you bless me.'

The man asked him, 'What is your name?'

'Jacob,' he answered.

Then the man said, 'Your name will no longer be Jacob, but Israel, because you have struggled with God and with men and have overcome.'

Jacob said, 'Please tell me your name.' But he replied, 'Why do you ask my name?' Then he blessed him there.

So Jacob called the place Peniel, saying, 'It is because I saw God face to face, and yet my life was spared.'

(Genesis 32:24–30)

It is when we 'wrestle' with God in prayer that God's biggest interventions in our lives often come.

Joseph

Joseph is an interesting character; for while there is no doubt that God intervened significantly in his life, and no doubt that Joseph was aware of it, there are no recorded instances of Joseph actually praying. (The same is true of Ruth and Esther.)

Throughout Joseph's story there are constant glimpses of God's intervention 'behind the scenes', whether in the amazing timing of things (Genesis 37:25), or the significance of what happened (Genesis 39:1), or the favour he constantly won (e.g. Genesis 39:3–6, 20–23), or the people he 'happened to meet' (Genesis 40:1–4), or the usefulness of God's gift of interpreting dreams (Genesis 40:6–22; 41:9–16). Even in all his hardships he kept his focus on God (e.g. Genesis 41:15–16), which suggests he had been maintaining a relationship with God through prayer.

It is when Joseph reveals his true identity to his brothers (remember, twenty years had passed since they had last seen him and he had only been a teenager at the time; so it is little wonder they didn't recognize him!) that his supreme confidence in God is expressed:

'I am your brother Joseph, the one you sold into Egypt! And now, do not be distressed and do not be angry with yourselves for selling me here, because it was to save lives that God sent me ahead of you. For two years now there has been famine in the land, and for the next five years there will not be ploughing and reaping. But God sent me ahead of you to preserve for you a remnant on earth and to save your lives by a great deliverance. So then, it was not you who sent me here, but God.'

(Genesis 45:4–8)

Hannah

Hannah, Samuel's mother, saw God's intervention in her own life in a way that ultimately affected the nation. For years she had been barren, with all the sadness that this can bring (1 Samuel 1:1–8). But Hannah didn't give up; and one day, her reaching out to God in a mixture of anguish and faith (1:10–11) was met with the assurance that she would conceive (1:17–18). Within the year she was holding Samuel ('Heard of God') in her arms (1:19–20), and within three years she was dedicating him to God's service as promised and leaving him with Eli the priest (1:21–28). From that point, Samuel's life, and Israel's, would never be the same again. God had intervened.

Hannah's prayer of thanksgiving to the intervening God has been described as the 'Magnificat of the Old Testament', since it is so similar to Mary's song (see Luke 1:46–55).

'My heart rejoices in the LORD;
in the LORD my horn is lifted high.
My mouth boasts over my enemies,
for I delight in your deliverance.
There is no-one holy like the LORD;
there is no-one besides you;
there is no Rock like our God.
Do not keep talking so proudly
or let your mouth speak such arrogance,
for the LORD is a God who knows,
and by him deeds are weighed.
The bows of the warriors are broken,
but those who stumbled are armed with strength.

Those who were full hire themselves out for food,
but those who were hungry hunger no more.
She who was barren has borne seven children,
but she who has had many sons pines away.
The LORD brings death and makes alive;
he brings down to the grave and raises up.
The LORD sends poverty and wealth;
he humbles and he exalts.
He raises the poor from the dust
and lifts the needy from the ash heap;
he seats them with princes
and has them inherit a throne of honour.
For the foundations of the earth are the LORD's;
upon them he has set the world.
He will guard the feet of his saints,
but the wicked will be silenced in darkness.
It is not by strength that one prevails;
those who oppose the LORD will be shattered.
He will thunder against them from heaven;
the LORD will judge the ends of the earth.
He will give strength to his king
and exalt the horn of his anointed.

(1 Samuel 2:1–10)

Thanks to the God who intervenes!

Knowing that God intervenes in our lives in such wonderful ways should cause us to be both humble and grateful. A prayer of King David's sums up his own sense of amazement at such a God:

'Who am I, O Sovereign LORD, and what is my family, that you have brought me this far? And as if this were not enough in your sight, O Sovereign LORD, you have also spoken about the future of the house of your servant. Is this your usual way of dealing with man, O Sovereign LORD?

What more can David say to you? For you know your servant, O Sovereign LORD. For the sake of your word and according to your will, you have done this great thing and made it known to your servant.

How great you are, O Sovereign LORD! There is no-one like you, and there is no God but you, as we have heard with our own ears.'

(2 Samuel 7:18–22)

God's intervention for nations

Of course, it is not just in the lives of individuals that God intervenes. Individuals make up nations, and there are plenty of examples of God intervening in the affairs of nations and in the grand sweep of history.

The Exodus: the great intervention

Throughout the Old Testament, *the* great intervention by God in the life of Israel was always seen as the Exodus, when God delivered his people from cruel slavery in Egypt. After the miraculous crossing of the Red Sea and the overthrow of Egypt's army (Exodus 14:1–31), Moses led the Israelites in this song of thanksgiving to the Lord for his great intervention on their behalf:

'I will sing to the LORD,
for he is highly exalted.
The horse and its rider
he has hurled into the sea.
The LORD is my strength and my song;
he has become my salvation.
He is my God, and I will praise him,
my father's God, and I will exalt him.
The LORD is a warrior;
the LORD is his name.
Pharaoh's chariots and his army
he has hurled into the sea.

The best of Pharaoh's officers
are drowned in the Red Sea.
The deep waters have covered them;
they sank to the depths like a stone.
Your right hand, O LORD,
was majestic in power.
Your right hand, O LORD,
shattered the enemy.
In the greatness of your majesty
you threw down those who opposed you.
You unleashed your burning anger;
it consumed them like stubble.
By the blast of your nostrils
the waters piled up.
The surging waters stood firm like a wall;
the deep waters congealed in the heart of the sea.
The enemy boasted,
"I will pursue, I will overtake them.
I will divide the spoils;
I will gorge myself on them.
I will draw my sword
and my hand will destroy them."
But you blew with your breath,
and the sea covered them.
They sank like lead
in the mighty waters.
Who among the gods is like you, O LORD?
Who is like you –
majestic in holiness,
awesome in glory,
working wonders?
You stretched out your right hand
and the earth swallowed them.
In your unfailing love you will lead
the people you have redeemed.
In your strength you will guide them
to your holy dwelling.
The nations will hear and tremble;
anguish will grip the people of Philistia.
The chiefs of Edom will be terrified,
the leaders of Moab will be seized with trembling,
the people of Canaan will melt away;
terror and dread will fall upon them.
By the power of your arm
they will be as still as a stone –
until your people pass by, O LORD,
until the people you bought pass by.
You will bring them in and plant them
on the mountain of your inheritance –
the place, O LORD, you made for your dwelling,
the sanctuary, O LORD, your hands established.
The LORD will reign
for ever and ever.'

(Exodus 15:1–18)

Again and again prophets and leaders looked back to this great event, reminding Israel of what God had done for them in the past, and encouraging them to trust him once again for the future.

Awake, awake! Clothe yourself with strength,
O arm of the LORD;
awake, as in days gone by,
as in generations of old.
Was it not you who cut Rahab to pieces,
who pierced that monster through?
Was it not you who dried up the sea,
the waters of the great deep,
who made a road in the depths of the sea
so that the redeemed might cross over?
The ransomed of the LORD will return.
They will enter Zion with singing;
everlasting joy will crown their heads.
Gladness and joy will overtake them,
and sorrow and sighing will flee away.

(Isaiah 51:9–11)

See also Deuteronomy 7:7–11,17–19; Joshua 2:10–11; 4:20–24; 24:5–7; Nehemiah 9:9–12; Psalm 77:10–20; 78:11–14, 40–55; 106:7–12; 114:1–8; 136:1–15; Isaiah 43:16–19; Jeremiah 2:5–6; Daniel 9:15; Hosea 11:1

The exile: the surprise intervention

Seeing themselves delivered *from* the hands of their enemies was easy for Israel to see as God's intervention; but what about being delivered *into* the hands of their enemies? Could that be God too? Oh yes, the prophets answered! For Israel had forgotten that God was the God of the nations; and he would use those pagan nations to bring his judgment on his people for their constant neglect of his covenant.

First, the northern kingdom of Israel was defeated and exiled by Assyria (described by God as 'the rod of my anger' in Isaiah 10:5) after the fall of Samaria in 722/721 BC (2 Kings 17:3–23). This was prophesied by Hosea (e.g. 8:1–10) and Amos (e.g. 3:1–15) in the north, and by Isaiah (e.g. 8:1–10) in the south. But Nahum's prophecy in the next century told how Assyria itself would then come under God's judgment.

Later, the southern kingdom of Judah, having failed to learn from the disaster that had befallen their northern neighbour Israel, was also defeated and exiled to Babylon in 586 BC (2 Kings 25:1–21). Isaiah and Jeremiah prophesied this (e.g. Isaiah 39:5–7; Jeremiah 1:11–16), as did Ezekiel (e.g.12:1–28) who was already exiled in Babylon. But all of them also prophesied the ultimate overthrow of Babylon itself and Judah's return (e.g. Isaiah 54:1–17; Jeremiah 33:1–26; Ezekiel 37:1–28).

But then here was the biggest surprise of all: it would be another pagan nation – Persia, the next great superpower – that God would use to intervene in history to bring his people back to the promised land! Cyrus, King of Persia, conquered Babylon; and then God conquered Cyrus, though he did not know it! We are told that 'in order to fulfil the word of the LORD spoken by Jeremiah, the LORD moved the heart of Cyrus' (2 Chronicles 36:22) to send all the Jews back home – and even financed them to do it (Ezra 1:1–11)!

This truly is amazing! God is at work, even through those who don't believe in him, even through those who oppose him. All must carry out his sovereign will!

The LORD controls rulers,
just as he determines the course of rivers.
(Proverbs 21:1, CEV)

His dominion is an eternal dominion;
his kingdom endures from generation to generation.
All the peoples of the earth
are regarded as nothing.
He does as he pleases
with the powers of heaven
and the peoples of the earth.
No-one can hold back his hand
or say to him: 'What have you done?'
(Daniel 4:34–35)

A FINAL PRAYER

Let thy mighty hand, O Lord God,
and outstretched arm
be our defence;
thy mercy and loving-kindness in
Jesus Christ, thy dear Son,
our salvation;
thy all-true word, our instruction;
the grace of the life-giving Spirit,
our comfort and consolation,
unto the end and in the end.

John Knox (c. 1513–1572), leader of the Reformed Church in Scotland

CONCLUSION

Like the potter moulding his clay, so God shapes our lives and our history. He loves to intervene – we need only ask!

Oh, that you would rend the heavens and come down.

(Isaiah 64:1)

Relevance for today

Looking back

God wants us to look back and remember the times when he has intervened to save us, our family or our nation. Gratefully remembering what he has done in the past encourages us to trust him for the future.

I will remember your great deeds, Lord;
I will recall the wonders you did in the past.
I will think about all that you have done;
I will meditate on all your mighty acts.

(Psalm 77:11–12, GNB)

Looking round

God still wants to intervene today. Are there situations where you need to see him act on your behalf? Does your church need to see this? Our nation certainly does! Why not tell him right now!

Save us and help us with your right hand,
that those you love may be delivered.

(Psalm 60:5)

Let us then approach the throne of grace with confidence, so that we may receive mercy and find grace to help us in our time of need.

(Hebrews 4:16)

Looking forward

Telling the next generation of how God has intervened in our family, church, or nation is so important. Without this 'generational transfer' we quickly become forgetful and are doomed to repeat the mistakes of the past. But with it, we build strong foundations for the next generation to move further into God's purposes. It was when Israel neglected to do this that they experienced centuries of dismal history during the period of the Judges, endlessly repeating the mistakes of their forebears (e.g. Judges 2:10–19).

Psalm 78 contains an appeal not to forget the interventions of God, but rather to ensure that their memory is passed on to the next generation.

I will open my mouth in parables,
I will utter hidden things, things from of old –
what we have heard and known,
what our fathers have told us.
We will not hide them from their children;
we will tell the next generation
the praiseworthy deeds of the Lord,
his power, and the wonders he has done.
He decreed statutes for Jacob
and established the law in Israel,
which he commanded our forefathers
to teach their children,
so that the next generation would know them,
even the children yet to be born,
and they in turn would tell their children.
Then they would put their trust in God
and would not forget his deeds
but would keep his commands.

(Psalm 78:2–7)

Chapter Five

Thanksgiving for God's Answers

God has promised to answer our prayers; when he does, it is only courteous to say 'Thank you!'

Lord, I thank you for answering me. (Psalm 118:21, NCV)

How do you feel when you've given a present to someone and they don't even say 'Thank you'? Or when you've done someone a favour and it isn't even appreciated? If you're like us, then you probably feel disappointed. It's not that you wanted an accolade of gratitude; it's simply that, well, saying thanks is just so appropriate.

But if gratitude to one another is appropriate, how much more so when it is due to God – especially when he has answered our prayers. If *we* can feel disappointed, how much more does *God* have the right to be disappointed if we don't thank him for his answers.

An outpouring of thanksgiving

As we shall see in Chapter 7 of this Part, thankfulness should be a way of life for us. But sometimes we are not thankful simply because we don't stop and think about the answers God has already given. We take his blessings and run! The following two psalms help slow us down and be thankful.

Psalm 136

Psalm 136 is a wonderful antidote to the 'take the blessing and run!' attitude. (Do take time to read it!) As a responsive psalm the first line would probably have been sung by a Levite, with the choir or worshippers replying with the refrain. The psalm sweeps majestically through its great themes: God, the only God (vv1–3); his creation of the universe (vv4–9); his delivering his people from Egypt (vv10–15); his leading them through the wilderness (v16); his giving them the promised land (vv17–22). It concludes by sweeping through the same themes in reverse: God's works in history for his people (vv23–24); his works in creation (v25); God, the only God (v26). Clearly the psalmist did not want people to forget! And to bring all this home, after every line they had to sing out the same refrain:

His love endures for ever . . . His love endures for ever . . . His love endures for ever . . .

The writer understood that God's people need to be constantly provoked to thank God for who he is and what he has done.

Psalm 107

The writer of Psalm 107 also stirs people to be grateful for God's answers to prayer in the various circumstances of life. Once again a recurring refrain brings home the point of gratitude.

The introductory call to give thanks (vv1–3) almost certainly sets this psalm at the time of the return from the Babylonian exile. This is followed by four stanzas covering areas of life where God had brought his deliverance. While these had a literal meaning at the time, they can still be relevant to us metaphorically today:

- *Some wandered in desert wastelands . . .* (vv4–9)
- *Some sat in darkness and the deepest gloom . . .* (vv10–16)
- *Some became fools through their rebellious ways . . .* (vv17–22)
- *Others went out to the sea in ships . . .* (vv23–32)

Two final stanzas (vv33–38 and vv39–42) then reflect on how God can reverse our adverse circumstances, and a conclusion (v43) calls upon us to 'heed these things and consider the great love of the LORD'.

Each of the central four stanzas sets a different scene, and then reminds us how people called out to God in these situations and found that he answered them, for which the psalmist urges thanksgiving. There are some poetic variations in this recurring theme, but all follow these lines:

Then they cried out to the LORD in their
trouble,
and he delivered them from their distress . . .
Let them give thanks to the LORD For his
unfailing love
and his wonderful deeds for men.

(vv6, 8)

When God answers, we should be grateful!

Thankfulness for answers to prayer

Here are a selection of prayers expressing gratitude for God's answers in various situations of life.

For encouragement given

Praise be to the God and Father of our Lord Jesus Christ, the Father of compassion and the God of all comfort, who comforts us in all our troubles, so that we can comfort those in any trouble with the comfort we ourselves have received from God.

(2 Corinthians 1:3–4)

See also 2 Corinthians 7:5–7,13–16; 1 Thessalonians 3:7–10

For wisdom received

'Praise be to the name of God for ever and
ever;
wisdom and power are his.
He changes times and seasons;
he sets up kings and deposes them.
He gives wisdom to the wise
and knowledge to the discerning.
He reveals deep and hidden things;
he knows what lies in darkness,
and light dwells with him.
I thank and praise you, O God of my
fathers:
You have given me wisdom and power,
you have made known to me what we
asked of you,
you have made known to us the dream
of the king.'

(Daniel 2:20–23)

See also Psalm 111:10; Romans 11:33–36; James 1:5

For provision made

Sing to the LORD with thanksgiving;
make music to our God on the harp.
He covers the sky with clouds;

he supplies the earth with rain
and makes grass grow on the hills.
He provides food for the cattle
and for the young ravens when they call.

(Psalm 147:7–9)

See also Psalm 65:9–13; 111:1–9; 145:13–16; 2 Corinthians 9:10–11; 1 Timothy 6:17

For healing given

O LORD, heal me, for my bones are in agony
. . . I am worn out from groaning;
all night long I flood my bed with weeping
and drench my couch with tears.
Away from me, all you who do evil,
for the LORD has heard my weeping.
The LORD has heard my cry for mercy;
the LORD accepts my prayer.

(Psalm 6:2, 6, 8–9)

See also Psalm 30:1–2; Isaiah 38:1–20; Jeremiah 17:14; Matthew 9:6–8; Luke 17:11–19; Acts 3:6–8

For help in avoiding danger or sin

Praise our God, O peoples,
let the sound of his praise be heard;
he has preserved our lives
and kept our feet from slipping.

(Psalm 66:8–9)

See also Psalm 56:12–13; 73:1–28; 94:18; 116:5–9; 121:1–8

For receiving mercy

I love the LORD, for he heard my voice;
he heard my cry for mercy.
Because he turned his ear to me,
I will call on him as long as I live.

(Psalm 116:1–2)

See also Psalm 28:6–7; 1 Peter 1:3–5; 2:9–10

For rescue from difficulties

Praise be to the LORD,
for he showed his wonderful love to me
when I was in a besieged city.
In my alarm I said,
'I am cut off from your sight!'
Yet you heard my cry for mercy
when I called to you for help.

(Psalm 31:21–22)

See also Psalm 40:1–3; 81:1–7; 107:6–9; Jonah 2:1–9

For victory won

All the nations surrounded me,
but in the name of the LORD I cut them off.
They surrounded me on every side,
but in the name of the LORD I cut them off.
They swarmed around me like bees,
but they died out as quickly as burning thorns;
in the name of the LORD I cut them off.
I was pushed back and about to fall,
but the LORD helped me.
The LORD is my strength and my song;
he has become my salvation.
Shouts of joy and victory
resound in the tents of the righteous:
'The LORD's right hand has done mighty things!
The LORD's right hand is lifted high;
the LORD's right hand has done mighty things!'

(Psalm 118:10–16)

See also Psalm 18:1–19; 44:4–8; 144:9–10; 1 Corinthians 15:57; 2 Corinthians 2:14

For deliverance from suffering

I will declare your name to my brothers;
in the congregation I will praise you.
You who fear the LORD, praise him!
All you descendants of Jacob, honour him!
Revere him, all you descendants of Israel!
For he has not despised or disdained
the suffering of the afflicted one;
he has not hidden his face from him
but has listened to his cry for help.

(Psalm 22:22–24)

See also Psalm 119:50; Isaiah 38:15–19

For deliverance from fears

I will extol the LORD at all times;
his praise will always be on my lips.
My soul will boast in the LORD;
let the afflicted hear and rejoice.
Glorify the LORD with me:
let us exalt his name together.
I sought the LORD, and he answered me;
he delivered me from all my fears.

(Psalm 34:1–4)

See also Psalm 56:10–13; Isaiah 12:1–6

For deliverance from the danger of death

I will exalt you, O LORD,
for you lifted me out of the depths
and did not let my enemies gloat over me.
O LORD my God, I called to you for help
and you healed me.
O LORD, you brought me up from the grave;
you spared me from going down into the pit.
Sing to the LORD, you saints of his;
praise his holy name.
For his anger lasts only a moment,
but his favour lasts a lifetime;
weeping may remain for a night,
but rejoicing comes in the morning.

(Psalm 30:1–5)

See also Psalm 56:12–13; 116:3–7; Isaiah 38:9–20; Lamentations 3:55–58

For deliverance for the nation

When the LORD brought back the captives to Zion,
we were like men who dreamed.
Our mouths were filled with laughter,
our tongues with songs of joy.
Then it was said among the nations,
'The LORD has done great things for them.'
The LORD has done great things for us,
and we are filled with joy.

(Psalm 126:1–3)

See also Genesis 14:20; Exodus 15:1–21; Isaiah 49:8–13

Thankfulness for answers to prayer about others

Paul is a great example of how to pray and give thanks for others. Each of Paul's letters written to a church congregation begins, after an introduction of writer and recipient, with a greeting, similar to this one from Romans 1:7.

Grace and peace to you from God our Father and from the Lord Jesus Christ.

This is then always followed by thanksgiving to God – with the notable exception of Galatians, where Paul was so infuriated at how the gospel was in danger of being undermined by legalism that he just launches straight in with the cry, 'I am astonished . . .!' (Galatians 1:6).

Let's look at the grateful expressions with which these letters begin. On many occasions, the thanksgiving then leads him on to further prayer.

Romans

First, I thank my God through Jesus Christ for all of you, because your faith is being reported all over the world. God, whom I serve with my whole heart in preaching the gospel of his Son, is my witness how constantly I remember you in my prayers at all times.

(Romans 1:8–10)

1 Corinthians

I always thank God for you because of his grace given you in Christ Jesus. For in him you have been enriched in every way – in all your speaking and in all your knowledge – because our testimony about Christ was confirmed in you. Therefore you do not lack any spiritual gift as you eagerly wait for our Lord Jesus Christ to be revealed. He will keep you strong to the end, so that you will be blameless on the day of our Lord Jesus Christ. God, who has called you into fellowship with his Son Jesus Christ our Lord, is faithful.

(1 Corinthians 1:4–9)

2 Corinthians

Praise be to the God and Father of our Lord Jesus Christ, the Father of compassion and the God of all comfort, who comforts us in all our troubles, so that we can comfort those in any trouble with the comfort we ourselves have received from God. For just as the sufferings of Christ flow over into our lives, so also through Christ our comfort overflows. If we are distressed, it is for your comfort and salvation; if we are comforted, it is for your comfort, which produces in you patient endurance of the same sufferings we suffer. And our hope for you is firm, because we know that just as you share in our sufferings, so also you share in our comfort.

(2 Corinthians 1:3–7)

Ephesians

Praise be to the God and Father of our Lord Jesus Christ, who has blessed us in the heavenly realms with every spiritual blessing in Christ . . . And you also were included in Christ when you heard the word of truth, the gospel of your salvation . . . For this reason, ever since I heard about your faith in the Lord Jesus and your love for all the saints, I have not stopped giving thanks for you, remembering you in my prayers. I keep asking that the God of our Lord Jesus Christ, the glorious Father, may give you the Spirit of wisdom and revelation, so that you may know him better. I pray also that the eyes of your heart may be enlightened in order that you may know the hope to which he has called you, the riches of his glorious inheritance in the saints, and his incomparably great power for us who believe.

(Ephesians 1:3, 13, 15–19)

Philippians

I thank my God every time I remember you. In all my prayers for all of you, I always pray with joy because of your partnership in the gospel from the first day until now, being confident of this, that he who began a good work in you will carry it on to completion until the day of Christ Jesus. It is right for me to feel this way about all of you, since I have you in my heart; for whether I am in chains or defending and confirming the gospel, all of you share in God's grace with me. God can testify how I long for all of you with the affection of Christ Jesus. And this is my prayer: that your love may abound more and more in knowledge and depth of insight, so that you may be able to discern what is best and may be pure and blameless until the day of Christ, filled with the fruit of righteousness that comes through Jesus Christ – to the glory and praise of God.

(Philippians 1:3–11)

Colossians

We always thank God, the Father of our Lord Jesus Christ, when we pray for you, because we have heard of your faith in Christ Jesus and of the love you have for all the saints – the faith and love that spring from the hope that is stored up for you in heaven and that you have already heard about in the word of truth, the gospel that has come to you. All over the world this gospel is bearing fruit and growing, just as it has been doing among you since the day you heard it and understood God's grace in all its truth . . . For this reason, since the day we heard about you, we have not stopped praying for you and asking God to fill you with the knowledge of his will through all spiritual wisdom and understanding. And we pray this in order that you may live a life worthy of the Lord and may please him in every way: bearing fruit in every good work, growing in the knowledge of God, being strengthened with all power according to his glorious might so that you may have great endurance and patience, and joyfully giving thanks to the Father, who has qualified you to share in the inheritance of the saints in the kingdom of light.

(Colossians 1:3–6, 9–12)

1 Thessalonians

We always thank God for all of you, mentioning you in our prayers. We continually remember before our God and Father your work produced by faith, your labour prompted by love, and your endurance inspired by hope in our Lord Jesus Christ.

(1 Thessalonians 1:2–3)

2 Thessalonians

We ought always to thank God for you, brothers, and rightly so, because your faith is growing more and more, and the love every one of you has for each other is increasing. Therefore, among God's churches we boast about your perseverance and faith in all the persecutions and trials you are enduring.

(2 Thessalonians 1:3–4)

Two of Paul's 'personal' letters also begin with thanksgiving.

2 Timothy

I thank God, whom I serve, as my forefathers did, with a clear conscience, as night and day I constantly remember you in my prayers. Recalling your tears, I long to see you, so that I may be filled with joy. I have been reminded of your sincere faith, which first lived in your grandmother Lois and in your mother Eunice and, I am persuaded, now lives in you also.

(2 Timothy 1:3–5)

Philemon

I always thank my God as I remember you in my prayers, because I hear about your faith in the Lord Jesus and your love for all the saints. I pray that you may be active in sharing your faith, so that you will have a full understanding of every good thing we have in Christ. Your love has given me great joy and encouragement, because you, brother, have refreshed the hearts of the saints.

(Philemon 4–7)

A FINAL PRAYER

Glory to God for all things!

John Chrysostom (c. 347–407),
Bishop of Constantinople

CONCLUSION

We need to ensure we stay a grateful people. Ingratitude leads to forgetfulness of God; but gratitude opens the way to even more of his blessings.

You turned my wailing into dancing;
you removed my sackcloth and clothed me with joy,
that my heart may sing to you and not be silent.
O LORD my God, I will give you thanks for ever.

(Psalm 30:11–12)

Relevance for today

To conclude this chapter, here are three simple things we can do to train ourselves further in thankfulness.

Be thankful in everyday life

Thankfulness is a mind-set. We won't express thankfulness towards God unless it is part of our ordinary, everyday living. Start saying 'Thank you!' much more each day – to the shopkeeper, the bus driver, your child's teacher, the canteen workers, the receptionist, the refuse collectors, the postman. Learn to say thank you for the little things in life, and to the people who normally never get thanked.

In every thing give thanks: for this is the will of God in Christ Jesus concerning you.

(1 Thessalonians 5:18, KJV)

Keep a list of answered prayers

Most of us have an amazing ability to remember trivia and to forget what is important. Surprisingly, we sometimes forget God's answers to prayer – even the 'big ones'! The prophets often had to chide God's people for their forgetfulness:

Does a maiden forget her jewellery,
a bride her wedding ornaments?
Yet my people have forgotten me,
days without number.

(Jeremiah 2:32)

See also Isaiah 17:10; Jeremiah 18:13–15; Ezekiel 23:35; Hosea 8:14

One simple way of 'not forgetting' is to write down the things God says to us and the answers to prayer he brings, along with the date that it happened. (The front of your Bible or the front of this book might be a good place to do it!) The more we remember, the more we will thank; the more we thank, the more we will see of God's resources released from heaven.

Go now, write it on a tablet for them,
inscribe it on a scroll,
that for the days to come
it may be an everlasting witness.

(Isaiah 30:8)

See also Deuteronomy 6:4–9; 11:18–21; 31:19–22; Isaiah 8:1–4; Habakkuk 2:2–3

Tell others what God has done for you

Why keep good things to yourself? If God has answered your prayer in a special way, tell others about it too. Not only does this glorify God, it will encourage others (if they are Christians) or stir them (if they are not!). Telling what God has done for us is, in itself, an expression of thanksgiving.

Praise the Lord, *and worship him. Tell everyone what he has done and how great he is. Sing praise to the* Lord, *because he has done great things. Let all the world know what he has done.*

(Isaiah 12:4–5, NCV)

Go home to your family and tell them how much the Lord has done for you and how good he has been to you.

(Mark 5:19, CEV)

Chapter Six

Thanksgiving for God's Blessings

In a world that is often so ungrateful, how important it is for God's people to be grateful for even the ordinary things in life, seeing them all as God's kind provision for us.

'He has shown kindness by giving you rain from heaven and crops in their seasons; he provides you with plenty of food and fills your hearts with joy.' (Acts 14:17)

Long ago, when the prophet Samuel wanted to remind Israel of how God had given them victory over the Philistines, he set up a physical monument:

Then Samuel took a stone and set it up between Mizpah and Shen. He named it Ebenezer, saying, 'Thus far has the LORD helped us.'

(1 Samuel 7:12)

'Ebenezer' (meaning, 'stone of help') was put there to make sure that God's people would not forget God's blessings. Every time they walked past it, they were to think, 'Ah yes! God helped us win that victory!' We too need to find ways of putting modern-day 'Ebenezers' into our lives, families, and churches so that we do not become forgetful of God's blessings – especially those 'ordinary' ones that we so easily take for granted.

The blessing of food

One of the most basic things we all need for life is our 'daily bread' (Matthew 6:11). As we saw earlier (Part One, Chapter 1) this was something that Jesus encouraged us to ask God for, including it in 'The Lord's Prayer' (Matthew 6:9–13) and assuring us that, basic as this need was, it was important to his Father (Matthew 6:25–34). The provision of food is a blessing of God for which we should be grateful.

Giving thanks for our food

Because our food is a blessing, Jesus set the example of thanking God for it at meal times:

Taking the five loaves and the two fish and looking up to heaven, he gave thanks and broke them. Then he gave them to the disciples to set before the people.

(Luke 9:16)

When he was at the table with them, he took bread, gave thanks, broke it and began to give it to them.

(Luke 24:30)

Leaders in the early church also continued this practice of giving thanks for food before a meal:

Just before dawn Paul urged them all to eat . . . After he said this, he took some bread and gave thanks to God in front of them all. Then he broke it and began to eat.

(Acts 27:33, 35)

Does all food have God's blessing?

The early church was quickly faced with the equivalent of today's 'vegetarian lobby' and had to resolve this issue. Did all foods have God's blessing, or only some foods? For those from Jewish backgrounds, certain foods had always been 'unclean' for them according to their Law (e.g. Leviticus 11:1–47). Did those rules now apply to Christians?

Jesus himself made clear that food cannot make us 'unclean'. What makes us unclean isn't what goes into the mouth, but what comes out of the heart (Matthew 15:16–20). Peter, brought up a Jew, had to grasp that the food regulations of the Law were no longer binding on Christians; but it took a vision from God to convince him (Acts 10:9–16). Paul warned Christians to beware of those who:

. . . forbid people to marry and order them to abstain from certain foods, which God created to be received with thanksgiving by those who believe and who know the truth. For everything God created is good, and nothing is to be rejected if it is received with thanksgiving, because it is consecrated by the word of God and prayer.

(1 Timothy 4:3–5)

In Romans 14 Paul tackled the issue of 'Can we eat meat?' or 'Should we just eat vegetables?' The conclusion he came to was this:

One man's faith allows him to eat everything, but another man, whose faith is weak, eats only vegetables. The man who eats everything must not look down on him who does not, and the man who does not eat everything must not condemn the man who does, for God has accepted him . . . He who regards one day as special, does so to the Lord. He who eats meat, eats to the Lord, for he gives thanks to God; and he who abstains, does so to the Lord and gives thanks to God.

(Romans 14:2–3, 6–8)

In a similar discussion in 1 Corinthians 8 (this time about 'food offered to idols') he came to this conclusion:

But food does not bring us near to God; we are no worse if we do not eat, and no better if we do.

(1 Corinthians 8:8)

The New Testament's conclusion, then, is that no food is 'off limits' to us; but any food that is eaten should be eaten thankfully and thoughtfully.

What about today?

If food and drink is something we are encouraged to ask God for, then is it not appropriate that we should also thank God when he provides it? The trouble is, most of us reduce this blessing to not being a blessing at all; it is simply the result of our hard-earned income and a trip to the local supermarket. But visit a Third World Christian home and your perspective will be changed.

Mike will never forget his first trip to Uganda, shortly after the civil war. He had been given a welcome cup of tea and was just about to drink when his host said, 'Shall we give thanks?' and proceeded with heartfelt thanksgiving for the refreshment they were about to take. What Mike had taken for granted was a miracle of provision for that family. What about you? Do you take your food for granted too?

Stopping to thank God for our food before eating is a good way to remember how dependent we are upon him and how we should be grateful for even the basic provisions in life. Of course, it can become a garbled ritual – but it doesn't have to!

The blessing of life and health

How many times have you heard someone say, 'As long as you've got your health, that's all that matters' – and then grumble about something they haven't got? There's nothing like a time of crisis – a sudden illness or hospitalization – to make us appreciate life and health. But God doesn't want us to appreciate this just in the bad times; he wants us to be grateful for it in the good times too.

Life as the gift of God

Throughout the Bible 'life' is seen as the gift of God.

The Spirit of God has made me;
the breath of the Almighty gives me life.

(Job 33:4)

See also Genesis 2:7; 1 Samuel 2:6; Acts 17:25

As the gift of God, life and health are therefore things for which we should be grateful and give God our thanks. King Belshazzar of Babylon was rebuked because he forgot this.

'You did not honour the God who holds in his hand your life and all your ways.'

(Daniel 5:23)

Thankfulness for life and health

In contrast to Belshazzar's attitude, what should characterize us is thankfulness 'for our creation, preservation, and all the blessings of this life' (The General Thanksgiving). When Hezekiah's lifespan was extended by God (Isaiah 38:1–5), he responded with thanksgiving:

You restored me to health
and let me live.
Surely it was for my benefit
that I suffered such anguish.
In your love you kept me
from the pit of destruction;
you have put all my sins
behind your back.
For the grave cannot praise you,
death cannot sing your praise;
those who go down to the pit
cannot hope for your faithfulness.
The living, the living – they praise you,
as I am doing today.

(Isaiah 38:16–19)

Since our life is something God holds in his hands, we should not be too presumptuous in our plans either!

Look here, you people who say, 'Today or tomorrow we are going to a certain town and will stay there a year. We will do business there and make a profit.' How do you know what will happen tomorrow? For your life is like the morning fog – it's here a little while, then it" gone. What you ought to say is, 'If the Lord wants us to, we will live and do this or that.' Otherwise you will be boasting about your own plans, and all such boasting is evil.

(James 4:13–16, NLT)

See also Proverbs 20:24; Jeremiah 10:23

Remembering that life is short and fragile is a healthy check to our arrogance and keeps us grateful to God.

Teach us to number our days aright,
that we may gain a heart of wisdom.

(Psalm 90:12)

See also Job 7:6–10; 9:25–26; 14:1–6; Psalm 39:4–7; 102:1–12; Ecclesiastes 11:8–12:7; Isaiah 40:6–8; Luke 12:16–21

The blessing of family

Our family is another of God's basic provisions which it is all too easy to take for granted.

Family life is not a social creation, but a gift of God. From the beginning God planned family (Genesis 2:23–24; 4:1–2) and said parents were to be honoured (Exodus 20:12). 'Family' flows out of God's fatherhood (Ephesians 3:14–15) and God reveals himself as one who takes care of families that honour him (e.g. Genesis 7:–5; 2 Samuel 6:11; Jeremiah 35:18–19; Matthew 2:13–23). Family life was seen as such a blessing that God made provision for those without immediate family to be provided for and drawn into 'extended families' (e.g. Deuteronomy 25:5–10; Ruth 4:1–10; Job 31:16–23; Psalm 68:6; 1 Timothy 5:3–8).

Jesus himself took family responsibilities seriously, almost certainly staying at home until the age of thirty to help bring up his younger brothers and sisters (mentioned, for example, in Matthew 13:55–56). Perhaps Joseph died while Jesus was a teenager, there being no further appearance by him after the journey to Jerusalem when Jesus was twelve (Luke 2:41–51). Even when dying on the cross, Jesus was thoughtful enough for his mother to entrust her to his cousin John's care (John 19:25–27). This again suggests that Joseph was dead by then.

All of this demonstrates that 'family' is close to God's heart. As his blessing to us, it is right that we thank him constantly for it and pray for our family to know his blessing, guidance, and protection.

In the land of Uz there lived a man whose name was Job. This man was blameless and upright; he feared God and shunned evil. He had seven sons and three daughters . . . His sons used to take turns holding feasts in their homes, and they would invite their three sisters to eat and drink with them. When a period of feasting had run its course, Job would send and have them purified. Early in the morning he would sacrifice a burnt offering for each of them, thinking, 'Perhaps my children have sinned and cursed God in their hearts.' This was Job's regular custom.

(Job 1:1–2, 4–5)

Then all the people left, each for his own home, and David returned home to bless his family.

(1 Chronicles 16:43)

See also Genesis 27:27–29; 2 Samuel 7:18–29; Matthew 19:14–15; Acts 10:1–2

A godly heritage

What a blessing it is when we have a godly heritage! When parents and grandparents and great-grandparents have the joy of seeing their prayers answered and their children following the Lord Jesus for themselves. Timothy is one such example in the Bible.

I thank God, whom I serve, as my forefathers did, with a clear conscience, as night and day I constantly remember you in my prayers. Recalling your tears, I long to see you, so that I may be filled with joy. I have been reminded of your sincere faith, which first lived in your grandmother Lois and in your mother Eunice and, I am persuaded, now lives in you also.

(2 Timothy 1:3–5)

We too should give thanks to God for any godly heritage in our own family, and should pray for our children and grandchildren to be able to do the same one day. Teaching them about God and his ways is a crucial part of this (e.g. Deuteronomy 4:9; 6:4–9).

A parent's prayer

Almighty God and heavenly father, we thank thee for the children which thou hast given us: give us also grace to train them in thy faith, fear and love; that as they advance in years they may grow in grace, and may hereafter be found in the number of thine elect children; through Jesus Christ our Lord.

John Cosin (1594–1672),
Bishop of Durham

The blessing of friends

The Bible contains such lofty themes. But then it surprises us by coming so down to earth that we can hardly believe it. Consider Paul, for example, the great apostle and pioneer of the early church; the man who wrote of cosmic mysteries (e.g. Ephesians 1:3–10; Philippians 2:5–11; Colossians 1:15–20), who grappled with how Israel still fitted into God's purposes (e.g. Romans 9–11), who wrestled with the doctrine of justification by faith (e.g. Romans 3:21–4:25). And yet, this was the man who wrote these words:

Now when I went to Troas to preach the gospel of Christ and found that the Lord had opened a door for me, I still had no peace of mind, because I did not find my brother Titus there . . . But God, who comforts the downcast, comforted us by the coming of Titus.

(2 Corinthians 2:12–13; 7:6)

From the heights of divine mysteries to the ordinariness of worrying about a friend's whereabouts and needing him to come and cheer you up! Paul clearly understood the value of God-given friendship!

Thankfulness for friends

Paul's letters are full of thankfulness to God for those he counted as his friends.

I thank my God every time I remember you. In all my prayers for all of you, I always pray with joy because of your partnership in the gospel from the first day until now.

(Philippians 1:3–5)

I always thank my God as I remember you in my prayers, because I hear about your faith in the Lord Jesus and your love for all the saints.

(Philemon 4–5)

See also Romans 16:1–16; Philippians 2:25–30; Colossians 4:7–15

The Wisdom literature has good advice about true friendships, which can serve as a basis for prayer and thanksgiving.

A friend loves at all times,
and a brother is born for adversity.

(Proverbs 17:17)

Some friends may ruin you,
but a real friend will be more loyal than a brother.

(Proverbs 18:24, NCV)

Wounds from a friend can be trusted . . .

(Proverbs 27:6)

Two are better than one,
because they have a good return for their work:
If one falls down,
his friend can help him up.

But pity the man who falls
and has no-one to help him up!
(Ecclesiastes 4:9–10)

Friends and the church

Sadly, the church is often seen by many as an institution, organization, or club. But this is not what God intends it to be. God's plan for the church is for it to be a *family* (e.g. Matthew 12:46–50; Galatians 6:10; Ephesians 2:19; 3:15; 1 Peter 4:17).

A recurring phrase in the New Testament letters is 'dear friends'. This was no formalized means of address, but was a genuine expression of the heart of the leaders in the early church. It was used by:

- Paul (e.g. Romans 16:5, 9, 12; 1 Corinthians 10:14; 2 Corinthians 7:1; Philippians 2:12).
- Peter (e.g. 1 Peter 2:11; 4:12; 2 Peter 3:1, 8, 14)
- John (e.g. 1 John 2:7; 3:2, 21; 3 John 1–13)
- Jude (3, 17, 20)
- The unknown writer of Hebrews (Hebrews 6:9)

Good friends

The Bible contains lots of examples of good friendships and the blessing that they bring. Examples include:

- Ruth and Naomi (Ruth 1:15–18)
- David and Jonathan (1 Samuel 18:1–4; 23:16; 2 Samuel 1:17–27)
- Elijah and Elisha (2 Kings 2:1–14)
- The paralysed man and his friends (Mark 2:1–5)
- Jesus and the Twelve (John 15:9–17)
- Paul and Luke (Colossians 4:14)
- Paul and Timothy (2 Timothy 1:2–5)

All of these could give thanks to God for the provision of good and loyal friends.

The church members were their 'friends' not just their 'flock'. That is why Paul could name so many of them at the end of Romans (16:1–23). Moreover, it is clear that the apostles were not 'colleagues' in ministry, but good friends who served the Lord together (e.g. Acts 15:25–27; 2 Peter 3:15).

A FINAL PRAYER

Almighty God,
Father of all mercies,
we thine unworthy servants do
give thee most humble
and hearty thanks
for all thy goodness and
lovingkindness to us
and to all men.
We bless thee for our creation,
preservation,
and all the blessings of this life;
but above all for thine
inestimable love
in the redemption of the world by
our Lord Jesus Christ;
for the means of grace,
and for the hope of glory.
And, we beseech thee, give us that
due sense of all thy mercies,
that our hearts may be
unfeignedly thankful,
and that we shew forth thy praise,
not only with our lips
but in our lives; by giving up
ourselves to thy service,
and by walking before thee in

holiness and righteousness
all our days;
through Jesus Christ our Lord,
to whom with thee and
the Holy Ghost
be all honour and glory,
world without end. Amen.

General Thanksgiving, Book of Common Prayer

CONCLUSION

We have so much in our ordinary everyday lives to give thanks for! Let us not miss those blessings or neglect to say 'Thank you!' to our Father for them.

So whether you eat or drink or whatever you do, do it all for the glory of God.

(1 Corinthians 10:31)

Relevance for today

Giving thanks for our food

- Do I give thanks ('say Grace') before my meals? If I do, are they prayers from the heart, or have they become a quick, formal ritual? If I don't give thanks, why not?
- Do I give thanks at home but not in public? If so, why? Am I embarrassed? Am I more concerned with what people might think than with what God might think?
- Do I see the source of my provision as my job or bank account, or my God? Which holds my heart?

Being grateful for life and health

- Am I grateful for the life God gives me each day? Do I tell him so? And do I live as someone who is grateful?
- Am I grateful for the lives and health of my family? Do I pray for that and do I thank God for that?
- Do I take care of my health, recognizing that I cannot ask God to do for me what I am not prepared to play my part in? Are my eating and lifestyle sensible and healthy?

Appreciating our friends

- Do I thank God for my friends and do I pray for them?
- Do I take my friends for granted? Do I tell them from time to time that I appreciate them? And do I thank God when they are honest enough to tell me the truth about myself or my actions?
- Do I see members of my church as my friends? Do I thank God for them as such and treat them as such?

Chapter Seven

A Life Full of Thanks

'Thanks-giving is good, but thanks-living is better.' (Matthew Henry)

Be joyful always; pray continually; give thanks in all circumstances, for this is God's will for you in Christ Jesus. (1 Thessalonians 5:16–18)

Imagine how you would feel if someone said 'Thanks' but then went away and did something that proved the very opposite. Perhaps they had said, 'Oh, what a wonderful present! Thank you so much,' and then you discovered they had thrown it straight in the dustbin. How would you feel? We don't imagine you would be too pleased, for this really would be a case of 'actions speak louder than words'. And that's exactly how God feels in the same situation. We may well go to church, or pray in our house group or the prayer meeting, or 'say our prayers'; but if the 'thanks' expressed in words there aren't matched by the 'thanks' lived out in our life, then the thanks weren't worth very much really – were they?

The Bible tells us that if we are really grateful to God, then it will not just be our words but our whole lives that will express it. Our life will in effect be a constant prayer of thanks to God.

An attitude of gratitude

God wants us to develop 'an attitude of gratitude'; an attitude where our *first* response is to be grateful rather than to grumble; where thankfulness permeates everything we are and do and pray; where appreciation – of God, his people and his world – is the atmosphere we breathe. But for most of, us let's face it, this does not come instinctively!

So, where we can work at displaying in our lives this 'attitude of gratitude'?

In our praying

Three times a day he got down on his knees and prayed, giving thanks to his God.

(Daniel 6:10)

For this reason, ever since I heard about your faith in the Lord Jesus and your love for all the saints, I have not stopped giving thanks for you, remembering you in my prayers.

(Ephesians 1:15–16)

Devote yourselves to prayer, being watchful and thankful.

(Colossians 4:2)

In our thinking

Therefore, I urge you, brothers, in view of God's mercy, to offer your bodies as living sacrifices, holy and pleasing to God – this is your spiritual act of worship. Do not conform any longer to the pattern of this world, but be transformed by the renewing of your mind. Then you will be able to test and approve what God's will is – his good, pleasing and perfect will.

(Romans 12:1–2)

Rejoice in the Lord always. I will say it again: Rejoice! Let your gentleness be evident to all. The Lord is near. Do not be anxious about anything, but in everything, by prayer and petition, with thanksgiving, present your requests to God. And the peace of God, which transcends all understanding, will guard your hearts and your minds in Christ Jesus.

Finally, brothers, whatever is true, whatever is noble, whatever is right, whatever is pure, whatever is lovely, whatever is admirable – if anything is excellent or praiseworthy – think about such things. Whatever you have learned or received or heard from me, or seen in me – put it into practice. And the God of peace will be with you.

(Philippians 4:4–9)

In our speaking

But among you there must not be even a hint of sexual immorality, or of any kind of impurity, or of greed, because these are improper for God's holy people. Nor should there be obscenity, foolish talk or coarse joking, which are out of place, but rather thanksgiving. For of this you can be sure: No immoral, impure or greedy person – such a man is an idolater – has any inheritance in the kingdom of Christ and of God. Let no-one deceive you with empty words, for because of such things God's wrath comes on those who are disobedient. Therefore do not be partners with them.

(Ephesians 5:3–7)

Do not get drunk on wine, which leads to debauchery. Instead, be filled with the Spirit. Speak to one another with psalms, hymns and spiritual songs. Sing and make music in your heart to the Lord, always giving thanks to God the Father for everything, in the name of our Lord Jesus Christ.

(Ephesians 5:18–20)

In our relating

Therefore, as God's chosen people, holy and dearly loved, clothe yourselves with compassion, kindness, humility, gentleness and patience. Bear with each other and forgive whatever grievances you may have against one another. Forgive as the Lord forgave you. And over all these virtues put on love, which binds them all together in perfect unity. Let the peace of Christ rule in your hearts, since as members of one body you were called to peace. And be thankful. Let the word of Christ dwell in you richly as you teach and admonish one another with all wisdom, and as you sing psalms, hymns and spiritual songs with gratitude in your hearts to God. And whatever you do, whether in word or deed, do it all in the name of the Lord Jesus, giving thanks to God the Father through him.

(Colossians 3:12–17)

The secret of contentment

One of the reasons we are not grateful is that we have not learned how to be content. We live in a society where we are constantly bombarded with messages telling us that we need something bigger, better, newer, nicer than what we have already; where we are told that our dresses our too long, our ties are too wide, our colours are too bright . . . until next year of course, when we are told that our dresses are too short, our ties are too narrow, our colours are too dull . . .

Sounds familiar? Of course it does! The trouble is, we believe it! Little wonder

Some quotations about gratitude

'Thanks-giving is good, but thanks-living is better.'

(Matthew Henry)

'No duty is more urgent than that of returning thanks.'

(St Ambrose)

'Thou that hast given me so much . . . Give me one thing more – a grateful heart.'

(George Herbert)

'The best way to show gratitude to God is to accept everything, even my problems, with joy.'

(Mother Teresa)

'The Christian is suspended between blessings received and blessings hoped for, so he should always give thanks.'

(M. R. Vincent)

we do not learn how to be content.

A missionary friend of Mike's was working in war-torn Burundi when she came across an old man in ragged clothing, his only possession in the world (other than the clothes he was wearing) being a tin cup held in his hand. She hardly knew what to say to him; but the old man looked up and said with a kindly smile, 'Madame Missionary, I never knew that Jesus was all I needed until Jesus was all I had.' To such faith and deep contentment in Jesus, Madame Missionary could give no answer.

So, what about us? Does our response to what God has provided us with reflect an 'attitude of gratitude', a godly contentment, a thankfulness of heart? Or do we get lost in covetousness, greed, materialism, avarice and ambition, anxiety about the future, which quickly lead to loss of contentment, and so to the loss of gratitude, and so to the loss of a sense of the closeness of God's presence?

The fear of the LORD leads to life:
Then one rests content, untouched by trouble.

(Proverbs 19:23)

Better one handful with tranquillity
than two handfuls with toil
and chasing after the wind.

(Ecclesiastes 4:6)

'Be content with your pay.'

(Luke 3:14)

I rejoice greatly in the Lord that at last you have renewed your concern for me. Indeed, you have been concerned, but you had no opportunity to show it. I am not saying this because I am in need, for I have learned to be content whatever the circumstances. I know what it is to be in need, and I know what it is to have plenty. I have learned the secret of being content in any and every situation, whether well fed or hungry, whether living in plenty or in want. I can do everything through him who gives me strength.

(Philippians 4:10–13)

But godliness with contentment is great gain. For we brought nothing into the world, and we can take nothing out of it. But if we have food and clothing, we will be content with that. People who want to get rich fall into temptation and a trap and into many foolish and harmful desires that plunge men into ruin and destruction. For the love of money is a root of all kinds of evil. Some people, eager for money, have wandered from the faith and pierced themselves with many griefs.

(1 Timothy 6:6–10)

Keep your lives free from the love of money and be content with what you have, because God has said, 'Never will I leave you; never will I forsake you.' So we say with confidence, 'The Lord is my helper; I will not be afraid. What can man do to me?'

(Hebrews 13:5–6)

Learning how to trust

One key to growing in contentment is learning how to trust God more. We so easily fall into 'comparison'. Why did God answer their prayer and not mine? Why can they afford a nicer house and car than we can? Why is it they can go abroad every year for a holiday and we can't? (Recognize any of those questions?)

While we would never acknowledge it, of course, such questions are fundamental challenges to God. We are telling him that he does not know how to run our lives (though we will, of course, piously sing on Sunday that he knows how to run the world!). A thankful heart to God is one that trusts his purposes in our lives, that gratefully receives what he gives us (without comparing it with others), and that trusts him even when things aren't working out as we would have liked them to.

In the following psalm the psalmist contrasts his feelings when he wasn't trusting God and when he felt 'hard done by' with how he felt when he came to God to let him deal with those things and began to trust him. As he did so, everything came back into perspective again.

When my heart was grieved
and my spirit embittered,
I was senseless and ignorant;
I was a brute beast before you.
Yet I am always with you;
you hold me by my right hand.
You guide me with your counsel,
and afterwards you will take me into glory.
Whom have I in heaven but you?
And earth has nothing I desire besides you.
My flesh and my heart may fail,
but God is the strength of my heart
and my portion for ever.

(Psalm 73:21–26)

See also Psalm 9:10; 13:1–6; 20:7; 31:9–16; 46:1–11; 62:5–8; 91:1–16

What is there to give thanks for?

Well, this whole part of the book should have given you some food for thought there! But sometimes, especially if we are feeling disappointed, discouraged, or low in spirits, we need some simple things that we can keep hold of to reassure us. It strikes us that there are four key truths that are unchanging and unchangeable. No matter what happens in life, these things stand firm and for these we can always give thanks.

God is good

Give thanks to the LORD, for he is good;
his love endures for ever.

(Psalm 106:1)

You are good, and what you do is good.

(Psalm 119:68)

See also 1 Chronicles 16:34; 2 Chronicles 7:3; Ezra 3:11; Psalm 107:1; 118:1, 29

God is in control

I know that you can do all things;
no plan of yours can be thwarted.

(Job 42:2)

And we know that in all things God works for the good of those who love him, who have been called according to his purpose.

(Romans 8:28)

See also Numbers 23:19; Daniel 4:34–35; John 10:27–29; Ephesians 1:11

His Spirit is always with us

'My Spirit remains among you. Do not fear.'

(Haggai 2:5)

'And I will ask the Father, and he will give you another Counsellor to be with you for ever – the Spirit of truth. The world cannot accept him, because it neither sees him nor knows him. But you know him, for he lives with you and will be in you. I will not leave you as orphans; I will come to you.'

(John 14:16–18)

See also Isaiah 59:21; John 7:37–39; 1 Corinthians 3:16; 6:19; Ephesians 2:22

Jesus is coming back

'Do not let your hearts be troubled. Trust in God; trust also in me. In my Father's house are many rooms; if it were not so, I would have told you. I am going there to prepare a place for you. And if I go and prepare a place for you, I will come back and take you to be with me that you also may be where I am.'

(John 14:1–3)

God is just: He will pay back trouble to those who trouble you and give relief to you who are troubled, and to us as well. This will happen when the Lord Jesus is revealed from heaven in blazing fire with his powerful angels.

(2 Thessalonians 1:6–7)

See also Matthew 24:3–44; Acts 1:11; Philippians 3:20–21; 2 Thessalonians 2:8; Hebrews 9:27–28; 1 Peter 1:3–7

A FINAL PRAYER

Thou hast giv'n so much to me,
Give one thing more,
a grateful heart . . .
Not thankful, when it
pleaseth me;
As if thy blessings had spare days:
But such a heart,
whose pulse may be
Thy praise.

George Herbert (1593–1633)

CONCLUSION

'Not only with our lips, but also in our lives' should be the watchword of all God's children when it comes to giving him thanks.

Through Jesus, therefore, let us continually offer to God a sacrifice of praise – the fruit of lips that confess his name. And do not forget to do good and to share with others, for with such sacrifices God is pleased.

(Hebrews 13:15–16)

Relevance for today

To conclude this section on thanks-giving, here are some questions for you to reflect on.

'Thanks-giving' or 'thanks-living'?

Do I model 'thanks-giving' or 'thanks-living' in my life? Is my enthusiasm for praising God in the meetings of the church matched by enthusiastic praise in my whole way of life?

Gratitude or grumbling?

Do I seek to maintain 'an attitude of gratitude'? Am I a grumbler or am I grateful? A worrier or a worshipper? Does 'an attitude of gratitude' permeate –

- My praying
- My thinking
- My speaking
- My relating to others

Comparison or contentment?

Do I constantly compare myself with others and how they seem to be being blessed? Am I resentful if they go on a holiday that I can't afford or get promotion when I don't? Am I learning to be content with what God gives me, believing that he knows what is best for me?

Testing God or trusting God?

Am I growing in my trust of God, or am I always putting him to the test, asking for yet more things to prove that he loves me? Do I trust him only when things are going well for me?

Part Four

Prayers that say 'Sorry!'

Chapter One

Why Say Sorry?

Saying 'sorry' doesn't come naturally; but it is the key to finding, and maintaining, friendship with a holy God.

He who conceals his sins does not prosper, but whoever confesses and renounces them finds mercy. (Proverbs 28:13)

When our children were young, one of the things we tried to work hard on as parents was getting them to say 'sorry' when it was needed. Such a small word, yet one that it could be so difficult to extract from them at times! Of course, adults are no different; it's just that we are far more subtle in the way we avoid saying it. But knowing how to say 'sorry' is one of the most important things in life. It is the key to a good relationship with God, and with others.

Saying 'sorry' reminds us who God is

The holy God

God is holy and cannot bear to look upon sin. This is hard for us to grasp, for we have all learned to live too easily with sin. But just as we instinctively feel repulsed if we see scenes of mass slaughter on the TV news, so that is exactly how God feels about sin when he sees it. He feels revolted and sickened by it – even by what we might see as 'trivial' sin – for it offends his holy nature.

Your eyes are too pure to look on evil;
you cannot tolerate wrong.

(Habakkuk 1:13)

Our sin offends God's holiness, his perfection, his love of what is good and right. Acknowledging our sinfulness, therefore, is the first step to receiving God's forgiveness. If we won't confess *our* sin, we can't receive *his* forgiveness.

So I confessed my sins and told them all to you.
I said, 'I'll tell the LORD each one of my sins.'
Then you forgave me and took away my guilt.

(Psalm 32:5, CEV)

'Woe is me! I am lost, for I am a man of unclean lips, and I live among a people of unclean lips; yet my eyes have seen the King, the LORD of hosts!' Then one of the seraphs

All have sinned

Romans 3:23 sums up so succinctly how we are all sinners and fail to come up to God's standards. Here is the verse from several different English translations:

For all have sinned, and come short of the glory of God. (KJV)

For all have sinned; all fall short of God's glorious standard. (NLT)

All have sinned and are not good enough for God's glory. (NCV)

Everyone has sinned and is far away from God's saving presence. (GNB)

flew to me, holding a live coal that had been taken from the altar with a pair of tongs. The seraph touched my mouth with it and said: 'Now that this has touched your lips, your guilt has departed and your sin is blotted out.'

(Isaiah 6:5–7, NRSV)

All sin is against God

Perhaps we wonder sometimes what a particular sin has got to do with God? Upsetting my friend, arguing with my boss, messing up my own life; how does all this affect *God*? Well, it affects him because all these things are an offence to his holiness and because he has made us all to live as his obedient children. All sin is sin against him, therefore, whether we see a direct connection to him or not.

In the well-known parable of the prodigal son, note what the wayward son says when he realizes what a mess he has made of his life:

'I will arise and go to my father, and will say to him, "Father, I have sinned against heaven and before you, and I am no longer worthy to be called your son."'

(Luke 15:18–19, NKJV)

Note the two dimensions of sin here: 'against heaven' (a common synonym for 'God' in those days to avoid using the divine name) and 'against you'. But note which came first – God! God is far more offended by our sin or failings than anyone else will ever be. That's why it is important that we confess our sin to *him* even if we don't think he is directly involved.

When Potiphar's wife attempted to seduce the godly young Joseph, look how he responded:

'No-one is greater in this house than I am. My master has withheld nothing from me except you, because you are his wife. How then could I do such a wicked thing and sin against God?'

(Genesis 39:9)

The sin, he saw, would not just have been against his master, by betraying his trust, but against God himself. It is seeing sin in this bigger context – as something that offends and hurts God – that helps keep us on the 'straight and narrow'.

David also understood that sin against an individual was sin against God. In the well-known incident of his adulterous relationship with Bathsheba, the prophet Nathan was told by God of the sin that David had committed and he came to confront him with it. David could have tried to cover it up (as he had tried to do along the way); but once confronted, his confession is short and to the point:

'I have sinned against the LORD.'

(2 Samuel 12:13)

Of all the people that David could have listed here – Bathsheba, her husband

Uriah, the child in her womb, the nation of which he was king – David focuses on just one: God himself. Sin is primarily sin against God. He expressed this further in Psalm 51:

Have mercy on me, O God,
according to your unfailing love;
according to your great compassion
blot out my transgressions.
Wash away all my iniquity
and cleanse me from my sin.
For I know my transgressions,
and my sin is always before me.
Against you, you only, have I sinned
and done what is evil in your sight,
so that you are proved right when you speak
and justified when you judge.

(Psalm 51:1–4)

See also Genesis 13:13; 20:3–6; Daniel 9:4–19

The fear of the LORD

The Bible speaks of 'the fear of the LORD'. By this it does not mean we are to be frightened of God, as we might be frightened of a lion attacking us; it means that we are to have a *profound and healthy respect for God* out of our understanding of his holiness and his absolute hatred of sin. It means we cannot reduce God to the level of a 'mate' who says, 'Well, never mind; we all get it wrong at times. Don't worry!' A proper 'fear of the LORD' helps us to see sin in its proper light, just as God sees it. It even helps us to avoid sin.

'The fear of God will be with you to keep you from sinning.'

(Exodus 20:20)

'Have you considered my servant Job? There is no-one on earth like him; he is blameless and upright, a man who fears God and shuns evil.'

(Job 1:8)

Through love and faithfulness sin is atoned for;
through the fear of the LORD a man avoids evil.

(Proverbs 16:6)

See also Job 2:3; Proverbs 3:7; 8:13; 14:16

Saying 'sorry' reminds us who we are

Not only does saying 'sorry' remind us who God is, it also reminds us who we are. We can so easily lose a proper perspective of ourselves and become convinced of our own importance and indispensability. How fortunate the company is to have us working for them! How blessed the church is to have us as a member. But owning up to our sin and saying 'sorry' to God has a way of healthily putting things back into perspective again, by reminding us who we really are – just sinners saved by grace.

Opening the door to God

Saying 'sorry' to God opens the door to friendship with him. Confessing that we have done wrong (e.g. Psalm 106:6), that we have fallen short of his standards (e.g. Romans 3:23), that we have gone our own way (e.g. Isaiah 53:6), that we have violated his commands (e.g. 1 Samuel 15:24), and that we have ruined our lives (e.g. Proverbs 5:11–14), is absolutely foundational to finding God's forgiveness and friendship. The Bible calls this 'repentance', and God never tires of calling people to it, for he knows that it is the way to eternal life for us.

This is what the LORD says: 'If you repent, I will restore you that you may serve me.'

(Jeremiah 15:19)

'Repent! Turn away from all your offences; then sin will not be your downfall. Rid

yourselves of all the offences you have committed, and get a new heart and a new spirit. Why will you die, O house of Israel? For I take no pleasure in the death of anyone, declares the Sovereign LORD. Repent and live!

(Ezekiel 18:30–32)

'The time has come,' he said. 'The kingdom of God is near. Repent and believe the good news!'

(Mark 1:15)

'In the past God overlooked such ignorance, but now he commands all people everywhere to repent.'

(Acts 17:30)

When we respond to God's call to repent and acknowledge our sin, then God is always quick to forgive us. Of this, we need have no doubt – no matter how bad we think our sin might have been.

Then I acknowledged my sin to you
and did not cover up my iniquity.
I said, 'I will confess
my transgressions to the Lord' –
and you forgave
the guilt of my sin.

(Psalm 32:5)

If we claim to be without sin, we deceive ourselves and the truth is not in us. If we confess our sins, he is faithful and just and will forgive us our sins and purify us from all unrighteousness.

(1 John 1:8–9)

See also Psalm 65:1–4; 78:32–39; Acts 2:38–39; Acts 3:19–20; Colossians 2:13–15

Keeping the door open to God

God hates arrogance. In fact, he holds arrogance and pride at a distance:

The arrogant cannot stand in your presence;
you hate all who do wrong.

(Psalm 5:5)

Though the LORD is supreme,
he takes care of those who are humble,
but he stays away from the proud.

(Psalm 138:6, NCV)

The eyes of the arrogant man will be humbled
and the pride of men brought low;
the LORD alone will be exalted in that day.

(Isaiah 2:11)

See also Psalm 18:27; 119:21; 147:6; Jeremiah 50:31–32; Daniel 5:18–21

However, humility and tenderness of heart keep the door to friendship with God wide open. When we humbly say 'sorry' for how we have failed him, God rushes in with his grace day by day.

'This is the one I esteem:
he who is humble and contrite in spirit,
and trembles at my word.'

(Isaiah 66:2)

God opposes the proud but gives grace to the humble.

(James 4:6)

See also Ezra 8:21–23; Psalm 149:1–4; Proverbs 3:34; Matthew 23:12; 1 Timothy 6:17

Saying 'sorry' reminds us who others are

Sometimes, despite our very best intentions, we hurt other people. Careless words, thoughtless actions, ungrateful attitudes – all can cut deep into the hearts of family, friends, colleagues, fellow church members. When we recognize that we have done this, we need to say sorry quickly – both to God and to them – as this reminds us that we are no different from them and that they too are made in the image of God and are to be treated as such. Saying sorry keeps things in perspective!

Saying 'sorry' to God when we treat others badly

Think again about David's adulterous relationship with Bathsheba (2 Samuel 11). He treated so many people badly through this incident: Bathsheba, whose marriage he violated; Uriah, whose death he conveniently arranged; Joab, his army commander, whom he drew in to his scheming; the soldiers, whose friend Uriah was; the child that was conceived, whose life would be cut so short. But as we noted earlier, the primary focus of David's repentance was towards God (2 Samuel 12:13). Let's make sure we say 'sorry' to God when we abuse other people in any way, by thoughts, words, or deeds.

Saying 'sorry' to others when we treat them badly

But, of course, just saying 'sorry' to God could be a 'cop-out', a convenient way of not facing up to our responsibilities or the consequences of what we have done. That's why it is important to take our courage in both hands and to apologize to the person we have wronged, face to face, and be ready to forgive them if they have wronged us. This is prayer being outworked in action.

The man who refused to forgive

Peter came up to the Lord and asked, 'How many times should I forgive someone who does something wrong to me? Is seven times enough?'

Jesus answered: Not just seven times, but seventy-seven times! This story will show you what the kingdom of heaven is like:

One day a king decided to call in his officials and ask them to give an account of what they owed him. As he was doing this, one official was brought in who owed him fifty million silver coins. But he didn't have any money to pay what he owed. The king ordered him to be sold, along with his wife and children and all he owned, in order to pay the debt.

The official got down on his knees and began begging, 'Have pity on me, and I will pay you every penny I owe!' The king felt sorry for him and let him go free. He even told the official that he did not have to pay back the money.

As the official was leaving, he happened to meet another official, who owed him a hundred silver coins. So he grabbed the man by the throat. He started choking him and said, 'Pay me what you owe!'

The man got down on his knees and began begging, 'Have pity on me, and I will pay you back.' But the first official refused to have pity. Instead, he went and had the other official put in jail until he could pay what he owed.

When some other officials found out what had happened, they felt sorry for the man who had been put in jail. Then they told the king what had happened. The king called the first official back in and said, 'You're an evil man! When you begged for mercy, I said you did not have to pay back a penny. Don't you think you should show pity to someone else, as I did to you?' The king was so angry that he ordered the official to be tortured until he could pay back everything he owed. That is how my Father in heaven will treat you, if you don't forgive each of my followers with all your heart.

(Matthew 18:21–35, CEV)

Be kind and compassionate to one another, forgiving each other, just as in Christ God forgave you.

(Ephesians 4:32)

Therefore, as God's chosen people, holy and dearly loved, clothe yourselves with compassion, kindness, humility, gentleness and patience. Bear with each other and forgive whatever grievances you may have against one another. Forgive as the Lord forgave you. And over all these virtues put on love, which binds them all together in perfect unity. Let the peace of Christ rule in your hearts, since as members of one body you were called to peace. And be thankful.

(Colossians 3:12–15)

A FINAL PRAYER

Almighty God,
unto whom all hearts be open,
all desires known,
and from whom no secrets are hid;
Cleanse the thoughts of our hearts
by the inspiration of thy Holy
Spirit, that we may perfectly love
thee, and worthily magnify
thy holy Name;
through Christ our Lord. Amen.

The Collect from The Communion,
Book of Common Prayer (1662)

CONCLUSION

Getting the word 'sorry' out of our mouths is not always easy; but when we do, it is the most liberating thing on earth!

I will declare mine iniquity; I will be sorry for my sin.

(Psalm 38:17, KJV)

Relevance for today

God is still holy

God does not change (Malachi 3:6), and so he is still holy today. This holiness means two things for us:

I cannot hide my sin from a holy God

For a man's ways are in full view of the
LORD,
and he examines all his paths.

(Proverbs 5:21)

Nothing in all creation is hidden from God's sight. Everything is uncovered and laid bare before the eyes of him to whom we must give account.

(Hebrews 4:13)

See also Psalm 33:13–15; Jeremiah 16:17; 23:24; Acts 5:1–11

I do not need to hide my sin from God

The thought of all our sin being known by the holy God could be terrifying! But God tells us this, not to terrify us – but to draw us to himself! He wants us to know that he knows – and that he is still ready to receive us despite it all!

If you, O LORD, kept a record of sins,
O Lord, who could stand?
But with you there is forgiveness;
therefore you are feared.

(Psalm 130:3–4)

'Come now, let us reason together,'
says the LORD.
'Though your sins are like scarlet,
they shall be as white as snow;
though they are red as crimson,
they shall be like wool.'

(Isaiah 1:18)

See also Psalm 51:7; Isaiah 55:6–7

God loves to hear our 'sorrys'

Saying sorry to God

When we get things wrong, we need to say 'sorry' to God – and quickly! But how easy do you find it to say 'sorry' to him? Do you put it off? Or make excuses? Or blame others?

'O LORD, have mercy on me;
heal me, for I have sinned against you.'

(Psalm 41:4)

Saying sorry to others

How easy do you find it to say 'sorry' to others? Jesus stressed the importance of doing so – and doing so quickly!

'Settle matters quickly with your adversary who is taking you to court. Do it while you are still with him on the way, or he may hand you over to the judge, and the judge may hand you over to the officer, and you may be thrown into prison. I tell you the truth, you will not get out until you have paid the last penny.'

(Matthew 5:25–26)

God is ready to hear your first 'sorry' today

It may be that, as you have read this chapter, you have realized for the first time in your life that you have something to say 'sorry' to God for – for living life without him this far, for neglecting him all these years, for something in the past you have buried away in your memory but which God is stirring up right now. If so, then this is as good a time as any to say your first 'sorry' to him. Remember, Jesus said this:

'Listen! I am standing and knocking at your door. If you hear my voice and open the door, I will come in and we will eat together.'

(Revelation 3:20, CEV)

In your own words, simply say something like, 'Jesus, I'm really sorry for …. Please forgive me because of your death on the cross. Please come in and share your life with me, and let me start life all over again with you.'

Chapter Two

Coming Clean

There is something within us that hates having to own up and say 'It was me!' But when we do 'come clean', God is always quick to forgive.

If I had cherished sin in my heart, the Lord would not have listened; but God has surely listened and heard my voice in prayer.
(Psalm 66:18–19)

On a hot and sticky day, after a hard day's work, what can be better than a refreshing shower? It feels so good to feel clean again! And the Bible tells us that it is possible to feel like that on the inside too. We can feel completely fresh and new, with all the 'dirt' washed away. But in order to get clean we have to 'come clean'. We have to own up to what we did and acknowledge it was wrong – with no excuses or blame-shifting. And then, a miracle happens! Through his Spirit, and because of the cross, God forgives us – just like that!

As old as the hills

Some things are as old as the hills, as the saying goes. And blame-shifting is one of the oldest, going right back to Adam and Eve. When God challenged Adam about his disobedience, he immediately blamed it on his wife. 'The woman you put here with me – she gave me some fruit from the tree, and I ate it' (Genesis 3:12). It wasn't really my fault – take it up with her! But his wife was ready with her excuses too. 'The serpent deceived me, and I ate' (Genesis 3:13). I was tricked so it wasn't my fault! (And if the story were being retold these days, no doubt the serpent would go to his psychiatrist who would tell him it wasn't his fault, but it was due to a traumatic experience when he was younger which still lay buried in his subconscious!) Trying to shift the blame onto others really is as old as the hills. But the Bible tells us that 'coming clean' – owning up to what we have done wrong – is an absolute prerequisite to finding God's forgiveness. Without this, we will never be forgiven.

People who tried to blame-shift

- **Abraham** blamed the reputation of the local area for lying about his wife and saying she was just his sister (Genesis 20:8–13)

- **Aaron** blamed the people for leading him into idolatry, even claiming that a gold calf just 'happened' to come out of the furnace! (Exodus 32:21–24)
- **Israel** blamed Moses for their hardships on leaving Egypt (Exodus 14:10–12; Numbers 20:2–5)
- **Saul** blamed his soldiers' fear for his disobedience to Samuel's command (1 Samuel 13:7–12; 15:20–21)
- **Abner** blamed Ish-Bosheth, Saul's son, for his own sin in sleeping with a royal concubine (2 Samuel 3:7–10)
- **King Ahab** blamed Elijah for bringing the trouble on Israel that he himself had caused (1 Kings 18:16–18)
- **Martha** blamed Jesus for the death of her brother Lazarus by failing to arrive on time (John 11:21)

Why do we blame-shift?

Clearly, this matter of trying to shift the blame is no new phenomenon! But, why do we do it? What is it in us that finds it so hard to 'come clean'?

Sometimes it is because of *pride*. We are too proud to admit that we made a mistake; or we want to maintain a good appearance before people and have them think well of us, like King Saul (e.g. 1 Samuel 15:30). Sometimes it is because of *fear*, perhaps from our circumstances (e.g. 1 Samuel 13:11–12) or from worrying about the outcome of our sin or even whether God will ever forgive us for it. Whatever the specific reason, behind them all lies what the Bible calls *the deceitfulness of sin*.

In Paul's argument in Romans 7 about how the very presence of the commandments provoked within him a desire to break them (rather like a 'Wet Paint' sign provokes us to touch, just to see!), he includes this phrase:

I found that the very commandment that was intended to bring life actually brought death. For sin, seizing the opportunity afforded by the commandment, deceived me, and through the commandment put me to death.

(Romans 7:10–11)

This is what sin does: it deceives us. It tells us things will be all right; but then once we have done wrong, we discover that things aren't right at all (which we probably suspected all along, but somehow thought it might be different this time!). Blame-shifting is an aspect of that deceitfulness of sin. It tells us that it wasn't really our fault and that there were others just as responsible; and, in believing it, we put ourselves outside the grace of God, for that grace can only be found where we are prepared to come clean.

Owning up to our sin: Psalm 51

Probably one of the most famous psalms in the Bible is this one, written 'when the prophet Nathan came to him after David had committed adultery with Bathsheba' (Psalm 51, title). In early Christian liturgical tradition it was one of the 'seven penitential psalms' (the others being Psalms 6, 32, 38, 102, 130, and 143), and provides a classic insight into true confession of sin.

Have mercy on me, O God,
according to your unfailing love;
according to your great compassion
blot out my transgressions.
Wash away all my iniquity
and cleanse me from my sin.
For I know my transgressions,
and my sin is always before me.
Against you, you only, have I sinned
and done what is evil in your sight,
so that you are proved right when you speak
and justified when you judge.
Surely I was sinful at birth,

sinful from the time my mother conceived
me.
Surely you desire truth in the inner parts;
you teach me wisdom in the inmost place.

Cleanse me with hyssop, and I shall be clean;
wash me, and I shall be whiter than snow.
Let me hear joy and gladness;
let the bones you have crushed rejoice.
Hide your face from my sins
and blot out all my iniquity.

Create in me a pure heart, O God,
and renew a steadfast spirit within me.
Do not cast me from your presence
or take your Holy Spirit from me.
Restore to me the joy of your salvation
and grant me a willing spirit, to sustain
me.

Then I will teach transgressors your ways,
and sinners will turn back to you.
Save me from bloodguilt, O God,
the God who saves me,
and my tongue will sing of your
righteousness.
O Lord, open my lips,
and my mouth will declare your praise.
You do not delight in sacrifice, or I would
bring it;
you do not take pleasure in burnt
offerings.
The sacrifices of God are a broken spirit;
a broken and contrite heart,
O God, you will not despise.

In your good pleasure make Zion prosper;
build up the walls of Jerusalem.
Then there will be righteous sacrifices,
whole burnt offerings to delight you;
then bulls will be offered on your altar.
(Psalm 51:1–19)

So, what does this psalm teach us about the way we should confess our sin, and so come into the forgiveness and freedom that David himself did (2 Samuel 12:20–25)?

Begin with God (v1)

David's prayer begins by focusing on God and not himself. He reminds himself that his God is a God of 'mercy ... unfailing love ... great compassion' (v1). These foremost characteristics, revealed to us by God himself (e.g. Exodus 34:6–7), are where we should begin. If we don't, our confession will be little more than a rehearsal of self-pity. Remember: Jesus himself encouraged us in the Lord's Prayer (Matthew 6:9–13) to focus on God and his goodness before we confess our sins (see Part One, Chapter 1). For it is when we start with remembering what God is really like that we can press on with the harder bit of 'coming clean', knowing that he will surely forgive us.

Acknowledge the sin (v3–6)

Unlike the blame-shifters we have looked at, David faced up to his sin 'square on'. He acknowledged:

The sinful act (v1–4)

David acknowledges his action as 'transgressions ... iniquity ... sin' (v1–2). His piling up of these words shows there is no attempt to 'soft-pedal' the issue. He 'calls a spade a spade' before God. All of this has clearly been very much on his mind (v3): 'For I recognize my shameful deeds – they haunt me day and night' (NLT). It is now time to get it 'off his chest' and with it, off his conscience.

As we saw in the previous chapter, he sees that his sin is primarily not against Bathsheba or Uriah, but against God himself. 'You are the only one I have sinned against; I have done what you say is wrong' (v4, NCV). As such, God's judgment on him is deserved (v4).

The sinful nature (v5–6)

But as he reflected on his sinful act, he began to see that the issue went far deeper. It wasn't just that he had sinned; it was that he was a sinner. He saw that this was his essential nature from his earliest days (v5), so he can't excuse it as a 'one-off'. He may not have done this particular sin before; but sin had been the story of his life! How this conflicts with what God is looking for (v6).

Ask for forgiveness (v7–9)

Having confessed his sin, David now calls out to God to forgive him, showing his seriousness by using a variety of imagery. First, he asks God to cleanse him with hyssop (v7), a plant used in the Old Testament in ritual cleansing (see e.g. Exodus 12:22; Leviticus 14:1–7, 48–53; Numbers 19:17–22). The Hebrew word 'cleanse' literally means to 'un-sin'. 'Oh God, get this sin out of me!' is David's cry. Then he calls out to be washed (v7), to have renewed what is broken and damaged (v8), to have his sin completely blotted out (v9).

Use whatever words it takes! Use whatever imagery helps you express your heart! But, like David, call out to the one who is waiting to forgive.

Ask for a change of heart (v10–12)

David is aware of how all too easily he could go away and do the same thing again, unless God works a change in his heart. He therefore asks (v10) for 'a pure heart' (so that he will not want to do this again) and 'a steadfast spirit' (so that he will have the strength to stay on the straight and narrow). Only God's Spirit can do this in him; and hence his cry in verse 11: 'Do not cast me from your presence or take your Holy Spirit from me.' Remember: he had seen King Saul losing God's Spirit (1 Samuel 16:14), so the fear of its possibility must have been great. Through the Spirit he knew that his joy would once again be restored (v12).

Look to the future once again

The psalm ends with David now looking ahead: to having a testimony that he can share with others (v13), to being able to praise God once again (v14–15), to being able to walk more humbly with his God out of the whole experience (v16–17), and to seeing the people of God being built up and established (v18–19), for in our blessing is their blessing.

The devil loves nothing more than trying to get us to look back at our past sin and failings. But when God has forgiven it, it is forgiven!

As far as the east is from the west,
so far has he removed our transgressions
from us.

(Psalm 103:12)

We don't need to look back to the past any more, but only to the future!

Some prayers of confession

There are many prayers of confession scattered throughout the Bible – some long, some short. Here are some of them that might help you when you need to say 'sorry' to God.

For the honour of your name, O LORD,
forgive my many, many sins.

(Psalm 25:11, NLT)

I confess my sins;
I am deeply sorry for what I have done.

(Psalm 38:18, NLT)

O LORD, have mercy on me;
heal me, for I have sinned against you.

(Psalm 41:4)

All of us have become like one who is
unclean,
and all our righteous acts are like filthy
rags;
we all shrivel up like a leaf,
and like the wind our sins sweep us
away.
No-one calls on your name
or strives to lay hold of you;
for you have hidden your face from us
and made us waste away because of our
sins.

Yet, O LORD, you are our Father.
We are the clay, you are the potter;
we are all the work of your hand.
Do not be angry beyond measure, O LORD;
do not remember our sins for ever.
Oh, look upon us we pray,
for we are all your people.

(Isaiah 64:6–9)

Return, O Israel, to the LORD your God.
Your sins have been your downfall!
Take words with you
and return to the LORD.
Say to him:
'Forgive all our sins
and receive us graciously,
that we may offer the fruit of our lips.'

(Hosea 14:1–2)

'O Lord GOD, forgive, I beg you!'

(Amos 7:2, NRSV)

'Forgive us our sins, just as we have forgiven
those who have sinned against us.'

(Matthew 6:12, NLT)

'God, have mercy on me, a sinner.'

(Luke 18:13)

See also Exodus 34:9; Numbers 14:19–20; 2 Samuel 24:10; Ezra 9:6–15; Nehemiah 1:4–11; Psalm 32:5; Daniel 9:4–19

Unconfessed sin

When we don't take God at his word, believing that he really wants to forgive our sin, but try to hide it instead, a number of things can happen.

It eats us up inside

The Bible knew all about psychology long before psychologists came onto the scene! It tells us that when we have unresolved conflicts or guilt, it eats away at us on the inside. In Psalm 32 David contrasts his experience of hiding his sin with the joy that followed when he confessed it.

Blessed is he
whose transgressions are forgiven,
whose sins are covered.
Blessed is the man
whose sin the LORD does not count
against him
and in whose spirit is no deceit.

When I kept silent,
my bones wasted away
through my groaning all day long.
For day and night
your hand was heavy upon me;
my strength was sapped
as in the heat of summer. *Selah*

Then I acknowledged my sin to you
and did not cover up my iniquity.
I said, 'I will confess
my transgressions to the LORD' –
and you forgave
the guilt of my sin. *Selah*

Therefore let everyone who is godly pray to
you
while you may be found;
surely when the mighty waters rise,
they will not reach him.
You are my hiding-place;
you will protect me from trouble

and surround me with songs of
deliverance. *Selah*
(Psalm 32:1–7)

See also Psalm 38:1–8

It hinders our prayers

Unconfessed sin hinders with our prayers. It stops us speaking boldly to God (for we are still hanging our heads in shame) and it stops God being able to answer us as he would like to.

Surely the arm of the LORD *is not too short*
to save,
nor his ear too dull to hear.
But your iniquities have separated
you from your God;
your sins have hidden his face from you,
so that he will not hear.
(Isaiah 59:1–2)

Your sins have deprived you of good.
(Jeremiah 5:25)

See also Isaiah 1:15–20; Jeremiah 11:9–11; Ezekiel 39:23

God does not look for us to be perfect before he can answer our prayers; but he does expect us to be humble and quick to confess our sins when we get things wrong. Saying 'sorry' helps to clear the spiritual airwaves.

If I had cherished sin in my heart,
the Lord would not have listened;
but God has surely listened
and heard my voice in prayer.
(Psalm 66:18–19)

A FINAL PRAYER

O Lord, the house of my soul is narrow; enlarge it, that you may enter in. It is ruinous, O repair it! It displeases your sight; I confess it, I know. But who shall cleanse it, to whom shall I cry but to you? Cleanse me from my secret faults, O Lord, and spare your servant from strange sins.

St Augustine (354–430)

CONCLUSION

While it is possible for God to 'turn a deaf ear to you' (Deuteronomy 1:45), confessing our sin is the one thing that ensures he will not.

Finally, I confessed all my sins to you
and stopped trying to hide them.
I said to myself, 'I will confess my rebellion
to the LORD.*'*
And you forgave me! All my guilt is gone.
(Psalm 32:5, NLT)

Relevance for today

Blame-shifting is still at large!

This disease is still as popular as ever and was last seen near your home! Being aware of it is the first step to dealing with it. When you feel it is taking hold in your life, resist it ruthlessly! Remember: God can't forgive blame-shifters! When you are tempted to shift the blame for something, stop and ask yourself why your are doing it.

No sin is too bad to be owned up to

We may feel our sin is bad – too bad for God to forgive – so why bother bringing it to him? No matter what our sin, there is someone who has done it before you – and who has received God's forgiveness too! Think of some in the Bible and what they had to confess: Abraham and his deceitfulness (Genesis 12:10–20; 20:1–18); Moses and his act of murder (Exodus 2:11–15); David and his adultery (Psalm 51:1–19); Peter and his outright denial of Jesus (Matthew 26:69–75); Paul and his persecution of Christians (Acts 7:58–8:1; 9:1–19; 1 Corinthians 15:9–10; Galatians 1:13–15); Zacchaeus and his fraudulent business practices (Luke 19:1–10) – the list is endless!

Only sin that is owned up to can be forgiven

God wants to forgive us; but his forgiveness is not something that drops out of the sky in some automatic way. It comes only to those who humbly seek it. Remember: the only sin that cannot be forgiven is the sin that will not be confessed. But all sin that is confessed will be forgiven!

Always start with God!

While instinctively we want to start with ourselves when we have something to confess, the Bible tells us to start with God. Recall what he is like, based on the truth of his word; for it is as we do so that we are assured that what we are about to confess will indeed be forgiven. Constantly tell yourself who he is: 'The LORD, the LORD, the compassionate and gracious God, slow to anger, abounding in love and faithfulness, maintaining love to thousands, and forgiving wickedness, rebellion and sin' (Exodus 34:6–7).

Remember the deceitfulness of sin

Sin, by its very nature, will always try to convince us that 'It wasn't too bad really' or that 'It will turn out all right' or that 'I won't do it again'. Don't believe it! Bring it to God and trust your Father's love of truth rather than sin's love of deceitfulness.

Be specific

Be specific when confessing your sin. 'He must confess in what way he has sinned' (Leviticus 5:5). Don't be vague, for that simply leaves us with an underlying lack of ease about whether we are truly forgiven or not. Tell God it all!

Chapter Three

The God Who Forgives

Forgiving our sin is not something that God does reluctantly – he delights to do it!
It is in his very nature to forgive sin whenever it is confessed.

If we confess our sins, he is faithful and just to forgive us our sins, and to cleanse us from all unrighteousness. (1 John 1:9, KJV)

Some things are just too big at times for us to get our minds around. The boundless expanse of outer space; the weird-looking creatures in the depths of the ocean; the infinite patterns of snowflakes; the amazing perfection of a baby's fingers. And the willingness of a holy God to forgive our sin! It seems beyond belief that God should be concerned with us, let alone forgive us. But that is why he is God and we are us! His very nature is compassion and forgiveness.

Why God forgives

God forgives because it is his nature to do so. Fish swim; birds fly; people breathe; rain falls; the sun shines – and God forgives! That's simply the way things are. Again and again in the Bible, the saints of old discovered – to their amazement and delight! – the truth that God revealed to Moses, that he is:

'The LORD, the LORD, the compassionate and gracious God, slow to anger, abounding in love and faithfulness, maintaining love to thousands, and forgiving wickedness, rebellion and sin.'

(Exodus 34:6–7)

See also Numbers 14:18; 2 Chronicles 30:9; Nehemiah 9:16–18; Psalm 86:5, 15; 103:8; 111:4; 145:8–9; Joel 2:13; Jonah 4:2

The basis of our confidence

It is this revelation of God himself as one who is forgiving by nature and who therefore delights to forgive that is the basis for our confidence. It is not us being presumptuous; we are simply taking God at his word.

King David captures this essential nature of the God who forgives in one of his prayers:

Praise the LORD, O my soul;
all my inmost being, praise his holy name.
Praise the LORD, O my soul,
and forget not all his benefits –
who forgives all your sins
and heals all your diseases,
who redeems your life from the pit
and crowns you with love and compassion,
who satisfies your desires with good things
so that your youth is renewed like the eagle's.

The LORD works righteousness
and justice for all the oppressed.

He made known his ways to Moses,
his deeds to the people of Israel:
The LORD is compassionate and gracious,
slow to anger, abounding in love.
He will not always accuse,
nor will he harbour his anger for ever;
he does not treat us as our sins deserve
or repay us according to our iniquities.
For as high as the heavens are above the earth,
so great is his love for those who fear him;
as far as the east is from the west,
so far has he removed our transgressions from us.
As a father has compassion on his children,
so the LORD has compassion on those who fear him;
for he knows how we are formed,
he remembers that we are dust.
As for man, his days are like grass,
he flourishes like a flower of the field;
the wind blows over it and it is gone,
and its place remembers it no more.
But from everlasting to everlasting
the LORD's love is with those who fear him,
and his righteousness with their children's children –
with those who keep his covenant
and remember to obey his precepts.

The LORD has established his throne in heaven,
and his kingdom rules over all.

Praise the LORD, you his angels,
you mighty ones who do his bidding,
who obey his word.
Praise the LORD, all his heavenly hosts,
you his servants who do his will.
Praise the LORD, all his works
everywhere in his dominion.
Praise the LORD, O my soul.

(Psalm 103:1–22)

The promises of God

Because it is in God's very nature to forgive sinners, it should not surprise us to find that he makes many promises in his word assuring us that we will be forgiven when we confess our sin. Try using some of these promises when you come to him to confess your own sin.

'Though your sins are like scarlet,
they shall be as white as snow;
though they are red as crimson,
they shall be like wool.'

(Isaiah 1:18)

'I, even I, am he who blots out
your transgressions, for my own sake,
and remembers your sins no more.'

(Isaiah 43:25)

Seek the LORD while he may be found;
call on him while he is near.
Let the wicked forsake his way
and the evil man his thoughts.
Let him turn to the LORD, and he will have mercy on him,
and to our God, for he will freely pardon.

(Isaiah 55:6–7)

If we say we have no sin, we are only fooling ourselves and refusing to accept the truth. But if we confess our sins to him, he is faithful and just to forgive us and to cleanse us from every wrong.

(1 John 1:8–9, NLT)

See also 2 Chronicles 7:14; Isaiah 44:21–22; Jeremiah 31:31–34; 33:8–9; Micah 7:18–19; Zechariah 3:4

The assurance of the cross

If God's promise alone is not enough for us, then what Jesus did on the cross should certainly settle things. For it was at the cross two thousand years ago that God himself paid the price of all our sins – past, present, and future; so the devil cannot claim that our sins have not been properly dealt with. In sending his own Son to pay the price for us, God was making it possible for sin to be paid for, once for all, absolutely and completely. Who can argue when God pays the price?

God demonstrates his own love for us in this: While we were still sinners, Christ died for us.

(Romans 5:8)

He personally carried away our sins in his own body on the cross so we can be dead to sin and live for what is right.

(1 Peter 2:24, NLT)

For Christ died for sins once for all, the righteous for the unrighteous, to bring you to God.

(1 Peter 3:18)

One of Paul's prayers reflects his amazement that God should show his love and forgiveness in such a way.

Praise be to the God and Father of our Lord Jesus Christ, who has blessed us in the heavenly realms with every spiritual blessing in Christ. For he chose us in him before the creation of the world to be holy and blameless in his sight. In love he predestined us to be adopted as his sons through Jesus Christ, in accordance with his pleasure and will – to the praise of his glorious grace, which he has freely given us in the One he loves. In him we have redemption through his blood, the forgiveness of sins, in accordance with the riches of God's grace that he lavished on us with all wisdom and understanding.

(Ephesians 1:3–8)

Who God forgives

If it is amazing to discover that God loves to forgive, then here is the next amazing thing: he loves to forgive *everybody*! Our minds can just about grasp the idea that God forgives the very religious, or those who pray a lot, or those who haven't sinned too badly. But God goes further than any of that. He tells us that he is prepared to forgive absolutely anyone for absolutely anything – as long as they are really sorry for what they have done.

Examples of those God forgave

As we dig into the Bible and discover the broad range of people that God forgave and the broad range of sins that they had committed, it really does get mind-blowing! It should certainly convince us that, if he forgave them, he can certainly forgive us. Let's look at just these examples.

King Manasseh

King Manasseh did not follow the godly path laid out by his father, King Hezekiah of Judah. Sadly he reverted to idolatry, star worship, sorcery, divination, spiritism and witchcraft; he set up pagan altars within God's temple; and, perhaps most unbelievable of all, he even sacrificed his own son to pagan gods (2 Kings 21:1–9; 2 Chronicles 33:1–9). Clearly this was a man most of us would write off. But this was a man that God forgave!

In his distress he sought the favour of the LORD his God and humbled himself greatly before the God of his fathers. And when he prayed to him, the LORD was moved by his entreaty and listened to his plea; so he brought him back to Jerusalem and to his kingdom. Then Manasseh knew that the LORD is God.

(2 Chronicles 33:12–13)

Paul

It's easy for us to forget what Paul had been like before his conversion. He led the persecution against the first Christians (Acts 9:1–2); he played a significant role in the stoning of Stephen (Acts 7:57–8:1); he was responsible for the arrest and death of other Christians (Acts 22:4–5); he attempted to destroy the church on a house-by-house basis (Acts 8:1–3). Can you imagine the horror he must have felt at all of this when he later became a Christian himself? Yet God was prepared to forgive him for it all.

For I am the least of the apostles, who am not worthy to be called an apostle, because I persecuted the church of God. But by the grace of God I am what I am, and His grace towards me was not in vain.

(1 Corinthians 15:9–10, NKJV)

Others

We could add many others, like Moses the murderer (Exodus 2:11–3:10), David the adulterer (2 Samuel 11:1–12:25), the unnamed prostitute (Luke 7:36–50), Zacchaeus the fraudulent tax collector (Luke 19:1–10). All of these had done dreadful things. But all discovered the kindness and mercy of God when they came to him with truly repentant hearts. No sinner has ever sinned too badly to be forgiven!

How God forgives

Ever felt wronged by someone, and forgiven them when they asked you to do so, but then found it difficult to 'get things back to normal' quickly? Perhaps you had to work at forgetting the issue; or perhaps your feelings needed to catch up with your will; or perhaps there was a measure of reserve in the relationship, just in case they let you down again. But God is never like that! When God forgives, he forgives!

God forgives freely

When God forgives us, he does so freely. There is no cost and no conditions to receiving the forgiveness; and no limits to its extent. God's forgiveness really is a free gift generously given.

For it is by grace you have been saved, through faith – and this not from yourselves, it is the gift of God – not by works, so that no-one can boast.

(Ephesians 2:8–9)

But when the kindness and love of God our Saviour appeared, he saved us, not because of righteous things we had done, but because of his mercy. He saved us through the washing of rebirth and renewal by the Holy Spirit, whom he poured out on us generously through Jesus Christ our Saviour, so that, having been justified by his grace, we might become heirs having the hope of eternal life.

(Titus 3:4–7)

See also Romans 3:23–24; Ephesians 1:5–6

The reason God can do this is quite simple: the price has been fully and completely paid already! It happened two thousand years ago when Jesus Christ died on the cross. All we now need to do is to believe it and to make it our own in our hearts.

Failure does not disqualify me

All across the world there are thousands of people who feel disqualified from knowing God's blessing or from ever being used by God again. The reason? At some point in their past they 'messed up'. Perhaps they experienced some moral failure; perhaps their family life fell apart; perhaps they got into a mess in business; perhaps they stole something; perhaps they ended up in trouble with the authorities. Whatever it might be, they have lived under the shadow of it ever since, feeling disqualified from being useful to God ever again and walking around as a 'second–rate' Christian.

If this is you, we've got good news for you! It's this simple message: failure does not disqualify me! If failure disqualified us from God's love and purposes, then the Bible would be a very thin book indeed. But rather, it is a very large book full of lots of people who ought to have been disqualified, but who discovered they weren't. Think of King David for example: he failed on countless occasions, as a husband, father, and king.

- Failure to deal with his sexual appetites, which led to deception and conspiracy to murder (2 Samuel 11:1–12:25)
- Failure to deal with his son Amnon's rape of Tamar, which led to endless family problems (2 Samuel 13:1–22)
- Failure to deal with his son Absalom's growing ambition, which led to civil war (2 Samuel 15–19)
- Failure in taking a census, which led to judgment on the nation (2 Samuel 24:1–25)
- Failure in clarifying his successor, which led to potential division in the nation (1 Kings 1:1–53)

These are significant failures! In fact, they are probably more significant than those of King Saul whom he replaced. So why the difference in how these two men were handled by God? The answer is simple: Saul was always a blame-shifter, whereas David confessed his sin. 'I have sinned against the LORD' was David's simple cry (2 Samuel 12:13). He was a 'man after God's heart' (1 Samuel 13:14) who sought to keep his heart soft towards God. And such a man knows that failure does not disqualify us – providing we handle the failure properly. And the way to handle failure is not to run away or excuse it or retreat into self-pity; but rather, to 'come clean', to face those we need to, and to embrace whatever process of restoration is appropriate. David did this and so discovered, like so many others in the Bible, that failure does not disqualify me.

If you feel disqualified because of something in your past, *today* can be the very day that this disqualification can end! Stop believing the lie of the devil, and start believing the truth of God. With God, your failure need never disqualify you – all you need do is repent.

God forgives fully

God does not keep a little bit of judgment in reserve, just I case he wants to change his mind about us later. Nor does he keep a memo of our past sins, just in case he needs it. When he forgives sin, he forgives it completely.

How great is God's love for all who worship him?
Greater than the distance between heaven and earth!
How far has the LORD taken our sins from us?
Further than the distance from east to west!
(Psalm 103:11–12, CEV)

What about penance?

'Penance' – the saying of prayers or the doing of good works as a precondition to receiving God's forgiveness – is something unknown in the Bible, although it developed quite early in the history of the church, and by the third century a system of public penance had developed. Penitents would often be separated from the rest of the congregation until the prescribed period of prayer, fasting, or good works that had been assigned to them was completed; only then could they receive 'absolution' (the declaration that their sins were forgiven) from the priest. This belief that sin must, at least in part, be atoned for by the sinner may seem so reasonable; but it is quite unbiblical. It contrasts strongly with the New Testament's teaching that the sacrifice of Jesus on the cross is alone sufficient for all our sins.

He offered a sacrifice once for all, when he gave himself.

(Hebrews 7:27, CEV)

Christ's death was ... a one-time event, but it was a sacrifice that took care of sins forever.

(Hebrews 9:28, The Message)

Once we understand how complete and sufficient is Christ's death for us, the need for penance becomes superfluous. Only those who doubt that his sacrifice has paid it all will feel the need to think that they must still somehow pay!

He forgave us all our sins.

(Colossians 2:13)

See also Psalm 85:1–2; 1 John 1:8–9

God forgives quickly

With God, there is no delay in forgiveness, no time lapse while he thinks about it or waits to see how we get on first. When we truly repent, God's forgiveness always comes quickly, as the thief who was crucified alongside Jesus discovered.

One of the criminals who hung there hurled insults at him: 'Aren't you the Christ? Save yourself and us!' But the other criminal rebuked him. 'Don't you fear God,' he said, 'since you are under the same sentence? We are punished justly, for we are getting what our deeds deserve. But this man has done nothing wrong.' Then he said, 'Jesus, remember me when you come into your kingdom.' Jesus answered him, 'I tell you the truth, today you will be with me in paradise.'

(Luke 23:39–43)

See also 2 Samuel 12:13; Mark 2:1–12

A FINAL PRAYER

Grant, we beseech thee, merciful Lord, to thy faithful people pardon and peace; that they may be cleansed from all their sins, and serve thee with a quiet mind; through Jesus Christ our Lord. Amen.

The Collect for the Twenty-first Sunday after Trinity, Book of Common Prayer (1662)

CONCLUSION

God delights to forgive – it is his nature! And there is nothing and no one that is not included in his offer of forgiveness.

There is no God like you. You forgive those who are guilty of sin; you don't look at the sins of your people who are left alive. You will not stay angry for ever, because you enjoy being kind.

(Micah 7:18, NCV)

Relevance for today

God's nature has not changed

'I am the LORD, and I do not change.'

(Malachi 3:6, NLT)

In the light of this, God is still the same today as when he first revealed himself to Moses as the one who is 'compassionate and gracious' and who delights to forgive 'wickedness, rebellion and sin' (Exodus 34:6–7).

God's forgiveness has not changed

If God's nature has not changed, then he is still the God who 'forgives all your sins' (Psalm 103:3). This 'all' includes all our sins – no matter what they might be or how guilty we feel because of them. God is committed to doing this for you. You only have to ask!

Failure does not disqualify me

Always remember this important truth that so many in the Bible themselves had to learn: failure does not disqualify me – providing I handle it right! Have you let failure disqualify you? If so, now's the time to put that right!

Believe God's word, not your feelings

The devil is very good at accusing God's people (e.g. Revelation 12:10). His very name, Satan, means 'adversary'. When he accuses us that our sins are not really forgiven, we need to listen to the truth of God's word rather than to the accusations of his lies or the doubts of our hearts.

When our hearts make us feel guilty, we can still have peace before God. God is greater than our hearts, and he knows everything.

(1 John 3:19–20, NCV)

Penance is unnecessary

Penance is not needed in order to win God's forgiveness. We do not need to do things in order to be forgiven; we do things only to show that we have been forgiven. God wants our hearts to respond out of gratitude, not fear.

Jesus is here!

Do you know God has forgiven you – absolutely and completely – because of what Jesus did on the cross for you? If you don't have that conviction in your heart, then don't go a step further until you have asked him to forgive you and to come and live within your life. He is here! And he will do it!

Chapter Four

Forgiven and Forgiving

God tells us that if we are going to *receive* his forgiveness, then we need to be ready to *give* ours.

'Forgive us our sins, just as we have forgiven those who sinned against us.' (Matthew 6:12, NCV)

Ever looked at a new-born baby and said to the proud parents, 'My word, he's got your eyes!' or 'She really looks like you!' It's called seeing the family likeness. And as our children get older, it's fascinating to see how that family likeness develops.

The same is true in the Christian life. When we are 'born again', we take on something of 'the family likeness'. Different ones of us reflect different aspects of our heavenly Father's character; but there are some features that he looks for in us all. High on his list is that our forgiving Father expects to see forgiving children.

Forgiving Father, forgiving children

As we have seen in previous chapters, forgiveness is part of God's very nature. As such, our forgiving Father expects to see his children reflect this characteristic. Its importance is seen in the fact that Jesus includes it in the Lord's Prayer (see Part One, Chapter 1).

Matthew's version of the prayer, reflecting the Jewish idea that sins were 'debts' to God, records this:

Forgive us our debts,
as we also have forgiven our debtors.

(Matthew 6:12)

Luke records the prayer this way:

Forgive us our sins,
for we also forgive everyone who sins against us.

(Luke 11:4)

Note that God's forgiving of us is not *conditional* on our forgiving of others, though some older English translations, such as the King James Version (and therefore the version of the Lord's Prayer that many of us have learned by heart), almost make it sound that way. In the King James translation of Matthew's version of the prayer, it reads, 'Forgive us our debts, as we forgive our debtors', making it sound as though the first action were conditional on the second. This is not the sense of the Greek however, as other versions make plain.

What Jesus is saying is something like this: 'Father, we come and ask you to forgive us our sins, because we – sinners as we are – have forgiven (Matthew), or are forgiving right now (Luke), others who have sinned against us. If we have done that, Father, how much more confident can we be that you will do the same for us!'

That's why it is so important to deal with issues of unforgiveness in our heart; for as long as they remain there, they undermine our assurance that our forgiving Father has truly forgiven us.

Dealing with issues quickly

This is why, when we are praying or worshipping, forgiveness takes priority over everything else.

'Therefore, if you are offering your gift at the altar and there remember that your brother has something against you, leave your gift there in front of the altar. First go and be reconciled to your brother; then come and offer your gift.'

(Matthew 5:23–24)

How many times have you sat through a church service, or tried to struggle through your own prayer time, with unresolved issues racing through your mind? 'What did she mean?' 'Why did he say that?' 'Didn't he know that was hurtful?' On and on our thoughts go. And what do we discover by the end of it all? That we might as well not have bothered to worship or pray, for all the good it did! So, go and sort things out first, Jesus said! Deal with issues quickly.

When we do not deal with issues promptly, they are left to fester, to the harm of both us and others. Think of how King David failed to deal with the issue when his son Amnon raped his half-sister Tamar. Rather than deal with this in the way that the law required, it was 'swept under the carpet' for everyone to trip over.

When King David heard all this, he was furious. Absalom never said a word to Amnon, either good or bad; he hated Amnon because he had disgraced his sister Tamar.

(2 Samuel 13:21–22)

In other words, everybody was mad, but nobody did anything about it! Nobody brought the issues out into the open so that they could be dealt with. And because nobody did anything about it, the whole thing got worse and worse and ultimately led to Absalom's murder of Amnon, which in turn, because this issue was not dealt with, led to Absalom's rebellion against David and civil war. What we leave in the darkness, Satan has power over; but when we bring things 'into the light', Jesus' forgiveness, healing, and power can break in (e.g. John 3:20–21; 1 John 1:5–7; 2:10–11).

Conditional forgiveness?

But what about those passages of the Bible that do seem to make our forgiveness conditional on whether we forgive others?

If you forgive those who sin against you, your heavenly Father will forgive you. But if you refuse to forgive others, your Father will not forgive your sins.

(Matthew 6:14–15, NLT)

'And when you stand praying, if you hold anything against anyone, forgive him, so that your Father in heaven may forgive you your sins.'

(Mark 11:26)

Such passages make it look like Jesus is saying that our receiving forgiveness from God is conditional on our giving forgiveness to others. But is that what he means? We believe it is not.

There is a basic principle of biblical interpretation which, put simply, says this: difficult passages must be interpreted in the light of straightforward passages, and not the other way round. Applying that principle here means this: the Bible repeatedly makes it plain that forgiveness is *God's free gift* (e.g. Romans 6:23; Ephesians 2:8), that it is based on Christ's death alone (e.g. Colossians 1:14), and that it is not something that we can in any way earn (Ephesians 2:8–9). Therefore Jesus cannot be saying here that forgiveness is either conditional or can in some ways be *earned* or *lost*, depending on our behaviour, for that would contradict the weight of teaching elsewhere. So what is he saying then?

We are struck by the fact that this teaching comes in the context, not of our acceptability before God, but of prayer. Here is a man or woman, coming to God in prayer and seeking his forgiveness. But how on earth can you expect to go away with a conviction that your own sins have been forgiven by your heavenly Father when you won't forgive others who have sinned against you? It will continue to get in the way and spoil fellowship between you and God until it is dealt with, says Jesus. So let it go! Otherwise you may well have God's 'Not guilty' as a fact, but you will certainly not have the feelings that go with it. There will be a gap between the legality and the reality.

The parable of the unmerciful servant (Matthew 18:21–35) helps to throw light on this whole matter. The servant, who had owed an enormous debt of millions of pounds, had begged for mercy and found the king writing off the entire debt. However, he then came across a fellow-servant who owed him the equivalent of just a few days' wages. Rather than treat him with the grace that he himself had just received, he threw the man into jail until the debt could be paid. But the king heard about it!

'Then the master called the servant in. "You wicked servant," he said, "I cancelled all that debt of yours because you begged me to. Shouldn't you have had mercy on your fellow-servant just as I had on you?" In anger his master turned him over to the jailers to be tortured, until he should pay back all he owed. This is how my heavenly Father will treat each of you unless you forgive your brother from your heart.'

(Matthew 18:32–35)

What Jesus is saying here is: when we don't forgive others, it is like locking ourselves in jail and throwing away the key. It is not *others* who are locked up – it is *us*! Just think about the truth of that: how many times have you felt angry towards someone for what they have done? Perhaps you have thrown mental daggers at them, or have rehearsed endless conversations of what you would like to say to them. But where did it get you? Absolutely nowhere! You were left as 'stewed up' as ever – and they hadn't even noticed! So who is in the prison, says Jesus? ... Just forgive them, and then you'll be able to come out.

James sums it up like this:

Speak and act as those who are going to be judged by the law that gives freedom, because judgment without mercy will be shown to anyone who has not been merciful. Mercy triumphs over judgment!

(James 2:12–13)

Unforgiveness hinders our prayers

Another reason we should be quick to forgive others is that unforgiveness can hinder our prayers.

In the morning, as they went along, they saw the fig-tree withered from the roots. Peter remembered and said to Jesus, 'Rabbi, look! The fig-tree you cursed has withered!' 'Have faith in God,' Jesus answered. 'I tell you the truth, if anyone says to this mountain, "Go, throw yourself into the sea," and does not doubt in his heart but believes that what he says will happen, it will be done for him. Therefore I tell you, whatever you ask for in prayer, believe that you have received it, and it will be yours. And when you stand praying, if you hold anything against anyone, forgive him, so that your Father in heaven may forgive you your sins.'

(Mark 11:20–26)

Note the context of Jesus' teaching about unforgiveness again. He is speaking about things that can hinder our faith in prayer. He says that if we don't have faith that God can deal with an issue that has arisen between me and someone else, how on earth can we have faith for the 'fig-trees' or the 'mountains' of life? Confess the unforgiveness, and then nothing will stand in the way of your boldly asking Father to do the things that are on your heart. But as long as there is unforgiveness in our hearts, our faith, and therefore our prayers, will be hindered.

Examples of those who forgave others

Joseph

When Joseph's brothers saw that their father was dead, they said, 'What if Joseph holds a grudge against us and pays us back for all the wrongs we did to him?' So they sent word to Joseph, saying, 'Your father left these instructions before he died: "This is what you are to say to Joseph: I ask you to forgive your brothers the sins and the wrongs they committed in treating you so badly." Now please forgive the sins of the servants of the God of your father.' When their message came to him, Joseph wept. His brothers then came and threw themselves down before him. 'We are your slaves,' they said. But Joseph said to them, 'Don't be afraid. Am I in the place of God? You intended to harm me, but God intended it for good to accomplish what is now being done, the saving of many lives. So then, don't be afraid. I will provide for you and your children.' And he reassured them and spoke kindly to them.

(Genesis 50:15–21)

Jesus

Jesus said, 'Father, forgive them, for they do not know what they are doing.'

(Luke 23:34)

Stephen

While they were stoning him, Stephen prayed, 'Lord Jesus, receive my spirit.' Then he fell on his knees and cried out, 'Lord, do not hold this sin against them.' When he had said this, he fell asleep.

(Acts 7:59–60)

Paul

If anyone has caused grief, he has not so much grieved me as he has grieved all of you, to some extent – not to put it too severely. The punishment inflicted on him by the majority is sufficient for him. Now instead, you ought to forgive and comfort him, so that he will not be overwhelmed by excessive sorrow. I urge you, therefore, to reaffirm your love for him. The reason I wrote to you was to see if you would stand the test and be obedient in everything. If you forgive anyone, I also forgive him. And what I have forgiven – if there was anything to forgive – I have forgiven in the sight of Christ for your sake, in order that Satan might not outwit us. For we are not unaware of his schemes.

(2 Corinthians 2:5–11)

Keep forgiving!

But how often should we forgive others? That was the question Peter asked Jesus one day. Feeling rather proud of his conclusion, Peter had tentatively suggested seven times – seven being the 'perfect' number in Judaism – expecting the Lord's approval. But then Jesus shocked him!

Then Peter came to Jesus and asked, 'Lord, how many times shall I forgive my brother when he sins against me? Up to seven times?' Jesus answered, 'I tell you, not seven times, but seventy-seven times.'

(Matthew 18:21–22)

'If your brother sins, rebuke him, and if he repents, forgive him. If he sins against you seven times in a day, and seven times comes back to you and says, "I repent," forgive him.'

(Luke 17:3)

Forgiveness is not something we can 'count'; it is the very atmosphere of the kingdom. That is why Christians are constantly urged to forgive – even when others don't forgive us.

Therefore, as God's chosen people, holy and dearly loved, clothe yourselves with compassion, kindness, humility, gentleness and patience. Bear with each other and forgive whatever grievances you may have against one another. Forgive as the Lord forgave you. And over all these virtues put on love, which binds them all together in perfect unity.

(Colossians 3:12–14)

No retaliation!

Retaliation is not an option for the Christian – despite that being what we might feel like doing at times! True forgiveness means letting things go and leaving things to God.

Do not say, 'I'll do to him as he has done to me;
I'll pay that man back for what he did.'

(Proverbs 24:29)

Do not repay anyone evil for evil. Be careful to do what is right in the eyes of everybody. If it is possible, as far as it depends on you, live at peace with everyone. Do not take revenge, my friends, but leave room for God's wrath, for it is written: 'It is mine to avenge; I will repay,' says the Lord. On the contrary: 'If your enemy is hungry, feed him; if he is thirsty, give him something to drink. In doing this, you will heap burning coals on his head.' Do not be overcome by evil, but overcome evil with good.

(Romans 12:17–21)

See also Matthew 5:38–48; Romans 12:14; 1 Corinthians 4:12–13; 1 Peter 3:9–12

Better to be kind than right

Sometimes, when we get into a disagreement with someone, it is so important to us that we are seen to be right. But for God, there is something far more important than being right; and that is being kind. The attitude that Jesus is looking for is summed up in the Sermon on the Mount:

Blessed are the poor in spirit, for theirs is the kingdom of heaven.

(Matthew 5:3)

Get rid of all bitterness, rage and anger, brawling and slander, along with every form of malice. Be kind and compassionate to one another, forgiving each other, just as in Christ God forgave you.

(Ephesians 4:31–32)

True love always forgives

One of the most beautiful passages in the New Testament is 1 Corinthians 13, where Paul sets out the pattern of true Christian love, which can provide an excellent framework for prayer.

If I speak in the tongues of men and of angels, but have not love, I am only a resounding gong or a clanging cymbal. If I have the gift of prophecy and can fathom all mysteries and all knowledge, and if I have a faith that can move mountains, but have not love, I am nothing. If I give all I possess to the poor and surrender my body to the flames, but have not love, I gain nothing.

Love is patient, love is kind. It does not envy, it does not boast, it is not proud. It is not rude, it is not self-seeking, it is not easily angered, it keeps no record of wrongs. Love does not delight in evil but rejoices with the truth. It always protects, always trusts, always hopes, always perseveres.

Love never fails. But where there are prophecies, they will cease; where there are tongues, they will be stilled; where there is knowledge, it will pass away. For we know in part and we prophesy in part, but when perfection comes, the imperfect disappears. When I was a child, I talked like a child, I thought like a child, I reasoned like a child. When I became a man, I put childish ways behind me. Now we see but a poor reflection as in a mirror; then we shall see face to face. Now I know in part; then I shall know fully, even as I am fully known.

And now these three remain: faith, hope and love. But the greatest of these is love.

(1 Corinthians 13:1–13)

Jesus went further in this area than anyone ever before or since; for not only did he call us to unconditionally love and forgive our friends, he called us to do the same with our enemies!

'You have heard that it was said, "Love your neighbour and hate your enemy." But I tell you: Love your enemies and pray for those who persecute you, that you may be sons of your Father in heaven.'

(Matthew 5:43–45)

See also Matthew 5:38–42

Love tears up the list

It is so easy to 'keep a list' of the wrongs that people have done to us. But the Bible urges us to tear it up. Here is part of 1 Corinthians 13:5 from several different English translations:

Love does not count up wrongs that have been done. (NCV)
It doesn't keep a record of wrongs that others do. (CEV)
It keeps no record of when it has been wronged. (NLT)
It does not take into account a wrong suffered. (NASB)
Love doesn't keep score of the sins of others. (The Message)

What about you? Have you got a mental list of where others have hurt you or disappointed you? If you have one, tear it up! After all, what good does it do you?

A FINAL PRAYER

O Holy and ever-blessed Lord, teach us, we beseech thee, to love one another, to exercise forbearance and forgiveness towards our enemies; to recompense no man evil for evil, but to be merciful even as thou, our Father in heaven, art merciful: that so we may continually follow after thee in all our doings, and be more and more conformed to thine image and likeness.

New Church Book of Worship (1876)

CONCLUSION

A forgiving Father produces forgiving children, who pass on to others what God has first passed on to them.

Do not repay evil with evil or insult with insult, but with blessing, because to this you were called so that you may inherit a blessing.

(1 Peter 3:9)

Relevance for today

Forgiving Father, forgiving children

Do I reflect the family likeness in this matter of forgiveness? My Father forgives freely – do I?

Dealing with issues quickly

Do I deal with issues promptly when they arise, or do I leave things and let them fester (Ephesians 4:26)?

Keeping on forgiving

Do I keep on forgiving people, even if they keep 're-offending'? Do I keep a mental list of what they did and when they did it, ready to be used against them? If I do, am I ready to tear it up today?

Not retaliating

Do I look to retaliate or 'get my own back' on people when they hurt me or let me down? Am I learning how to 'turn the other cheek' (Matthew 5:39)?

The greatest is love

Paul's 'hymn to love' in 1 Corinthians 13 is a powerful basis for prayer. Try substituting the words 'I am' wherever the words 'love is' occur – 'I am patient and kind ...' – and ask God to make you more like that.

Chapter Five

'Sorry' Means Changing

Just as words without action are meaningless, so saying 'sorry' without demonstrating it is meaningless too.

'I preached that they should repent and turn to God and prove their repentance by their deeds.' (Acts 26:20)

Change. You either love it or you hate it. Some of us, like Mike, find change exciting and we love the thought of constant change in our life. For us, keeping things the same is boring! For others, like Martin, change is far more challenging, and we prefer the steady certainty that keeps everything in its proper place in life. For us, keeping things the same is wonderful!

But whatever our natural inclinations and character, 'change' is something that God looks for in all of us. For 'change' lies at the very heart of God's call on our lives.

The challenge to change

God loves us too much to let us stay the same! He wants to see us change. In fact, if we serious about living as his children, we cannot claim to know him and yet stay the same.

Jeremiah lived in days when people's religion blinded them to the need to change. The focus of their security was the temple in Jerusalem. As long as that stood there, they felt they were safe and nothing could prevail against them. 'Wrong!' said Jeremiah, and called them to profound change in the way they were living to show they were truly sorry for their sin.

'This is what the LORD Almighty, the God of Israel, says: Reform your ways and your actions, and I will let you live in this place. Do not trust in deceptive words and say, "This is the temple of the LORD, the temple of the LORD, the temple of the LORD!" If you really change your ways and your actions and deal with each other justly, if you do not oppress the alien, the fatherless or the widow and do not shed innocent blood in this place, and if you do not follow other gods to your own harm, then I will let you live in this place, in the land I gave to your forefathers for ever and ever. But look, you are trusting in deceptive words that are worthless. Will you steal and murder, commit adultery and perjury, burn incense to Baal and follow other gods you have not known, and then come and stand before me in this house, which bears my Name, and say, "We are

safe" – safe to do all these detestable things? Has this house, which bears my Name, become a den of robbers to you? But I have been watching! declares the LORD.'

(Jeremiah 7:3–11)

Being sorry for their sin meant changing their ways and their actions (v3), not just going through religious rituals, living as though everything were fine when it wasn't. Real sorrow meant changing!

This challenge to change also lay at the heart of Jesus' message.

He called a little child and had him stand among them. And he said: 'I tell you the truth, unless you change and become like little children, you will never enter the kingdom of heaven.'

(Matthew 18:2–3)

Remember: there was religion in abundance in Jesus' day too, especially among the Pharisees. Yet, for all their religion, they had missed the heart of things. For all their fasting and pious demonstrations of remorse (e.g. Matthew 6:16), they had missed the essence of demonstrating true repentance – changing! And without changing, Jesus said, we will never get into God's kingdom.

Repent!

This call to change is what lies behind the word 'repent'. In fact, the very word means 'to change'. The main Hebrew word used in the Old Testament means 'to turn', either literally or metaphorically; but it came to be used of people turning *from* their sin (e.g. 1 Kings 8:35) and turning *to* God (e.g. 1 Kings 8:33). The Greek word used in the New Testament means 'a change of mind or heart that leads to a change of action'. Both words bring home to us the need for a change of behaviour if we have truly turned away from what is wrong and turned to God and what is right. Repentance is not just about saying 'sorry' to God, but then living life exactly the same as before. Such an attitude has more to do with feeling sorry for ourselves, or feeling sorry that we were 'caught out' in our sin, than true repentance. True repentance, the Bible tells us, means saying sorry and then living sorry; that is, changing our behaviour to show we really mean what we say.

John's call to repent

A call to repentance lay at the heart of John the Baptist's ministry. This meant, for him, an acknowledgment of one's sinfulness, expressed in baptism (Matthew 3:6; Mark 1:4–5), followed up by a change in the pattern of ordinary daily life (Matthew 3:8; Luke 3:8–14). He summed this up in one short sentence:

'Produce fruit in keeping with repentance.'

(Luke 3:8)

Jesus' call to repent

Repentance also lay at the very heart of Jesus' message, as Mark makes clear in his introductory summary of Jesus' ministry:

'The time has come,' he said. 'The kingdom of God is near. Repent and believe the good news!'

(Mark 1:15)

See also Matthew 4:17; 11:20–24; 21:31–32; Mark 6:7–12; Luke 5:31–32; 10:13–15; 11:29–32; 13:1–5; 15:3–10; 24:45–47

The church's call to repent

The call to repentance remained central as the church engaged in its ministry. In fact, Peter's first sermon climaxed in a call to repent:

Peter replied, 'Repent and be baptised, every

one of you, in the name of Jesus Christ for the forgiveness of your sins. And you will receive the gift of the Holy Spirit. The promise is for you and your children and for all who are far off – for all whom the Lord our God will call.'

(Acts 2:38–39)

See also Acts 3:19–26; 5:31; 8:22; 11:19–21; 14:14–17; 17:30; 20:21; 26:15–20

The fact that this call to 'repent' was seen, not merely as a private and inward spiritual experience, but also as a change that led to action, is demonstrated in the change in lifestyle that followed among those who responded to the message (e.g. Acts 2:44–45).

Change that costs

The sort of change that the Bible calls us to when we repent can be costly – not in the sense of it costing us to gain God's forgiveness for, as we have already seen, his forgiveness is a free gift (e.g. Ephesians 2:8–9); but in the sense of there being a cost to us in following its consequences through. Let's look at some examples.

A man called Zacchaeus

As a 'chief tax collector' (Luke 19:2), Zacchaeus had become an extremely wealthy man. The 'tax man' in those days was hated even more than nowadays! The tax system operated like this: a rich man would buy the right to gather taxes in a defined area in exchange for a fixed payment to Rome. For Rome, this had the advantage of getting all its taxes 'up front', with no delays or difficulties; but where the advantage came for the tax collector was that, having paid his money to Rome, Rome now backed him (complete with army) in his tax demands on others – with, of course, the inevitable surcharges that he put on them for his own profit. It was a veritable gold mine of a job – and no one could escape its demands! This is how Zacchaeus had spent his life, and he had clearly made a fine living from it.

But when Jesus came into Zacchaeus' life, his repentance touched his money – proof indeed that his heart had changed!

Jesus entered Jericho and was passing through. A man was there by the name of Zacchaeus; he was a chief tax collector and was wealthy. He wanted to see who Jesus was, but being a short man he could not, because of the crowd. So he ran ahead and climbed a sycamore-fig tree to see him, since Jesus was coming that way. When Jesus reached the spot, he looked up and said to him, 'Zacchaeus, come down immediately. I must stay at your house today.' So he came down at once and welcomed him gladly. All the people saw this and began to mutter, 'He has gone to be the guest of a "sinner".' But Zacchaeus stood up and said to the Lord, 'Look, Lord! Here and now I give half of my possessions to the poor, and if I have cheated anybody out of anything, I will pay back four times the amount.' Jesus said to him, 'Today salvation has come to this house, because this man, too, is a son of Abraham. For the Son of Man came to seek and to save what was lost.'

(Luke 19:1–9)

Can you imagine the cheer that must have gone up in Jericho that day! To get back four times the tax you had overpaid would have brought joy to every family in the district. Zacchaeus' action demonstrated that his repentance had gone deep and that God's forgiveness had truly flooded his heart. His 'sorry' had gone deeper than words, and it had cost him; but it had also released him!

Burning your past

In Acts 19 we read of Paul's ministry in Ephesus, where he had seen a powerful move of God's Spirit as he preached about Jesus, resulting in conversions, miracles, and people being filled with the Holy Spirit (Acts 19:1–12). The expression of the people's repentance there is very striking:

Many of those who believed now came and openly confessed their evil deeds. A number who had practised sorcery brought their scrolls together and burned them publicly. When they calculated the value of the scrolls, the total came to fifty thousand drachmas. In this way the word of the Lord spread widely and grew in power.

(Acts 19:18–20)

Parchment was extremely expensive in those days; hence, the note about its value. When we bear in mind that a drachma was the equivalent of a day's wages, we begin to see the cost to them of their repentance. Fifty thousand days' wages; or the total annual salaries of about 140 workers! That was some repentance! But they didn't stop to count the cost – literally or metaphorically. Their past needed to be burnt up; and the burning of the scrolls was what it took to do it.

Putting things right

Sometimes the cost may not be a monetary cost, but may be the cost of putting things right in our lives. In the days of Ezra and Nehemiah, at the return from the exile, there was a family cost, where men had to 'put away' unbelieving wives that they had married. (The women were not simply abandoned; they would have been supported, but they could not live as the wives of the men concerned.)

While Ezra was praying and confessing, weeping and throwing himself down before the house of God, a large crowd of Israelites – men, women and children – gathered round him. They too wept bitterly. Then Shecaniah son of Jehiel, one of the descendants of Elam, said to Ezra, 'We have been unfaithful to our God by marrying foreign women from the peoples around us. But in spite of this, there is still hope for Israel. Now let us make a covenant before our God to send away all these women and their children, in accordance with the counsel of my lord and of those who fear the commands of our God. Let it be done according to the Law.' … Then Ezra the priest stood up and said to them, 'You have been unfaithful; you have married foreign women, adding to Israel's guilt. Now make confession to the L*ORD, the God of your fathers, and do his will. Separate yourselves from the peoples around you and from your foreign wives.' The whole assembly responded with a loud voice: 'You are right! We must do as you say. But there are many people here and it is the rainy season; so we cannot stand outside. Besides, this matter cannot be taken care of in a day or two, because we have sinned greatly in this thing. Let our officials act for the whole assembly. Then let everyone in our towns who has married a foreign woman come at a set time, along with the elders and judges of each town, until the fierce anger of our God in this matter is turned away from us.'*

(Ezra 10:1–3, 10–14)

See also Nehemiah 9:1–3; 13:23–31

True repentance will sometimes mean putting things right from our past. For one couple Mike knows it meant taking back to the shop goods that they had stolen – to the complete amazement of the manager!

When the cost is too much

Sometimes the cost of repentance seems just too much for some people. Perhaps the best example in the New Testament is the rich young man. When asked by him what he must do to inherit eternal life, having assured Jesus that he had kept all the commandments, this was Jesus' reply:

'If you want to be perfect, go, sell your possessions and give to the poor, and you will have treasure in heaven. Then come, follow me.' When the young man heard this, he went away sad, because he had great wealth. Then Jesus said to his disciples, 'I tell you the truth, it is hard for a rich man to enter the kingdom of heaven.'

(Matthew 19:21–23)

The cost was too much for him. He was not yet desperate enough for God. When we are, we will bring about any change, whatever the cost.

The principle of restitution

Almost neglected in most modern law systems today, restitution was an important aspect of Old Testament law that helped people express their sorrow for what they had done wrong. Restitution meant 'making good' your offence in some tangible way to the benefit of the person you had wronged.

'When a man or woman wrongs another in any way and so is unfaithful to the LORD, that person is guilty and must confess the sin he has committed. He must make full restitution for his wrong, add one fifth to it and give it all to the person he has wronged.'

(Numbers 5:6–7)

See also Exodus 22:1–15; Leviticus 5:14–16; 6:1–7; 24:17–22

This law of restitution ensured that no one 'got away' with sin or crime, but had to fully pay back and make amends for what they had done. It is yet another expression of the principle that 'sorry' means changing.

Confessing to others

The Bible makes it clear that there is no need for us to confess our sins to a third party, whether priest or anyone else. After all, we all have free and direct access to God himself and Jesus Christ is the only 'go-between' that we need:

For there is one God, and one mediator between God and men, the man Christ Jesus.

(1 Timothy 2:5, KJV)

However, sometimes it can be helpful to unburden ourselves with someone else that we trust, and to see that, if they do not condemn us, how much more will the Lord not condemn us. Hearing someone declare scriptural promises of forgiveness over us (such as 1 John 1:8–9), can be a powerful and liberating experience.

Confess your sins to each other and pray for each other so that you may be healed. The earnest prayer of a righteous person has great power and wonderful results.

(James 5:16, NLT)

See also 2 Samuel 12:13; Luke 15:17–24

Repentance means happiness!

Part of our problem with repentance is that we think it will bring such misery. Of course, the devil does a good job here at sowing his lies. He convinces us that it will be painful, embarrassing, awkward; that we will never hear the end of it; that we would be better if we just moved on and forgot all about it; and anyway, God is loving so he doesn't really require it, does he?

Well, the truth is, repentance may feel painful at first. It may seem embarrassing to acknowledge you were wrong or to start living a different way. But, rather like a medical operation, the wounding is brief and the healing is lasting. In fact, rather than bringing sadness or embarrassment, the Bible tells us that repentance is always ultimately characterized by joy.

Sing to the LORD, you saints of his;
praise his holy name.
For his anger lasts only a moment,
but his favour lasts a lifetime;
weeping may remain for a night,
but rejoicing comes in the morning.
(Psalm 30:4–5)

'Look, here is water. Why shouldn't I be baptised?' And he gave orders to stop the chariot. Then both Philip and the eunuch went down into the water and Philip baptised him. When they came up out of the water, the Spirit of the Lord suddenly took Philip away, and the eunuch did not see him again, but went on his way rejoicing.
(Acts 8:36, 38–39)

Godly sorrow brings repentance that leads to salvation and leaves no regret, but worldly sorrow brings death.
(2 Corinthians 7:10)

A FINAL PRAYER

Good and gracious Lord, as thou givest me grace to acknowledge my sins, so give me grace in both word and heart to repent them and utterly forsake them. And forgive me those sins which my pride blinds me from discerning. Glorious God, give me thy grace to turn my back on the things of this world, and to fix my heart solely on thee.

Sir Thomas More (1478–1535),
Lord Chancellor to King Henry VIII

CONCLUSION

If we are truly sorry, it will show in our actions.

'Produce fruit in keeping with repentance.'
(Matthew 3:8)

Relevance for today

Responding to change

How do I respond to change? Whatever my natural character and inclinations, how do I respond when God challenges me, or the church that I am part of, to change?

Responding to repentance

Have I responded to God's call to me to repent? Do I know that he has completely forgiven me, and is that expressed in the different way that I now live my life?

Cutting off the past

Are there things from my past that need to be burnt – literally or metaphorically? What we cling on to has a way of clinging on to us.

Putting things right

Are there issues that I need to go and put right with people? What I leave 'swept under the carpet' will trip someone up one day – and it might be me!

Paying things back

Are there things that I need to give back or pay back that were the result of past sin? Is the Holy Spirit prompting me to take action in any area?

Confessing to others

Would confessing my sin to a trusted friend or pastor help me to accept God's forgiveness in some area where I have been struggling to receive it?

Chapter Six

Prayers of Corporate Repentance

Repentance must always be *personal*,
but it may not always be *private*.

'Come, let us return to the LORD. He has torn us to pieces but he will heal us; he has injured us but he will bind up our wounds.'
(Hosea 6:1)

A strong sense of individualism pervades life in the West. For most of us the individual is sacrosanct and, like democracy, only a hair's breadth away from God's heart. But the Bible is surprisingly quiet about such concepts. In fact, its world view is quite different from our own. For it tells us that, while God certainly deals with us as individuals, his purposes are not individualistic, but corporate. His desire is not just to save lots of individuals, but to gather 'a chosen people, a royal priesthood, a holy nation, a people belonging to God' (1 Peter 2:9). The Christian life is far more corporate than we often think; and repentance is part of this.

Corporate confession

Whatever our church tradition, we are probably accustomed to the confession of sin being a rather private matter. Even if we are led in a prayer of confession in a service, it will probably be very general; and most of us would be horrified if it were not! So it perhaps comes as a shock to discover that the Bible has much to say about corporate confession.

Confessing sin together

The Bible contains many examples of God's people coming together to confess their sin.

Then Samuel said, 'Assemble all Israel at Mizpah and I will intercede with the LORD for you.' When they had assembled at Mizpah, they drew water and poured it out before the LORD. On that day they fasted and there they confessed, 'We have sinned against the LORD.'

(1 Samuel 7:5–6)

On the twenty-fourth day of the same month, the Israelites gathered together, fasting and wearing sackcloth and having dust on their heads. Those of Israelite descent had separated themselves from all foreigners. They stood in their places and confessed their sins and the wickedness of their fathers. They stood where they were and read from the Book of the Law of the LORD their God for a quarter of the day, and spent another quarter in confession and in worshipping the LORD their God.

(Nehemiah 9:1–3)

See also Numbers 14:39–40; 21:7; Judges 10:6–16; 2 Chronicles 6:36–39; Psalm 106:6–47; Matthew 3:1–6; Luke 3:7–18; Acts 19:18–20; James 5:16

Representing others

Sometimes leaders represent God's people by leading them in confession – not as their *substitute*, but as their *representative.* Here are some varied examples:

Prophets praying for the nation

O LORD, we acknowledge our wickedness
and the guilt of our fathers;
we have indeed sinned against you.
For the sake of your name do not despise us;
do not dishonour your glorious throne.
Remember your covenant with us
and do not break it.
Do any of the worthless idols of the nations
bring rain?
Do the skies themselves send down
showers?
No, it is you, O LORD our God.
Therefore our hope is in you,
for you are the one who does all this.

(Jeremiah 14:20–22)

See also 1 Samuel 12:19; 2 Kings 19:1–4; Isaiah 59:12–15; 64:6–7; Jeremiah 3:22–25; 14:7–9; 42:1–4; Lamentations 5:1–22

Leaders praying for the nation

'O LORD, God of heaven, the great and awesome God, who keeps his covenant of love with those who love him and obey his commands, let your ear be attentive and your eyes open to hear the prayer your servant is praying before you day and night for your servants, the people of Israel. I confess the sins we Israelites, including myself and my father's house, have committed against you. We have acted very wickedly towards you. We have not obeyed the commands, decrees and laws you gave your servant Moses.

'Remember the instruction you gave your servant Moses, saying, "If you are unfaithful, I will scatter you among the nations, but if you return to me and obey my commands, then even if your exiled people are at the farthest horizon, I will gather them from there and bring them to the place I have chosen as a dwelling for my Name."

'They are your servants and your people, whom you redeemed by your great strength and your mighty hand. O Lord, let your ear be attentive to the prayer of this your servant and to the prayer of your servants who delight in revering your name. Give your servant success today by granting him favour in the presence of this man.'

(Nehemiah 1:5–11)

See also 2 Samuel 24:17; 1 Kings 8:22–53; 2 Kings 19:14–19; 2 Chronicles 30:18–20; 32:20; 33:10–13; Ezra 9:1–15; Jonah 3:6–10

Others praying for the nation

Daniel is a good example of someone who was not a leader praying for his nation, even though he was in exile in Babylon.

'O Lord, the great and awesome God, who keeps his covenant of love with all who love him and obey his commands, we have sinned and done wrong. We have been wicked and have rebelled; we have turned away from your commands and laws. We have not listened to your servants the prophets, who spoke in your name to our kings, our princes and our fathers, and to all the people of the land.

'Lord, you are righteous, but this day we are covered with shame – the men of Judah and people of Jerusalem and all Israel, both near and far, in all the countries where you

have scattered us because of our unfaithfulness to you. O LORD, we and our kings, our princes and our fathers are covered with shame because we have sinned against you. The Lord our God is merciful and forgiving, even though we have rebelled against him; we have not obeyed the LORD our God or kept the laws he gave us through his servants the prophets. All Israel has transgressed your law and turned away, refusing to obey you ...

'Now, O Lord our God, who brought your people out of Egypt with a mighty hand and who made for yourself a name that endures to this day, we have sinned, we have done wrong. O Lord, in keeping with all your righteous acts, turn away your anger and your wrath from Jerusalem, your city, your holy hill. Our sins and the iniquities of our fathers have made Jerusalem and your people an object of scorn to all those around us.

'Now, our God, hear the prayers and petitions of your servant. For your sake, O Lord, look with favour on your desolate sanctuary. Give ear, O God, and hear; open your eyes and see the desolation of the city that bears your Name. We do not make requests of you because we are righteous, but because of your great mercy. O Lord, listen! O Lord, forgive! O Lord, hear and act! For your sake, O my God, do not delay, because your city and your people bear your Name.'

(Daniel 9:4–11,15–19)

Note two key things from this prayer:

- ***He identifies himself with the nation's past sin***
  Rather than standing apart and aloof from it all, he sees himself as part of the people who had sinned against God. His confession of sin does not use the words 'they' but 'we'.
- ***He appeals to God's character and promises***
  Daniel knew that the judgment upon his nation was deserved; so his appeal is not on the basis of what they have or have not done, but on the basis of God's character and promises (v7–9, 15–19).

While our own nation is not a theocratic nation in a special relationship to God in the way that Israel was, Daniel's prayer can nevertheless provide a good model for interceding for our own nation in these days.

Identifying with others

As we have just seen, confession sometimes goes beyond simply leading others in prayer; it may include identifying oneself with those who have sinned. This is not some sort of 'mystical experience', whereby we somehow translate ourselves into the past or bring their sin into the present; it is simply an acknowledgment that we do not stand apart from others, that we are part of the same people, and that we would probably have acted exactly as they did if we had been in their place.

Ezra is a good example of someone who prayed like this. Having discovered the extent to which the Israelites had intermarried outside of God's people, in disobedience to God's law (e.g. Deuteronomy 7:1–4), he was appalled. But rather than simply condemn them, he identified himself with them. Such a gentle attitude generally attracts a better response from people than the 'finger wagging' approach. Note how, like Daniel, he constantly uses 'us' and 'our' in this prayer.

'O my God, I am too ashamed and disgraced to lift up my face to you, my God, because our sins are higher than our heads and our guilt has reached to the heavens.

From the days of our forefathers until now, our guilt has been great. Because of our sins, we and our kings and our priests have been subjected to the sword and captivity, to pillage and humiliation at the hand of foreign kings, as it is today ...

'But now O our God, what can we say after this? For we have disregarded the commands you gave through your servants the prophets when you said: "The land you are entering to possess is a land polluted by the corruption of its peoples. By their detestable practices they have filled it with their impurity from one end to the other. Therefore, do not give your daughters in marriage to their sons or take their daughters for your sons. Do not seek a treaty of friendship with them at any time, that you may be strong and eat the good things of the land and leave it to your children as an everlasting inheritance."

'What has happened to us is a result of our evil deeds and our great guilt, and yet, our God, you have punished us less than our sins have deserved and have given us a remnant like this. Shall we again break your commands and intermarry with the peoples who commit such detestable practices? Would you not be angry enough with us to destroy us, leaving us no remnant or survivor? O LORD, God of Israel, you are righteous! We are left this day as a remnant. Here we are before you in our guilt, though because of it not one of us can stand in your presence.'

(Ezra 9:6–7, 10–15)

Calling others to repent

Sometimes we find calls to corporate repentance in the Bible. The letters to the seven churches in Revelation contain examples. Sin had so invaded the life, not just of individuals, but of the church as a whole, that the whole church was called to repent.

'You have patiently suffered for me without giving up. But I have this complaint against you. You don't love me or each other as you did at first! Look how far you have fallen from your first love! Turn back to me again and work as you did at first. If you don't, I will come and remove your lampstand from its place among the churches.'

(Revelation 2:3–5, NLT)

'I know your deeds; you have a reputation of being alive, but you are dead. Wake up! Strengthen what remains and is about to die, for I have not found your deeds complete in the sight of my God. Remember, therefore, what you have received and heard; obey it, and repent. But if you do not wake up, I will come like a thief, and you will not know at what time I will come to you.'

(Revelation 3:1–3)

See also Revelation 2:14–16, 20–22; 3:14–20

Can our confession affect others?

But can we actually confess sin *on behalf of others*? Can our prayers count as though they were the prayers of others and can those prayers then be heard by God as such? Well, while we can certainly *identify ourselves with other sinners*, in the sense of not standing apart from them, acknowledging we are no better than they and that we would probably have acted as they did, the Bible doesn't seem to make provision for our *repenting on behalf of others*. The recent concept of 'identificational repentance', in which, for example, we repent for the cruelties of the Crusades in order to impact Islamic nations, would not seem to be a particularly biblical practice, though we understand its purpose. Identifying ourselves with others who have sinned may certainly be good for *us* and our humility; but there seem to be no biblical grounds for believing that it affects *others* in any way.

What about praying for the dead?

What about the practice of praying for the dead, the ultimate expression of repenting on behalf of others, whether by prayer or the lighting of candles or the saying of Masses? Does such prayer somehow 'cover' the sins they have committed or influence in any way how God deals with them? The Bible's answer is a straightforward 'No'. It tells us that each of us is responsible for our own sin.

The soul who sins is the one who will die. The son will not share the guilt of the father, nor will the father share the guilt of the son. The righteousness of the righteous man will be credited to him, and the wickedness of the wicked will be charged against him.

(Ezekiel 18:20)

We are entirely responsible for our own sins. However, the Bible is clear that the only way that our sins can be atoned for is not through our own prayers, and not through the prayers of others, but only as we personally trust in Christ to forgive us. And the only opportunity for us to do that is in this life, not the next. Jesus made this clear in the parable of the rich man and Lazarus (Luke 16:19–31), where he told us that there is 'a great chasm' between this life and the next and that there is no way in which this can be breached.

John writes in his first letter about 'a sin that leads to death', telling us not to pray about such sin (1 John 5:16). In the Catholic tradition this verse has been used to distinguish between 'venial sin' (which can be forgiven and prayed for) and 'mortal sin' (which cannot). Such an interpretation, however, is at variance with John's context and purpose, and it would involve introducing a major doctrine in what is a 'throw-away' closing line. Far more likely is that John is thinking here of sin that literally leads to death – as in the story of Ananias and Sapphira (Acts 5:1–11) and in Paul's reference to those who died because of their abuse of the Lord's Supper (1 Corinthians 11:27–30). What John is simply saying is this: there is no point praying about sin that has led to people's death. They are dead now, so it's simply too late to pray about it. Our prayers *here* cannot affect their destiny *there*.

A FINAL PRAYER

Almighty and most merciful Father; We have erred and strayed from thy ways like lost sheep. We have followed too much the devices and desires of our own hearts. We have offended against thy holy laws. We have left undone those things which we ought to have done; And we have done those things which we ought not to have done; and there is no health in us. But thou, O Lord, have mercy upon us, miserable offenders. Spare thou them, O God, which confess their faults. Restore thou them that are penitent; According to thy promises declared unto mankind in Christ Jesu our Lord. And grant, O most merciful Father, for his sake, That we may hereafter live a godly, righteous, and sober life, To the glory of thy holy Name. Amen.

General Confession,
Book of Common Prayer (1662)

CONCLUSION

God invites us to bring our repentance to him corporately at times, thereby experiencing his healing and release for us as the people of God.

'Return, faithless people; I will cure you of backsliding.' 'Yes, we will come to you, for you are the LORD our God.'

(Jeremiah 3:22)

Relevance for today

Corporate confession in our church services

Do our church services and other meetings make room for us to confess our sins to God?

Intercession for our nation

God is still looking for those who will intercede on behalf of their nation, identifying themselves with their own people and calling out to God for mercy. Do you pray for your nation in this way? Does your church?

Readiness to repent

If we get things wrong as a church at times, are we ready to acknowledge it and repent, or do we simply 'sweep things under the carpet' and try to move on as if nothing had happened?

The barrenness of 'finger-wagging'

The church too easily falls into 'wagging its finger' and 'tut-tutting' at the failures of society around us at times. How much more effective our prayers and witnessing might be if we turned our disappointments into prayer and confession on our nation's behalf.

Praying for the living not the dead

If you have been accustomed to praying for the dead (and we understand that the motive behind it is love for one you have lost), we would encourage you to stop doing it. The Bible shows us that such prayers have no effect, and we could more usefully use our energies in praying for the living. Trust the dead to God!

Chapter Seven

Will God ever say 'No'?

Despite our fears and doubts to the contrary, the Bible assures us that God will never say 'no' when we come to him in true repentance.

'The LORD your God is gracious and compassionate. He will not turn his face from you if you return to him.' (2 Chronicles 30:9)

It's amazing how hesitant we can be about asking someone for something when we think their answer might be 'no'. We put it off; we make excuses; we convince ourselves we can manage – anything, but going and asking, just in case we don't get the answer we want. Who knows – the answer might turn out to be 'yes'! But we never find out because we never ask.

Thankfully, it's not like that with God. We are not left wondering what his answer might be if we go and seek forgiveness. God has committed himself in his word to never saying 'no' to those who come to him in true repentance.

The fearful heart

One of the main reasons we hesitate asking God for his forgiveness is that we fear his answer might be 'no'. We convince ourselves we have sinned too badly or have committed that particular sin just once too often. At such times, our fearful hearts need to listen to the truth of God's word, not the lies of the devil.

So, what is the basis of our assurance that God will not say 'no'?

God's character

The first ground of assurance that God will forgive us is based on his revelation of himself as a gracious and compassionate God.

'But you are a forgiving God, gracious and compassionate, slow to anger and abounding in love.'

(Nehemiah 9:17)

Yet the LORD longs to be gracious to you;
he rises to show you compassion.
For the LORD is a God of justice.
Blessed are all who wait for him!

(Isaiah 30:18)

See also Exodus 34:6–7; 2 Kings 13:22–23; 2 Chronicles 30:6–9; Psalm 86:15; 103:8–14; 145:8–9; Isaiah 33:2; Lamentations 3:31–33; Joel 2:13; Jonah 4:2

God's heart

God has revealed himself as a God whose heart is to see everyone saved.

'Do I take any pleasure in the death of the wicked? declares the Sovereign L*ORD. Rather, am I not pleased when they turn from their ways and live?'*

(Ezekiel 18:23)

God our Saviour … desires all men to be saved and to come to the knowledge of the truth.

(1 Timothy 2:3–4, NASB)

See also Ezekiel 18:30–32; Micah 7:18; John 3:16–17; 1 Timothy 4:9–10; 2 Peter 3:9

God's patience

Unlike us, God is patient! He constantly shows his patience in his dealings with people.

'I revealed myself to those who did not ask
for me;
I was found by those who did not seek me.
To a nation that did not call on my name,
I said, "Here am I, here am I."
All day long I have held out my hands
to an obstinate people,

(Isaiah 65:1–2)

Don't you realise how kind, tolerant and patient God is with you? Or don't you care? Can't you see how kind he has been in giving you time to turn from your sin?

(Romans 2:4, NLT)

God is patient, because he wants everyone to turn from sin and no one to be lost.

(2 Peter 3:9, CEV)

See also Nehemiah 9:30–31; Isaiah 7:13; Romans 9:22–24; 1 Timothy 1:15–16; 2 Peter 3:15

God's discipline

The very fact that God brings discipline into our lives, perhaps through our circumstances, is proof that he has not washed his hands of us but is still working to bring us gently back to himself.

'You disciplined me like an unruly calf,
and I have been disciplined.
Restore me, and I will return,
because you are the L*ORD my God.*
After I strayed,
I repented;
after I came to understand,
I beat my breast.
I was ashamed and humiliated
because I bore the disgrace of my youth.'

(Jeremiah 31:18–19)

'Come, let us return to the L*ORD.*
He has torn us to pieces
but he will heal us;
he has injured us
but he will bind up our wounds.
After two days he will revive us;
on the third day he will restore us,
that we may live in his presence.

(Hosea 6:1–2)

'Those whom I love I rebuke and discipline.
So be earnest, and repent.'

(Revelation 3:19)

See also Deuteronomy 8:1–5; Job 5:17; Psalm 38:1–22; Proverbs 3:11–12; Jeremiah 46:28; Hosea 2:5–7; 1 Corinthians 11:32; Hebrews 12:5–12

God's promise

This God, so compassionate and patient, so eager to see people be saved, has promised to forgive our sin whenever we come to him and acknowledge it.

He who conceals his sins does not prosper,
but whoever confesses and renounces them
finds mercy.

(Proverbs 28:13)

If we claim to be without sin, we deceive ourselves and the truth is not in us. If we confess our sins, he is faithful and just and will forgive us our sins and purify us from all unrighteousness.

(1 John 1:8–9)

See also 2 Chronicles 7:14; Isaiah 1:18; 43:25; 55:6–7; Jeremiah 31:33–34; Micah 7:18; Acts 2:37–39; 3:19; Hebrews 10:19–23; 1 John 2:1–2

Does God ever refuse to forgive?

Having stressed how very much God wants to forgive us, we now need to turn to some difficult Bible passages; for there *are* occasions where God does *not* forgive. However, make sure you read to the end of this section before you begin to panic!

For [Manasseh] had filled Jerusalem with innocent blood, and the LORD was not willing to forgive.

(2 Kings 24:4)

And the LORD said to Hosea, 'Name your daughter Lo–ruhamah – "Not loved" – for I will no longer show love to the people of Israel or forgive them.'

(Hosea 1:6, NLT)

For if you forgive men when they sin against you, your heavenly Father will also forgive you. But if you do not forgive men their sins, your Father will not forgive your sins.

(Matthew 6:14–15)

See also Deuteronomy 29:18–20; Judges 10:11–14; 1 Samuel 15:24–26; Jeremiah 5:7–9; Lamentations 3:40–42; Amos 7:8; 8:1–7

All of this sounds rather worrying, doesn't it? But take note that God's declarations that he will not forgive come at the end of a long process of appeal to people to repent and receive his forgiveness. It is only when people persistently refuse to repent that God abandons them to the consequence of their own decisions. But even when God declares that judgment is coming, it is never to late to seek him; and if we do, God will withhold the judgment and forgive our sin (e.g. Jonah 3:1–10). God will gladly change his intent if we will change our heart.

God's declarations that he will not forgive are really designed, then, to make us throw ourselves on his mercy so that he might forgive!

Joshua said to the people, 'You are not able to serve the LORD. He is a holy God; he is a jealous God. He will not forgive your rebellion and your sins. If you forsake the LORD and serve foreign gods, he will turn and bring disaster on you and make an end of you, after he has been good to you.' But the people said to Joshua, 'No! We will serve the LORD.' Then Joshua said, 'You are witnesses against yourselves that you have chosen to serve the LORD.' 'Yes, we are witnesses,' they replied. 'Now then,' said Joshua, 'throw away the foreign gods that are among you and yield your hearts to the LORD, the God of Israel.' And the people said to Joshua, 'We will serve the LORD our God and obey him.'

(Joshua 24:19–24)

On the first day, Jonah started into the city. He proclaimed: 'Forty more days and Nineveh will be overturned.' The Ninevites believed God. They declared a fast, and all of them, from the greatest to the least, put on sackcloth. When the news reached the king of Nineveh, he rose from his throne, took off his royal robes, covered himself with sackcloth and sat down in the dust … When God saw what they did and how they turned from their evil ways, he had compassion and did not bring upon them the destruction he had threatened.

(Jonah 3:4–6, 10)

What about 'the unforgivable sin'?

In all his years' experience as a pastor, Mike has lost count of the number of times that someone has come to him, fearful they have committed 'the unforgivable sin' – and of the range of things of what they felt that sin might be. The answer he has always given is that if you are worried you might have committed the unforgivable sin, then your worry assures you that you have not!

Let's remind ourselves what Jesus said and the context in which he said it.

'I tell you the truth, all the sins and blasphemies of men will be forgiven them. But whoever blasphemes against the Holy Spirit will never be forgiven; he is guilty of an eternal sin.'

(Mark 3:28–29)

Clearly this is serious teaching, and we don't want to take away from that. But let's look at its context. In both Matthew 12:22–32 and Mark 3:20–30, which record this particular saying, the context is one of Jesus' opponents ascribing his work by the power of the Spirit to the work of the devil. In fact Mark specifically adds the explanation, 'He said this because they were saying, "He has an evil spirit."'

So, the sin in question is ascribing to the devil what Jesus is doing. Such a sin, Jesus says, can't be forgiven. Why? Because Jesus is the sole grounds of our salvation; and if we reject him, then we are rejecting the only basis on which we can be forgiven and saved. If we are worried we might have committed this sin, then we haven't committed it; for the very fact that we are worried shows that we are still sensitive to Jesus and his requirements on our life – the very opposite of those who reject his work and teaching.

Remember this: the only sin God will not forgive is the sin that will not be confessed.

But I've sinned too badly!

As we saw in Chapter 3 of this Part, no one has ever sinned too badly to be forgiven – though the devil tries to convince us otherwise. Consider some of the people who must have felt that their sin excluded them from God's purposes, but who found that God forgave them:

- **Abraham** – deceitfulness (Genesis 12:10–20; 20:1–18)
- **Moses** – murder (Exodus 2:10–15)
- **David** – adultery and conspiracy to murder (2 Samuel 11:1–12:13; Psalm 51)
- **Manasseh** – idolatry, witchcraft, and child sacrifice (2 Chronicles 33:1–13)
- **Zacchaeus** – fraudulent business practice (Luke 19:1–10)
- **Peter** – denial of Jesus (Matthew 26:69–75)
- **Paul** – persecution of Christians (Acts 7:58–8:1; 9:1–19; 22:4–5; 1 Corinthians 15:9–10; Galatians 1:13–15)

None of us should let past sin keep us from enjoying God's forgiveness and friendship. We simply need to come to him and 'come clean'.

Jesus said to them, 'It is not the healthy who need a doctor, but the sick. I have not come to call the righteous, but sinners'.

(Mark 2:17)

What hinders repentance?

The only thing that can prevent God's forgiveness, then, is our refusal to repent. So, what sort of things hinder repentance?

Pride

The whole book of Obadiah is a challenge to pride. The nation of Edom, descended from Esau, lay to the south of the Dead Sea. With its high–cliff capital, it saw itself as impregnable, in contrast to puny Israel which was currently being invaded by Babylon. But who could possibly defeat Edom? Pride comes before a fall, warns Obadiah!

'The pride of your heart has deceived you,
you who live in the clefts of the rocks
and make your home on the heights,
you who say to yourself,
"Who can bring me down to the ground?"
Though you soar like the eagle
and make your nest among the stars,
from there I will bring you down,' declares the LORD.

(Obadiah 3–4)

Pride in our own abilities, security, or reputation can still be a hindrance to our coming to seek God's forgiveness.

Unbelief

A refusal to believe in God, and in his promises or his judgment, can make us glib about dealing with our sin.

They wilfully put God to the test
By demanding the food they craved.
They spoke against God, saying,
'Can God spread a table in the desert?
When he struck the rock, water gushed out,
and streams flowed abundantly.
But can he also give us food?
Can he supply meat for his people?'
When the LORD heard them, he was very angry;
his fire broke out against Jacob,
and his wrath rose against Israel,
for they did not believe in God
or trust in his deliverance.

(Psalm 78:18–22)

The deceitfulness of sin

Sin, by its very nature, seeks to explain itself away, finding excuses for our behaviour and telling us 'it wasn't that bad really'.

See to it, brothers, that none of you has a sinful, unbelieving heart that turns away from the living God. But encourage one another daily, as long as it is called Today, so that none of you may be hardened by sin's deceitfulness.

(Hebrews 3:12–13)

Unwillingness to change

In Chapter 5 of this Part, we saw that 'sorry means changing'. An unwillingness to change will always hinder true repentance and our ability to receive God's forgiveness.

Even after this, Jeroboam did not change his evil ways, but once more appointed priests for the high places from all sorts of people. Anyone who wanted to become a priest he consecrated for the high places. This was the sin of the house of Jeroboam that led to its downfall and to its destruction from the face of the earth.

(1 Kings 13:33–34)

Can backsliders be forgiven?

Yes! The Bible has many examples of people who trusted in God, but who then drifted from him. But where there is repentance, a backslider is treated no different from anyone else.

Return, faithless people;
I will cure you of backsliding.'

'Yes, we will come to you,
for you are the LORD our God.'
(Jeremiah 3:22)

'I will save them from all their sinful backsliding, and I will cleanse them. They will be my people, and I will be their God.'
(Ezekiel 37:23)

My brothers, if one of you should wander from the truth and someone should bring him back, remember this: Whoever turns a sinner from the error of his way will save him from death and cover over a multitude of sins.
(James 5:19–20)

See also Jeremiah 14:7–9; John 21:15–19; 1 John 5:16; Revelation 3:1–3

But doesn't Hebrews chapter 6 suggest that backsliders cannot be restored? Let's look at what it says:

But what about people who turn away after they have already seen the light and have received the gift from heaven and have shared in the Holy Spirit? What about those who turn away after they have received the good message of God and the powers of the future world? There is no way to bring them back. What they are doing is the same as nailing the Son of God to a cross and insulting him in public!
(Hebrews 6:4–6, CEV)

Once again, the context is so important. Hebrews was written to people who had been Jews, but who had become Christians. Under pressure from other Jews, some of them were considering going back to their old Judaism again. Against this background the writer says: 'How on earth can you think of doing that and still hope to be saved? You left your old Judaism because you saw it was inadequate to save you – and now you want to go back and think you will still be saved? That's impossible! So keep pressing on with your Christian faith.' We must take care, then, not to misuse this passage, nor to make it contradict what the Bible says elsewhere about how God always receives those who return and repent. What may have been an early Christian hymn sums up our assurance in this area, but brings a challenge to us too:

Here is a trustworthy saying:

If we died with him,
we will also live with him;
if we endure,
we will also reign with him.
If we disown him,
he will also disown us;
if we are faithless,
he will remain faithful,
for he cannot disown himself.
(2 Timothy 2:11–13)

A FINAL PRAYER

Almighty and everlasting God, who art always more ready to hear, than we to pray, and art wont to give more than either we desire, or deserve; pour down upon us the abundance of thy mercy, forgiving us those things whereof our conscience is afraid, and giving us those good things which we are not worthy to ask, save through the merits and mediation of Jesus Christ thy Son our Lord. Amen.

The Gelasian Sacramentary
(Fifth Century)

CONCLUSION

The only sin that cannot be forgiven is the sin that will not be confessed.

Then I acknowledged my sin to you
and did not cover up my iniquity.
I said, 'I will confess
my transgressions to the LORD' –
and you forgave
the guilt of my sin.

(Psalm 32:5)

Relevance for today

The importance of listening to God not the devil

In this matter of forgiveness, listen to God's promises and not the devil's lies.

When he lies, he speaks his native language, for he is a liar and the father of lies.

(John 8:44)

The devil's accusation that God will not forgive you is a lie!

The importance of responding now!

While God is gracious, the Bible tells us not to presume on his grace, but to respond as soon as we become aware of our sin. If we keep putting it off, we harden our heart against God; and ultimately, God then has no option but to underline the choice we have made.

See to it, brothers, that none of you has a sinful, unbelieving heart that turns away from the living God. But encourage one another daily, as long as it is called Today, so that none of you may be hardened by sin's deceitfulness. We have come to share in Christ if we hold firmly till the end the confidence we had at first. As has just been said:

'Today, if you hear his voice,
do not harden your hearts
as you did in the rebellion.'

(Hebrews 3:12–15)

See also Isaiah 6:9–10; Matthew 13:14–15; Acts 28:23–29; 2 Corinthians 6:1–2

The importance of pressing on

Like a ship adrift at sea, if we stop moving ahead, we start drifting back. So, keep pressing on, the Bible encourages us, and in this way there will be no fear of your drifting away from God.

So do not throw away your confidence; it will be richly rewarded. You need to persevere so that when you have done the will of God, you will receive what he has promised. For in just a very little while,
'He who is coming will come and will not delay.
But my righteous one will live by faith.
And if he shrinks back,
I will not be pleased with him.'
But we are not of those who shrink back and are destroyed, but of those who believe and are saved.

(Hebrews 10:35–39)

See also Hosea 6:3; 1 Corinthians 10:11–13; Philippians 3:12–16; Colossians 1:21–23; Hebrews 12:1–12; 2 Peter 3:17–18

The unforgivable sin?

Remember: the only sin that cannot be forgiven is the sin that will not be confessed.

Welcome home, backslider!

If you have recognized that you have drifted away from God, why not make the decision right now to return to him? Just like the father welcomed his prodigal son (Luke 15:11–32), so your heavenly Father is ready to welcome you – no matter how far you have drifted and no matter what you have done. It is never too late to come home!

Part Five

Prayers that ask 'Why?'

Chapter One

Prayers in Confusing Times

The more we get to know God personally, the more we can be real with him and express what is in our hearts.

Pour out your heart like water in the presence of the Lord.
(Lamentations 2:19)

Some years ago Mike and Martin both had the privilege of meeting Prince Charles (although we only discovered this as this book was being compiled). For months after this meeting Mike was kicking himself for the rather inane replies he gave to the Prince's questions. The trouble was, no matter how nice Prince Charles was trying to be, Mike was overwhelmed by the occasion; and so, for once in his life, was rather lost for words. Martin, on the other hand was, surprisingly, a little more confident. When we don't really know someone, it is hard to 'be ourselves'; but once we've got to know them, it is so much easier.

That's exactly how it is with God. Once we've got to know him, we can really be ourselves and 'pour out our hearts to him' – complaints, questions, and all.

God is neither embarrassed nor angered by our questions. He is big enough to take them all on board, and he does not wants us to feel awkward in bringing them to him. In this section of the book, we are going to look at some prayers that ask God 'Why?' Some of them may sound shocking; but none of them shock God! God wants a relationship with us where we feel free to bring these sorts of questions – and where we will be ready to listen to his answers.

Let's begin by looking at some of the questions that have been asked in confusing times.

Where is God?

When life gets confusing and we don't understand what is happening, a common question is, 'Where is God in all of this?' The psalmists clearly enjoyed wonderful intimacy with God; but there were also times when they felt that God was a million miles away, and told him so!

Why, O LORD, do you stand far off?
Why do you hide yourself in times of trouble?

(Psalm 10:1)

How long will you forget me, LORD?
For ever?
How long will you hide from me?
How long must I worry
and feel sad in my heart all day?
(Psalm 13:1–2, NCV)

My God, my God, why have you forsaken me?
Why are you so far from saving me,
so far from the words of my groaning?
O my God, I cry out by day, but you do not answer,
by night, and am not silent.
(Psalm 22:1–2)

See also Job 13:24–27; Psalm 22:11; 35:22–23; 38:21–22; 42:9–10; 44:23–26; Lamentations 5:20–22

The blessing of God's absence

When we do not sense God's nearness, we can feel lonely or even fearful, but such times can, in fact, prove precious in the long run. First, they strengthen our faith, for we have to trust what at that moment we cannot 'feel'. Second, they remind us not to take God for granted, as though he were some mere friend who calls by when needed, rather than the Lord of Glory. But third, the times of God's 'absence' (though in truth, he is never absent!) make us appreciate so much more the times of his presence. And it is often when we feel that he is absent, that things that have lain hidden in our souls (like anger or fear) come to the surface. And when that happens, God can, at last, deal with them.

Remember: God is *always* there, even if we do not *feel* his presence or *see* his activity. There is nowhere his presence cannot be found (e.g. Psalm 139:7–12) and no sin his grace cannot deal with (e.g. Psalm 51:1–12); so we need not fear we have been abandoned. The secret is simply to keep waiting for him!

I am still confident of this:
I will see the goodness of the LORD
in the land of the living.
Wait for the LORD;
be strong and take heart
and wait for the LORD.
(Psalm 27:13–14)

I will wait for the LORD,
who is hiding his face from the house of Jacob.
I will put my trust in him.
(Isaiah 8:17)

See also Psalm 5:1–3; 33:20–22; 37:1–9; 38:13–15; 130:5–7; Proverbs 8:34; Isaiah 64:4; Lamentations 3:19–26; Micah 7:7; Habakkuk 2:1

Why am I experiencing troubles?

David was a man who experienced more than his fair share of troubles in life. Consider some of the things he faced:

- Being despised by his brothers (1 Samuel 17:20–29)
- Attempts made on his life by Saul (1 Samuel 18:10–15; 19:8–24; 23:7–8)
- Being on the run for years (e.g. 1 Samuel 19:11–13; 20:1; 21:10; 22:1–2)
- Having to feign insanity to preserve his life (1 Samuel 21:10–15)
- Losing his best friend Jonathan (2 Samuel 1:17–27)
- Experiencing trouble with his children (2 Samuel 13:1–39)
- Facing a rebellion led by his own son (2 Samuel 15:1–19:8)
- Facing a rebellion by the northern tribes (2 Samuel 20:1–23)
- Being responsible for judgment upon his people (2 Samuel 24:1–25)
- Experiencing frailty in his closing years (1 Kings 1:1–2)

This wide range of life's troubles underlines how David's psalms weren't written from some comfortable 'ivory tower', but out of the hard knocks of life. That's what makes them so relevant. He had experienced the hardships of life, yet had learnt how to bring them to God.

Do not withhold your mercy from me,
O LORD;
may your love and your truth always protect me.
For troubles without number surround me;
my sins have overtaken me, and I cannot see.
They are more than the hairs of my head,
and my heart fails within me.
Be pleased, O LORD, to save me;
O LORD, come quickly to help me.
May all who seek to take my life
be put to shame and confusion;
may all who desire my ruin
be turned back in disgrace.
May those who say to me, 'Aha! Aha!'
be appalled at their own shame.
But may all who seek you
rejoice and be glad in you;
may those who love your salvation always say,
'The LORD be exalted!'
Yet I am poor and needy;
may the Lord think of me.
You are my help and my deliverer;
O my God, do not delay.

(Psalm 40:11–17)

See also Exodus 5:22–23; Numbers 11:10–15; Job 14:1–22; Psalm 10:1; Lamentations 3:1–26

Honestly expressing our emotions

The psalms contain the whole range of human emotions. God wants us to be free in what we bring to him and how we bring it. He knows everything we are thinking anyway (e.g. Psalm 139:1–4); so why try to hide things from him?

Here are some of the varied emotions expressed in the psalms:

- Abandonment (e.g. Psalm 31)
- Anger (e.g. Psalm 109)
- Depression (e.g. Psalm 42)
- Desertion by God (e.g. Psalm 22)
- Discouragement (e.g. Psalm 55)
- Distress (e.g. Psalm 102)
- Doubt (e.g. Psalm 10)
- Facing old age (e.g. Psalm 71)
- Fear (e.g. Psalm 27)
- Gratitude (e.g. Psalm 116)
- Impatience (e.g. Psalm 13)
- Loneliness (e.g. Psalm 3)
- Opposition (e.g. Psalm 35)
- Persecution (e.g. Psalm 7)
- Sadness (e.g. Psalm 43)
- Sickness (e.g. Psalm 6)
- Sorrow over sin (e.g. Psalm 51)
- Stress (e.g. Psalm 142)
- Weariness (e.g. Psalm 69)

There really is a psalm for all seasons!

And yet, despite the honesty with which these people expressed their troubles to God, and despite questioning why they were facing them, they held on to an underlying confidence that, even in the midst of trouble, God would keep them safe.

The LORD is a refuge for the oppressed,
a stronghold in times of trouble.
Those who know your name will trust in you,
for you, LORD, have never forsaken those who seek you.

(Psalm 9:9–10)

God is our refuge and strength,
an ever-present help in trouble.

(Psalm 46:1)

See also Psalm 18:1–6; 27:5; 32:6–7; 37:39–40; 61:2–3; 73:25–26; 91:1–16; Lamentations 3:55–57; Nahum 1:7

Why is there suffering?

Let's face it, there is much suffering in life. But the main reason for it is – us! Suffering is often the direct result of our own *actions* (e.g. smoking leading to lung cancer), *emotions* (e.g. anger leading to violence), *selfish passions* (e.g. lust leading to adultery), *stupidity* (e.g. drinking and driving), or *lifestyle* (e.g. using fossil fuels which affect global weather). So it hardly seems fair to blame God for the things that *we* do. Having said all that, some suffering seems inexplicable: things like earthquakes, disease, freak accidents. And these have often caused people to ask God, 'Why?'

Why is my pain unending and my wound grievous and incurable?

(Jeremiah 15:18)

As Jesus was walking along, he saw a man who had been blind from birth. 'Teacher,' his disciples asked him, 'why was this man born blind? Was it a result of his own sins or those of his parents?'

(John 9:1–2, NLT)

See also Judges 6:13; 21:3; Job 3:20–23; Luke 13:1–5

The Bible tells us that all suffering is rooted, ultimately, in human sin that has somehow invaded the very fabric of life (e.g. Romans 5:12) and creation itself (e.g. Romans 8:19–22). Yet God does not stand indifferent to our suffering: he comes and strengthens us in it (e.g. Psalm 86:15–17), identifies with us in it through his Son's suffering on the cross (e.g. Hebrews 2:9), and promises to rid the world of it when Jesus returns (e.g. Revelation 21:1–4).

Keeping focused on God

Through all our sufferings, the Bible encourages us to keep focused on God and his promises.

Cast your cares on the LORD and he will sustain you.

(Psalm 55:22)

My comfort in my suffering is this: Your promise preserves my life.

(Psalm 119:50)

At the end of the day, where else can we turn, but to God? When we have asked all our questions and expressed all our anger, what can we do but say, 'God I will continue to trust you; for life is better with you than without you'? Having asked all his questions and expressed all his longings, the writer of Psalm 42 ends on this positive note of turning again to God:

Why are you downcast, O my soul?
Why so disturbed within me?
Put your hope in God,
for I will yet praise him,
my Saviour and my God.

(Psalm 42:11)

Seeing good coming out of suffering

But suffering can have its good side. King Hezekiah was one who looked back and saw that positive benefit had come out of his suffering for him.

I said, 'In the prime of my life
must I go through the gates of death
and be robbed of the rest of my years?'
I said, I will not again see the LORD,
the LORD, in the land of the living;
no longer will I look on mankind,
or be with those who now dwell in this world.
Like a shepherd's tent my house
has been pulled down and taken from me.
Like a weaver I have rolled up my life,
and he has cut me off from the loom;
day and night you made an end of me.

I waited patiently till dawn,
but like a lion he broke all my bones;
day and night you made an end of me.
I cried like a swift or thrush,
I moaned like a mourning dove.
My eyes grew weak as I looked to the heavens.
I am troubled; O Lord, come to my aid!'
But what can I say?
He has spoken to me, and he himself has done this.
I will walk humbly all my years
because of this anguish of my soul.
Lord, by such things men live;
and my spirit finds life in them too.
You restored me to health
and let me live.
Surely it was for my benefit
that I suffered such anguish.
In your love you kept me
from the pit of destruction;
you have put all my sins
behind your back.

(Isaiah 38:10–17)

See also Genesis 50:20; Romans 5:1–5; 8:28–39; 2 Corinthians 1:8–11; Hebrews 12:11; 1 Peter 1:3–9; 4:12–19

Why do the wicked prosper?

One of the big questions that people often ask is: Why do the wicked always seem to 'get away with it'? Jeremiah was one who asked this question; and such was his relationship with God, that his questions and complaints seem almost blasphemous at times!

You are always righteous, O LORD,
when I bring a case before you.
Yet I would speak with you about your justice:
Why does the way of the wicked prosper?
Why do all the faithless live at ease?
You have planted them, and they have taken root;
they grow and bear fruit.
You are always on their lips
but far from their hearts.
Yet you know me, O LORD;
you see me and test my thoughts about you.
Drag them off like sheep to be butchered!
Set them apart for the day of slaughter!

(Jeremiah 12:1–3)

See also Job 10:3; 21:7–21; Psalm 73:1–12; 94:1–7; Habakkuk 1:1–4; Malachi 3:14–15

The strong feelings we often find in such prayers ('Drag them off like sheep to be butchered!') have sometimes troubled Christians. How can such a prayer be in the Bible? Well, remember this: just because that's how Jeremiah felt doesn't mean it's how God felt! These were Jeremiah's words, not God's words; but they are recorded for us in the Bible to bring home that it is all right to be so honest with God. Of course, when we have 'got it all off our chest', we then need to listen to what God has to say! There will no doubt be attitudes in us that need to change; but God also promises us that the wicked will not get away with their wickedness for ever. Ultimately, they will be punished for it, as surely as the righteous will be rewarded.

Do not fret because of evil men
or be envious of those who do wrong;
for like the grass they will soon wither,
like green plants they will soon die away.

Trust in the LORD and do good;
dwell in the land and enjoy safe pasture.
Delight yourself in the LORD
and he will give you the desires of your heart.
Commit your way to the LORD;
trust in him and he will do this:
He will make your righteousness shine like the dawn,
the justice of your cause like the noonday sun.

Be still before the LORD and wait patiently
for him;
do not fret when men succeed in their
ways,
when they carry out their wicked schemes.

Refrain from anger and turn from wrath;
do not fret – it leads only to evil.
For evil men will be cut off,
but those who hope in the LORD will
inherit the land.

(Psalm 37:1–9)

See also Psalm 1:1–6; 37:10–40; 49:13–20; 73:1–28; Proverbs 10:9, 23–25; 11:18–21; Ecclesiastes 8:11–13; Romans 2:5–11

Why was I born?

Job is a good example of someone bringing his honest questions and complaints to God. He had sought to live a godly life (Job 1:1–5, 8); but what had he got out of it? Everything was now crumbling around him. His cattle and camels had been stolen, his sheep struck by lightning, and his children killed in a freak disaster (Job 1:13–19). He had contracted some strange disease: his body was covered in painful sores (2:7; 7:5), his appearance so revolted others (2:11–12; 19:19–20) that they avoided him (19:13–16), his breath stank (19:17), he had lost weight (17:7; 19:20), he had dreadful nightmares (7:13–15), he was feverish (30:30) and in constant pain (30:16–17). Little wonder he had some questions for God! And little wonder that he wished he had never been born:

'May the day of my birth perish,
and the night it was said, "A boy is
born!"
That day – may it turn to darkness;
may God above not care about it;
may no light shine upon it.
May darkness and deep shadow claim it
once more;
may a cloud settle over it;
may blackness overwhelm its light.
That night – may thick darkness seize it;
may it not be included among the days
of the year
nor be entered in any of the months.
May that night be barren;
may no shout of joy be heard in it.
May those who curse days curse that day,
those who are ready to rouse Leviathan.
May its morning stars become dark;
may it wait for daylight in vain
and not see the first rays of dawn,
for it did not shut the doors of the womb
on me
to hide trouble from my eyes.
'Why did I not perish at birth,
and die as I came from the womb?
Why were there knees to receive me
and breasts that I might be nursed?
For now I would be lying down in peace;
I would be asleep and at rest
with kings and counsellors of the earth,
who built for themselves places now lying
in ruins,
with rulers who had gold,
who filled their houses with silver.
Or why was I not hidden in the ground
like a stillborn child,
like an infant who never saw the light of
day?
There the wicked cease from turmoil,
and there the weary are at rest.

(Job 3:3–17)

See also Job 10:18–19; Ecclesiastes 4:1–3; 6:3–6; Jeremiah 20:14–18

Here is honest praying! Yet in all his perplexity, Job never did what his wife urged him to do – 'Curse God and die' (Job 2:9). He held on in faith until God revealed himself wonderfully to him (Job 38:1–41:34). Interestingly, Job never did get the answers to his questions! But once we have met with God afresh, it is enough. His presence *is* the answer.

A FINAL PRAYER

We beseech thee, Master,
to be our helper and protector.
Save the afflicted among us;
have mercy on the lowly;
raise up the fallen;
appear to the needy;
heal the ungodly;
restore the wanderers of thy people;
feed the hungry;
ransom our prisoners;
raise up the sick;
comfort the fainthearted.

Clement of Rome (died c. AD 100),
Bishop of Rome

CONCLUSION

There are often confusing times in life; but God invites us to bring all our questions to him.

I am full of confusion; therefore see thou mine affliction.

(Job 10:15, KJV)

Relevance for today

Pour out your heart

God invites us to 'pour out your heart like water in the presence of the Lord' (Lamentations 2:19). Don't hold things back; tell him what you are thinking and how you are feeling. He is big enough to handle it!

The value of God's 'absence'

The times of God's 'absence' make us appreciate the times of God's presence. He has not abandoned us; he is simply giving us opportunity to see more clearly the things that matter.

Tell God everything

If you are holding on to things that you feel you can't express to God – don't! Tell him everything – he will not be shocked.

Ask the questions

Real faith is not afraid to ask God the hard questions of life. He may not always answer your 'Why?', but he will certainly come and meet with you.

'I wish I'd never been born'

If you are ever tempted to say this, remember that your birth was not an accident, but the specific plan of God. He made you, loves you, and has a purpose for you. Take encouragement from Psalm 139.

Chapter Two

Prayers of Complaint

God welcomes our complaints –
providing we complain in the right way!

I pour out my complaint before him; before him I tell my trouble.
(Psalm 142:2)

Historically, the British haven't been very good at complaining – or at least, complaining in the right way. Our complaints generally are *about* people rather than *to* people. In fact, the traditional British method of complaining is to go to the local pub, find some listening ears, and 'get it all off your chest'.

The trouble is, that's how we can be with God, whatever our nationality. We tend to complain *about* him, rather than *to* him. God hates the former, but gladly welcomes the latter!

Complain to God!

For many, the idea of complaining to God seems inappropriate, if not downright blasphemous. After all, doesn't the Bible tell us of some who complained and came under God's judgment?

Now the people complained about their hardships in the hearing of the LORD, and when he heard them his anger was aroused. Then fire from the LORD burned among them and consumed some of the outskirts of the camp.

(Numbers 11:1)

See also Exodus 16:1–12; Numbers 14:1–4, 20–35; 16:1–35; 20:1–13; Psalm 106:24–27; 1 Corinthians 10:1–13

This makes complaining look rather dangerous, doesn't it? And yet, the Bible contains so many prayers of complaint; and those who prayed them got away with it! So, what makes the difference? The difference concerns *how* we complain. In the examples above, the Israelites complained about their circumstances, blaming Moses (e.g. Exodus 16:2; 17:3; Numbers 20:2–5); but actually, they were really complaining against God (Exodus 16:8).

Our complaints should not be *about* God, but *to* God. This is what makes the difference. Don't tell others – tell God! When we complain to others, we are really saying, 'God, *you* don't know what you are doing!' But when we complain to *God*, we're saying, 'God, *I* don't know what you are doing; but I really would like to!'

Let's look at some 'godly complaints' in the Bible.

Complaints about what God does

How often have you said, 'It's not fair'? Perhaps something hadn't worked out as you wanted, or you got less than you felt you deserved; and so your cry of 'unfair!' went up. The trouble is, we bring that attitude into our thinking about God. So when he does something how we would not have done it, we cry, 'Unfair!' And that's where our problem lies: for God *isn't* fair; he is *more than fair.* That's what the Bible means by *grace.*

Jonah appreciated God's grace – as long as it was for him and his fellow Israelites. But he couldn't cope with the idea of God blessing others. At the time when Amos and Hosea were prophesying to Israel that unless they repented judgment would come in the form of Assyria, God called Jonah to go to Nineveh (Assyria's capital) to call them to repent too (Jonah 1:1–2). Jonah ran in the opposite direction (1:3); not because he was afraid, but because he thought God might be gracious and the Assyrians might actually repent (4:1–2). After a slight detour via the belly of a great fish, where he learned his lesson (1:17–2:10), Jonah eventually went to Nineveh and proclaimed his message of judgment. To his surprise, and displeasure, they repented (3:3–9).

When God saw what they did and how they turned from their evil ways, he had compassion and did not bring upon them the destruction he had threatened. But Jonah was greatly displeased and became angry. He prayed to the LORD, 'O LORD, is this not what I said when I was still at home? That is why I was so quick to flee to Tarshish. I knew that you are a gracious and compassionate God, slow to anger and abounding in love, a God who relents from sending calamity. Now, O LORD, take away my life, for it is better for me to die than to live.'

(Jonah 3:10 – 4:3)

The problem was, Jonah didn't want Nineveh saved; he wanted it destroyed. But God hadn't gone along with Jonah's plan, because God isn't like that. Deep down, Jonah knew this – and didn't like it! So much so, he thought he'd be better off dead (4:3, 9). Jonah's self-pity and self-concern blinded him to what God is really like. Yet God allowed him to express his complaint to him and then gently showed him why he was wrong (4:5–11). God didn't give Jonah what he wanted; but he did give him what he needed.

When we complain about what God does or doesn't do, it is often because we are narrow and mean-hearted. But God can change this if we honestly come to him.

Complaints about how God works

Not only is it sometimes hard to see what God is doing, it is hard to see *how* he is doing it. In fact, it can even seem like God is making things worse! Let's look at an occasion when Moses felt like that.

When God sent Moses to demand freedom for the Israelites, Pharaoh responded by increasing their burdens (Exodus 5:1–18), which didn't bless the people (5:19–21). Moses, bruised from the lashing of their tongues, took his complaint to God.

Moses returned to the LORD and said, 'O Lord, why have you brought trouble upon this people? Is this why you sent me? Ever since I went to Pharaoh to speak in your name, he has brought trouble upon this people, and you have not rescued your people at all.'

(Exodus 5:22–23)

'You've made things worse!' was the heart of Moses' prayer. But God didn't chastise him for it. He understood that it came, not out of self-righteousness, but out of a heart for the people. God therefore welcomed his complaint. He reassured Moses that they would indeed see God's power (Exodus 6:1), reminded him of the revelation he had received (6:2–4), and repeated his promise that they would be freed (6:5–6) and brought to the promised land (6:7–8).

We sometimes complain about how God works because we don't see things from his viewpoint. That's why God brought this challenge through Isaiah:

'For my thoughts are not your thoughts,
neither are your ways my ways,' declares
the LORD.
'As the heavens are higher than the earth,
so are my ways higher than your ways
and my thoughts than your thoughts.
As the rain and the snow
come down from heaven,
and do not return to it
without watering the earth
and making it bud and flourish,
so that it yields seed for the sower and
bread for the eater,
so is my word that goes out from my
mouth:
It will not return to me empty,
but will accomplish what I desire
and achieve the purpose for which I
sent it.'

(Isaiah 55:8–11)

When things don't work out as we had hoped, by all means let us bring our complaints to God. But we also need to listen to him, trusting that his ways are higher than ours and that he always, ultimately, 'causes everything to work together for the good of those who love God' (Romans 8:28, NLT).

Complaints about how God deals with us

Jeremiah exercised a difficult ministry. A prophet for some forty years in the period leading up to the Babylonian invasion of Judah in 586 BC, his message – that Jerusalem would be destroyed unless God's people repented – was bitterly opposed by his fellow-countrymen. He had nowhere to turn but to God. In what have been called his 'Confessions' (though they might be better described as 'Straight talks with God'!), Jeremiah laid bare his feelings before God (see Jeremiah 11:18–12:4; 15:10–21; 17:14–18; 18:19–23; 20:7–18). He was clearly a man of strong emotions: he wept much (9:1; 13:17), despaired of finding comfort (8:18–22), cursed the day he was born (15:10; 20:14–18), prayed for judgment upon his opponents (18:21–23), and frequently wanted to give up his prophetic ministry but couldn't (20:9).

Let's look at one of his complaints. Having been beaten and put into the stocks because of his prophecies, he complained bitterly to God upon his release, even accusing God of deceiving him.

O LORD, you deceived me, and I was
deceived;
you overpowered me and prevailed.
I am ridiculed all day long;
everyone mocks me.
Whenever I speak, I cry out
proclaiming violence and destruction.
So the word of the LORD has brought me
insult and reproach all day long.
But if I say, 'I will not mention him
or speak any more in his name,'
his word is in my heart like a fire,
a fire shut up in my bones.
I am weary of holding it in;
indeed, I cannot.

(Jeremiah 20:7–9)

What he was saying was, 'This just isn't fair, God! I didn't sign up for all this; but nor can I get out of it now! You've deceived me!' But then, in the midst of his complaint, he has a surge of faith:

But the LORD is with me like a mighty
warrior;
so my persecutors will stumble and not
prevail.
They will fail and be thoroughly
disgraced;
their dishonour will never be forgotten.
O LORD Almighty, you who examine the
righteous
and probe the heart and mind,
let me see your vengeance upon them,
for to you I have committed my cause.
Sing to the LORD!
Give praise to the LORD!
He rescues the life of the needy
from the hands of the wicked.

(Jeremiah 20:11–13)

But no sooner has he declared this than he curses the day he was born (20:14–18)! Isn't this so true to life, especially in stressful times? Don't our feelings and emotions go up and down and fly off in all directions?

Note two important things from Jeremiah's prayers. First, he knew he could be utterly honest with God. All his emotions, questions, and frustrations were brought before God without embarrassment. Second, his *decisions* weren't governed by his *emotions.* What he *did* and what he *felt like doing* weren't necessarily the same. Despite everything he was experiencing, Jeremiah 'got things off his chest' and then pressed on with declaring God's word.

His complaints received a variety of answers from God:

- It's going to get worse! (12:5)
- I'll deliver you (15:11)
- Repent, Jeremiah! (15:19–21)
- Just get on with your ministry! (17:19–20; 19:1–6)

God has no stock answers. But if we honestly bring our complaints to him, he meets us at our point of need – some way or other!

Complaints about things not working out

Some people's complaints were based on things not 'working out'. Let's look at two examples where this happened, but for quite different reasons.

Hitting breaking point

Let's return to Moses, now on his journey to the promised land. Life in the desert was hard, and it wasn't long before the Israelites were grumbling and wishing they were back in Egypt (Numbers 11:1–6). (It's amazing what short memories people have, isn't it?) Eventually Moses had had enough and took his complaint to God.

He asked the LORD, 'Why have you brought this trouble on your servant? What have I done to displease you that you put the burden of all these people on me? Did I conceive all these people? Did I give them birth? Why do you tell me to carry them in my arms, as a nurse carries an infant, to the land you promised on oath to their forefathers? Where can I get meat for all these people? They keep wailing to me, "Give us meat to eat!" I cannot carry all these people by myself; the burden is too heavy for me. If this is how you are going to treat me, put me to death right now – if I have found favour in your eyes – and do not let me face my own ruin.'

(Numbers 11:11–15)

Things certainly weren't working out

as Moses had imagined and he couldn't take any more. His complaint is very forthright; but note how God does not rebuke him. God recognized that this was the cry of a man who had come to breaking point. God's response was to provide a very practical solution. Moses had made himself almost indispensable; so God simply told him to share the load around a little (Numbers 11:16–30). Sometimes the solution to a spiritual problem can be very practical! – just as he had already told him to do so (Exodus 18:1–27).

Hiding sin

Our second example of things not working out as expected happened for very different reasons. The Israelites had just experienced a miraculous victory at Jericho (Joshua 6:1–27) and were now heading west to take Ai in the Judean foothills. But suddenly, everything went terribly wrong. Rather than winning another victory, they experienced a dramatic defeat (Joshua 7:2–5). Joshua was quick to bring his complaint to God.

And Joshua said, 'Ah, Sovereign LORD, why did you ever bring this people across the Jordan to deliver us into the hands of the Amorites to destroy us? If only we had been content to stay on the other side of the Jordan! O Lord, what can I say, now that Israel has been routed by its enemies? The Canaanites and the other people of the country will hear about this and they will surround us and wipe out our name from the earth. What then will you do for your own great name?'

(Joshua 7:7–9)

Once again, God did not rebuke this complaint, for he understood it came out of a mixture of fear (v5), confusion (v7) and concern for God's honour (v8–9). But God's reply on this occasion came in the form of a challenge.

The LORD said to Joshua, 'Stand up! What are you doing down on your face? Israel has sinned; they have violated my covenant, which I commanded them to keep. They have taken some of the devoted things; they have stolen, they have lied, they have put them with their own possessions. That is why the Israelites cannot stand against their enemies; they turn their backs and run because they have been made liable to destruction. I will not be with you any more unless you destroy whatever among you is devoted to destruction.'

(Joshua 7:10–12)

Sometimes our straight questions and complaints will meet with straight answers from God! If we respond positively, as Joshua did (7:16–26), God will redeem the mess we have got into, and things will begin to work out again.

Complaints about what God allows

Our final type of complaint concerns challenges to God about some of the things he allows to happen.

Complaints about tragedies

When tragedy occurs, a frequent human response is to question God about it.

Some time later the son of the woman who owned the house became ill. He grew worse and worse, and finally stopped breathing. She said to Elijah, 'What do you have against me, man of God? Did you come to remind me of my sin and kill my son?' 'Give me your son,' Elijah replied. He took him from her arms, carried him to the upper room where he was staying, and laid him on his bed. Then he cried out to the LORD, 'O LORD my God, have you brought tragedy also upon this widow I am staying with, by causing her son to die?' Then he stretched himself out on the boy three times and cried to the LORD, 'O

LORD my God, let this boy's life return to him!' The LORD heard Elijah's cry, and the boy's life returned to him, and he lived.
(1 Kings 17:17–22)

'Is it nothing to you, all you who pass by?
Look around and see.
Is any suffering like my suffering
that was inflicted on me,
that the LORD brought on me
in the day of his fierce anger?'
(Lamentations 1:12)

'Lord,' Martha said to Jesus, 'if you had been here, my brother would not have died.'
(John 11:21)

Complaints about evil

Another common question is, 'Why is there so much evil?' Habakkuk asked God some very frank questions about this:

'Why does evil go unpunished?'

Habakkuk couldn't work out why God wasn't punishing evildoing in Judah. Why didn't he do something?

How long, O LORD, must I call for help,
but you do not listen?
Or cry out to you, 'Violence!'
but you do not save?
Why do you make me look at injustice?
Why do you tolerate wrong?
Destruction and violence are before me;
there is strife, and conflict abounds.
Therefore the law is paralysed,
and justice never prevails.
The wicked hem in the righteous,
so that justice is perverted.
(Habakkuk 1:2–4)

How can a holy God use a wicked nation?

If Habakkuk couldn't understand why God wasn't punishing wickedness in Judah, he certainly couldn't understand how God could then say he would punish that wickedness, but through an even more wicked nation, Babylon.

O LORD, are you not from everlasting?
My God, my Holy One, we will not die.
O LORD, you have appointed them to
execute judgment;
O Rock, you have ordained them to punish.
Your eyes are too pure to look on evil;
you cannot tolerate wrong.
Why then do you tolerate the treacherous?
Why are you silent while the wicked
swallow up those more righteous than
themselves?
(Habakkuk 1:12–13)

God's answers

God always has an answer to such complaints, though not always ones we would want. His answer to Habakkuk was that he would just have to wait and see.

Then the LORD replied:
'Write down the revelation
and make it plain on tablets
so that a herald may run with it.
For the revelation awaits an
appointed time;
it speaks of the end
and will not prove false.
Though it linger, wait for it;
it will certainly come and will not
delay.'
(Habakkuk 2:2–3)

Sometimes, 'waiting and seeing' is all we can do. But ultimately, God's purposes will be fulfilled and 'the earth will be filled with the knowledge of the glory of the LORD,° as the waters cover the sea' (Habakkuk 2:14).

A FINAL PRAYER

God of love, whose compassion never fails; we bring before thee the troubles and perils of people and nations, the sighing of prisoners and captives, the sorrows of the bereaved, the necessities of strangers, the helplessness of the weak, the despondency of the weary, the failing powers of the aged. O Lord, draw near to each; for the sake of Jesus Christ our Lord.

St Anselm (1033–1109),
theologian and philosopher

CONCLUSION

God is big enough to handle our complaints; he simply wants us to bring them to him, not to others.

'I will give free rein to my complaint
and speak out in the bitterness of my soul.'
(Job 10:1)

Relevance for today

Complain to God, not to others

Make your complaints *to* God not *about* God. He's big enough to cope!

Don't cover things up

Don't pretend everything is fine when it isn't, or put on a smile when you can't (Job 9:27–28). God wants you to be honest with him.

Don't let your emotions rule your decisions

Jeremiah was an emotional man who expressed himself frankly to God; but having done so, he then 'got on with it'. His decisions weren't determined by his emotions; don't let yours be.

Be ready for straight answers

God is happy to hear our straight complaints; are we happy to hear his straight answers?

Complain – but remember!

Don't let your complaints fail to take account of what God is like.

Why do you say, O Jacob,
and complain, O Israel,
'My way is hidden from the LORD;
my cause is disregarded by my God'?
Do you not know?
Have you not heard?
The LORD is the everlasting God,
the Creator of the ends of the earth.
He will not grow tired or weary,
and his understanding no-one can fathom.
He gives strength to the weary
and increases the power of the weak.
Even youths grow tired and weary,
and young men stumble and fall;
but those who hope in the LORD
will renew their strength.
They will soar on wings like eagles;
they will run and not grow weary,
they will walk and not be faint.
(Isaiah 40:27–31)

Chapter Three

Prayers in Dark Days

Dark days come to all of us at times; but as we turn to God in them, we can find his strength.

We were crushed and completely overwhelmed,
and we thought we would never live through it.
In fact, we expected to die. But as a result,
we learned not to rely on ourselves,
but on God who can raise the dead.
(2 Corinthians 1:8–9, NLT)

Someone once said, 'An optimist is someone who has had never had much experience'. Of course, he was probably a pessimist! What this saying brings home is that, for everyone, life has its difficulties. But sometimes those difficulties seem almost overwhelming. The days are dark and there seems little hope breaking through. How should we pray at such times? 'Honestly', God tells us!

Prayers in times of depression

Depression, that feeling of deep sadness and an inability to do anything about it, was experienced by a number of people in the Bible. Perhaps one of the best-known examples is Elijah.

Elijah: from mountaintop to valley

Elijah had just had an exciting experience. He had challenged the prophets of Baal to a contest on Mount Carmel to determine who really was God (1 Kings 18:20–24). Despite their frenzied praying (18: 26–29), 'there was no response, no-one answered, no-one paid attention' (18:29). Elijah had then built his altar to the Lord, prayed to him, and fire fell from heaven (18:30–39). The people had repented (v39), the false prophets had been slain (v40), and King Ahab had been challenged (v41). Elijah's emotions were running high. But he had not counted on the wicked Queen Jezebel, whose threats suddenly threw him into a valley of despair.

Now Ahab told Jezebel everything Elijah had done and how he had killed all the prophets with the sword. So Jezebel sent a messenger to Elijah to say, 'May the gods deal with me, be it ever so severely, if by this time tomorrow I do not make your life like that of one of them.' Elijah was afraid and ran for his life. When he came to Beersheba in Judah, he left his servant there, while he himself went a day's journey into the desert. He came to a broom tree, sat down under it and prayed that he might die. 'I have had enough, LORD,' he said. 'Take my life; I am no better than my ancestors.' Then he lay down under the tree and fell asleep.

(1 Kings 19:1–5)

This incident illustrates how there is often no rational explanation for depression. Elijah had just seen God's power demonstrated in an amazing way. But now, after just one threat, he plummets into the depth of despondency.

God does not rebuke Elijah for his depression, however; and nor will he rebuke us. In fact, note the tender way God deals with him:

- He gives him sleep (19:5–6)
- He gets him to eat properly (19:5–8)
- He encourages him to express what he's struggling with (19:9–10)
- He meets with him gently (19:11–13)
- He lets him express his self-pity (19:14)
- He gets him to do something practical (19:15–16)
- He gives him a friend and successor in Elisha (19:16)
- He reassures him he is not alone (19:18)

There was a lot of self-pity in Elijah *before* his depression developed (1 Kings 18:22), not just during it (19:10). (Sometimes depression simply highlights what has always been there!) But God did not rebuke Elijah for it (a good 'telling off' rarely helps at such times); he simply drew him out of it step by step. And God will do the same for us.

Some causes of depression

While, as the example of Elijah shows us, there might be no obvious cause of depression, there sometimes can be. Wherever we can, we should deal with the issue so that the darkness can lift. Causes of depression can include:

- Circumstances (e.g. Job 9:21–35; Joel 1:10–12; 2 Corinthians 1:8–10)
- Closeness to death (e.g. Psalm 88:1–18; Acts 27:20)
- Disobedience (e.g. Deuteronomy 28:58–68)
- Fear of others (e.g. 1 Kings 19:1–3)
- Hope constantly deferred (e.g. Proverbs 13:12)
- Illness (e.g. Psalm 6:1–10; 31:9–12; Isaiah 38:1–3)
- Losing a sense of God's presence (e.g. Psalm 22:1–2)
- Responsibilities that feel too heavy (e.g. Numbers 11:10–15)
- Seeing life as meaningless (e.g. Ecclesiastes 2:17–23)
- Sin (e.g. Psalm 25:16–18; Ezekiel 7:23–27; Matthew 27:3–5)

Others who experienced depression

When we feel depressed, we should take encouragement from the fact that many of the great figures in the Bible had times when they felt like this.

- David (Psalm 22)
- Hagar (Genesis 21:8–19)
- Job (Job 10:1–22)
- Jonah (Jonah 4:5–10)
- Joshua (Joshua 7:6–10)
- Moses (Numbers 11:10–15)
- Naomi (Ruth 1:8–18)
- Paul (2 Corinthians 1:8–11)

God brought all of these through their depression and made them useful again. Why should we think it will be any different with us?

Don't assume that all these must be true of you if you are feeling depressed! But one of them may be its root. If God highlights something as you pray, lay it before him.

Prayers in times of anxiety

Anxiety – worrying about what might happen – can hit all of us at times. Sometimes the anxiety is 'free-floating', but sometimes it has specific causes. Here are some common ones:

Causes of anxiety

- Concern about the future (e.g. John 14:1–4)
- Disobedience to God (e.g. Deuteronomy 28:15, 64–68)
- Being under pressure to get things done (e.g. Luke 10:38–42)
- Stressful circumstances (e.g. Luke 2:41–48)
- Worldliness (e.g. Matthew 6:25–34; 13:22)
- Worry about other people (e.g. Philippians 2:25–30)

Bringing anxiety to God

Let's look at one of David's prayers, where he mixes honest expression of anxiety with declaration of trust in God.

Listen to my prayer, O God,
do not ignore my plea;
hear me and answer me.
My thoughts trouble me and I am distraught
at the voice of the enemy,
at the stares of the wicked;
for they bring down suffering upon me
and revile me in their anger.
My heart is in anguish within me;
the terrors of death assail me.
Fear and trembling have beset me;
horror has overwhelmed me.
I said, 'Oh, that I had the wings of a dove!
I would fly away and be at rest –
I would flee far away
and stay in the desert; *Selah*
I would hurry to my place of shelter,
far from the tempest and storm' …
… But I call to God,
and the LORD saves me.
Evening, morning and noon
I cry out in distress,
and he hears my voice …
Cast your cares on the LORD
and he will sustain you;
he will never let the righteous fall.
But you, O God, will bring down the wicked
into the pit of corruption;
bloodthirsty and deceitful men
will not live out half their days.
But as for me, I trust in you.

(Psalm 55:1–8, 16–17, 22–23)

Whatever our anxieties, the Bible encourages us to bring them to God:

Do not worry about anything, but pray and ask God for everything you need, always giving thanks. And God's peace, which is so great we cannot understand it, will keep your hearts and your minds in Christ Jesus.

(Philippians 4:6–7, NCV)

See also Psalm 139:23–24; Matthew 6:31–34

It is as we bring them to God that he is able to come and help us.

I said, 'I am falling';
But your constant love, O LORD, held me up.
Whenever I am anxious and worried,
you comfort me and make me glad.

(Psalm 94:18–19, GNB)

See also Psalm 55:22; Matthew 11:28–30; Luke 22:41–44; 2 Corinthians 4:7–9; 1 Peter 5:7

Prayers in times of spiritual darkness

Sometimes the darkness we experience can be of a more spiritual nature. Let's look at two common expressions of it.

Spiritual dryness

We all have times when we feel spiritually 'dry', when God seems a million miles away (though in reality he hasn't moved an inch!). When feeling like this, it's important we don't stop praying, worshipping, or going to church services. That's just what the devil wants; but it's the last thing we need. We need to maintain a spiritual atmosphere where we can meet with God – even if we have to wait. Remember, as we saw in the previous chapter, the times of God's 'absence' make us appreciate the times of his presence.

Honestly expressing to God our feelings and our questions is an important part of coming through such times. In the following psalm, the writer expresses his dryness and longing for God, but also intermingles expressions of confidence that God will once again be the object of his praise.

As the deer pants for streams of water,
so my soul pants for you, O God.
My soul thirsts for God, for the living God.
When can I go and meet with God?
My tears have been my food
day and night,
while men say to me all day long,
'Where is your God?'
These things I remember
as I pour out my soul:
how I used to go with the multitude,
leading the procession to the house of God,
with shouts of joy and thanksgiving
among the festive throng.

Why are you downcast, O my soul?
Why so disturbed within me?
Put your hope in God,
for I will yet praise him,
my Saviour and my God.

(Psalm 42:1–5)

See also Psalm 63:1–8; 84:1–12; 143:5–12; Isaiah 33:2

Spiritual confusion

Sometimes we want to ask God 'Why?' because we just don't understand what is going on or why. Perhaps things are going in a different direction from what we felt God promised. Gideon once found himself in such a situation and brought his honest questions before God.

'Sir,' Gideon replied, 'if the LORD is with us, why has all this happened to us? And where are all the miracles our ancestors told us about? Didn't they say, "The LORD brought us up out of Egypt?" But now the LORD has abandoned us and handed us over to the Midianites.'

(Judges 6:13, NLT)

See also Judges 21:1–3; Jeremiah 13:22–23

Prayers in times of desolation

All of us experience loneliness at times; but how dark things seem when we feel, not just lonely, but desolate – completely abandoned by everyone. That's how Jesus felt on the cross:

About the ninth hour Jesus cried out in a loud voice, 'Eloi, Eloi, lama sabachthani?' – which means, 'My God, my God, why have you forsaken me?'

(Matthew 27:46)

These words clearly impacted Jesus' followers; hence, the fact that the Aramaic phrase Jesus used was remembered and recorded. They couldn't believe what they were hearing! But this was not merely poetic language; it expressed the reality of Jesus' abandonment from the Father at that moment. As 'he himself bore our sins in his body on the tree' (1 Peter 2:24), the Father had to turn away from his beloved Son, for he could not look upon sin. This was the ultimate abandonment! And Jesus embraced it for you and me. However, Easter Sunday demonstrated that abandonment is never God's final word. There is always the hope of resurrection!

Jesus' cry was taken from a prayer of abandonment written by David a thousand years earlier. Note the mixture of despair and faith, so true to human experience.

My God, my God, why have you forsaken me?
Why are you so far from saving me,
so far from the words of my groaning?
O my God, I cry out by day, but you do not answer,
by night, and am not silent.

Yet you are enthroned as the Holy One;
you are the praise of Israel.
In you our fathers put their trust;
they trusted and you delivered them.
They cried to you and were saved;
in you they trusted and were not disappointed.

But I am a worm and not a man,
scorned by men and despised by the people.
All who see me mock me;
they hurl insults, shaking their heads:
'He trusts in the LORD;
let the LORD rescue him.
Let him deliver him,
since he delights in him.'

Yet you brought me out of the womb;
you made me trust in you
even at my mother's breast.
From birth I was cast upon you;
from my mother's womb you have been my God.
Do not be far from me,
for trouble is near
and there is no-one to help ...

... But you, O LORD, be not far off;
O my Strength, come quickly to help me.
Deliver my life from the sword,
my precious life from the power of the dogs.
Rescue me from the mouth of the lions;
save me from the horns of the wild oxen.

I will declare your name to my brothers;
in the congregation I will praise you.
You who fear the LORD, praise him!
All you descendants of Jacob, honour him!
Revere him, all you descendants of Israel!
For he has not despised or disdained
the suffering of the afflicted one;
he has not hidden his face from him
but has listened to his cry for help ...

(Psalm 22:1–11, 19–24)

Prayers in the face of dying and death

Nothing raises the question 'Why?' more in people's minds than dying and death. It is certainly something that none of us can avoid, for, as George Bernard Shaw said, 'Death is the ultimate statistic; one out of one die'. Facing death can be hard; but for those who trust in Christ, death is not the end.

Facing our own death

Death is an uncertain doorway for most people. But if we trust in God, we need not fear it, but rather can approach it with confidence.

I know that my Redeemer lives,
and that he will stand upon the earth at last.
And after my body has decayed,
yet in my body I will see God.

(Job 19:25–27, NLT)

God will redeem my life from the grave;
he will surely take me to himself.

(Psalm 49:15)

'Lord, now I can die in peace! As you promised me, I have seen the Saviour ...'

(Luke 2:29, NLT)

See also Numbers 23:10; Psalm 116:15; John 11:25–26; Acts 7:59–60; 1 Corinthians 15:55–57; Philippians 1:21–23; 2 Timothy 4:6–8; Revelation 7:13–17

Facing the death of others

Seeing loved ones die is never easy. The Bible encourages us to freely express our grief at such times, but to be strengthened by our hope in the resurrection. Paul wrote that he didn't want us 'to grieve like the rest of men, who have no hope' (1 Thessalonians 4:13). Grieve – but grieve with hope!

Job got up and tore his robe and shaved his head. Then he fell to the ground in worship and said:
'Naked I came from my mother's womb,
and naked I shall depart.
The LORD gave and the LORD has taken away;
may the name of the LORD be praised.'

(Job 1:20–21)

See also Genesis 23:1–2; 2 Samuel 1:17–27; 12:19–23; Psalm 23; John 11:21–27; Acts 8:2

A FINAL PRAYER

Comfort, we ask you, most gracious God, all who are cast down and faint of heart amidst the sorrows and difficulties of the world; and grant that, by the quickening power of the Holy Spirit, they may be lifted up to you with hope and courage, and enabled to go upon their way rejoicing in your love; through Jesus Christ our Lord.

Richard Meux Benson (1824–1915), Founder of the Society of St. John the Evangelist

CONCLUSION

Even in dark days, God has not abandoned us. As we wait, he will come to us.

Say to those with fearful hearts, 'Be strong, do not fear; your God will come.'

(Isaiah 35:4)

Relevance for today

When we face dark days, there are steps we can take to help ourselves:

Focus on God again

When we are depressed, we tend to focus on ourselves. The Bible encourages us to focus on God and see his greatness once again.

'Go out and stand on the mountain in the presence of the LORD, for the LORD is about to pass by.'

(1 Kings 19:11)

See also 2 Chronicles 20:5–12; Isaiah 26:1–8; Jeremiah 17:5–8

Remember God does not reject us

No matter how we feel, God doesn't reject or forsake us. He accepts us on the basis of Christ's work on the cross, not on how we feel today – good or bad!

For the LORD will not reject his people;
he will never forsake his inheritance.

(Psalm 94:14)

See also Leviticus 26:40–45; Deuteronomy 31:6; Joshua 1:5; Psalm 27:10; Romans 11:1–6; Hebrews 13:5–6

Remember God is faithful

Read some of the Scriptures that remind us of God's faithfulness.

Yet this I call to mind
and therefore I have hope:
Because of the LORD's great love we are not consumed,
for his compassions never fail.
They are new every morning;
great is your faithfulness.

(Lamentations 3:22–23)

See also Psalm 145:13–14; 146:5–6; 1 Corinthians 1:8–9; 10:13; 1 Thessalonians 5:24; 2 Thessalonians 3:3; 2 Timothy 2:11–13; Hebrews 10:19–23

Remember God's deeds in the past

In dark days, we need to remember what God has done for us in the past.

I will remember the deeds of the LORD;
yes, I will remember your miracles of long ago.
I will meditate on all your works
and consider all your mighty deeds.

(Psalm 77:11–12)

See also Psalm 30:1–5; 105:1–7;143:3–5; Lamentations 3:19–24; Hebrews 10:32–39

Praise God

While this is often the last thing we *feel* like doing, it is often the key to seeing the darkness lift. As we praise, we look away from ourselves to the one who can help us. Our praise doesn't need to be extravagant; simply heartfelt.

'I will praise you, O LORD.
Although you were angry with me,
your anger has turned away
and you have comforted me.
Surely God is my salvation;
I will trust and not be afraid.
The LORD, the LORD, is my strength and my song;
he has become my salvation.'
With joy you will draw water
from the wells of salvation.

(Isaiah 12:1–3)

See also Psalm 16:1–11; 22:22–28; 57:7–11; 136:1–26; Matthew 5:11–12; Philippians 4:4

(Continued overleaf)

Trust God

Trust, by its very nature, really comes into play when we are helpless. We don't have to *feel* good to tell God we still trust him.

Though the fig-tree does not bud
and there are no grapes on the vines,
though the olive crop fails
and the fields produce no food,
though there are no sheep in the pen
and no cattle in the stalls,
yet I will rejoice in the LORD,
I will be joyful in God my Saviour.

(Habakkuk 3:17–18)

See also Psalm 22:22–31; 37:1–9; 42:11; 118:5–9; Isaiah 26:3–4; Nahum 1:7

Claim God's promise

Claim God's promise that his Spirit will lift our heaviness and restore our joy.

The Spirit of the Sovereign LORD is on me,
because the LORD has anointed me
to preach good news to the poor.
He has sent me to bind up the broken-hearted,
to proclaim freedom for the captives
and release from darkness for the prisoners,
to proclaim the year of the LORD's favour
and the day of vengeance of our God,
to comfort all who mourn,
and provide for those who grieve in Zion –
to bestow on them a crown of beauty
instead of ashes,
the oil of gladness
instead of mourning,
and a garment of praise
instead of a spirit of despair.
They will be called oaks of righteousness,
a planting of the LORD
for the display of his splendour.

(Isaiah 61:1–3)

See also Psalm 51:10–12; Luke 10:21; Acts 13:52; Romans 14:17; 15:13; Galatians 5:22–23

Pray!

Praying is often the last thing we feel like doing in hard times; but it needs to be the first thing! You don't need to 'feel' good to pray – just pray!

Is any one of you in trouble? He should pray.

(James 5:13)

See also Psalm 32:6–7; 50:15; 91:15; Jeremiah 29:11–14; Philippians 4:6–7

Chapter Four

Prayers that Question God's Ways

There are times when all of us wonder why God does, or allows, certain things. He invites us to bring such questions to him, but to listen as well as to speak.

'Yet you say, "The way of the Lord is not just." Hear, O house of Israel: Is my way unjust? Is it not your ways that are unjust?'
(Ezekiel 18:25)

Let's face it: we don't always find God's ways easy to understand. Why he does certain things, but doesn't do other things, is often hard to grasp. And this has sometimes led people to question his ways, or even to doubt his existence. God is big enough to cope with these sort of questions, however; but the challenge to us is, are we big enough to listen to his answers?

Questioning God's morality

The thought of questioning God's morality might almost seem blasphemous; but some people knew God so well that that's exactly what they did.

The example of Abraham

Perhaps the best-known challenge to God's morality was the one that Abraham brought. Abraham had had three visitors – two angels and, almost certainly, the Lord himself – who came to tell him that the son they had been promised would be with them within the year (Genesis 18:1–15). As they were about to leave, the Lord resolved not to hide his plans from Abraham (v17), but to let him into them: Abraham would become a nation through which all other nations would be blessed (v18–19), and Sodom and Gomorrah, sinful cities that they were (Genesis 13:13), were about to be weighed and judged (Genesis 18:20–21). Since Lot, his nephew, had settled in that area, Abraham had vested interests in God's plan and was quick to challenge him about it. The heart of his plea, however, was not Lot, but the Lord. 'How on earth can you think about doing something like this, Lord?' he asked.

The men turned away and went towards Sodom, but Abraham remained standing before the LORD. *Then Abraham approached him and said: 'Will you sweep away the righteous with the wicked? What if there are fifty righteous people in the city?*

Will you really sweep it away and not spare the place for the sake of the fifty righteous people in it? Far be it from you to do such a thing – to kill the righteous with the wicked, treating the righteous and the wicked alike. Far be it from you! Will not the Judge of all the earth do right?"

(Genesis 18:22–25)

What Abraham was struggling with was how a moral God could do, what to his eyes, seemed such an 'immoral' thing. It violated Abraham's sense of right and wrong; and surely 'the Judge of all the earth' had to do what was right (v25)? Of course he did; but the problem was, Abraham didn't know the whole story as God did; and so his assessment of what was 'right' differed from God's. But God agreed with Abraham: if he could find fifty righteous men he would spare the cities (v26). What follows is a fascinating insight into the intimacy of prayer of someone who really knows God. Abraham begins to 'chip away' at that number fifty – not as an attempt at 'bargaining with God' (you don't bargain with the Judge of all the earth!), but out of compassion. With a mixture of boldness and humility, Abraham gets the number down – to forty-five, then to forty, thirty, twenty, ten (Genesis 18:27–32) – and God agrees!

The unfolding of the story shows how little Abraham knew in comparison to God; for when the angels visited the cities to investigate their renowned ungodliness, they were appalled at what they saw and how rampant immorality had become (Genesis 19:1–11). The next morning they struggled to overcome the reluctance of Lot and his family to leave, and barely got Lot, his wife, and two daughters out of the danger area before the burning sulphur (perhaps thrown up from an earthquake) engulfed the cities. Sadly, the disobedient hesitation of Lot's wife, perhaps looking back on the destruction of their worldly possessions, caused her death (19:23–26).

So what can we learn from this story? Abraham had thought God was less righteous than he should be, but discovered God was far more righteous than he himself was. Abraham would have let nine righteous people suffer judgment as the price of punishing the wicked; but God wouldn't! God could ultimately find only four righteous people (and one of those didn't make it); but they were spared, no matter what the number Abraham had set. God showed that he was more concerned for others than Abraham could ever be.

When we are tempted to question God's morality, we shouldn't be embarrassed about bringing the issue to him in prayer. But as we do so, we will discover that he alone knows the full picture. It is because he does that he can truly be seen as the Judge of all the earth, who always does what is right.

Other examples

Other examples of people who questioned God's morality include:

- Abimelech (Genesis 20:3–7)
- Amos (Amos 7:1–6)
- Habakkuk (Habakkuk 1:2–4; 1:12–2:1)
- Jonah (Jonah 4:1–11)
- Job (Job 9:1–24)
- The psalmist (Psalm 94:1–7)

Questioning God's principles

Sometimes we find people questioning how God 'operates'. We saw in Chapter 2 of this Part how Habakkuk challenged God about using sinful Babylon to bring about his purposes (Habakkuk 1:12–2:1). Now let's look at Ezekiel who had to answer people who were questioning God about the principle of sin and retribution.

There was a common saying in those days – quoted also by Jeremiah (Jeremiah 31:29) – which summed up the popular view on this matter:

'The fathers eat sour grapes,
and the children's teeth are set on edge.'
(Ezekiel 18:1)

In some ways, this proverb simply expressed what was found in the Ten Commandments: that God would punish 'the sin of the fathers to the third and fourth generation' (Exodus 20:5). But this was a *comment* not a *curse*. Those who break God's laws pass on their ways to their families, thereby affecting generations to come; but things don't *have* to be like that. By Ezekiel's time, however, people had turned this into a law; and, as a result, a very fatalistic view of God and how he operated had developed, denying any sense of basic justice.

Ezekiel therefore set about to correct their false theology and their wrong conclusions about how God worked. He did so by imagining the lives of three generations of one family (Ezekiel 18:5–18). The conclusion he came up with was simple:

'The soul who sins is the one who will die. The son will not share the guilt of the father, nor will the father share the guilt of the son. The righteousness of the righteous man will be credited to him, and the wickedness of the wicked will be charged against him.'
(Ezekiel 18:20)

But it's clear from their response that they felt this was a very unfair principle!

'Yet you say, "The way of the Lord is not just." Hear, O house of Israel: Is my way unjust? Is it not your ways that are unjust?'
(Ezekiel 18:25)

God ended the discussion with a question and a challenge to them:

'Do I take any pleasure in the death of the wicked? declares the Sovereign LORD. Rather, am I not pleased when they turn from their ways and live?'
(Ezekiel 18:23)

'Therefore, O house of Israel, I will judge you, each one according to his ways, declares the Sovereign LORD. Repent! Turn away from all your offences; then sin will not be your downfall. Rid yourselves of all the offences you have committed, and get a new heart and a new spirit. Why will you die, O house of Israel? For I take no pleasure in the death of anyone, declares the Sovereign LORD. Repent and live!'
(Ezekiel 18:30–31)

Our theology, beliefs and traditions may sometimes cause us to question God's principles or methods, especially if he does things in a way that we wouldn't or think that he shouldn't! At such times we need to keep an open heart to God's answers, lest we find ourselves defending something for him that he doesn't want defending!

Questioning God's calling

'What, me, God? Why pick me?' That's probably how most of us feel when God calls us to do something for him. And it's how some leading figures in the Bible felt when God called them too. They really felt he'd got it wrong, and weren't slow in telling him so!

The example of Moses

Moses, born an Israelite but brought up an Egyptian (Exodus 2:1–10), found his life completely turned around the day he met God. God revealing himself to him (Exodus 3:1–6) was one thing; but when

God started speaking about having a task for Moses to do, the excuses started to tumble out. 'You've picked the wrong person!' was the gist of his reply. Just look at the list of excuses he makes in the conversation that ensued:

But Moses said to God, 'Who am I, that I should go to Pharaoh and bring the Israelites out of Egypt?' …

Moses said to God, 'Suppose I go to the Israelites and say to them, "The God of your fathers has sent me to you," and they ask me, "What is his name?" Then what shall I tell them?' …

Moses answered, 'What if they do not believe me or listen to me and say, "The LORD did not appear to you"?' …

Moses said to the LORD, 'O Lord, I have never been eloquent, neither in the past nor since you have spoken to your servant. I am slow of speech and tongue.' …

But Moses said, 'O Lord, please send someone else to do it.'

(Exodus 3:11, 13; 4:1, 10, 13)

Moses really felt that God had got it wrong – and didn't hesitate to tell him so. But if you read Exodus chapters 3 and 4 you will see that to each objection Moses raised, God provided a gentle answer; until, by the fifth objection, he became impatient with his prevarications and told him just to get on with it (4:14–17)! God will answer our questions; but the point comes where we need to hear what he is saying and act on it.

The example of Jeremiah

Jeremiah was another who was significant in God's purposes, but who was very reluctant about God's calling on his life.

The word of the LORD came to me, saying, 'Before I formed you in the womb I knew you, before you were born I set you apart; I appointed you as a prophet to the nations.' 'Ah, Sovereign LORD,' I said, 'I do not know how to speak; I am only a child.' But the LORD said to me, 'Do not say, "I am only a child." You must go to everyone I send you to and say whatever I command you. Do not be afraid of them, for I am with you and will rescue you, declares the LORD.

(Jeremiah 1:4–8)

Note four things that God says to Jeremiah:

- **'I formed you'** God's position as our Creator gives him the right to do with us as he wills, just like a potter with his clay (Jeremiah 18:1–6; see also Romans 9:19–21). Who are we to argue or prevaricate?
- **'I knew you'** Even before he was conceived, God 'knew' Jeremiah – that is, had made a commitment to him and entered into relationship with him. If God's choice of us is so personal and relational, should this not cause us to respond with grateful hearts and willing dedication?
- **'I set you apart'** The Hebrew word used here denotes being set apart from all other uses to God's special use. As Paul put it many years later, 'You are not your own; you were bought at a price. Therefore honour God with your body' (1 Corinthians 6:19–20). If we are set apart for God's sole use, how can we then complain when he uses us?
- **'I appointed you'** Jeremiah's call was not vague, but specific. It was a divine appointment to carry out a task, a task that wasn't just confined to Judah, but extended to the nations. God is God over the whole earth. Can he not therefore do with us as he wills and send us where he wills?

Jeremiah often struggled with his ministry over the years; but he could never get away from this call of God on his life (e.g. Jeremiah 20:7–18). We may question God about his call; but we should always be grateful to God for his call.

Both Moses and Jeremiah felt inadequate to the task God had called them to, as did others like Gideon (Judges 6:11–40) and Paul (1 Corinthians 15:7–9). They felt God had made a mistake. But God doesn't make mistakes and he doesn't take back his call and find someone else when the person he has chosen doesn't instantly respond. We may ask 'Why?' But, as Paul would write, 'God's gifts and his call are irrevocable' (Romans 11:29). God doesn't make mistakes and he doesn't change his mind. Question him by all means; but then do what he says! He has called you, and he will enable you.

When the questioning is over

If anyone could understandably question God about his ways, it was perhaps Job. As we saw in Chapter 1 of this Part, Job had lived a godly life, but then everything had gone wrong for him (Job 1:1–2:10). He had a few things he wanted the answers to! But when all his questioning was over, he was no further forward. His friends had tried their best to give him answers, though often they were trite or stock answers which failed to 'scratch where things itched' for Job. What really changed things for Job was not *questioning* God, but *meeting God.* He had said, 'Let the Almighty answer me' (Job 31:35); and now he got his answer – but not in the way he expected. In Job chapters 38–41 God revealed himself in a powerful and dramatic way through a storm and started to ask Job some questions of his own. The questions ranged far and wide: Do you know how creation came into being (38:4–11)? Can you tell the morning to come (38:12)? Do you know where light lives (38:19)? Do you know where snow is kept (38:22)? Do you understand the universe (38:31–33)? Can you make it rain (38:34)? Do you understand the ways of wildlife (38:39–39:30)? Do you understand justice (40:8–14)? Can you tame the monsters of the sea (41:1–34)?

By the time God had finished, Job felt as small as it is possible to feel. Suddenly, his questioning of God and his ways didn't seem so important any more. He didn't have his answers; but he had met God, and that had put a whole different slant on things. So this is what Job could now say:

You asked why I talk so much when I know
so little.
I have talked about things
that are far beyond my understanding.
You told me to listen and answer your
questions.
I heard about you from others;
now I have seen you with my eyes.
(Job 42:3–5, CEV)

Let us ask our questions of God by all means. But the real answers are to be found, not in arguments or explanations, but in meeting with the living God.

A FINAL PRAYER

Give me, O Lord,
a steadfast heart,
which no unworthy thought
can drag downwards,
an unconquered heart, which no
tribulation can wear out;
an upright heart, which
no unworthy purpose
may tempt aside.

Bestow upon me also,
O Lord my God,
understanding to know thee,
diligence to seek thee,
wisdom to find thee,
and a faithfulness that may
finally embrace thee;
Through Jesus Christ our Lord.

St Thomas Aquinas (1225–74),
Dominican theologian and philosopher

CONCLUSION

Because God's ways are so different to our ways it will sometimes lead us to ask searching questions of him. But we must also be ready to let him bring searching answers to us.

'Do you still want to argue with the Almighty? You are God's critic, but do you have the answers?'

(Job 40:2, NLT)

Relevance for today

We will find it easier to understand God and his ways the more we get to know him and the more we bring our thinking into line with what God reveals about himself in the Bible. When we are struggling with God's ways, we need to remember and reflect on the following fixed points that the Bible gives us:

God's ways are different

'For my thoughts are not your thoughts,
neither are your ways my ways,'
declares the LORD.
'As the heavens are higher than the earth,
so are my ways higher than your ways
and my thoughts than your thoughts.

(Isaiah 55:8–9)

God's ways are eternal

His ways are eternal.

(Habakkuk 3:6)

God's ways are faithful

All the ways of the LORD are loving and faithful
for those who keep the demands of his covenant.

(Psalm 25:10)

God's ways are holy

Your ways, O God, are holy.

(Psalm 77:13)

God's ways are just

He is the Rock, his works are perfect,
and all his ways are just.
A faithful God who does no wrong,
upright and just is he.

(Deuteronomy 32:4)

God's ways are loving

All the ways of the LORD are loving and faithful
for those who keep the demands of his covenant.

(Psalm 25:10)

God's ways are right

Who is wise? He will realise these things.
Who is discerning? He will understand them.
The ways of the LORD are right;
the righteous walk in them,
but the rebellious stumble in them.

(Hosea 14:9)

God's ways are righteous

The LORD is righteous in all his ways
and loving towards all he has made.

(Psalm 145:17)

God's ways are true

'Great and marvellous are your deeds,
Lord God Almighty.
Just and true are your ways,
King of the ages.'

(Revelation 15:3)

Chapter Five

Prayers of Trust in the Face of Difficulties

Trusting God when things are going well is easy; but real faith keeps trusting God when circumstances are hard and when questions aren't answered.

Trust in him at all times, O people; pour out your hearts before him, for God is our refuge.
(Psalm 62:8)

Not many of us will recognize the name of Jean-Francois Gravelet. But perhaps we are more familiar with his stage name: Blondin, the famous nineteenth-century tightrope walker who became famous by crossing the Niagara Falls on a tightrope 1,100 feet long, suspended 160 feet above the rushing waters. In fact, he did it several times, with increasing level of difficulty: in a sack, with a wheelbarrow, on stilts, sitting down half way across to cook an omelette. But perhaps the best known of his attempts was when he asked a bystander if he believed he could do it. 'Absolutely!' the man replied. 'I've got every faith in you.' 'Then why don't you come and sit on my shoulders and cross it with me?' asked Blondin. No doubt the man's face turned pale; but he clambered on his shoulders and risked it – and, yes, they made it safely across to the other side. Now, that's faith!

And that's rather how it is with God. God invites us to, as it were, 'climb on his shoulders' and to trust him, rather than to simply stand on the sidelines with our comments, questions, or advice thrown safely from a distance.

Few of us go through life without facing difficulties: sickness, tragedy, family worries, financial problems, unemployment, bereavement – life in a fallen world throws up plenty of challenges. Not surprisingly, at such times, we have questions for God. While God is always happy to receive our questions and complaints, we make most progress when such prayers are mixed with affirmations of trust in him. In this chapter we are going to look at some of the varied circumstances of life in which people brought their problems to God in prayer, but also expressed their underlying trust in him. But first, let's look at a well-known psalm that expresses absolute trust in God and which encourages others to trust him too.

The blessing of trusting in God: Psalm 91

This psalm is a wonderful testimony to how God can keep us safe through all the varied troubles of life.

Its introduction (v1–2) begins by focusing on God himself, reminding us who he is: the Most High (El Elyon), the Almighty (El Shaddai), the LORD (Yahweh), my God (Elohim). Such a one can surely be trusted to protect us!

He who dwells in the shelter of the Most
High
will rest in the shadow of the Almighty.
I will say of the LORD, *'He is my refuge and*
my fortress,
my God, in whom I trust.'

The first half of the psalm then speaks, in powerful poetic and metaphorical language, of *God's commitment* to protect us from a wide range of troubles (v3–8):

Surely he will save you from the fowler's
snare
and from the deadly pestilence.
He will cover you with his feathers,
and under his wings you will find refuge;
his faithfulness will be your shield and
rampart.
You will not fear the terror of night,
nor the arrow that flies by day,
nor the pestilence that stalks in the
darkness,
nor the plague that destroys at midday.
A thousand may fall at your side,
ten thousand at your right hand,
but it will not come near you.
You will only observe with your eyes
and see the punishment of the wicked.

The second half of the psalm (v9–13) then invites us to make a *personal response* to all this by putting our own trust in God and enjoying the blessings that this brings.

If you make the Most High your dwelling –
even the LORD, *who is my refuge –*
then no harm will befall you,
no disaster will come near your tent.
For he will command his angels concerning
you
to guard you in all your ways;
they will lift you up in their hands,
so that you will not strike your foot
against a stone.
You will tread upon the lion and the cobra;
you will trample the great lion and the
serpent.

The conclusion (v14–16) then underlines *our reassurance* in the form of a personal promise from God.

'Because he loves me,' says the LORD, *'I will*
rescue him;
I will protect him, for he acknowledges my
name.
He will call upon me, and I will answer
him;
I will be with him in trouble,
I will deliver him and honour him.
With long life will I satisfy him
and show him my salvation.'

Knowing such a God is a firm basis for meeting life's varied difficulties.

Trusting God in life's difficulties

Having seen the general reassurance of Psalm 91, let's now look at some specific areas of difficulties in life and God's reassurances for each of them.

When facing trouble

We don't have to go looking for trouble in

life; it has a way of coming to look for us! As one of Job's friends put it, 'Man is born to trouble as surely as sparks fly upward' (Job 5:7). At such times, God can sometimes feel far away:

Why, O LORD, do you stand so far away?
Why do you hide when I need you the most?

(Psalm 10:1, NLT)

But no matter how we feel, and no matter how big our troubles seem, God is never far away. In fact, we are never in any situation where he is not close (e.g. Psalm 139:7–10). Because of this, he invites us to spread out our troubles before him, and then to 'climb onto his shoulders' (like the man did with Blondin) and to trust him to carry us through them.

Look at these declarations of trust in God, expressed by some who had to walk through hard times:

Therefore let everyone who is godly pray to you
while you may be found;
surely when the mighty waters rise,
they will not reach him.
You are my hiding-place;
you will protect me from trouble
and surround me with songs of deliverance.

(Psalm 32:6–7)

The LORD hears his people when they call to him for help.
He rescues them from all their troubles.
The LORD is close to the broken-hearted;
He rescues those who are crushed in spirit.

The righteous face many troubles,
but the LORD rescues them from each and every one.

(Psalm 34:17–19, NLT)

In the day of my trouble I will call to you,
for you will answer me.

(Psalm 86:7)

The LORD is good,
a refuge in times of trouble.
He cares for those who trust in him.

(Nahum 1:7)

See also 2 Kings 18:5–8; 1 Chronicles 5:20; Psalm 20:1–8; 25:1–3; 37:1–9; 46:1–7; Jeremiah 17:5–8; Daniel 6:1–23; John 14:1

When facing fear

Fear, by its very nature, can be quite paralysing; but this is a time for turning to God in our own helplessness and letting him know that we are looking to him for help, whatever our feelings or questions might be at that moment. Once again, the psalms are a rich resource for such prayers.

The LORD is my light and my salvation –
whom shall I fear?
The LORD is the stronghold of my life –
of whom shall I be afraid?
When evil men advance against me
to devour my flesh,
when my enemies and my foes attack me,
they will stumble and fall.
Though an army besiege me,
my heart will not fear;
though war break out against me,
even then will I be confident.

(Psalm 27:1–3)

When I am afraid,
I will trust in you.
In God, whose word I praise,
in God I trust; I will not be afraid.
What can mortal man do to me?

(Psalm 56:3–4)

See also Joshua 1:6–9; 2 Kings 6:16–17; 2 Chronicles 32:7–8; Nehemiah 4:14; Psalm 115:9–11; Isaiah 12:2; 35:3–4; 41:8–10

A hymn of strong trust

John Newton (1725–1807), a former captain and slave trader of fiery temperament, was converted in 1779 and became a great preacher and hymn writer. Here is one of his hymns, declaring a strong trust in God in the face of all difficulties.

Begone, unbelief;
My Saviour is near,
And for my relief
Will surely appear.
By prayer let me wrestle,
And He will perform;
With Christ in the vessel,
I smile at the storm.

His love in time past
Forbids me to think
He'll leave me at last
In trouble to sink.
Each sweet Ebenezer
I have in review
Confirms His good pleasure
To help me quite through.

Why should I complain
Of want or distress,
Temptation or pain ?
He told me no less:
The heirs of salvation,
I know from His word,
Through much tribulation
Must follow their Lord.

How bitter that cup,
No heart can conceive,
Which He drank quite up,
That sinners might live.
His way was much rougher
And darker than mine;
Did Jesus thus suffer,
And shall I repine?

Since all that I meet
Shall work for my good,
The bitter is sweet,
The medicine food.
Though painful at present,
'Twill cease before long;
And then, O how pleasant
The conqueror's song!

When running out of resources

God loves it when we run out of our own resources! This is not because he takes delight in seeing us struggle; but because, at last, we have come to the place where we recognize that we can't do it ourselves and that we have nowhere else to go but to him. It is when we come empty-handed to God in this way that he can begin to fill those empty hands.

I said to the LORD, 'You are my Lord;
apart from you I have no good thing.'
(Psalm 16:2)

Whom have I in heaven but you?
And there is nothing on earth that I desire
other than you.
My flesh and my heart may fail,
but God is the strength of my heart
and my portion for ever.
(Psalm 73:25–26, NRSV)

See also Judges 16:28–30; Nehemiah 4:10–15; Job 1:20–21; Psalm 31:9–24; Isaiah 40:27–31; Habakkuk 3:16–19; Philippians 4:12–13

When confronted by enemies

There were many in the Bible who had to face enemies and their verbal or physical attacks. While everything within us wants to retaliate, God encourages us to commit our cause to him and to allow him to act on our behalf.

To you, O LORD, I lift up my soul;
in you I trust, O my God.
Do not let me be put to shame,
nor let my enemies triumph over me.
No-one whose hope is in you
will ever be put to shame,
but they will be put to shame
who are treacherous without excuse.

(Psalm 25:1–3)

Though I walk in the midst of trouble,
you preserve me against the wrath of my enemies;
you stretch out your hand
and your right hand delivers me.
The LORD will fulfil his purpose for me;
your steadfast love, O LORD, endures for ever.
Do not forsake the work of your hands.

(Psalm 138:7–8, NRSV)

'When you are brought to trial in the synagogues, and before rulers and authorities, don't worry about what to say in your defence, for the Holy Spirit will teach you what needs to be said even as you are standing there.'

(Luke 12:11–12, NLT)

See also Psalm 27:1–3; 56:1–11; 59:1–17; 69:16–18; Romans 12:17–21

When facing sickness

Having a serious or prolonged illness can be a challenge to all of us. But just because we are ill does not mean God has abandoned us or forgotten us. We need to keep trusting him through it.

Be merciful to me, O LORD, for I am in distress;
my eyes grow weak with sorrow,
my soul and my body with grief.
My life is consumed by anguish
and my years by groaning;
my strength fails because of my affliction,
and my bones grow weak …
But I trust in you, O LORD;
I say, 'You are my God.'

(Psalm 31:9–10, 14)

To keep me from becoming conceited because of these surpassingly great revelations, there was given me a thorn in my flesh, a messenger of Satan, to torment me. Three times I pleaded with the Lord to take it away from me. But he said to me, 'My grace is sufficient for you, for my power is made perfect in weakness.' Therefore I will boast all the more gladly about my weaknesses, so that Christ's power may rest on me. That is why, for Christ's sake, I delight in weaknesses, in insults, in hardships, in persecutions, in difficulties. For when I am weak, then I am strong.

(2 Corinthians 12:7–10)

See also 2 Kings 20:1–11; Job 2:7–10; Matthew 8:5–13; Mark 5:21–43; John 4:43–54

When facing death

Death is something that none of us can avoid. It is the ultimate trouble that we must face in this life, the 'last enemy', as Paul describes it (1 Corinthians 15:26), that must be faced. When we put our trust in Jesus, its sting is suddenly drawn however.

The LORD is my shepherd,
I shall not want.
He makes me lie down in green pastures;
He leads me beside quiet waters.
He restores my soul;
He guides me in the paths of righteousness
For His name's sake.
Even though I walk through the valley of
the shadow of death,
I fear no evil: for You are with me;
Your rod and Your staff, they comfort me.

(Psalm 23:1–4, NASB)

'My soul is overwhelmed with sorrow to the point of death,' he said to them. 'Stay here and keep watch.' Going a little farther, he fell to the ground and prayed that if possible the hour might pass from him. 'Abba, Father,' he said, 'everything is possible for you. Take this cup from me. Yet not what I will, but what you will.'

(Mark 14:34–36)

Jesus called out with a loud voice, 'Father, into your hands I commit my spirit.' When he had said this, he breathed his last.

(Luke 23:46)

See also 2 Samuel 12:15–23; Isaiah 38:9–20; John 11:1–43; 1 Corinthians 15:50–57

God's promise to help

Not only does the Bible contain many heart cries to God in times of varied troubles, it also assures us of God's commitment to his people and his promise to help them in their time of need.

'Call upon me in the day of trouble;
I will deliver you, and you will honour me.'

(Psalm 50:15)

'Because he loves me,' says the LORD, 'I will rescue him;
I will protect him, for he acknowledges my name.
He will call upon me, and I will answer him;
I will be with him in trouble,
I will deliver him and honour him.
With long life will I satisfy him
and show him my salvation.'

(Psalm 91:14–16)

We do not have a high priest who is unable to sympathise with our weaknesses, but we have one who has been tempted in every way, just as we are – yet was without sin. Let us then approach the throne of grace with confidence, so that we may receive mercy and find grace to help us in our time of need.

(Hebrews 4:15–16)

A FINAL PRAYER

What is before us, we know not, whether we shall live or die; but this we know, that all things are ordered and sure. Everything is ordered with unerring wisdom and unbounded love, by thee, our God, who art love. Grant us in all things to see thy hand; through Jesus Christ our Lord.

Charles Simeon (1759–1836),
Cambridge vicar, leader of the
Evangelical Revival

CONCLUSION

The more we take time to get to know God in the good times, the more we will be able to trust him in the hard times.

Those who know your name will trust in you, for you, LORD, have never forsaken those who seek you.

(Psalm 9:10)

Relevance for today

Can God still be trusted today to come and help and strengthen us in our times of difficulty and trouble? Yes he can! Here are just some of the reasons for believing that.

God loves us

'... you are my dearest son,
the child I love best.
Whenever I mention your name,
I think of you with love.
My heart goes out to you;
I will be merciful.'

(Jeremiah 31:20, GNB)

God is always with us

'The LORD himself goes before you and will be with you; he will never leave you nor forsake you. Do not be afraid; do not be discouraged.'

(Deuteronomy 31:8)

God will help us

'I am holding you by your right hand – I, the LORD, your God. And I say to you, "Do not be afraid. I am here to help you."'

(Isaiah 41:13, NLT)

God is in control

The LORD has made the heavens his throne;
From there he rules over everything.

(Psalm 103:19, NLT)

God works everything together for good

We know that in everything God works for the good of those who love him.

(Romans 8:28, NCV)

God has a plan for our lives

'For I know the plans I have for you,' declares the LORD, 'plans to prosper you and not to harm you, plans to give you hope and a future.'

(Jeremiah 29:11)

Chapter Six

Does God Change His Mind?

The unchanging and unchangeable God tells us there are times when he will gladly change his mind!

'I searched for someone to stand in the gap …' (Ezekiel 22:30, NLT)

Let's face it: some things in life are just a mystery. Most men put women into that category – and most women put men there too! But when it comes to God, everything is a mystery. How God could become a man; how Jesus could rise from the dead; how God's Spirit can live within us; why God should bother with people like us; – and why God seems prepared to 'change his mind' when people 'stand in the gap' and pray. Is this a measure of his weakness? No! It is a measure of his greatness!

At the heart of pagan religion is the idea that you can 'manipulate' the gods to do what is favourable to you by offering the right sacrifices or saying the right prayers. Such a manipulative view of religion is a far cry from biblical faith. And yet, the Bible tells us that God sometimes 'changed his mind' in response to people's prayers, and that sometimes he would have acted differently if only someone had prayed (e.g. Ezekiel 22:30–31). So, how do we make sense of all this? Well, in looking for our answer, let's begin by reminding ourselves of what God is like.

What is God like?

The God of truth

'WYSIWYG' – 'what you see is what you get' – is an expression well known to computer users. It means what shows on your computer screen is exactly what you get when printed out on paper. This is exactly how it is with God: what you see is what you get! With him, there is no distortion, trickery, deception or lies; just absolute truth. The concept of 'absolute truth' does not rest easily in a postmodern world; but this is exactly what God is – absolute truth. His words, promises and plans have absolute integrity and are absolutely dependable. What he says, he means; what he says, he does. He is completely dependable and reliable, unchanging and unchangeable.

God is not a man, that he should lie …

(Numbers 23:19)

But the plans of the LORD stand firm for ever,
the purposes of his heart through all generations.

(Psalm 33:11)

'I the LORD do not change.'

(Malachi 3:6)

Jesus answered, 'I am the way and the truth and the life.'

(John 14:6)

Though everyone else in the world is a liar, God is true.

(Romans 3:4, NLT)

… God who does not lie …

(Titus 1:2)

'… it is impossible for God to lie … '

(Hebrews 6:18)

Every good and perfect gift is from above, coming down from the Father of the heavenly lights, who does not change like shifting shadows.

(James 1:17)

The God of compassion

Let there be no misunderstanding, God judges sin (e.g. Job 34:21–27; Psalm 1:4–6; 98:7–9; Romans 2:12–16; 2 Peter 2:4–9; Jude 14–15). However, God makes it plain that his heart is to see everyone repent and be saved, so avoiding his judgment upon sin. Again and again, he is revealed as a God of compassion.

'When they cried out to you again, you heard from heaven, and in your compassion you delivered them time after time.'

(Nehemiah 9:28)

The LORD is gracious and righteous;
our God is full of compassion.

(Psalm 116:5)

'For a brief moment I abandoned you,
but with deep compassion I will bring you back.
In a surge of anger
I hid my face from you for a moment,
but with everlasting kindness
I will have compassion on you,'
says the LORD your Redeemer.

(Isaiah 54:7–8)

When he saw the crowds, he had compassion on them, because they were harassed and helpless, like sheep without a shepherd.

(Matthew 9:36)

The Lord is full of compassion and mercy.

(James 5:11)

See also Exodus 33:19; 34:6–7; Deuteronomy 30:1–10; Judges 2:18; Psalm 102:13; 145:8–9; Isaiah 30:18; Jeremiah 31:18–20; Lamentations 3:22–23; Joel 2:13–14; 2 Peter 3:9

What this means for our theme is that whenever God says judgment is coming, he means it; but, as a God of compassion, he would far rather that people responded to his warnings and repented, so that he can then change his judgment into mercy, just as he said he would (e.g. Jeremiah 18:5–10).

Yahweh, not Allah

Some Christians reduce the God of the Bible – Yahweh, the great 'I AM' – to little more than the Muslim god, Allah. But he is not! For Muslims, whatever Allah wills, happens, inexorably and relentlessly; all people can do is to receive it, for good or for bad. Sadly, this is the God that some Christians have; but it is not the God of the Bible. God certainly has an ultimate will and plan; but he brings it about, not through fixed and unchangeable events, but through dynamic interaction with his people as they live and pray. Hence, prayer is not about resigning ourselves to his iron will, but about engaging with his heart and becoming 'God's fellow-workers' (2 Corinthians 6:1) out of our sharing with him and his sharing with us. Our God is a dynamic God with dynamic purposes, which is why Paul could write that 'God causes all things to work together for good to those who love God' (Romans 8:28, NASB) – the good and the bad, the planned and the unexpected, our praying and the lack of it.

Having laid this foundation of these three basic truths, let's now apply it to our question: does God change his mind? Well, we can give two apparently contradictory answers!

The God who *does* change his mind!

In saying that God sometimes changes his mind, we are not suggesting for one minute that he is unreliable or that we can't depend on him and take him at his word. As we saw earlier, he is always trustworthy and true. But in order to maintain that 'truth' towards his character and purposes, there are times when God changes his declared plan – but not because we have somehow 'won him over' (rather like some children do when their parents have said 'No'). This is not about *our overcoming of his reluctance*; it is about *his winning of our hearts.* God changes his mind when we grasp his bigger salvation purposes and then appeal to him to do what he always wanted to do all along. Let's look at some examples.

Abraham

We looked at how Abraham pleaded with God for Sodom and Gomorrah in Chapter 4 of this Part. While we won't retell the story, it is worth noting that this was a clear example of God 'changing his mind'. His intention, it is clear from Abraham's prayer (Genesis 18:23–25), had been to destroy everyone. But Abraham's debating with God in prayer led to at least some being saved.

Jeremiah

Jeremiah prophesied repeatedly that judgment was coming upon Judah because of disobedience. Here is one example where God promises this judgment in unmistakable and irrevocable terms:

This is what the LORD says:
'The whole land will be ruined,
though I will not destroy it completely.
Therefore the earth will mourn
and the heavens above grow dark,
because I have spoken and will not relent,
I have decided and will not turn back.'
(Jeremiah 4:27–28)

God's purpose seems fairly clear there, doesn't it? But now let's look just a few chapters further ahead:

Then the word of the LORD came to me: 'O house of Israel, can I not do with you as this potter does?' declares the LORD. 'Like clay in the hand of the potter, so are you in my hand, O house of Israel. If at any time I announce that a nation or kingdom is to be uprooted, torn down and destroyed, and if that nation I warned repents of its evil, then I will relent and not inflict on it the disaster I had planned. And if at another time I announce that a nation or kingdom is to be built up and planted, and if it does evil in my sight and does not obey me, then I will reconsider the good I had intended to do for it.'

(Jeremiah 18:5–10)

God himself says he will change his mind! Does this contradict what Jeremiah had just prophesied? No. It merely reflects the depths of God's heart in wanting sinners to repent and be saved. When they do, God gladly changes his mind and does not bring on them the promised judgment for sinners.

Amos

Amos was another prophet who understood God's heart and his desire to extend mercy and forgiveness to everyone. Amos was simply appealing to this; and when he did, he saw God 'change his mind'.

This is what the Sovereign LORD showed me: He was preparing swarms of locusts after the king's share had been harvested and just as the second crop was coming up. When they had stripped the land clean, I cried out, 'Sovereign LORD, forgive! How can Jacob survive? He is so small!' So the LORD relented.' This will not happen,' the LORD said. This is what the Sovereign LORD showed me: The Sovereign LORD was calling for judgment by fire; it dried up the great deep and devoured the land. Then I cried out, 'Sovereign LORD, I beg you, stop! How can Jacob survive? He is so small!' So the LORD relented. 'This will not happen either,' the Sovereign LORD said.

(Amos 7:1–6)

Jonah

Jonah is another excellent example of how God changes his mind and does not bring about his declared judgment when people turn to him and repent.

Jonah obeyed the word of the LORD and went to Nineveh. Now Nineveh was a very important city – a visit required three days. On the first day, Jonah started into the city. He proclaimed: 'Forty more days and Nineveh will be overturned.' The Ninevites believed God. They declared a fast, and all of them, from the greatest to the least, put on sackcloth. When the news reached the king of Nineveh, he rose from his throne, took off his royal robes, covered himself with sackcloth and sat down in the dust. Then he issued a proclamation in Nineveh: 'By the decree of the king and his nobles: Do not let any man or beast, herd or flock, taste anything; do not let them eat or drink. But let man and beast be covered with sackcloth. Let everyone call urgently on God. Let them give up their evil ways and their violence. Who knows? God may yet relent and with compassion turn from his fierce anger so that we will not perish.' When God saw what they did and how they turned from their evil ways, he had compassion and did not bring upon them the destruction he had threatened.

(Jonah 3:1–10)

A parable of persistence

Jesus' parable of the persistent widow also encourages us to believe that things can change as we keep praying about them.

Then Jesus told his disciples a parable to show them that they should always pray and not give up. He said: 'In a certain town there was a judge who neither feared God nor cared about men. And there was a widow in that town who kept coming to him with the plea, "Grant me justice against my adversary." For some time he refused. But finally he said to himself, "Even though I don't fear God or care about men, yet because this widow keeps bothering me, I will see that she gets justice, so that she won't eventually wear me out with her coming!"' And the Lord said, 'Listen to what the unjust judge says. And will not God bring about justice for his chosen ones, who cry out to him day and night? Will he keep putting them off? I tell you, he will see that they get justice, and quickly. However, when the Son of Man comes, will he find faith on the earth?'

(Luke 18:1–8)

Jesus says that if an unrighteous judge can respond to such persistence, how much more will our righteous God respond! As we saw in Part One, Chapter 5, this parable encourages us to 'stick at it in prayer'. What God does not answer at first hearing, he may well 'change his mind about'; and if he doesn't, he will at least change something in us as we pray!

A lesson learnt

All of this does not mean, however, that we can push God into making decisions that suit our own purposes. Even Mary, Jesus' mother, had to learn this lesson.

Three days later Mary, the mother of Jesus, was at a wedding feast in the village of Cana in Galilee. Jesus and his disciples had also been invited and were there. When the wine was all gone, Mary said to Jesus, 'They don't have any more wine.' Jesus replied, 'Mother, my time hasn't yet come! You must not tell me what to do.' Mary then said to the servants, 'Do whatever Jesus tells you to do.'

(John 2:1–5, CEV)

Mary, having kept the secret of who her son was for thirty years, felt that now would be a good time for him to launch his ministry by doing something special and saving the family from major social embarrassment. She was trying (ever so nicely, as only mothers can do!) to 'twist his arm' into acting; but she was lovingly, but firmly, put in her place. Jesus would act only in response to his heavenly Father, not his earthly mother. Strangely enough, once she had learnt this lesson (and she learned quickly, as her words to the servants show), Jesus was then free to do what his Father had in mind, and miraculous provision was released (John 2:6–11).

This story brings home to us that the discovery that God sometimes 'changes his mind' is not a blank cheque for us to try to manipulate him into doing whatever we want. It is more to do with God getting hold of our hearts and our getting hold of his purposes, than our 'getting our own way'.

The God who *doesn't* change his mind?

Having seen some examples of where God *does* 'change his mind' let's now look at some passages that seem to state he *doesn't* change his mind and see how these relate to our theme.

A pagan prophet's testimony

'God is not a man, that he should lie,
nor a son of man, that he should change his mind.
Does he speak and then not act?
Does he promise and not fulfil?'

(Numbers 23:19)

This passage seems to say quite plainly that God doesn't change his mind – end of story! But can we use this passage to conclude that God never changes his mind about *anything*? We don't think that's what it's saying.

Let's look at the context: King Balak of Moab had hired the services of the pagan soothsayer, Balaam, to curse Israel. But instead of cursing them, Balaam blessed them (much to the annoyance of Balak), for God intervened and commanded him what to say. As far as Balak was concerned, Balaam was devious and unreliable. But the writer wants us to know that God isn't like that! His yes is yes and his no is no. If God has spoken a blessing over Israel, he isn't going to change his mind just because some pagan soothsayer has been paid to curse them. God's blessing is God's blessing! This does not mean, however, that there are no occasions when God changes his mind, as we have seen; he was simply resolved not to do so in *this* situation.

A true prophet's testimony

'He who is the Glory of Israel does not lie or change his mind; for he is not a man, that he should change his mind.'

(1 Samuel 15:29)

Once again, at first sight, this looks as if the Bible is saying that there are never occasions where God changes what he has said he will do. But let's look at the context once again. King Saul, twice rejected from his position as Israel's first king because of disobedience (1 Samuel 13:5–14; 15:1–23), was trying to 'twist God's arm' to let him carry on ruling. Had he been genuinely repentant, who knows what the outcome might have been? (See 1 Samuel 13:13.) But Saul's repentance was shallow, more concerned for what people thought about him than what God thought about him (15:30). He had thereby removed the only ground on which he could stand before God; and so God's judgment was assured. God would not change his mind now, and Samuel underlines this with this declaration. Once again, it is not a generalized statement about every situation; it is God's declaration about *this* situation.

David's testimony

In Psalm 110 David also seems to imply that God never changes his mind.

The LORD has sworn
and will not change his mind:
'You are a priest for ever,
in the order of Melchizedek.'

(Psalm 110:4)

Once again, the context is important in understanding what is being said. David is writing about the absolute reliability of God's purposes and promises. This psalm was interpreted by Jesus (Matthew 22:43–45), Peter (Acts 2:34–36) and the writer of Hebrews (Hebrews 1:13; 5:6–10; 7:11–28) as a Messianic psalm, in which David looked ahead and saw the ultimate priest-king, the Lord Jesus Christ. David saw him as *the victorious king* (v1–3), ruling over everything and triumphant over his enemies; and as *the eternal priest* (v4–7), having the right to judge all people. In this context, our verse in question is *an oath*; a declaration of God's promise of the eternal nature of Christ's priesthood – one that never fails, is wearied or is incomplete, in contrast to the priesthood of the old covenant. The verse is not a declaration that God never changes his mind about *anything*, but simply that God will never change his mind about *this* thing.

Verses which *appear* to say that God will never change his mind, then, are specific statements about specific situations, not general statements about all situations.

A FINAL PRAYER

O Lord Jesus Christ, the Way, the Truth and the Life, grant that we may never stray from you who are the Way, nor distrust you who are the Truth, not rest in any thing other than you, who are the Life. Teach us by your Holy Spirit what to believe, what to do, and wherein to take our rest. For your own name's sake we ask it, O Jesus Christ our Lord. Amen.

Erasmus (c. 1467–1536),
Christian humanist and scholar

CONCLUSION

God is dependable and trustworthy, never changing his ultimate goal; but he will change his *declared word* into his *desired word* whenever people repent, so that they can avoid his judgment and come into his blessing.

Mercy triumphs over judgment!

(James 2:13)

Relevance for today

God can be trusted

God is the God of truth, absolutely dependable and faithful to his promises. He will never deceive us, never trick us, never change his mind about us. Do *you* trust him?

We can always ask!

No matter what the situation, we can bring it before God. Ask! Who knows whether he may not 'change his mind'? But we will never know if we never ask. Do *you* ask?

We should not sulk

If God doesn't answer our particular prayer, we shouldn't sulk, but should trust his wisdom and his knowledge of the facts that we don't know. Do *you* sulk when you don't get your own way with God?

Who will 'stand in the gap'?

God is still looking for those who will 'stand in the gap' in prayer (Ezekiel 22:30) in order that more of his graciousness might be demonstrated. Do *you* stand in the gap for people and situations known to you?

Chapter Seven

Why Isn't Prayer Answered Sometimes?

God *always* answers prayer – with 'Yes', 'No', or 'Wait'.

'Why do you complain to him that he answers none of man's words? For God does speak – now one way, now another – though man may not perceive it.' (Job 33:13–14)

'Why didn't God answer my prayer?' is probably a question we have all asked at times. But actually, God *always* answers, though not as we may expect or wish. Sometimes his answer is 'yes'; sometimes, 'no'; and sometimes, 'wait'. He always answers; it's just that we don't always understand – or like! – the answer that he gives.

If we are going to grow in our relationship with God, it is important that we understand *why* he doesn't always answer our prayers as we had hoped. We can summarize the reasons under three broad headings:

Reasons concerning God

God's knowledge

The first reason why God doesn't seem to answer our prayers at times is that he knows more than us (which is not unreasonable, if he is God!). Our knowing the fuller picture would often change our attitude – especially when we are about to pass judgment on someone. But God always knows 'one fact more' than us; and it's this knowledge that sometimes prevents him from answering our prayer, for if he did, the outcome might be disastrous. Like the parent withholding matches from their toddler, what seems so 'unfair' (from the child's viewpoint) is, in fact, a blessing that comes out of greater knowledge.

One example of this is where God gave Job neither physical relief nor answers to his questions because he knew wider issues were involved (Job 1:6–12; 2:1–8) and that Job had bigger lessons to learn (Job 33:8–10; 40:1–5; 42:1–6).

God is a 'God who knows', and his knowledge will always shape his answering of our prayers.

'Do not keep talking so proudly
or let your mouth speak such arrogance,
for the LORD *is a God who knows,*
and by him deeds are weighed.'

(1 Samuel 2:3)

O the depth of the riches both of the wisdom and knowledge of God! How unsearchable are His judgments, and His ways past finding out!

(Romans 11:33, NKJV)

God's timing

Sometimes prayers aren't answered, not because what we asked for was wrong, but because the timing wasn't right. Mary and Martha's request to Jesus to come and heal their brother Lazarus comes into this category. Jesus didn't respond immediately because he knew God had a greater miracle in store (John 11:1–6), which would never have happened had he rushed to answer. Only later did they see God's bigger purpose (John 11:21–27, 38–44). At such times, when God's answer is, 'Wait', we need to trust him, for his timing is always perfect.

Jesus told them, 'The right time for me has not yet come; for you any time is right.'

(John 7:6)

But when the fullness of the time had come, God sent forth His Son …

(Galatians 4:4, NKJV)

God's purposes

Sometimes it looks like our prayers aren't answered because we simply don't understand what God is doing in the bigger scheme of things. While we don't have recorded examples of Joseph praying, it is impossible to believe that someone who had such revelations from God didn't pray. Over a period of thirteen years (see Genesis 37:2 and 41:46) things kept 'going wrong' for Joseph and God didn't seem to intervene. Joseph must have often wondered why God had lots of things to say to others through him (through his gift of interpreting dreams), but had nothing to say to him personally. However, at the end of the whole process, Joseph saw what God had been doing and why he had not answered him earlier:

'You weren't really the ones who sent me here – it was God.'

(Genesis 45:8, CEV)

'You intended to harm me, but God intended it for good to accomplish what is now being done, the saving of many lives.'

(Genesis 50:20)

God's prerogative

A further reason why God may not always answer our prayers as we would like is simply that he is *God.* He is indebted to no man, can do as he pleases, and certainly doesn't have to 'dance to our tune'.

'Does a clay pot ever argue with its maker? Does the clay dispute with the one who shapes it, saying, "Stop, you are doing it wrong!"'

(Isaiah 45:9, NLT)

But who are you, O man, to talk back to God? 'Shall what is formed say to him who formed it, "Why did you make me like this?"'

(Romans 9:20)

What we can be sure of, however, is that God will never act in an arbitrary or unjust way, and that Abraham's question, 'Will not the Judge of all the earth do right?' (Genesis 18:25), will always be answered with a resounding 'Yes!'

Reasons concerning us

The second group of reasons for why our prayers don't always seem to be answered concerns us.

Our wrong requests

Sometimes we simply ask for the wrong things. Some requests would seem obviously wrong, if only we stopped to think about them ('Oh God, please let me win the lottery!'). Some may not appear wrong to us, but are wrong from God's perspective of higher love and wisdom (like the parent refusing to give matches to the toddler). We simply can't expect God to answer our wrong requests. He has promised only to answer those that are in line with his will.

And we can be confident that he will listen to us whenever we ask him for anything in line with his will. And if we know he is listening when we make our requests, we can be sure that he will give us what we ask for.

(1 John 5:14–15, NLT)

Our wrong motives

Sometimes we might ask for the right thing, but with wrong or self-serving motives. Because God is far more interested in our hearts than anything else, he sometimes refuses our request to enable us to see the far more important issues.

When you ask, you do not receive, because you ask with wrong motives, that you may spend what you get on your pleasures.

(James 4:3)

Dear friends, if our hearts do not condemn us, we have confidence before God and receive from him anything we ask, because we obey his commands and do what pleases him.

(1 John 3:21–22)

Our lack of faith

While we may not like it, the Bible tells us that sometimes our prayers aren't answered because of our lack of faith.

When they arrived at the foot of the mountain, a huge crowd was waiting for them. A man came and knelt before Jesus and said, 'Lord, have mercy on my son, because he has seizures and suffers terribly. He often falls into the fire or into the water. So I brought him to your disciples, but they couldn't heal him.' Jesus replied, 'You stubborn, faithless people! How long must I be with you until you believe? How long must I put up with you? Bring the boy to me.' Then Jesus rebuked the demon in the boy, and it left him. From that moment the boy was well. Afterwards the disciples asked Jesus privately, 'Why couldn't we cast out that demon?' 'You didn't have enough faith,' Jesus told them. ' I assure you, even if you had faith as small as a mustard seed you could say to this mountain, "Move from here to there," and it would move. Nothing would be impossible.'

(Matthew 17:14–21, NLT)

It is, of course, important not to assume that 'lack of faith' (whether in quality or quantity) is *always* the reason for unanswered prayer. Nothing is more unhelpful to someone who is ill than being told it is because they don't have enough faith. As we are seeing throughout this chapter, there are often other issues at stake.

Our lack of prayer

We sometimes don't see what we would like to for the simple reason that we didn't pray! It is often easier to *talk* about praying, or to *promise* you will pray, than to actually *do* it!

You do not have, because you do not ask God.

(James 4:2)

Moses' praying in Exodus 17 is a wonderful example of the difference that prayer, or the lack of it, can make. The Israelites were on their way to the promised land when the Amalekites attacked them. But the battle that day wasn't won primarily down in the valley with a sword, but up on the hill with prayer, as Moses stretched out his hands before the Lord.

So Joshua fought the Amalekites as Moses had ordered, and Moses, Aaron and Hur went to the top of the hill. As long as Moses held up his hands, the Israelites were winning, but whenever he lowered his hands, the Amalekites were winning. When Moses' hands grew tired, they took a stone and put it under him and he sat on it. Aaron and Hur held his hands up – one on one side, one on the other – so that his hands remained steady till sunset. So Joshua overcame the Amalekite army with the sword.

(Exodus 17:10–13)

Of course, we must remember that there is no intrinsic power in prayer as such; the power does not reside in the *prayer*, but in *God*. Prayer merely acknowledges our helplessness and his greatness. The trouble is, most of us don't like to acknowledge we are helpless! So, as individuals and as churches, we would rather do anything than pray. What a contrast to John Wesley, who believed, 'God does nothing but in answer to prayer.'

Our sin

Another reason prayer may not be answered is because of sin. Of course, if God were to wait until we had no sin before he answered our prayers, he would wait a long time! The truth is, we are all sinners, and denying that is to fool ourselves (1 John 1:8). But the harbouring of serious or ongoing sin inevitably hinders what God can do through us. For example, Achan's sin, stealing some of what God had commanded should be destroyed when Jericho was captured, meant that God couldn't answer the people's prayer for victory at the next city they reached (Joshua 7:1–12). It was only when the sin was exposed and dealt with (7:13–26) that God could give them victory again (8:1–29).

If I had cherished sin in my heart,
the Lord would not have listened;
but God has surely listened
and heard my voice in prayer.

(Psalm 66:18–19)

When we are aware of sin, we should confess it quickly and receive God's forgiveness so that nothing hinders our prayers. But an absence of answers to prayer should not automatically be interpreted as a sign of sin, as Jesus reminded his disciples (John 9:1–3).

Our need

A final reason concerning us why prayer may not always be answered is our need to stay humble and dependent. We would probably become unbearable if all our prayers were answered every time. Why, God might even have to move sideways on his throne! Paul saw Satan's original rebellion as rooted in conceitedness (1 Timothy 3:6; see also Isaiah 14:12–15; Ezekiel 28:12–19), and it is one of the tools Satan has tried to use ever since. Not having our prayers answered sometimes, therefore, can help to keep us humble and dependent on God, as Paul himself discovered.

To keep me from becoming conceited because of these surpassingly great revelations, there was given me a thorn in my flesh, a messenger of Satan, to torment me. Three times I pleaded with the Lord to take it away from me. But he said to me, 'My grace is sufficient for you, for my power is made perfect in weakness.' Therefore I will boast all the more gladly about my weaknesses, so that Christ's power may rest on me. That is why, for Christ's sake, I delight in weaknesses, in insults, in hardships, in persecutions, in difficulties. For when I am weak, then I am strong.

(2 Corinthians 12:7–10)

Reasons concerning the devil

The third category of reasons why our prayers aren't always answered is to do with the devil.

Satan's opposition

His opposition to God's purposes

From the day of his expulsion from heaven, Satan has opposed God and all his purposes. When Jesus came to earth, Satan did all he could to oppose him: he tried to kill him at birth (Matthew 2:16), tempted him to disobey his Father (Luke 4:3–13), stirred up a lynch mob against him (Luke 4:28–30), inspired Judas to betray him (Luke 22:3–6), and provoked the authorities to execute him (Mark 14:43–50; 15:1–15). Throughout the New Testament Satan is seen as the opponent of God's purposes and, as the book of Revelation shows, he remains so to the very end (e.g. Revelation 20:7–10).

His opposition to God's people

Because he opposes God and his purposes, he inevitably opposes God's people in every way that he can, both corporately (e.g. 1 Chronicles 21:1) and individually (e.g. Job 2:7; 1 Thessalonians 2:18). We should not be surprised therefore (e.g. 1 Peter 4:12) when we find him opposing us too.

His opposition to God's plans

The devil's opposition is not just general, but also specific. For example, Daniel had been praying and fasting for three weeks about his nation's future (Daniel 10:1–3). Having someone discover God's plans at this point was the last thing the devil wanted; so he organized some spiritual opposition. When God's angelic messenger finally broke through, he explained the delay to Daniel:

Then he continued, 'Do not be afraid, Daniel. Since the first day that you set your mind to gain understanding and to humble yourself before your God, your words were heard, and I have come in response to them. But the prince of the Persian kingdom resisted me twenty-one days. Then Michael, one of the chief princes, came to help me, because I was detained there with the king of Persia. Now I have come to explain to you what will happen to your people in the future, for the vision concerns a time yet to come.'

(Daniel 10:12–14)

The 'prince of the Persian kingdom' was apparently a demon that exercised influence over Persia (where Daniel was in exile) and that was resisting God's answer to Daniel's prayers. This was not about God's weakness, however, but about Daniel learning to battle in prayer and to be a co-worker with God.

Our response

How then should we respond to Satan's opposition?

Seeing the unseen

The spiritual realm is a place of ongoing warfare that we do not see, but that affects us. Elisha once prayed for his servant's eyes to be opened to see what was going on at this level.

When the servant of the man of God got up and went out early the next morning, an army with horses and chariots had surrounded the city. 'Oh, my lord, what shall we do?' the servant asked. 'Don't be afraid,' the prophet answered. 'Those who are with us are more than those who are with them.' And Elisha prayed, 'O LORD, open his eyes so that he may see.' Then the LORD opened the servant's eyes, and he looked and saw the hills full of horses and chariots of fire all round Elisha.

(2 Kings 6:15–17)

Paul summed up the unseen battle like this:

For our struggle is not against flesh and blood, but against the rulers, against the authorities, against the powers of this dark world and against the spiritual forces of evil in the heavenly realms.

(Ephesians 6:12)

Spiritual warfare

Because we are in the midst of this unseen battle all around us, the Bible calls us to engage in spiritual warfare. Some Christians turn this into binding and loosing all sorts of demons; but the Bible's approach seems, perhaps surprisingly, to be much 'down to earth'. It tells us that spiritual warfare involves such things as:

- **Praying and fasting** as Daniel did for revelation (e.g. Daniel 10:1–19)
- **Submitting to God** and seeing the devil flee as we do (James 4:7)
- **Being self-controlled and alert** for the devil prowls around looking for prey to devour (1 Peter 5:8–9)
- **Recalling Christ's victory** at the cross, where Jesus stripped Satan and all his hosts of their power (Colossians 2:13–15)
- **Changing ways of thinking** which become strongholds that need demolishing (2 Corinthians 10:3–5)
- **Putting on 'the armour of God'** (Ephesians 6:10–18) – not as a spiritual exercise for the moment of battle, but as a lifestyle that prepares us for such times ('Therefore put on the full armour of God, so that *when* the evil day comes …', verse 13).
- **Getting back to God** as the seven churches in the Book of Revelation were called to do (Revelation 2:1–3:22). It is very striking that churches that were facing such satanic opposition and persecution, were told to deal with this spiritual warfare, not by binding up demons in heavenly places, but by getting back to their first love (2:4–5), being faithful (2:10), repenting (2:16), holding on (2:25), waking up (3:2), taking advantage of open doors (3:8), and restoring their fervour (3:15–20).

Fighting God's way

Having said all this, there may well be times when we need to confront demonic powers more directly, as Jesus himself did. If we are wise, however, we will not do so personally, but rather will call on the Lord to act on our behalf.

The LORD said to Satan, 'The LORD rebuke you, Satan! The LORD, who has chosen Jerusalem, rebuke you!'

(Zechariah 3:2)

But even the archangel Michael, when he was disputing with the devil about the body of Moses, did not dare to bring a slanderous accusation against him, but said, 'The Lord rebuke you!'

(Jude 9)

A FINAL PRAYER

Holy Spirit, think through me
till your ideas are my ideas.

Amy Carmichael (1868–1951)

CONCLUSION

When God does not seem to answer our prayers, we should *wait* and *trust*, for in due time his reasons will become clear.

Trust in the LORD with all your heart
and lean not on your own understanding;
in all your ways acknowledge him,
and he will make your paths straight.

(Proverbs 3:5–6)

Relevance for today

We need to know our God

The less we invest in our relationship with God in the good times, the less we will be able to trust him in the hard times; the more we get to know him, the more we will be able to stand, trust, and be victorious.

'The people that do know their God shall be strong, and do exploits.'

(Daniel 11:32, KJV)

We need to know ourselves

When our prayers aren't answered, we need to make a sober assessment of ourselves. As we look honestly at our requests, motives, faith, prayerlessness, sin and the extent to which we are keeping humble, unanswered prayer has a way of taking its proper perspective.

Do not think of yourself more highly than you ought, but rather think of yourself with sober judgment, in accordance with the measure of faith God has given you.

(Romans 12:3)

We need to know our enemy

While our interest and focus should always be primarily on God, we should also be aware of the devil's tactics so we can take both evasive and proactive steps to counteract his work.

We do this so that we may not be outwitted by Satan; for we are not ignorant of his designs.

(2 Corinthians 2:11, NRSV)

Part Six

Prayers that say 'Please'

Chapter One

Praying for Ourselves

We should never be embarrassed to bring our personal needs to God. He is our heavenly Father who delights to hear the heartfelt cries of his children and to answer them out of his rich resources.

And my God will meet all your needs according to his glorious riches in Christ Jesus. (Philippians 4:19)

'But isn't praying for yourself rather selfish?' people sometimes ask. Well, no, it isn't. In fact, we are on very safe ground in praying for ourselves and our own needs, for Jesus included this aspect of prayer when he gave us the Lord's Prayer as our model for praying (Matthew 6:9–13; see Part One, Chapter 1). He encouraged us to pray about our present need ('daily bread'), past sin ('forgive us our debts'), and future welfare ('And lead us …'). If this is good enough for Jesus, then it's good enough for us! And it's certainly good enough for God our Father who has promised to 'meet all your needs according to his glorious riches in Christ Jesus'.

When we begin to explore the Bible, we find ourselves almost overwhelmed with the sheer breadth of personal needs that were brought by people before God in prayer. Their relationship with God was such that there was nothing that they felt they couldn't bring to him. Let's look at some common examples.

Wisdom

While this is probably not something that many of us would think of asking for, it is frequently found in Bible prayers. God wants us to ask him for his wisdom: that is, the ability to do the *right thing* in the *right way* at the *right time.*

At Gibeon the LORD appeared to Solomon during the night in a dream, and God said, 'Ask for whatever you want me to give you.' Solomon answered, '… Now, O LORD my God, you have made your servant king in place of my father David. But I am only a little child and do not know how to carry out my duties … So give your servant a discerning heart to govern your people and to distinguish between right and wrong. For who is able to govern this great people of yours?' The Lord was pleased that Solomon had asked for this.

(1 Kings 3:5–7, 9–10)

If any of you lacks wisdom, he should ask God, who gives generously to all without finding fault, and it will be given to him.

(James 1:5)

See also 2 Chronicles 1:7–12; Job 28:12–28; Psalm 90:12; Proverbs 2:1–11; 3:13–18; 4:5–9; Daniel 2:17–23; Ephesians 1:17; Philippians 1:9–10

Daily provision

God does not want us to take the daily provision of our basic needs, such as food and clothing, for granted, nor to see it as something that comes solely from us (because, as we sometimes think, it was *our* money that paid for it!). Asking God for daily provision keeps us both grateful and humble.

Give me neither poverty nor riches, but give me only my daily bread. Otherwise, I may have too much and disown you and say, 'Who is the LORD?' Or I may become poor and steal, and so dishonour the name of my God.

(Proverbs 30:8–9)

Give us each day our daily bread.

(Luke 11:3)

See also Genesis 22:13–14; Deuteronomy 8:10–18; 1 Kings 17:1–16; Psalm 65:9–13; Matthew 6:25–34; 7:9–11; 14:15–21; 1 Timothy 6:17

Financial needs

Countless individuals and churches have experienced God's provision in this area of finances. Having handled their finances well and honoured God in their giving, they perhaps found that their resources had run out, for either the basics, or for some special treat, or for some expansion that they felt God calling them to. But then when they called out to God in prayer, they experienced his wonderful provision – often way beyond what they could have imagined. Sometimes the provision may seem quite miraculous, at other times, more 'ordinary'; but either way, God can provide. Try him out in this area and see – he is truly faithful!

'Go and cast a line into the lake and pull out the first fish you hook. Open its mouth, and you will find a coin. Use it to pay your taxes and mine.'

(Matthew 17:27, CEV)

God will generously provide all you need. Then you will always have everything you need and plenty left over to share with others.

(2 Corinthians 9:8, NLT)

See also Malachi 3:10; 2 Corinthians 8:1–15; 9:6–15; Philippians 4:14–19

A marriage partner

If we want a husband or wife, then God should be the first person we talk to about it! It is so important that we do not base our choice on merely external factors, such as good looks or good prospects, for, as the writer of Proverbs puts it, 'Charm is deceptive, and beauty is fleeting' (Proverbs 31:30). What we need more than anything else is the man of God who will help us become more of a woman of God, or the woman of God who will help us become more of a man of God.

One of the most delightful stories in the Bible of a man finding a wife is the account of Isaac finding Rebekah. The story is laced with references to prayer all along the way (Genesis 24:12, 15, 45, 48, 52). When the servant explains how clearly God has been involved in the whole incident, Bethuel her father and Laban her brother can only say, 'This is from the LORD; we can say nothing to you one way or the other. Here is Rebekah; take her and go, and let her become the wife of your master's son, as the LORD has directed' (Genesis 24:50–51).

See also Genesis 2:18–24; Ruth 3:1–4:12; Proverbs 18:22; 31:10–31

Health and healing

Sickness and disease came into the world as a result of the fall. We should therefore be no slower to pray confidently about our need for health and healing than we should about our need for forgiveness of sin.

Be merciful to me, LORD, for I am faint;
O LORD, heal me, for my bones are in agony.
My soul is in anguish.
How long, O LORD, how long?

Turn, O LORD, and deliver me;
save me because of your unfailing love.
No-one remembers you when he is dead.
Who praises you from his grave?

I am worn out from groaning;
all night long I flood my bed with weeping
and drench my couch with tears.
My eyes grow weak with sorrow;
they fail because of all my foes.

Away from me, all you who do evil,
for the LORD has heard my weeping.
The LORD has heard my cry for mercy;
the LORD accepts my prayer.

(Psalm 6:2–9)

Heal me, O LORD, and I shall be healed;
save me and I shall be saved,
for you are the one I praise.

(Jeremiah 17:14)

See also Exodus 15:22–26; Psalm 103:1–5; Isaiah 38:1–22; Matthew 9:20–22; James 5:13–16

Barrenness

The inability to have children can be a great trial to a couple. While none of us has the *right* to have children (they are, after all, a *gift* from God), the Bible gives us many examples of people who were barren but brought their desperate desire for children before God and who found that their prayers were answered. In days of modern medical advances, it is all too easy to look for help everywhere, except God!

'I prayed for this child, and the LORD has granted me what I asked of him.'

(1 Samuel 1:27)

By faith Abraham, even though he was past age – and Sarah herself was barren – was enabled to become a father because he considered him faithful who had made the promise.

(Hebrews 11:11)

See also Genesis 15:1–5; 21:1–7; Exodus 23:25–26; 1 Samuel 1:1–28; 2 Kings 4:8–17; Psalm 113:1–9; Luke 1:5–25

Help in hard times

All of us experience hard times in life. Sometimes it may be the consequence of our own mistakes or sin; sometimes it may just be 'one of those things'. Whatever the cause of the hardship, we can bring it before God in prayer and ask him to both strengthen us and to change the circumstances.

The Israelites groaned in their slavery and cried out, and their cry for help because of their slavery went up to God. God heard their groaning and he remembered his covenant with Abraham, with Isaac and with Jacob. So God looked on the Israelites and was concerned about them.

(Exodus 2:23–25)

Have mercy on me, O God, have mercy on me,
for in you my soul takes refuge.
I will take refuge in the shadow of your wings
until the disaster has passed.

(Psalm 57:1)

See also Psalm 27:1–14; 71:1–24; 102:1–28; Daniel 3:1–30; 6:1–28; 2 Corinthians 12:7–10; Philippians 1:12–26

Protection

While we do not need to live fearfully, we should not take our safety for granted. Committing ourselves to God, whether in crisis times or routinely, is a wise and godly thing to do.

And there by the Ahava Canal, I gave orders for all of us to fast and humble ourselves before our God. We prayed that he would give us a safe journey and protect us, our children, with our goods as we travelled. For I was ashamed to ask the king for soldiers and horsemen to accompany us and protect us from enemies along the way. After all, we had told the king, 'Our God protects all those who worship him, but his fierce anger rages against those who abandon him.' So we fasted and earnestly prayed that our God would take care of us, and he heard our prayer.

(Ezra 8:21–23, NLT)

And pray that we may be delivered from wicked and evil men, for not everyone has faith. But the Lord is faithful, and he will strengthen and protect you from the evil one.

(2 Thessalonians 3:2–3)

See also Psalm 27:4–5; 32:6–7; 35:1–28; 64:1–10; 91:1–16; 140:1–13; 143:1–12; John 17:9–15; 1 John 5:18

Being kept from temptation

Make no mistake about it, the devil is our enemy and is out to attack us in any way he can. He doesn't play fair, and that's why Jesus encouraged us to pray about this. We all know where we are weak and can get tempted; so bring these to God.

'And lead us not into temptation, but deliver us from the evil one.'

(Matthew 6:13)

This High Priest of ours understands our weaknesses, for he faced all of the same temptations we do, yet he did not sin. So let us come boldly to the throne of our gracious God. There we will receive his mercy, and we will find grace to help us when we need it.

(Hebrews 4:15–16)

See also Matthew 4:1–11; Luke 17:1–3; 22:39–46; 1 Corinthians 7:1–5; 10:13; Galatians 6:1; Hebrews 2:18

Forgiveness

As we saw in Part Four, God always welcomes us when we say 'Sorry' for our shortcomings, failures, and sins. We can be sure he will *always* forgive us and *never* turn us away.

Then I acknowledged my sin to you
and did not cover up my iniquity.
I said, 'I will confess
my transgressions to the LORD' –
and you forgave
the guilt of my sin

(Psalm 32:5)

'Forgive us our sins – just as we forgive those who have sinned against us.'

(Luke 11:4, NLT)

See also 2 Samuel 12:13; Psalm 32:1–5; 51:1–19; 103:1–18; Proverbs 28:13; Isaiah 6:5–7; 64:8–9; Luke 18:9–14; 1 John 1:8–9

We must remember, however, that *this life* is the only opportunity there is to have our sins forgiven. While God's door is always open to the very end (e.g. Luke 23:39–43), once death comes, it is then too late to seek God and his forgiveness (e.g. Luke 16:19–31).

Guidance

Our God, who is all-seeing and all-knowing, loves it when his children come seeking his guidance, both for the broad strategy of our lives and the specific steps we should take.

Show me your ways, O LORD,
teach me your paths;
guide me in your truth and teach me,
for you are God my Saviour,
and my hope is in you all day long.

(Psalm 25:4–5)

Whether you turn to the right or to the left, your ears will hear a voice behind you, saying, 'This is the way; walk in it.'

(Isaiah 30:21)

See also Exodus 33:12–14; 1 Samuel 23:1–5; 2 Samuel 2:1; 5:17–19; Psalm 143:8; Proverbs 3:5–6; Jeremiah 6:16; Matthew 2:19–20; Luke 6:12–13; Acts 16:9–10

Opening up the way

Sometime it is not so much guidance that we need, as for God to open up the way for us to move ahead into what we know he has for us. At such times we can pray for God to remove the circumstances or people that are the hindrance, or to bring new openings or opportunities.

'Oh, that you would bless me and enlarge my territory!'

(1 Chronicles 4:10)

Seeking signs

When younger, Martin was once on a train journey, praying and agonizing over whether to marry a particular girl. Eventually he asked God to intervene miraculously and to show him his will through a sign. There was suddenly a surprising intervention when cows invaded the railway line and brought the journey to a standstill. The trouble was: Martin wasn't quite sure whether this was God answering his prayer or not – and if it was, what the sign meant anyway! And so he (wisely!) decided that perhaps this wasn't quite what God meant by seeking his guidance!

While there are times when God gives 'signs' to assure people of his presence or guidance (e.g. 2 Kings 19:29; Luke 2:8–12), or sometimes even of his coming judgment (e.g. Ezekiel 12:1–11), asking for signs is generally seen as a mark of an inability to trust God (e.g. Exodus 4:1–17; 2 Kings 20:8–11), and a *demand* for signs is always resisted (e.g. Matthew 12:38–40). Gideon's laying out of a fleece (Judges 6:36–40) has often been taken by Christians as a 'model' of how to receive guidance; but it is clear from the context that, for a man who had just encountered the angel of the LORD (v11–12), had been commissioned by him (v13–16), had experienced a miracle (v20–22) and had received an empowering of the Holy Spirit (v34), his exercise with the fleece was a measure of his *lack* of faith, not the abundance of it.

As Christians we do not need to look for such external 'signs'. Through God's Word, God's Spirit and God's people, God has provided ample means for us to receive his guidance. We only need to ask!

'... knock and the door will be opened to you.'

(Matthew 7:7)

God, whom I serve with my whole heart in preaching the gospel of his Son, is my witness how constantly I remember you in my prayers at all times; and I pray that now at last by God's will the way may be opened for me to come to you.

(Romans 1:9–10)

See also Psalm 107:4–9; Isaiah 40:3–5; 43:18–22; 57:14; Acts 16:25–40; 18:21; Colossians 4:2–4

Boldness

God does not want his children to be fearful, but to be confident in both our dealing with people and our sharing the gospel with them, and in the way we approach him in prayer. When we lack confidence or courage, we should ask God for it.

When I called, you answered me;
you made me bold and stout-hearted.

(Psalm 138:3)

Now, Lord, consider their threats and enable your servants to speak your word with great boldness. Stretch out your hand to heal and perform miraculous signs and wonders through the name of your holy servant Jesus.' After they prayed, the place where they were meeting was shaken. And they were all filled with the Holy Spirit and spoke the word of God boldly.

(Acts 4:29–31)

See also 1 Chronicles 17:25; Proverbs 28:1; Romans 15:15; 2 Corinthians 3:7–18; Philemon 8–21; Hebrews 4:14–16

In old age

As we get older, we should not fear that God has any less time for us (perhaps because we cannot always 'do' as much for him) or that he will abandon us. God remains faithful to us, and we can continue to bring our changing needs before him just as much as we have done throughout our lives, whether that be our increasing aches and pains, or our desire to stay useful to him.

Since my youth, O God, you have taught me,
and to this day I declare your marvellous deeds.
Even when I am old and grey,
do not forsake me, O God,
till I declare your power to the next generation,
your might to all who are to come.

(Psalm 71:17–18)

See also Joshua 14:10–14; Job 42:10–17; Psalm 39:4–7; 61:1–8; 92:12–15; Isaiah 46:3–4

A FINAL PRAYER

Almighty God, who knowest our necessities before we ask,
and our ignorance in asking:
Set free thy servants from all anxious thoughts for the morrow;
give us contentment
with thy good gifts;
and confirm our faith that,
according as we seek thy kingdom,
thou wilt not suffer us to lack
any good thing;
through Jesus Christ our lord.

St Augustine of Hippo (354–430)

CONCLUSION

The wide breadth of topics brought before God in prayer by people in the Bible encourages us to believe that there is absolutely nothing that we cannot bring to our heavenly Father who wants to satisfy our needs.

The LORD will guide you always;
he will satisfy your needs …

(Isaiah 58:11)

Relevance for today

Pray for yourself boldly!

Remember: Jesus shows us, through the Lord's prayer, that it isn't selfish to pray for ourselves. (It becomes selfish when we *only* pray for ourselves and never for others.) Jesus has made it possible for us to bring our requests to our heavenly Father boldly (e.g. Hebrews 4:14–16), so let us do so! Bring bold and big requests to God!

Pray for yourself broadly!

Try not to be too narrow in what you pray about for yourself, always covering the same one or two topics. Why not use the headings of this chapter as a framework for expanding the sort of personal things that you could pray about? You could perhaps work through the list, taking one topic each day to ensure you maintain breadth and variety.

Pray for yourself beseechingly!

Jesus encouraged us not to give up when praying, including when praying for ourselves. In the parables in Luke 11:5–10 (the neighbour who needed bread) and Luke 18:1–7 (the widow and the judge), both requests were for very personal needs, not some vague spiritual benefit for the world at large. Because they weren't afraid to keep asking, they received what they needed. We too need to keep beseeching God, earnestly pleading with him, for those things that are on our heart. We will certainly never receive if we do not ask (James 4:2)!

Chapter Two

Praying for Others

> Praying for others is both a privilege and a responsibility, in which the Holy Spirit comes to help us.
>
> ***'And I will pour out a spirit of compassion and supplication on the house of David'***
> (Zechariah 12:10, NRSV)

With over twenty different words used in the original Bible languages to denote various types of prayer, it is clear that the people of Bible times loved to pray. But their praying was not totally self-centred; much of it was directed towards others. Still today the Holy Spirit wants to teach us how to pray for others so that, as we listen for his promptings, we can then bring our intercessions effectively before our Father God.

If we saw in the previous chapter a breadth of topics to pray about for ourselves, then there is an even broader range of things to pray about for others, as we shall see in this and the following chapter. Like Paul, we perhaps sometimes feel that 'we do not know what we ought to pray for' (Romans 8:26); but if we just stay still, we will often find that the Holy Spirit drops a thought into our minds about a particular person or situation. We just need to stop and listen!

The following headings may help stimulate you in your praying for others.

Praying for family

Our family is one of God's most precious gifts to us, and one about which we should be constantly praying to see God's blessing released. We will never see our prayers affect the nations if we cannot have faith to see them affect our family.

David returned home to bless his family.
(1 Chronicles 16:43)

If we are parents, our children are our greatest inheritance. We need to invest in them, not just materially, but also spiritually, praying for them regularly, teaching them God's word, and training them how to pray themselves.

And Abraham said to God, 'If only Ishmael might live under your blessing!'
(Genesis 17:18)

Then Manoah prayed to the LORD: 'O Lord, I beg you, let the man of God you sent to us come again to teach us how to bring up the boy who is to be born.'

(Judges 13:8)

See also Genesis 27:27–29; 48:12–49:28; 1 Samuel 1:27–28; Ezra 8:21; Job 1:1–5; Psalm 78:1–8; Proverbs 22:6; Matthew 19:13–14; Luke 1:67–79; 2:21–40; 2 Timothy 3:14–15

Praying for friends

For blessing

Even if we don't know specific things to pray about for our friends, we can at least ask God to bless them (though don't let this become a lazy option!).

The priests and the Levites stood to bless the people, and God heard them, for their prayer reached heaven, his holy dwelling-place.

(2 Chronicles 30:27)

May the God of peace, who through the blood of the eternal covenant brought back from the dead our Lord Jesus, that great Shepherd of the sheep, equip you with everything good for doing his will, and may he work in us what is pleasing to him, through Jesus Christ, to whom be glory for ever and ever. Amen.

(Hebrews 13:20–21)

See also Numbers 6:24–26; Deuteronomy 10:8; Joshua 14:13; Ruth 2:19–20; Psalm 3:8; 128:5–6; Matthew 16:17–19

For spiritual growth

Paul's ministry took him to the Gentile world where philosophy and human wisdom were highly prized and where, consequently, the message of the gospel seemed 'foolishness' (1 Corinthians 1:18). The temptation to be led astray by apparently 'fine sounding arguments' (Colossians 2:4) was therefore strong, just as it is today in a post-modern world. Against this background, Paul prayed for strong and true spiritual growth among his Christian friends.

For this reason, since the day we heard about you, we have not stopped praying for you and asking God to fill you with the knowledge of his will through all spiritual wisdom and understanding. And we pray this in order that you may live a life worthy of the Lord and may please him in every way: bearing fruit in every good work, growing in the knowledge of God, being strengthened with all power according to his glorious might so that you may have great endurance and patience, and joyfully giving thanks to the Father, who has qualified you to share in the inheritance of the saints in the kingdom of light.

(Colossians 1:9–12)

Epaphras … is always wrestling in prayer for you, that you may stand firm in all the will of God, mature and fully assured.

(Colossians 4:12)

See also 2 Corinthians 13:9; Galatians 4:19; Ephesians 1:15–19; 3:14–19; 2 Thessalonians 1:11–12

For health and healing

It is impossible to read the New Testament without concluding that praying for the sick formed a key part of the ministry of both Jesus and the early church. To remove such prayer from our ministry today, therefore, is to leave ourselves only half-clothed in the gospel. Go to the doctor by all means – but at least pray before you go!

Is any one of you sick? He should call the elders of the church to pray over him and anoint him with oil in the name of the Lord. And the prayer offered in faith will make the sick person well; the Lord will raise him up. If he has sinned, he will be forgiven. Therefore confess your sins to each other and pray for each other so that you may be healed. The prayer of a righteous man is powerful and effective.

(James 5:14–16)

Dear friend, I pray that you may enjoy good health and that all may go well with you, even as your soul is getting along well.

(3 John 2)

See also Numbers 12:13; 2 Kings 5:1–15; Psalm 103:1–5; 147:3; Matthew 8:5–13; 9:18–26; Mark 1:32–34; 16:15–18; Acts 3:1–16; 5:12–16; 9:32–42; 28:7–9

For protection

Praying for one another for protection is important – whether in difficult or dangerous circumstances, or just in routine travelling. It was because the wife of a colleague, nudged by the Holy Spirit, prayed a prayer of protection for Mike that he survived a potentially fatal accident with a Land Rover in Kenya. It certainly taught him not to take prayers for protection for granted!

But let all who take refuge in you be glad;
let them ever sing for joy.
Spread your protection over them,
that those who love your name may rejoice in you.
For surely, O LORD, you bless the righteous;
you surround them with your favour as with a shield.

(Psalm 5:11–12)

The power of blessing

The Bible sees 'blessings' as powerful. They are not merely the offering of 'spiritual best wishes', but are a powerful declaratory prayer based on the promises of God.

'The LORD bless you
and keep you;
the LORD make his face shine upon you
and be gracious to you;
the LORD turn his face towards you
and give you peace.'

(Numbers 6:24–26)

May the LORD bless you from Zion
all the days of your life;
may you see the prosperity of Jerusalem,
and may you live to see your children's children.

(Psalm 128:5–6)

Then little children were brought to Jesus for him to place his hands on them and pray for them.

(Matthew 19:13)

Bless those who curse you, and pray for those who spitefully use you.

(Luke 6:28, NKJV)

After spending some time there, they were sent off by the brothers with the blessing of peace to return to those who had sent them.

(Acts 15:33)

See also Genesis 27:27–29; 28:1–5; 48:15–16; 49:1–28; Deuteronomy 33:1–29; Ruth 2:4; 2 Samuel 7:28–29; 19:39; Psalm 3:8; Proverbs 11:11; Matthew 5:1–11; Romans 15:29; 1 Peter 3:9

In both our prayers and our conversations, what a difference it would make if we were to learn the power of blessing others, based on the promises of God's word and the inspiration of his Holy Spirit!

So Peter was kept in prison, but the church was earnestly praying to God for him.

(Acts 12:5)

See also Ezra 8:21–23; Psalm 20:1–2; 91:1–16; Luke 22:31; John 17:9–15; Romans 15:30–33; 2 Thessalonians 3:1–3

For filling with the Holy Spirit

We can pray for others to receive the Holy Spirit. In the New Testament, the Spirit was often given as a believer laid hands on someone and prayed. While this is not the only way the Spirit is given (see e.g. Acts 10:44–46), it is certainly the most common, perhaps as a sign of the need that we have of one another in the body of Christ.

When the apostles in Jerusalem heard that Samaria had accepted the word of God, they sent Peter and John to them. When they arrived, they prayed for them that they might receive the Holy Spirit, because the Holy Spirit had not yet come upon any of them; they had simply been baptised into the name of the Lord Jesus. Then Peter and John placed their hands on them, and they received the Holy Spirit.

(Acts 8:14–17)

Then Ananias went to the house and entered it. Placing his hands on Saul, he said, 'Brother Saul, the Lord – Jesus, who appeared to you on the road as you were coming here – has sent me so that you may see again and be filled with the Holy Spirit.'

(Acts 9:17)

See also Matthew 3:11; Luke 3:21–22; John 20:21–22; Acts 1:1–8; 4:23–31; 19:1–7; Romans 15:13; Ephesians 5:18–20

For doors to open

Sometimes our friends need to see doors opening up so that they can move ahead into all that God has promised. We can help to see those doors opened through our prayers of intercession.

Devote yourselves to prayer, being watchful and thankful. And pray for us, too, that God may open a door for our message, so that we may proclaim the mystery of Christ, for which I am in chains. Pray that I may proclaim it clearly, as I should.

(Colossians 4:2–4)

See also Isaiah 40:3–5; Matthew 7:7–8; Acts 12:5–19; 1 Corinthians 16:8–9; 2 Corinthians 2:12; 2 Thessalonians 3:1–2; Revelation 3:7–8

Praying for enemies

Praying for our friends is not a great burden; but what about praying for our enemies? Our enemies? Well, yes; for that's exactly what the Bible tells us to do. Why? Because when we do, we are reflecting the character of our compassionate God, and are thereby giving God opportunity to deal with people in his own way.

Do not take revenge, my friends, but leave room for God's wrath, for it is written: 'It is mine to avenge; I will repay,' says the Lord. On the contrary:

'If your enemy is hungry, feed him;
if he is thirsty, give him something to drink.
In doing this, you will heap burning coals on his head.'
Do not be overcome by evil, but overcome evil with good.

(Romans 12:19–21)

Do not repay evil with evil or insult with insult, but with blessing, because to this you were called so that you may inherit a blessing.

(1 Peter 3:9)

See also Leviticus 19:18; Proverbs 20:22; 25:21–22; Luke 6:27–31; Romans 12:14, 17; 1 Corinthians 4:12–13

Praying in tongues

Only a couple of decades ago, a section on 'praying in tongues' (prayer language that you have neither learned nor understand) would probably not have been found in a mainstream Christian book like this one. But so widespread has been charismatic renewal, across the whole spectrum of churches, that not to include it now would be a serious omission.

The authors' own experiences are different: Martin doesn't exercise the gift, whereas Mike uses it often. But both are convinced it is a genuine gift of the Spirit, as explained by Paul in 1 Corinthians 12:4–11, 27–31; 14:1–33. In corporate gatherings, praying in tongues requires interpretation (1 Corinthians 14:13–17) so everybody may be 'edified' (v17) or 'strengthened' (v26). In private use, however, it needs no interpretation, for it is a means of personal edification (v4) and of our spirit being able to pray beyond the level of our knowledge or understanding, which can be especially useful when we don't know the details of a particular situation.

Paul believed in the value of praying both 'with my mind' (i.e. in our own language) and 'with my spirit' (i.e. in tongues) (v15). He gave testimony to his own frequent use of tongues (v18) and this may also have been what was in his mind when he referred to the Spirit's 'groans' (Romans 8:26). If God has given you this gift, use it! Your intercession on behalf of others in this way may well be expressing things that your natural mind could never think of nor could ever know.

Praying for the church

The church is still the major vehicle through which God acts in this world. Praying for the church that we are part of, therefore, should very much be on our agenda so that together we might be more effective in seeing God's will 'done on earth as it is in heaven' (Matthew 6:10). So, what sort of things can we pray for the church?

For its growth

Jesus wants his church to grow, not so that we can have the pleasure of seeing our buildings full on Sundays, but out of his heart of compassion to see people respond to the good news of the kingdom and so be saved.

Jesus went through all the towns and villages, teaching in their synagogues, preaching the good news of the kingdom and healing every disease and sickness. When he saw the crowds, he had compassion on them, because they were harassed and helpless, like sheep without a shepherd. Then he said to his disciples, 'The harvest is plentiful, but the workers are few. Ask the Lord of the harvest, therefore, to send out workers into his harvest field.'

(Matthew 9:35–38)

Note that Jesus urges prayer here, not for some vague concept of 'church growth', but rather for *workers* to go out and do the job! The harvest is ready, he said; all it needs is people (i.e. you and me!) to go and bring it in. We need to pray for one another, therefore, that we will play our part as those workers.

Praying for growth is often the first step to *participating* in growth. In the church which Mike pastors in Oxford, for example, they have experienced significant growth among students, all arising from a small group of students who felt burdened to pray for the harvest in the University. As they prayed, something happened: they discovered that God was making them willing workers and that they were starting to participate in the harvest with growing ease and effectiveness.

Paul was convinced that it is as we are active in sharing our faith that our understanding of what it really means to be a Christian grows:

I pray that you may be active in sharing your faith, so that you will have a full understanding of every good thing we have in Christ.

(Philemon 6)

See also Luke 10:1–21; John 4:35–38; Acts 9:31; 2 Corinthians 10:15–16; Colossians 1:3–12

For its leaders

The prophecy 'strike the shepherd and the sheep will be scattered' (Zechariah 13:7) was fulfilled in Jesus at the cross (Matthew 26:31; Mark 14:27). It is still a strategy that the devil uses against the church today. If he can cause its leaders to get weary or discouraged, or attack them and cause them to stumble, then he can significantly weaken the church. This is why church leaders (whether pastors, group leaders, or youth leaders) should be the object of our constant prayers rather than our constant criticism.

I urge you, brothers, by our Lord Jesus Christ and by the love of the Spirit, to join me in my struggle by praying to God for me. Pray that I may be rescued from the unbelievers in Judea and that my service in Jerusalem may be acceptable to the saints there, so that by God's will I may come to you with joy and together with you be refreshed.

(Romans 15:30–31)

He has delivered us from such a deadly peril, and he will deliver us. On him we have set our hope that he will continue to deliver us, as you help us by your prayers. Then many will give thanks on our behalf for the gracious favour granted us in answer to the prayers of many.

(2 Corinthians 1:10–11)

See also Acts 6:6; 14:23; Ephesians 6:19–20; Philippians 1:19; 1 Thessalonians 5:25; 2 Thessalonians 3:1; Hebrews 13:18–19

For its unity

Unity is tremendously important to God, for his very being is a perfect unity of Father, Son, and Holy Spirit ('the Trinity'). His children, therefore, should be eager to express unity in their own lives, not necessarily in outward form (belonging to one mega-church or organization), but certainly in terms of heart and purpose. We should therefore pray for unity within our own church, and between the churches in our locality. Such unity undoubtedly attracts the blessing of God, and makes a powerful impact on the world.

How good and pleasant it is
when brothers live together in unity!
It is like precious oil poured on the head,
running down on the beard,
running down on Aaron's beard,
down upon the collar of his robes.
It is as if the dew of Hermon
were falling on Mount Zion.
For there the LORD bestows his blessing,
even life for evermore.

(Psalm 133:1–3)

'My prayer is not for them alone. I pray also for those who will believe in me through their message, that all of them may be one, Father, just as you are in me and I am in you. May they also be in us so that the world may believe that you have sent me. I have

given them the glory that you gave me, that they may be one as we are one.'

(John 17:20–21)

See also Psalm 122:6–9; Micah 4:1–5; John 17:1–19, 22–23; Acts 1:12–14; 2:1; 1 Corinthians 1:10; 10:16–17; Ephesians 1:3–10

Prayer: a priority for church leaders

As a pastor Mike knows all too well how easy it is to get caught up in 'doing things'. There is always one more person to visit, one more phone call to make, one more message to prepare, one more crisis to resolve; and meanwhile, God stands by, watching. But if our churches are going to have God's blessing released, then leaders need to understand that the first call on their life is not to *do*, but to *pray*. This was a lesson the early church had to learn quickly. The Jerusalem church became overwhelmed with the consequences of rapid growth, and prayer and the study of God's word were getting squeezed out. So the leaders took decisive action to get things in their proper order again.

But as the believers rapidly multiplied, there were rumblings of discontent. Those who spoke Greek complained against those who spoke Hebrew, saying that their widows were being discriminated against in the daily distribution of food. So the Twelve called a meeting of all the believers. 'We apostles should spend our time preaching and teaching the word of God, not administering a food programme,' they said. 'Now look around among yourselves, brothers, and select seven men who are well respected and are full of the Holy Spirit and wisdom. We will put them in charge of this business. Then we can spend our time in prayer and preaching and teaching the word.'

(Acts 6:1–4, NLT)

Not only could everyone immediately see the wisdom of the proposal (v5), it led to new significant growth (v7). But then, that should hardly surprise us, for God had been given first place again!

A FINAL PRAYER

Be gracious to all our friends
and neighbours.
Bless our relations with
the best of thy blessings,
With fear and love.
Preserve us from our enemies,
And reconcile them both to us
and to thyself.

John Wesley (1703–1791)

CONCLUSION

Praying for others is a wonderful, Spirit-inspired privilege! Let's make the most of it!

'... I will intercede with the LORD for you.'

(1 Samuel 7:5)

Relevance for today

Privilege and responsibility
Praying for others within our spiritual family is both a privilege and a responsibility. How seriously are *you* taking this?

Don't promise to pray – pray!
How easy it is to say, 'I'll remember to pray for you' – and then to forget! Having seen the power that there is in praying for others, let's not just promise; let's pray!

Use godly imagination
When praying for others, try to imagine yourself in their situation. It will help you to be creative in what you pray for and how you pray.

Ask for the Spirit's help
The Holy Spirit wants to help us to pray (e.g. Romans 8:26) and we are told to 'pray in the Spirit' (Ephesians 6:18). Therefore, ask the Spirit for help in what to pray and how to pray it. Use both your mind and your spirit (1 Corinthians 14:15).

Stop and listen
Intercession is not just about bringing God our spiritual shopping list. We need to be still and listen for those quiet nudges of the Spirit, and then bring these as prayers to God. A sudden thought, a picture, a name, a nation: all can be the leading of the Holy Spirit to pray.

Chapter Three

Praying for Nations and Leaders

God is God *over* every nation, but he wants us to pray that he might also be seen as God *in* every nation.

Blessed is the nation whose God is the Lord.
(Psalm 33:12)

Would you love to see our nation not only blessed by God, but also more godly? A nation living by the Ten Commandments, a nation where love for God and one's neighbour (Matthew 22:37–40) is the norm rather than the exception? If your answer is 'Yes', then ask yourself: how often do you pray for that? How much do you pray for your nation, your government (whatever political party you might support), and your leaders? Apart from those who do so briefly as part of their church's liturgy, we suspect that the answer is, 'Not very much.' So, maybe it's not very surprising that our nation is not as godly as it might be. But of course, things can change!

Worlds within a world

The world of the Bible is a complex patchwork of nations and rulers. In it we see the good and the bad, the godly and the godless. But two societies stand out in the way that they lived and related to that wider, more complex world.

The first is the world of Israel. Israel stood in a unique relationship, a covenant, with God in a way that no other nation did at that time or has done since. God promised that if Israel would keep that covenant by being obedient to his ways, then he would bless them (e.g. Genesis 12:1–3; Deuteronomy 6:1–25; 28:1–68; 2 Samuel 7:5–16). History proved the promise to be true: whenever Israel was obedient to God, it prospered as a nation; but, whenever it was disobedient, it declined, was defeated and even destroyed. However, since we are not part of that covenant with Israel, we cannot claim those same blessings directly today. We are not a theocratic nation (i.e. one ruled by God), but a scattered people in an alien and unbelieving world. This leads us to the second main world in the Bible.

In contrast to Israel's theocratic status, the New Testament church belonged to no nation, yet permeated them all – nations that were anything but favourable to it. And yet, church leaders boldly declared that all governing authorities were appointed by God and should therefore be obeyed (e.g. Romans 13:1–7) – even when, as was the case when Paul wrote Romans, the authority in question was the mad Emperor Nero who would take his pleasure in persecuting Christians. A world further removed from the Old Testament world cannot be imagined.

Through these two very different worlds, however, certain principles remain constant in God's word and are effective in God's world: godliness is better than ungodliness; obedience is better than disobedience; authority is better than anarchy; blessing is better than curse; 'righteousness exalts a nation, but sin is a disgrace to any people' (Proverbs 14:34). Whether people believe in him or not, God is the God over all the nations, and as such all nations can be brought to him in prayer, for him to challenge, change, and bless.

Let's look, then, at some of the prayers from these two worlds offered for nations and leaders to see what principles we can glean for praying for nations and leaders in our own time.

Prayer for blessing

God would far rather bless people and nations than curse them; so let's pray for his blessing!

Blessing on a godly nation

In Old Testament times, the name of the capital city was often used to represent the whole nation (just as today with 'London' or 'Washington'). Prayers were offered for Jerusalem therefore, not simply because it was marked out as God's dwelling place (e.g. Psalm 132:13–14), but because it represented the whole nation.

Pray for the peace of Jerusalem:
'May those who love you be secure.
May there be peace within your walls
and security within your citadels.'
For the sake of my brothers and friends,
I will say, 'Peace be within you.'
For the sake of the house of the LORD our God,
I will seek your prosperity.

(Psalm 122:6–7)

Because Christians are no longer part of the old covenant, there is no obligation on us to pray for Jerusalem (as some Christians have insisted we should do). But the underlying principle remains true: if you want *your* nation to be blessed, pray for it! And especially pray for its capital where the seat of government lies and where important decisions are made that affect us all.

See also Deuteronomy 1:11; 15:6; 28:1–14; 33:1–29; 2 Samuel 7:18–29; Psalm 28:8–9; 67:1–7; 115:9–15; 132:13–18; Jeremiah 31:23–25; Ezekiel 34:25–31

Blessing on a godless nation

Perhaps of more relevance to us is knowing whether we can ask God to bless our godless nation. Because God is 'the great King over all the earth' (Psalm 47:2), the God who 'reigns over the nations' (Psalm 47:8), all nations are ultimately subject to him and can therefore be brought to him for his blessing. In praying for blessing on our own nation, we are wanting people to see more of God – whether through his interventions or through his people – and so have opportunity to turn to him.

This is exactly what Jeremiah encouraged his fellow countrymen, exiled into pagan Babylon, to do:

This is what the LORD Almighty, the God of Israel, says to all those I carried into exile from Jerusalem to Babylon: 'Build houses and settle down; plant gardens and eat what they produce. Marry and have sons and daughters; find wives for your sons and give your daughters in marriage, so that they too may have sons and daughters. Increase in number there; do not decrease. Also, seek the peace and prosperity of the city to which I have carried you into exile. Pray to the L*ORD for it, because if it prospers, you too will prosper.'*

(Jeremiah 29:4–7)

In a different world and a different time, Paul encouraged Timothy to do the same:

I urge, then, first of all, that requests, prayers, intercession and thanksgiving be made for everyone – for kings and all those in authority, that we may live peaceful and quiet lives in all godliness and holiness. This is good, and pleases God our Saviour, who wants all men to be saved and to come to a knowledge of the truth.

(1 Timothy 2:1–4)

Daniel was another who grasped the importance of blessing the pagan nation where he lived. Taken into exile to Babylon as a young teenager, Daniel had been trained as a government official for the very nation that had enslaved him. He diligently carried out his duties, seeking to stay faithful to his God and useful to his king. Prayer three times a day was the backbone of his life (Daniel 6:10–13); but his prayer was not just for himself and his own people; it was also for the blessing of the pagan king and nation in whose service he now found himself. We even find him seeking God for interpretations of the king's dreams; and, as he did so, God answered – even for the benefit of a pagan!

Then Daniel returned to his house and explained the matter to his friends Hananiah, Mishael and Azariah. He urged them to plead for mercy from the God of heaven concerning this mystery, so that he and his friends might not be executed with the rest of the wise men of Babylon. During the night the mystery was revealed to Daniel in a vision ... Arioch took Daniel to the king at once and said, 'I have found a man among the exiles from Judah who can tell the king what his dream means.' The king asked Daniel (also called Belteshazzar), 'Are you able to tell me what I saw in my dream and interpret it?' Daniel replied, 'No wise man, enchanter, magician or diviner can explain to the king the mystery he has asked about, but there is a God in heaven who reveals mysteries.'

(Daniel 2:17–19, 25–27)

Daniel was careful to give God the credit as he outlined the dream and its meaning to the king, which led to an increased awareness of the living God in Nebuchadnezzar's life (Daniel 2:46–47; 4:34–37) and promotion and new opportunities for Daniel and his friends. Our prayers and godly work can still make a difference in our own nation today.

Prayer for deliverance

Deliverance from foes

Having conquered the northern kingdom of Israel in 721 BC and scattered its people across its empire, Assyria tried the same with the southern kingdom of Judah twenty years later. Jerusalem was surrounded by its armies, but Hezekiah 'tore his clothes and put on sackcloth and went into the temple of the LORD' (2 Kings 19:1), as a result of which Assyria withdrew because of threats from Egypt (19:5–9). However, Sennacherib sent Hezekiah a letter saying that he would be back! Undaunted, Hezekiah spread out the letter before the Lord and prayed for deliverance for his nation.

Hezekiah received the letter from the messengers and read it. Then he went up to the temple of the LORD and spread it out before the LORD. And Hezekiah prayed to the LORD: 'O LORD, God of Israel, enthroned between the cherubim, you alone are God over all the kingdoms of the earth. You have made heaven and earth. Give ear, O LORD, and hear; open your eyes, O LORD, and see; listen to the words Sennacherib has sent to insult the living God. It is true, O LORD, that the Assyrian kings have laid waste these nations and their lands. They have thrown their gods into the fire and destroyed them, for they were not gods but only wood and stone, fashioned by men's hands. Now, O LORD our God, deliver us from his hand, so that all kingdoms on earth may know that you alone, O LORD, are God.'

(2 Kings 19:14–19)

(You'll need to read 2 Kings 19:32–37 to find out what happened next and to see the miraculous deliverance God brought about!)

While our nation doesn't stand in the same relationship to God as Hezekiah's nation did, the principle of calling out to God to deliver us from evil still holds good, for God hates evil. The great leaders of the West during the Second World War didn't hesitate to do this; sadly, modern leaders are either too godless, or too conscious of their political image, to be seen to need to call upon the Almighty for help in times of crisis. But Christians don't need their permission, or their clarion call, to do so!

See also Exodus 14:13–22; Judges 3:7–11; 2 Kings 13:4–5; 2 Chronicles 14:9–15; 20:1–23; Nehemiah 9:5–37; Psalm 3:1–8; 18:1–50

Deliverance from reproach

God's people are one of the main ways that the world can 'see' God. Hence, if God's people are seen to be weak or the object of reproach, then God himself will be seen as the same. That is why the Bible contains prayers for God to deliver his people from reproach, so that his name might not be dishonoured.

'Hear us, O our God, for we are despised. Turn their insults back on their own heads. Give them over as plunder in a land of captivity. Do not cover up their guilt or blot out their sins from your sight, for they have thrown insults in the face of the builders.'

(Nehemiah 4:4–5)

Let the priests, who minister before the LORD,
weep between the temple porch and the altar.
Let them say, 'Spare your people, O LORD.
Do not make your inheritance an object of scorn,
a byword among the nations.
Why should they say among the peoples,
"Where is their God?"'

(Joel 2:17)

See also Joshua 5:9; Psalm 44:1–26; 79:1–13; Isaiah 51:7–16; Daniel 9:4–19; Micah 7:8–20

Deliverance from disaster

You don't have to look too far nowadays to come across disasters, and the ancient world was no different. That is because creation groans under the effects of human sin (Romans 8:20–21). But just because sin lies at its root doesn't mean we should sit by dispassionately. We can call out to God for his protection when disaster approaches or his help when disasters have struck.

Joel lived at a time when Israel – the land that was meant to be 'flowing with milk and honey' (e.g. Exodus 3:8) – had been devastated by locusts and severe drought. Confronted with this crisis, he prayed and called his nation to prayer, challenging them to see what *God* might be saying through all of this (a notion no more popular in his days than today!).

To you, O LORD, I call,
for fire has devoured the open pastures
and flames have burned up all the trees of the field.
Even the wild animals pant for you;
the streams of water have dried up
and fire has devoured the open pastures.

Blow the trumpet in Zion;
sound the alarm on my holy hill.
Let all who live in the land tremble,
for the day of the LORD is coming.

(Joel 1:19–2:1)

See also Genesis 49:18; 1 Samuel 17:37; Esther 4:12–16; Psalm 18:1–50; 107:1–43; Joel 2:15–18; Amos 7:1–6

Thanks to TV, newspapers and the Internet, we are more informed of events in our world than any previous generation, and therefore have less excuse than any of them for not praying. When you see some disaster, impending or actual, don't just feel sorry – pray!

Deliverance from judgment on sin

As we saw in Part Four, God is always ready to hear our prayers that say, 'Sorry'. Sometimes we need to seek forgiveness, not just for our personal sin, but for the sin that we as a nation have committed. Our longing should be for a huge wave of repentance and salvation to sweep through our land.

I lay prostrate before the LORD those forty days and forty nights because the LORD had said he would destroy you. I prayed to the LORD and said, 'O Sovereign LORD, do not destroy your people, your own inheritance that you redeemed by your great power and brought out of Egypt with a mighty hand. Remember your servants Abraham, Isaac and Jacob. Overlook the stubbornness of this people, their wickedness and their sin.'

(Deuteronomy 9:25–27)

Brothers, my heart's desire and prayer to God for the Israelites is that they may be saved.

(Romans 10:1)

See also Ezra 9:6–15; Nehemiah 9:5–37; Psalm 79:8–9; Amos 7:1–6

Prayer for revival

Much energy has been expended debating whether we should be praying for *renewal*, *revival*, or *restoration*; or whether we have been through one phase and are entering another. The more pragmatic approach simply says that, whatever it is that our nation needs, we want it! All of us should be longing to see the church come even more alive so that backsliders are restored, sinners are born again in their thousands, and the nation is changed.

Many prayers for revival are found in the Old Testament, and so aren't directly applicable to us today, because we are not a covenant nation like Israel was. But, as we saw earlier, there are still underlying principles that we can use as we pray.

'If my people, who are called by my name, will humble themselves and pray and seek my face and turn from their wicked ways, then will I hear from heaven and will forgive their sin and will heal their land.'

(2 Chronicles 7:14)

Will you not revive us again,
that your people may rejoice in you?

(Psalm 85:6)

Oh, that you would rend the heavens and
come down,
that the mountains would tremble before
you!
As when fire sets twigs ablaze
and causes water to boil,
come down to make your name known to
your enemies
and cause the nations to quake before you!
For when you did awesome things that we
did not expect,
you came down, and the mountains
trembled before you.
Since ancient times no-one has heard,
no ear has perceived,
no eye has seen any God besides you,
who acts on behalf of those who wait for
him.

(Isaiah 64:1–4)

LORD, I have heard of your fame;
I stand in awe of your deeds, O LORD.
Renew them in our day,
in our time make them known;
in wrath remember mercy.

(Habakkuk 3:2)

'Repent, then, and turn to God, so that your sins may be wiped out, that times of refreshing may come from the Lord.'

(Acts 3:19)

See also 1 Kings 8:46–53; Ezra 9:6–15; Psalm 80:1–19; Jeremiah 33:6–11; Lamentations 5:21–22; Ezekiel 37:1–14; Daniel 9:17–19; Hosea 6:1–3; Joel 2:12–14; Revelation 2:4–7; 3:1–6; 3:14–20

For prayers of repentance, often a precondition to revival, see Part Four, Chapter 6.

A FINAL PRAYER

Almighty Father,
whose will is to restore all things
in your beloved Son,
the king of all:
govern the hearts and minds
of those in authority,
and bring the families
of the nations,
divided and torn apart by the
ravages of sin,
to be subject to his just
and gentle rule;
who is alive and reigns with you
and the Holy Spirit,
one God, now and for ever.

Alternative Service Book (1980)

CONCLUSION

The privilege of intercession stretches beyond me, my friends, and my church, to the nation and the nations. God wants to be God of them all!

'Be still, and know that I am God;
I will be exalted among the nations,
I will be exalted in the earth.'

(Psalm 46:10)

Relevance for today

Let's conclude with some practical suggestions for how we can pray for our nation and the nations.

Pray in your own prayer times

Try to include praying for your own nation in your personal prayer times twice a week.

Pray when watching TV

When there is a news item of national or international importance, pray for it briefly there and then. God is always near, so praying doesn't need a 'warm-up' time for the prayer to be heartfelt or effective.

Pray on prayer walks

Walk through your village, town or city; open your eyes and *look*. What do you *see*? It may be something obvious: you walk past the police station, so pray about law and order; you walk past some offices, so pray for righteousness in business. Or it may be that you walk down a certain street and suddenly feel burdened to pray about marriage. Our experience is that this often proves to be a real need in that particular area at that time; so trust the Holy Spirit, and pray! You can do this on your own or in pairs.

Pray in church meetings

Apart from churches where prayer for the nation is included (if somewhat briefly) in their liturgy, probably few churches pray for our nation or government in any consistent way. (This is not the case, however, if you go to some African nations, for example, where Christians have had to pray in order to survive.) Encourage your leaders (nicely!) to include prayer for the nation more regularly in Sunday services or midweek groups.

Pray for other nations

The Great Commission (Matthew 28:18–20) calls the church to look beyond its own doorstep to the nations of the world. We don't necessarily have to establish special 'missionary prayer meetings' to focus on the nations; we can pray for nations when they appear in the news or if we go abroad on holiday. If your church has missionaries in other nations, put a photo of them on your kitchen notice board or by your computer screen to remind you to pray for them.

Chapter Four

Doing it Right

While there are no 'magic formulas' or set patterns for Christian prayer as in other religions, there are, nevertheless, certain ways of 'doing it right'.

'And when you pray, do not keep on babbling like pagans ...'
(Matthew 6:7)

Mike has a favourite plumbing story. It started early one Saturday when he needed to repair a toilet cistern at home. Of course, the easiest way to do it would have been to hire a plumber; but plumbers don't come cheap! So Mike went to the local DIY store, bought the required part, and started the job. Of course, as the morning unfolded various fittings now proved not to fit, one new part led to the need for another, and one joint obstinately refused to seal (witness the wet bathroom floor!) Nine hours later (!) Mike swallowed his pride and phoned a church member (who was rather better at DIY!) who rushed to the rescue. Twenty minutes later, the job was done!

Doing things right is always so much easier. And funnily enough, prayer is no different!

Prayer isn't magic!

In talking about 'doing it right' we aren't for one minute suggesting that prayer must be done in a certain way. If that were true, then it would be no different to primitive magic. The truth is, because prayer is about *a relationship* with God, it has as many different expressions as there are people. Some people are noisy and extrovert, and so their prayers will reflect that; some people are quiet and reflective, and so their prayers will reflect this. No one way will be 'right'. Nevertheless, there are certain things that can help, or hinder, our prayers. What are they?

Keys to praying aright

Praying according to God's will

Jesus' anguish must have been enormous. Indeed, it was so great that 'his sweat was like drops of blood falling to the ground' (Luke 22:44). What caused this was not merely the thought of a martyr's death; after all, countless of his followers would face the same. No, what caused Jesus such anguish was knowing that he was about to carry the weight of the world's sin and drink what the prophets called 'the cup of God's wrath' (e.g. Jeremiah 25:15–16), God's righteous judgment on sin. Little wonder he prayed as he did:

'Father, if you are willing, take this cup from me.'

(Luke 22:42)

And yet, that was only half of his prayer; for he continued,

'Yet not my will, but yours be done.'

(Luke 22:42)

For Jesus, the most important thing was praying for his Father's will to be done, whatever the personal cost; for in praying for this, he knew he was praying for what was best.

Sadly, Jesus' submission of his prayer to the condition 'if it be your will' has sometimes become little more than a 'lazy man's cop-out' for many Christians. That is, we can pray for whatever we like; but add the postscript 'if it be your will, Lord', and then we won't have to discover what God's will is before we pray, and nor will we have to worry if our prayers aren't answered, as we can always put it down to, 'Ah well, it wasn't God's will anyway'.

The far more exciting and faith-building approach, however, is to take time to try to discover what God's will is first – through the Bible, through prophecy, through waiting upon God, and so on – and then to pray it. If we find out what God wants in this way, then we can be confident our prayers will be answered, for we will be in tune with his thoughts.

'Your kingdom come, your will be done on earth as it is in heaven.'

(Matthew 6:10)

For this reason, since the day we heard about you, we have not stopped praying for you and asking God to fill you with the knowledge of his will through all spiritual wisdom and understanding.

(Colossians 1:9)

This is the confidence we have in approaching God: that if we ask anything according to his will, he hears us.

(1 John 5:14)

See also 2 Samuel 7:18–20; Psalm 40:7–8; 143:10; Hebrews 10:5–10; James 1:5–8

One key to discovering God's will is staying close to Jesus; what the Bible describes as 'remaining' or 'abiding' (KJV, NASB) in Christ. The closer we stay to Jesus in daily life, the easier it will be to hear him share what is on the Father's heart.

'I am the vine; you are the branches. If a man remains in me and I in him, he will bear much fruit; apart from me you can do nothing ... If you remain in me and my words remain in you, ask whatever you wish, and it will be given you. This is to my Father's glory, that you bear much fruit, showing yourselves to be my disciples.'

(John 15:5,7–8)

Praying in faith

Faith should characterize our relationship with God from start to finish. It is how we started that relationship, and how the relationship is maintained and grows. Hebrews sums it up like this:

And without faith it is impossible to please God, because anyone who comes to him must believe that he exists and that he rewards those who earnestly seek him.

(Hebrews 11:6)

The trouble is, the longer we are a Christian, the easier it is for us to stop exercising those 'faith muscles' and to become presumptuous. But we won't see our prayers answered unless faith remains central, as the disciples discovered. Peter, James, and John had been up a mountain with Jesus, witnessing the transfiguration (Matthew 17:1–13). Meanwhile, down at the bottom, the other disciples had experienced an embarrassing failure: a man had brought his demonized son to them, 'but they could not heal him' (Matthew 17:16). Jesus rebuked them for their failure (v17) and then healed the boy instantly. When they asked why it hadn't worked for them, Jesus replied:

'Because you have so little faith. I tell you the truth, if you have faith as small as a mustard seed, you can say to this mountain, "Move from here to there" and it will move. Nothing will be impossible for you.'

(Matthew 17:20–21)

What can we learn from this incident?

- **Past authority is no substitute for present faith**
  Jesus had already given them 'authority to drive out evil spirits and to heal every disease and sickness' (Matthew 10:1), but they hadn't taken hold of that authority right now when it was needed. As Christians today, the effectiveness of our prayers doesn't depend on the authority God gave our church in the past, but on what we do with that authority in the present.

- **Past experience is no substitute for present faith**
  Having been given Jesus' authority, the disciples had gone out and used it. 'They set out and went from village to village, preaching the gospel and healing people everywhere' (Luke 9:6). A little later they returned excitedly saying, 'Lord, even the demons submit to us in your name' (Luke 10:17). So, what had gone wrong? It seems they had become presumptuous because of their very success, and so had ended up not exercising faith (v20). But with faith, why, even mountains could be moved!

Jesus replied, 'I tell you the truth, if you have faith and do not doubt, not only can you do what was done to the fig-tree, but also you can say to this mountain, "Go, throw yourself into the sea," and it will be done. If you believe, you will receive whatever you ask for in prayer.'

(Matthew 21:21–22)

If any of you lacks wisdom, he should ask God, who gives generously to all without finding fault, and it will be given to him. But when he asks, he must believe and not doubt, because he who doubts is like a wave of the sea, blown and tossed by the wind. That man should not think he will receive anything from the Lord; he is a double-minded man, unstable in all he does.

(James 1:5–8)

We never get beyond the stage where we have to exercise faith on a daily basis. With faith, anything can happen; without it, only dismal failure awaits us.

See also 1 Chronicles 5:20; Matthew 8:5–10; 9:20–22, 27–30; Mark 6:5–6; Hebrews 10:22; James 5:14–15

Praying in Jesus' name

Another key to effective prayer is praying 'in Jesus' name'. We cannot stress enough that this is not a 'magic formula', as some Jewish exorcists, who tried to use it that way, discovered (Acts 19:13–16). Yet Jesus encouraged us to pray boldly in his name:

'And I will do whatever you ask in my name, so that the Son may bring glory to the Father. You may ask me for anything in my name, and I will do it.'

(John 14:13–14)

'You did not choose me, but I chose you and appointed you to go and bear fruit – fruit that will last. Then the Father will give you whatever you ask in my name.'

(John 15:16)

See also Matthew 18:19–20; Mark 9:39–40; 16:15–18; John 16:23–24; Acts 3:6, 16; 4:8–10, 30–31; 16:16–18; Ephesians 5:18–20; Hebrews 13:15

So what does it mean to pray 'in Jesus' name'? It is about:

- **Praying on the basis of who Jesus is**
  In Bible times, the 'name' of someone summed up who they were, the very essence of their character or role. When we pray 'in Jesus' name' we are recognizing that we ourselves have no claims in our own right when we approach God; we are coming solely on the basis of who Jesus is – God's Son, the perfect God-man.
- **Praying on the basis of what Jesus has done**
  When we pray 'in Jesus' name' we are recalling what he did at the cross, where he defeated sin and Satan. We are remembering that it was there that our own sins were dealt with, and so the devil has no grounds for accusing us now as we pray.
- **Praying on the basis of what Jesus is like**
  Jesus promised, 'You may ask me for anything in my name, and I will do it' (John 14:14); but the 'anything' of our prayer has to first get past the 'everything' that Jesus is. He is holy; so can we ask him to let us commit that sin just once more before we give it up? He is just; so can we ask him to let us win the lottery while millions are starving? He is righteous; so can we ask him to turn the manager's eyes while we 'borrow' something from the office?

Praying in Jesus' name and recalling what he is like should have a healthy sifting effect on our prayers!

Praying in the Spirit

As we saw in Part One, Chapter 5, we are not left alone in this task of prayer; Jesus has sent his Spirit to help us. Without the Spirit, we will never be able to 'do it right'.

Pray in the Spirit at all times with all kinds of prayers, asking for everything you need.

(Ephesians 6:18, NCV)

What did Paul mean by 'praying in the Spirit'? He meant that we should expect the Holy Spirit to:

- **Remind us** of our relationship with God our Father (e.g. Romans 8:14–16; Galatians 4:6–7), from which a strong basis of prayer comes.
- **Convict us** when there is sin in our life that needs to be confessed (e.g. Psalm 51:10–12; John 16:8), so that nothing hinders our prayers.
- **Show us** God's heart, plans, and truth (e.g. John 14:16–17, 25–26; 16:13–14), so that we know what to pray.
- **Guide us** in how to pray (e.g. Romans 8:26–27). The expression translated as the Spirit 'helps us' literally means 'he takes hold of us at our side'. He really does support us in this matter of praying, if only we will ask him!
- **Help us** to pray appropriately, whether with our own language or with the gift of tongues (e.g. 1 Corinthians 14:14–15)

Praying with humility

When we pray, God wants us to do so boldly and without fear (e.g. Hebrews 10:19–23). But he also wants us to do so with humility, remembering he is God. God hates arrogance (e.g. 1 Samuel 15:22–23; Psalm 5:5; Isaiah 2:11–17) but delights in humility (e.g. Isaiah 66:2; Micah 6:6–8; Luke 1:52). If we come arrogantly before God, therefore, parading our own virtues, rehearsing our own successes, or requiring our own demands, God cannot answer us. Even if we ask for something right, but do so without humility, then God is unlikely to answer, for the matter of our heart is always a bigger priority for God, whatever we might be praying for. When we come humbly, however, the way is open for God to answer.

Jesus told this story to some people who thought they were very good and looked down on everyone else. 'A Pharisee and a tax collector both went to the Temple to pray. The Pharisee stood alone and prayed, "God, I thank you that 1 am not like other people who steal, cheat, or take part in adultery, or even like this tax collector. I give up eating twice a week, and 1 give one-tenth of everything 1 get!" The tax collector, standing at a distance, would not even look up to heaven. But he beat on his chest because he was so sad. He said, "God, have mercy on me, a sinner." I tell you, when this man went home, he was right with God, but the Pharisee was not. All who make themselves great will be made humble, but all who make themselves humble will be made great.'

(Luke 18:9–14, NCV)

See also 2 Chronicles 7:14; Ezra 8:21–23; Zephaniah 2:3; James 4:6–10

Praying with perseverance

We have seen several times throughout this book the importance of 'sticking at it' when we pray. If God were always to answer our prayers first time, we wouldn't learn how to grow in faith, trust, patience, perseverance and so on – qualities that should be our hallmarks as Christians. If your prayers aren't answered at the first time of asking, therefore, don't give in. It doesn't mean God doesn't want to answer; it just means there are other issues that he is dealing with.

Having taught his disciples the Lord's Prayer, Jesus went on to stress the importance of 'sticking at it' when we pray. In Luke's Gospel the prayer is followed by the parable of the friend who came at midnight (Luke 11:5–8), with its message that persistence wins the day. This emphasis on persistence then comes out in the well-known saying that follows, though it is lost in most English translations. But here is one that brings it out:

'So I say to you, Ask and keep on asking, and it shall be given to you; seek and keep on seeking, and you shall find; knock and keep on knocking, and the door shall be opened to you. For everyone who asks and keeps on asking receives; and he who seeks and keeps on seeking finds; and to him who knocks and keeps on knocking the door shall be opened.'

(Luke 11:9–10, The Amplified Bible)

See also Genesis 18:23–33; 32:24–28; Psalm 88:1; Micah 7:7; Luke 11:5–8; 18:1–7; Acts 1:14; 2:42; Romans 1:9–10; 12:12; 1 Thessalonians 5:17

Praying with holiness

Does a lack of holiness hinder our prayers? The amazing thing is that God will often answer our prayers even when we aren't holy, as all of us have experienced. That's his grace! But as one of Mike's colleagues, who exercises a significant prophetic ministry, once said, 'All I know is this: when I walk cleaner, I prophesy better!' Likewise, when we pray 'cleaner', our prayers are more effective. For if God, in his grace, answers us when there is still known sin in

Some hindrances to prayer

Sometimes we can put hindrances in the way of our prayers being answered. Some common hindrances include:

- **Disobedience** (e.g. Proverbs 28:9)
- **Doubt** (e.g. James 1:5–7)
- **Hardness of heart** (e.g. Proverbs 21:13)
- **Injustice** (e.g. Isaiah 1:12–17)
- **Insincerity** (e.g. Malachi 1:6–10)
- **Lack of self-control** (e.g. 1 Peter 4:7)
- **Pride** (e.g. Job 35:12–13)
- **Self-righteousness** (e.g. Luke 18:9–14)
- **Sin** (e.g. Psalm 66:18)
- **Wrong motives** (e.g. James 4:3)

The good news, however, is that *all* of these can be forgiven! As we confess them to God, he will wash us clean so that nothing need get in the way of our prayers.

our life, how much more effective would our prayers be if we dealt with the sin! If we keep clinging on to sin, however, we shouldn't be surprised if God 'turns a deaf ear' to our prayers.

If I had cherished sin in my heart,
the Lord would not have listened.

(Psalm 66:18)

The earnest prayer of a righteous person has great power and wonderful results.

(James 5:16, NLT)

See also Deuteronomy 1:45; Psalm 34:15; 145:18; Proverbs 15:8; Isaiah 1:15–17; 59:1–2; Lamentations 3:40–44; John 9:31; 1 Peter 3:12

Praying in unity

As we saw in Chapter 6 of this Part, unity amongst God's people is tremendously important to God, being a reflection of his Trinitarian nature. Unity is also very important when it comes to praying together. If there are unresolved issues between us and another Christian, then how can we say 'Yes!' (which is what 'Amen' really means) to their prayers? Our hearts are too full of resentment, suspicion, or bitterness to be able to do that with integrity. But when there is nothing between us, then there are no limits to what can be achieved through the power of agreement in prayer.

'Again, I tell you that if two of you on earth agree about anything you ask for, it will be done for you by my Father in heaven. For where two or three come together in my name, there am I with them.'

(Matthew 18:19–20)

May the God who gives endurance and encouragement give you a spirit of unity among yourselves as you follow Christ Jesus, so that with one heart and mouth you may glorify the God and Father of our Lord Jesus Christ.

(Romans 15:5–6)

See also Psalm 133:1–3; Ecclesiastes 4:9–12; Acts 2:1; 4:31–33; 1 Corinthians 1:10; 10:16–17; Ephesians 4:1–16

A FINAL PRAYER

Almighty God, who hast promised to hear the petitions of them that ask in thy Son's name: We beseech thee mercifully to incline thine ears to us that have made now our prayers and supplications unto thee; and grant that those things, which we have faithfully asked according to thy will, may effectually be obtained, to the relief of our necessity, and to the setting forth of thy glory; through Jesus Christ our Lord. Amen.

The Book of Common Prayer (1549), Holy Communion

CONCLUSION

'Doing it right' is not about following certain techniques, but about pursuing God with all our heart and dealing with anything that would get in the way.

'You will seek me and find me when you seek me with all your heart.'

(Jeremiah 29:13)

Relevance for today

Heart before words

God wants our heart rather than our words. It doesn't matter if we can't get the right words out; as long as our heart is in it, our prayer is acceptable to God. Equally, we can recite the most profound words of great divines or composers from the past; but if our heart is not in it, it is meaningless to God.

You are always on their lips
but far from their hearts.
Yet you know me, O LORD;
you see me and test my thoughts about you.

(Jeremiah 12:2–3)

Content before format

There is no right format or way of praying. God is not interested in the beauty of our language or the structure of our prayer, but in the content of our words. He wants each of us to talk with him in our own words and in our own way, no matter how simple it might be.

From the lips of children and infants
you have ordained praise.

(Psalm 8:2)

Growing before getting

So often, we come to God because we want to 'get' something; but God is far more interested in our spiritual growth than simply giving us all we ask for. So, are *you* growing in the areas we have looked at in this chapter?

- Praying according to God's will
- Praying in faith
- Praying in Jesus' name
- Praying in the Spirit
- Praying with humility
- Praying with perseverance
- Praying with holiness
- Praying in unity

Ask God to highlight those where he wants you to grow, in order that you might 'do it right'.

Chapter Five

Praying from the Promises

When we pray on the basis of God's promises, we are on sure and strong ground for praying boldly and expecting our prayers to be answered.

For no matter how many promises God has made, they are 'Yes' in Christ. And so through him the 'Amen' is spoken by us to the glory of God. (2 Corinthians 1:20)

'I promise to pay the bearer on demand the sum of ten pounds.' So reads the wording on Bank of England currency notes. That promise, backed by the signature of the Governor of the Bank (and made secure by a whole host of anti-fraud designs and devices on the note!), is what guarantees our piece of paper is worth something and that it has real purchasing power. And that's exactly what the promises of God are like. They are God's promises with Jesus' signature, Jesus' 'Yes!', on them. That's what makes them so valuable when it comes to prayer. When we pray on the basis of these promises, we can be sure we are on firm ground and that we will not be turned away.

The God of the promises

Effective prayer goes hand in hand with discovering more about God. The more we come to know and trust *the God of the promises,* the more we will come to know and trust *the promises of God.* The best place to start is the Bible, God's inspired word (e.g. 2 Timothy 3:16), for it is here as nowhere else that God has revealed to us what he is like, how he acts, and what his plans are. And it is here that his supreme revelation, Jesus Christ his Son, is made known. It is as we get to know *the person of God* better through *the word of God* that we can call on *the promises of God* with increasing confidence as we pray.

There are three key things we need to remember about the God of the promises if we are going to trust the promises of God.

- **God is truthful**

God is true and speaks the truth. There is nothing deceptive about him, and he never plays tricks on us.

God is not a man, that he should lie …
(Numbers 23:19)

Though everyone else in the world is a liar, God is true.

(Romans 3:4, NLT)

See also John 14:6; Titus 1:2; Hebrews 6:18; James 1:17

• **God is faithful**

Because God is truthful, we can trust him to stay faithful whenever he makes a promise.

Not one of all the LORD's good promises to the house of Israel failed; every one was fulfilled.

(Joshua 21:45)

Let us hold unswervingly to the hope we profess, for he who promised is faithful.

(Hebrew 10:23)

See also Deuteronomy 32:4; Joshua 23:14; Nehemiah 9:8; Psalm 145:13

• **God is dependable**

Because God is truthful and faithful, he is dependable. We can be sure that he will not change his mind about something halfway through. What he starts, he always finishes.

'I am with you and will watch over you wherever you go, and I will bring you back to this land. I will not leave you until I have done what I have promised you.'

(Genesis 28:15)

Every good and perfect gift is from above, coming down from the Father of the heavenly lights, who does not change like shifting shadows.

(James 1:17)

See also Deuteronomy 31:6; Psalm 18:2; Malachi 3:6; Philippians 1:4–6

The promises of God

It is because God is so truthful, faithful, and dependable that we can trust the promises he makes. God has made plain that when he makes a promise, it is there to be claimed; when he speaks a word, it will surely come to pass.

As the rain and the snow
come down from heaven,
and do not return to it
without watering the earth
and making it bud and flourish,
so that it yields seed for the sower and
bread for the eater,
so is my word that goes out from my mouth:
It will not return to me empty,
but will accomplish what I desire
and achieve the purpose for which I sent it.

(Isaiah 55:10–11)

See also Numbers 11:23; Proverbs 19:21; Isaiah 40:8; 45:23; Ezekiel 12:21–25; Habakkuk 2:3; Romans 4:18–21; Hebrews 6:13–18

Appealing to the promises

Again and again in the Bible we find people appealing to God's promises. They came to him and said, 'Oh God, I want to remind you of what you once said ... And because you are a faithful God, I'm calling on you to fulfil that promise right now.' Such prayers were certainly daring, as they were bringing a challenge to the living God! But they were also based on solid ground, for it was the very promises of God himself that these people were appealing to.

Prayers based on promises

Let's look at some of the prayers in the Bible that appealed to God's specific promises in particular areas.

Appeals to promises made to Abraham

'You are the LORD God, who chose Abram and brought him out of Ur of the Chaldeans and named him Abraham. You found his heart faithful to you, and you made a

covenant with him to give to his descendants the land of the Canaanites, Hittites, Amorites, Perizzites, Jebusites and Girgashites. You have kept your promise because you are righteous.'

(Nehemiah 9:7–8)

See also Genesis 28:10–22; 32:9–12; 48:15–16; Exodus 32:11–14; Deuteronomy 9:25–29; 2 Chronicles 20:5–12; Psalm 105:1–15, 42–45; Micah 7:18–20; Luke 1:46–55

Appeals to promises made to Moses

'May your eyes be open to your servant's plea and to the plea of your people Israel, and may you listen to them whenever they cry out to you. For you singled them out from all the nations of the world to be your own inheritance, just as you declared through your servant Moses when you, O Sovereign LORD, brought our fathers out of Egypt.'

(1 Kings 8:52–53)

See also 1 Kings 2:2–4; Nehemiah 1:8–11; 9:9–21; Psalm 99:6–9; 105:23–41; Isaiah 63:11–14; Daniel 9:4–19; 2 Corinthians 3:12–18; Revelation 15:1–4

Appeals to promises made to David

'And now, LORD God, keep for ever the promise you have made concerning your servant and his house. Do as you promised, so that your name will be great for ever. Then men will say, "The LORD Almighty is God over Israel!"'

(2 Samuel 7:25–26)

See also 1 Kings 8:22–26; 2 Kings 20:1–6; 2 Chronicles 1:7–10; Psalm 89:1–4, 19–37; Isaiah 55:1–3; Hosea 3:4–5; Luke 1:67–75; Acts 4:23–31

Appeals to promises made about Israel

- **The land**

'Look down from heaven, your holy dwelling-place, and bless your people Israel and the land you have given us as you promised on oath to our forefathers, a land flowing with milk and honey.'

(Deuteronomy 26:15)

See also Genesis 28:10–15; Exodus 32:11–14; 2 Chronicles 7:11–22; Nehemiah 9:5–37; Jeremiah 32:16–44

- **Jerusalem and the temple**

'May your eyes be open towards this temple night and day, this place of which you said, "My Name shall be there," so that you will hear the prayer your servant prays towards this place. Hear the supplication of your servant and of your people Israel when they pray towards this place. Hear from heaven, your dwelling-place, and when you hear, forgive.'

(1 Kings 8:29–30)

See also 1 Kings 9:1–9; 2 Kings 20:1–6; 2 Chronicles 6:1–21; 7:11–16; Nehemiah 1:1–10; Isaiah 64:11–12; Daniel 9:17–19

- **Restoration**

'Remember the instruction you gave your servant Moses, saying, "If you are unfaithful, I will scatter you among the nations, but if you return to me and obey my commands, then even if your exiled people are at the farthest horizon, I will gather them from there and bring them to the place I have chosen as a dwelling for my Name."'

(Nehemiah 1:8–9)

See also Psalm 80:1–19; 85:1–9; 126:1–6; Isaiah 6:11–13; 64:8–12; Jeremiah 33:1–26; Ezekiel 37:1–14; Hosea 6:1–3

What does this tell us?

What does all of this tell us? That the saints of old were not afraid to remind God of what he had promised and to challenge him to keep his word! Hence, we often find them saying to God, 'You said … ' (e.g. Judges 6:36–37; 1 Kings 8:25–26; Psalm 89:3–4). This is not arrogance, but confidence; for it is based on nothing less than God's own words, God's own commitment.

Appealing to the promises today

Such confidence is not just for people of Bible times; it can be ours also. Whenever we pray like they did, appealing to God's promises, we can be sure that our prayers will be all the more effective and powerful – whether we are praying for ourselves, or with or for others. So, what are some of the things that God has made promises about to which we can appeal?

Salvation

'Everyone who calls on the name of the Lord will be saved.'

(Acts 2:21)

Forgiveness

'If my people, who are called by my name, will humble themselves and pray and seek my face and turn from their wicked ways, then will I hear from heaven and will forgive their sin and will heal their land.'

(2 Chronicles 7:14)

Daily needs

And my God will supply all your needs according to His riches in glory in Christ Jesus.

(Philippians 4:19, NASB)

Provision

'Bring the whole tithe into the storehouse, that there may be food in my house. Test me in this,' says the LORD *Almighty, 'and see if I will not throw open the floodgates of heaven and pour out so much blessing that you will not have room enough for it.'*

(Malachi 3:10)

Satisfaction

'Come, all you who are thirsty,
come to the waters;
and you who have no money,
come, buy and eat!
Come, buy wine and milk
without money and without cost.
Why spend money on what is not bread,
and your labour on what does not satisfy?
Listen, listen to me, and eat what is good,
and your soul will delight in the richest of fare.

(Isaiah 55:1–2)

Comfort

'I, even I, am he who comforts you.'

(Isaiah 51:12)

Peace

Do not be anxious about anything, but in everything, by prayer and petition, with thanksgiving, present your requests to God. And the peace of God, which transcends all understanding, will guard your hearts and your minds in Christ Jesus.

(Philippians 4:6–7)

Guidance

Whether you turn to the right or to the left, your ears will hear a voice behind you, saying, 'This is the way; walk in it.'

(Isaiah 30:21)

Revelation

'Call to me and I will answer you and tell you great and unsearchable things you do not know.'

(Jeremiah 33:3)

The Holy Spirit

'If anyone is thirsty, let him come to me and drink. Whoever believes in me, as the Scripture has said, streams of living water will flow from within him.' By this he meant the Spirit …

(John 7:37–38)

A new beginning

Therefore, if anyone is in Christ, he is a new creation; old things have passed away; behold, all things have become new.

(2 Corinthians 5:17, NKJV)

Healing

'I am the LORD, *who heals you.'*

(Exodus 15:26)

Power

But you will receive power when the Holy Spirit comes on you; and you will be my witnesses in Jerusalem, and in all Judea and Samaria, and to the ends of the earth.

(Acts 1:8)

Temptation

'And lead us not into temptation, but deliver us from the evil one.'

(Matthew 6:13)

Protection

He who dwells in the shelter of the Most High
will rest in the shadow of the Almighty.
I will say of the LORD, *'He is my refuge and my fortress,*
my God, in whom I trust.'

(Psalm 91:1–2)

And these are only just *some* of the promises God makes in his word to us! (For further promises, see Chapters 1–3 of this Part of the book.) Take hold of these promises when you pray; and pray, therefore, all the more confidently!

The Father who answers

But will God answer when we come to him? Yes he will! For one of the best promises we have, repeated again and again by Jesus, is that our Heavenly Father is good and will answer our prayers when we ask in faith.

'Which of you, if his son asks for bread, will give him a stone? Or if he asks for a fish, will give him a snake? If you, then, though you are evil, know how to give good gifts to your children, how much more will your Father in heaven give good gifts to those who ask him!'

(Matthew 7:9–11)

'I tell you that if two of you on earth agree about anything you ask for, it will be done for you by my Father in heaven.'

(Matthew 18:19)

'If you believe, you will receive whatever you ask for in prayer.'

(Matthew 21:22)

'Whatever you ask for in prayer, believe that you have received it, and it will be yours.'

(Mark 11:24)

'And I will do whatever you ask in my name, so that the Son may bring glory to the Father. You may ask me for anything in my name, and I will do it.'

(John 14:13–14)

'If you remain in me, and my words remain in you, ask whatever you wish, and it will be given you.'

(John 15:7)

'You did not choose me, but I chose you and appointed you to go and bear fruit – fruit that will last. Then the Father will give you whatever you ask in my name.'

(John 15:16)

'In that day you will no longer ask me anything. I tell you the truth, my Father will give you whatever you ask in my name. Until now you have not asked for anything in my name. Ask and you will receive, and your joy will be complete.'

(John 16:23–24)

[We] receive from him anything we ask, because we obey his commands and do what pleases him.

(1 John 3:22)

This is the confidence we have in approaching God: that if we ask anything according to his will, he hears us.

(1 John 5:14)

We need to remember these promises when we come to God with our requests. He *is* good; he *does* want to bless us; he *does* want to answer! However, the promises aren't automatic; we have to play our part. Look back over these promises of Jesus that we have just listed and you will see that there are conditions attached to them all: asking in faith, asking 'in Jesus name', agreeing with others, bearing fruit, etc. It is as we fulfil these conditions that God responds to our claims on the promises, releases his hand in heaven, and allows the promises to be fulfilled.

A FINAL PRAYER

O Lord Jesus Christ, who as a child didst learn and grow in wisdom: grant me so to learn thy holy Word, that I may walk in thy ways and daily grow more like unto thee, who are my Saviour and my Lord.

Church of Ireland,
Book of Common Prayer

CONCLUSION

The promises of God are given so that we might come to know better the God of the promises, and so be confident in bringing our requests to him who is faithful.

'God is not a man, that he should lie,
nor a son of man, that he should change his mind.
Does he speak and then not act?
Does he promise and not fulfil?'

(Numbers 23:19)

Relevance for today

God's word is full of promises; but those promises don't get into our hearts and lives by some sort of spiritual osmosis. It doesn't just 'happen'! We need to put the promises within us, just as Jesus himself did. It is interesting that, when Jesus was tempted by the devil in the wilderness, all the Scriptures he quoted were drawn from Deuteronomy. How did he know these? He had clearly taken time over the years to learn them, so that now, in his moment of need, he could pull them out of his treasure chest within and let them do their powerful work.

If we are going to be able to pray from the promises, then it will involve –

Listening to God's word

Ezra the priest brought the scroll of the law before the assembly, which included the men and women and all the children old enough to understand. He faced the square just inside the Water Gate from early morning until noon and read aloud to everyone who could understand. All the people paid close attention to the Book of the Law.

(Nehemiah 8:2–3, NLT)

Studying God's word

Do your best to present yourself to God as one approved, a workman who does not need to be ashamed and who correctly handles the word of truth.

(2 Timothy 2:15)

Meditating on God's word

'Do not let this Book of the Law depart from your mouth; meditate on it day and night, so that you may be careful to do everything written in it. Then you will be prosperous and successful.'

(Joshua 1:8)

Memorizing God's word

I have hidden your word in my heart
that I might not sin against you.

(Psalm 119:11)

Digesting God's word

Then he said to me, 'Son of man, eat this scroll I am giving you and fill your stomach with it.' So I ate it, and it tasted as sweet as honey in my mouth.

(Ezekiel 3:3)

Claiming God's word

'And now, O LORD, do as you have promised concerning me and my family. May it be a promise that will last for ever.'

(1 Chronicles 17:23, NLT)

Fulfil your promise to your servant,
so that you may be feared.

(Psalm 119:38)

Using God's word

Take the sword of the Spirit, which is the word of God.

(Ephesians 6:17, NLT)

Living God's word

Do not merely listen to the word, and so deceive yourselves. Do what it says.

(James 1:22)

Chapter Six

Praying and Fasting

Fasting is a way of our demonstrating seriousness of purpose when we come to God with our prayers.

'When you fast …' (Matthew 6:16)

'Have whatever you want, whenever you want it.' This could almost be the slogan of Western consumer society. If you can't afford something, charge it to your credit card or take out a loan. But whatever you do, don't deny yourself or wait. After all, you deserve to have it *now*!

Sadly, this attitude sometimes spills over into the Christian life. The thought of denying oneself anything is anathema to many Christians. Yet the Bible tells us that denying ourselves can be the very way of receiving what we are looking for!

What is fasting?

Fasting is about *denying oneself.* It is the practice of abstaining from food, partially or totally, for a period of time in order to devote oneself more fully to God. It is *not* about simply skipping a meal (and then calling it 'fasting'!) for, let's face it, many people skip breakfast when they get up too late or skip lunch when they stay to complete a job. This isn't fasting – it's dieting, or working too hard! Fasting is about denying oneself in order to focus on *God.* In fact, the Hebrew word signifies 'humbly submitting oneself to God'.

Fasting is a way of saying, 'Lord, there is nothing more important in my life than you – not even eating.' It is an opportunity to loosen our dependence on the 'material' aspects of life (including, Paul says, sexual relations between a husband and wife for a time, see 1 Corinthians 7:3–6) in order to concentrate more on the 'spiritual'. But let's be honest, it's not easy; for you feel hungry, as Jesus himself experienced.

After fasting for forty days and forty nights, he was hungry.

(Matthew 4:2)

Fasting was generally seen as voluntary in Scripture; the only fast actually commanded was on the Day of Atonement, underlining its solemnity (Leviticus 16:29–31). It was still observed by Jews in New Testament times (Acts 27:9). After the exile other fasts were introduced (Esther 9:29–32;

Zechariah 7:2–5; 8:18–19): in the fourth month (to lament the destruction of the walls of Jerusalem by Nebuchadnezzar), the fifth month (to lament the destruction of the temple), the seventh month (to commemorate the assassination of Gedaliah, Governor of Judah) and the tenth month (to lament the beginning of Nebuchadnezzar's siege of Jerusalem). By the time of Jesus, Judaism had turned fasting into a twice-weekly requirement for the devout (Luke 18:12) and it had become, sadly, an outward demonstration of piety and a legal bondage. Because of this, and because the same thing happened in church history, some Christians have shunned fasting; yet it is, as we shall see, a thoroughly biblical practice.

Types of fasting

The normal fast

This involved abstaining from all food, but not from water.

Jesus, full of the Holy Spirit, returned from the Jordan and was led by the Spirit in the desert, where for forty days he was tempted by the devil. He ate nothing during those days, and at the end of them he was hungry.

(Luke 4:1–2)

Luke specifies that Jesus 'ate nothing' and was 'hungry'; but there is no mention of his not drinking (as in Acts 9:9). Taking water, but not food, was the normal biblical fast. It generally lasted for one day, either from sunrise to sunset (e.g. Judges 20:26) or for a twenty-four hour period (e.g. Leviticus 23:32), though it could last as long as three days (e.g. Esther 4:16), seven days (e.g. 1 Samuel 31:11–13) or an unspecified length of time (e.g. Nehemiah 1:4).

See also 1 Samuel 7:5–6; 2 Samuel 12:15–17; Ezra 8:21–23; 9:4–5; Nehemiah 9:1–3; Daniel 9:1–3; Joel 1:13–14

The partial fast

This involved abstaining from certain foods for a period of time. Daniel often practised this. Exiled to Babylon in 605 BC, he was appointed a royal administrator, which gave him both challenges and opportunities. The first time we find him partially fasting (Daniel 1:8–20) was for dietary reasons, since Jews considered royal food to be contaminated, having been offered to idols. His fasting produced both physical (v15) and spiritual (v17) benefits.

'Please test your servants for ten days: Give us nothing but vegetables to eat and water to drink.' ... At the end of the ten days they looked healthier and better nourished than any of the young men who ate the royal food ... To these four young men God gave knowledge and understanding of all kinds of literature and learning. And Daniel could understand visions and dreams of all kinds.

(Daniel 1:12, 15, 17)

Through his loyal service, Daniel was able to bring increasing godly influence into the royal palace, not least through his ability to bring divine revelation for these pagan kings. It was often out of his partial fasting and seeking God that such revelation came (e.g. Daniel 10:1–14).

The complete fast

This involved abstaining from *both* food *and* water.

Then Esther sent this reply to Mordecai: 'Go, gather together all the Jews who are in Susa, and fast for me. Do not eat or drink for three days, night or day.'

(Esther 4:15–16)

See also Ezra 10:6; Jonah 3:6–9; Acts 9:9

Such a fast can only be undertaken for short periods, for while the body can for go long periods without food (and actually benefit from it), it can only go for short periods without water. It was therefore an exceptional measure for exceptional circumstances, as when Esther and the Jews were confronted with Haman's attempt to annihilate their entire nation.

The special fast

This lasted forty days and is found only at very key times, such as when Jesus faced Satan's temptations about his messiahship in the wilderness (Matthew 4:1–11; Luke 4:1–13), when Moses received the Ten Commandments (Exodus 34:28; Deuteronomy 9:9), and when Elijah travelled to Sinai to encounter God at the height of the clash with Baal worship (1 Kings 19:7–9). Moses is the only person who is specified as having fasted from both food and water for the forty days, clearly upheld supernaturally by God over such a lengthy period. (So, as they say on TV, 'Don't try this one at home!')

Occasions for fasting

Fasting was used to demonstrate seriousness of purpose in a wide range of circumstances.

To seek God

Fasting need not be linked to praying for specific things; it can simply be an expression of our seeking God with all our heart.

There was also a prophetess, Anna, the daughter of Phanuel, of the tribe of Asher. She was very old; she had lived with her husband seven years after her marriage, and then was a widow until she was eighty-four. She never left the temple but worshipped night and day, fasting and praying.

(Luke 2:36–37)

To humble oneself

Pride creeps into our lives so easily; but nothing reminds us of our humanity so much as an empty stomach, and nothing cause us to neglect him so much as a full one. We often think of Sodom's sin immorality; but God rebuked the city for being 'arrogant, overfed and unconcerned' (Ezekiel 16:49). Too much food and too much pride often go together!

… I humbled my soul with fasting …,

(Psalm 69:10, NRSV)

See also Deuteronomy 8:2–3, 10–14; Ezra 8:21

To be heard by God

Fasting can help our prayers be heard by God, for it demonstrates to him our determination. It is not, however, a 'hunger strike' to force God to answer!

So we fasted and petitioned our God about this, and he answered our prayer.

(Ezra 8:23)

See also 2 Samuel 12:16–25; Ezra 8:21; Isaiah 58:6–9; Joel 2:12–14

To discover God's direction

Both personally and corporately, there are times when we need to know God's direction for us. Fasting shows our resolve to find his guidance, whatever the personal cost to us.

In the church at Antioch there were prophets and teachers … While they were worshipping the Lord and fasting, the Holy Spirit said, 'Set apart for me Barnabas and Saul for the work to which I have called them.'

(Acts 13:1–2)

To mark a new stage

At key stages in life, fasting demonstrates how very much we are looking to God to bless us in what lies ahead.

Paul and Barnabas appointed elders for them in each church and, with prayer and fasting, committed them to the Lord, in whom they had put their trust.

(Acts 14:23)

See also Acts 13:3

To seek God's help

When we really need to see God's help in the face of difficulty or danger – whether as individuals, God's people, or a nation – or when we need to see God intervene on our behalf, fasting demonstrates our complete dependence on him to come and rescue us.

Then Esther sent this reply to Mordecai: 'Go, gather together all the Jews who are in Susa, and fast for me. Do not eat or drink for three days, night or day. I and my maids will fast as you do. When this is done, I will go to the king, even though it is against the law. And if I perish, I perish.'

(Esther 4:15–16)

See also Judges 20:24–28; 1 Samuel 20:34; 2 Samuel 12:15–16; 2 Chronicles 7:13–14; 20:1–4; Ezra 8:21–23; Esther 4:3; Joel 2:12–14

To bring spiritual release

While fasting is 'external', it is the 'internal' that really matters to God. A change in our attitudes or a breaking of spiritual strongholds in our life can all be assisted by fasting. The Pharisees turned fasting into bondage; God means fasting to release people from bondage!

'Is not this the kind of fasting I have chosen:
to loose the chains of injustice
and untie the cords of the yoke,
to set the oppressed free
and break every yoke?

(Isaiah 58:6)

To see a breakthrough

When Daniel realized from the Scriptures (Daniel 9:2) that the Babylonian exile would only last seventy years, as Jeremiah had prophesied, and that Israel would then return home (Jeremiah 25:8–14), he started seeking God with prayer and fasting (Daniel 9:3). It is interesting to note the answer Gabriel brings to him:

'Daniel, I have now come to give you insight and understanding. As soon as you began to pray, an answer was given, which I have come to tell you, for you are highly esteemed.'

(Daniel 9:22–23)

The words 'as soon as you began to pray' indicate that something was released in heaven the very moment Daniel began to fast and pray, even though he didn't see the outworking of it just yet. Fasting brings spiritual breakthroughs!

To release spiritual power

What we do not experience in our normal walk with the Lord will often be released as we fast and pray. When the disciples failed to cast out a demon from a young boy and asked Jesus why, he replied:

'This kind can come out by nothing but prayer and fasting.'

(Mark 9:29, NKJV)

To seek guidance

God really does want to speak, whether through the Bible, spiritual gifts, or the inner voice of conviction. In the Bible, there is frequently a close link between fasting and receiving God's guidance.

While they were worshipping the Lord and fasting, the Holy Spirit said, 'Set apart for me Barnabas and Saul for the work to which I have called them.'

(Acts 13:2)

See also Judges 20:26–28; Daniel 9:1–3, 20–23; 10:1–14

To demonstrate sincerity of repentance

Sometimes it is all too easy to just say 'sorry'. While nothing can add to, or take away from, the sacrifice of Jesus on the cross for our sins, fasting can demonstrate to God just how sorry we are and how seriously we are taking the need to repent and change.

'Even now,' declares the LORD,
'return to me with all your heart,
with fasting and weeping and mourning.'

'Rend your heart
and not your garments.
Return to the LORD your God,
for he is gracious and compassionate,
slow to anger and abounding in love,
and he relents from sending calamity.'

(Joel 2:12–13)

See also 1 Samuel 7:5–6; 1 Kings 21:27–29; Nehemiah 9:1–3; Daniel 9:3–19; Joel 1:13–14; Jonah 3:1–5

To deal with cravings

Ever since Satan tempted Adam and Eve in the Garden of Eden with a tasty piece of fruit, it has always been true that the quickest way to our hearts is through our stomachs. Esau sold his birthright for a meal (Genesis 25:29–34), Israel would have returned to Egypt because of food (Exodus 16:2–3; Numbers 11:4–5), Eli's sons despised their priesthood by taking the best meat for themselves (1 Samuel 2:12–17, 27–29), the Corinthians turned the Lord's Supper into a gluttonous feast (1 Corinthians 11:20–22). Let's make no mistake: our earthly appetites can rule our lives. Our body is a good servant but a poor master, and fasting helps to keep our natural desires in their proper place and to stop them from spoiling or even destroying our lives.

The tempter came to him and said, 'If you are the Son of God, tell these stones to become bread.' Jesus answered, 'It is written: "Man does not live on bread alone, but on every word that comes from the mouth of God."'

(Matthew 4:3–4)

See also Matthew 24:36–39; John 4:31–34; 1 Corinthians 6:12–13; 9:25–27

To express grief or mourning

Denying ourselves food allows us to share the pain of those who are bereaved and to express our own sadness.

Then David and all the men with him took hold of their clothes and tore them. They mourned and wept and fasted till evening for Saul and his son Jonathan, and for the army of the LORD and the house of Israel, because they had fallen by the sword.

(2 Samuel 1:11–12)

See also 1 Samuel 31:11–13; 2 Samuel 3:31–35; 1 Chronicles 10:11–12

Fasting and our attitudes

Because fasting has the potential for becoming a mere outward show (e.g. Matthew 6:16–18; Luke 18:9–12), the Bible lays great stress on the importance of the inner attitudes that accompany it. Without the right heart and attitudes, fasting is meaningless.

Wrong attitudes

'Look how spiritual I am!'

The Pharisees of Jesus' day fasted twice a week, on Mondays and Thursdays. But their fasting was not really for God, but for others – so they could be seen as tremendously spiritual people.

The Pharisee stood up and prayed about himself: 'God, I thank you that I am not like other men – robbers, evildoers, adulterers – or even like this tax collector. I fast twice a week and give a tenth of all I get.'

(Luke 18:11–12)

See also Matthew 6:16

'Why haven't you noticed, God?'

If we find ourselves wondering why God hasn't noticed our fasting, we have started to see it as something 'automatic', something that twists God's arm. Such an attitude blinds us to other factors.

'"Why have we fasted," they say,
"and you have not seen it?
Why have we humbled ourselves,
and you have not noticed?"
'Yet on the day of your fasting, you do as you please
and exploit all your workers.
Your fasting ends in quarrelling and strife,
and in striking each other with wicked fists.
You cannot fast as you do today
and expect your voice to be heard on high.'

(Isaiah 58:3–4)

See also Jeremiah 14:11–12; Zechariah 7:4–10

'Everyone should fast!'

Fasting cannot be made compulsory, for it is a matter of the heart. The Bible warns us to beware of anyone who tries to make it compulsory or a touchstone of spirituality.

Therefore do not let anyone judge you by what you eat or drink, or with regard to a religious festival, a New Moon celebration or a Sabbath day.

(Colossians 2:16)

See also Colossians 2:20–23; 1 Timothy 4:1–5

Jesus' attitude to fasting

While Jesus challenged wrong attitudes about fasting, he didn't abolish the practice; indeed, he himself fasted – on one occasion for forty days. What he did stress however was:

Fasting has no value in itself

When John the Baptist's disciples couldn't cope with Jesus' disciples not fasting, Jesus said that it wasn't an appropriate religious exercise at that moment, and that therefore there was no point in doing it. When the time was right and needful, then they would fast.

Then John's disciples came and asked him, 'How is it that we and the Pharisees fast, but your disciples do not fast?' Jesus answered, 'How can the guests of the bridegroom mourn while he is with them? The time will come when the bridegroom will be taken from them; then they will fast.'

(Matthew 9:14–15)

Fasting is not about displaying piety

The Pharisees turned fasting into an opportunity for letting everyone know how pious they were (Matthew 6:1–4). Jesus said this missed the whole point!

'When you fast, do not look sombre as the hypocrites do, for they disfigure their faces to show men they are fasting. I tell you the truth, they have received their reward in full. But when you fast, put oil on your head and wash your face, so that it will not be obvious to men that you are fasting, but only to your Father, who is unseen; and your Father, who sees what is done in secret, will reward you.'

(Matthew 6:16–18)

A FINAL PRAYER

Let our fasting be done unto the Lord, with our eye singly fixed on Him. Let our intention herein be this, and this alone, to glorify our Father which is in heaven; to express our sorrow and shame for our manifold transgressions of His holy law; to wait for an increase of purifying grace, drawing our affections to things above; to add seriousness and earnestness to our prayers; to avert the wrath of God; and to obtain all the great and precious promises which He hath made to us in Jesus Christ.

John Wesley (1703–1791)

CONCLUSION

If we think we couldn't possibly fast, then our stomach has become our master rather than our servant and we have closed the door to what God can do through fasting.

A man is a slave to whatever has mastered him.

(2 Peter 2:19)

Relevance for today

Not whether, but when

As Christians, the issue is not *whether* we will fast, but *when* we will start doing it. Jesus took it for granted that his followers would fast, just as they would pray and give to the poor.

'When you give to the needy … when you pray … when you fast …'

(Matthew 6:2, 5, 16)

How to begin

Perhaps having read this chapter, you would now like to 'give it a go'. How can you start?

- ***Resolve the issue!*** Has God spoken to you about fasting or not? Decide first, for the devil will challenge you once you begin!
- ***Start small*** Try a partial fast, or fasting until the evening meal, or missing lunch in order to pray. Build up gradually.
- ***Watch your motives*** Spiritual pride is subtle!
- ***Don't go by feelings*** Its effectiveness is not based on how you feel!
- ***Don't 'binge eat' at the end*** – it really doesn't help!

Common side effects

Don't be surprised if you experience some common side effects when fasting:

- ***Cravings for food*** (you won't die!) A desire for food is not the same thing as hunger.
- ***Weakness or faintness*** Keeping up your fluid intake helps.
- ***A headache*** (it will pass!) This is generally a withdrawal symptom from caffeine (found in tea and coffee).
- ***Bad taste in the mouth/bad breath*** (a sign of the body doing a 'spring clean'!) Brush your teeth; use a mouth spray.

The time is now!

Jesus expected his followers to fast once he had completed his work and returned to heaven. He's been gone a long time – surely the time to fast must be now!

'The time will come when the bridegroom will be taken from them; then they will fast.'

(Matthew 9:15)

Chapter Seven

Prayer Changes Things!

Prayer makes a difference! When we pray, things change; when we don't, we may miss what God wants to do.

He will rescue us because you are helping by praying for us.
(2 Corinthians 1:11, NLT)

'But can you *prove* that prayer makes a difference?' the sceptics ask. 'And how do you know that what you prayed for wouldn't have happened anyway? Maybe it was just a coincidence.' Well, maybe it was. But our own experience, along with countless Christians through the ages, is this: a remarkable number of coincidences seem to happen when we pray!

As authors, we would be the first to admit that we haven't learned everything about prayer that there is to learn and that, at times, we still feel like novices. But as we look back over the years of our faltering experience, we are convinced that prayer changes things. Prayer is not a meaningless exercise; God hears our prayers, God answers our prayers, and those prayers change things. Of course, the change may be in circumstances; but it is just as likely to be in us!

Prayer changes situations

While prayer is never seen in the Bible as 'twisting God's arm' to get what we want, the truth is that prayer does change situations. As we discover God's purposes and turn them into prayer, we are giving God the opportunity to act in our world, just as he wants to.

Expectation that prayer would be answered

It is clear that the central figures of the Bible expected their prayers to be answered. How different that is from today when many people pray, but often without any real expectation that anything will change. But if we don't expect answers, then what is the point of praying? We are engaging in a meaningless spiritual exercise. This is certainly not the attitude we find in the Bible, where there was tremendous confidence that God would answer prayer and that things would therefore change.

Consider, for example, Paul's confidence that the prayers of others on his behalf would be answered:

He has delivered us from such a deadly peril, and he will deliver us. On him we have set our hope that he will continue to deliver us, as you help us by your prayers. Then many will give thanks on our behalf for the gracious favour granted us in answer to the prayers of many.

(2 Corinthians 1:10–11)

I know that through your prayers and the help given by the Spirit of Jesus Christ, what has happened to me will turn out for my deliverance.

(Philippians 1:19)

And one thing more: Prepare a guest room for me, because I hope to be restored to you in answer to your prayers.

(Philemon 22)

Examples of prayer changing things

The Bible is packed with examples of people who prayed and saw things change. Here is an overview of just some of the key characters who did so.

Abraham

As we saw earlier (Part Five, Chapter 4) Abraham's bold prayers for Sodom and Gomorrah (Genesis 18:16–33) couldn't spare the cities as a whole because of their tremendous ungodliness (Genesis 19:1–9); but his prayers did see things change for his family living there (19:12–28).

So when God destroyed the cities of the plain, he remembered Abraham, and he brought Lot out of the catastrophe that overthrew the cities where Lot had lived.

(Genesis 19:29)

Moses

Moses saw things change through prayer many times. As each of the ten plagues visited Egypt, it was only as Moses prayed that they were lifted:

Then Moses left Pharaoh and prayed to the LORD, and the LORD did what Moses asked.

(Exodus 8:30–31)

When confronted with the Red Sea, it was as Moses lifted his staff in prayer that the waters withdrew:

Then Moses stretched out his hand over the sea, and all that night the LORD drove the sea back with a strong east wind and turned it into dry land. The waters were divided, and the Israelites went through the sea on dry ground, with a wall of water on their right and on their left.

(Exodus 14:21–22)

It was as that same staff was lifted in prayer that Israel won her battles:

So Joshua fought the Amalekites as Moses had ordered, and Moses, Aaron and Hur went to the top of the hill. As long as Moses held up his hands, the Israelites were winning, but whenever he lowered his hands, the Amalekites were winning. When Moses' hands grew tired, they took a stone and put it under him and he sat on it. Aaron and Hur held his hands up – one on one side, one on the other – so that his hands remained steady till sunset. So Joshua overcame the Amalekite army with the sword.

(Exodus 17:10–13)

Hannah

But it was not just for great national affairs that people in Bible times prayed. Personal needs were just as boldly brought to him, as we see with Hannah who experienced her own circumstances of barrenness changing as the result of faithful, persistent prayer.

'I prayed for this child, and the LORD has granted me what I asked of him.'

(1 Samuel 1:27)

David

David saw many situations change, both in his personal life and the life of the nation, as a result of prayer. In his later years, his pride took the better of him when he decided he wanted to know the true strength of his nation and so ordered a census, which even Joab saw as a wrong thing to do (2 Samuel 24:1–4). David's error led to judgment in the form of a plague coming upon the nation; but his crying out to God saw the situation change completely:

David built an altar to the LORD there and sacrificed burnt offerings and fellowship offerings. Then the LORD answered prayer on behalf of the land, and the plague on Israel was stopped.

(2 Samuel 24:25)

Elijah

Elijah too saw many answers to prayer during his ministry. One significant example was when his prayers brought an end to a significant period of drought which had come upon the land as judgment for King Ahab's turning to Baal. Baal, god of fertility and rain though he was supposed to be, had not been able to send rain; but now Elijah called on the Lord and things changed!

And Elijah said to Ahab, 'Go, eat and drink, for there is the sound of a heavy rain.' So Ahab went off to eat and drink, but Elijah climbed to the top of Carmel, bent down to the ground and put his face between his knees. 'Go and look towards the sea,' he told his servant. And he went up and looked. 'There is nothing there,' he said. Seven times Elijah said, 'Go back.' The seventh time the servant reported, 'A cloud as small as a man's hand is rising from the sea.' So Elijah said, 'Go and tell Ahab, "Hitch up your chariot and go down before the rain stops you."' Meanwhile, the sky grew black with clouds, the wind rose, a heavy rain came on and Ahab rode off to Jezreel.

(1 Kings 18:41–45)

Hezekiah

Hezekiah saw two very significant changes in situations as a result of prayer. The first concerned deliverance for Jerusalem from an impossible situation (2 Kings 19:14–37); the second concerned restoration of his own life when he was struck with a terminal illness:

In those days Hezekiah became ill and was at the point of death. The prophet Isaiah son of Amoz went to him and said, 'This is what the LORD says: Put your house in order, because you are going to die; you will not recover.' Hezekiah turned his face to the wall and prayed to the LORD, 'Remember, O LORD, how I have walked before you faithfully and with wholehearted devotion and have done what is good in your eyes.' And Hezekiah wept bitterly. Before Isaiah had left the middle court, the word of the LORD came to him: 'Go back and tell Hezekiah, the leader of my people, "This is what the LORD, the God of your father David, says: I have heard your prayer and seen your tears; I will heal you. On the third day from now you will go up to the temple of the LORD. I will add fifteen years to your life."'

(2 Kings 20:1–6)

Nehemiah

Nehemiah, a senior official in the Persian palace, was once caught without a smile on his face in the king's presence (a capital offence in that culture). He had been praying and fasting for some days (Nehemiah 1:4) because of the news he had received about the plight of the Jews who had returned to the Promised Land. He wanted to do something about it, and here was his chance. It would be either success, or the executioner's block! It was his prayer that changed things:

The king said to me, 'What is it you want?' Then I prayed to the God of heaven, and I answered the king, 'If it pleases the king and if your servant has found favour in his sight, let him send me to the city in Judah where my fathers are buried so that I can rebuild it.' Then the king, with the queen sitting beside him, asked me, 'How long will your journey take, and when will you get back?' It pleased the king to send me; so I set a time.

(Nehemiah 2:4–6)

Daniel

Daniel was a real man of prayer (e.g. Daniel 6:10) who saw many situations changed by praying. When he refused to abandon his devotion to God in response to a new law (6:6–9), he was thrown into a lions' den, sealed 'so that Daniel's situation might not be changed' (6:17). But God changed it!

Very early the next morning, the king hurried out to the lions' den. When he got there, he called out in anguish, 'Daniel, servant of the living God! Was your God, whom you worship continually, able to rescue you from the lions?' Daniel answered, 'Long live the king! My God sent his angel to shut the lions' mouths so that they would not hurt me, for I have been found innocent in his sight. And I have not wronged you, Your Majesty.' The king was overjoyed and ordered that Daniel be lifted from the den. Not a scratch was found on him because he had trusted in his God.

(Daniel 6:19–23, NLT)

Peter

Peter saw countless examples of prayer changing things. Indeed, it was while he and the other disciples were praying in the upper room that they experienced the biggest answer to prayer in their lives: the promised baptism in the Holy Spirit (Acts 1:8; 2:1–4). From that point on, Peter saw prayer changing things again and again, whether through his own prayers, such as the healing of the crippled beggar (Acts 3:1–10), or through the prayers of others, such as when he was miraculously released from jail (Acts 12:1–19). Little wonder he would later write, quoting from Psalm 34, 'For the eyes of the Lord are on the righteous and his ears are attentive to their prayer' (1 Peter 3:12).

So Peter was kept in prison, but the church was earnestly praying to God for him. The night before Herod was to bring him to trial, Peter was sleeping between two soldiers, bound with two chains, and sentries stood guard at the entrance. Suddenly an angel of the Lord appeared and a light shone in the cell. He struck Peter on the side and woke him up. 'Quick, get up!' he said, and the chains fell off Peter's wrists. Then the angel said to him, 'Put on your clothes and sandals.' And Peter did so. 'Wrap your cloak around you and follow me,' the angel told him. Peter followed him out of the prison, but he had no idea that what the angel was doing was really happening; he thought he was seeing a vision. They passed the first and second guards and came to the iron gate leading to the city. It opened for them by itself, and they went through it. When they had walked the length of one street, suddenly the angel left him.

(Acts 12:5–10)

Paul

Like Peter, Paul also saw countless instances of prayer changing things. As a good Pharisee, prayer had always played an important part in his life; but once he encountered Jesus, his prayer life left the realms of the required and the ritualistic and became an exciting adventure with God. He saw prayer do everything from changing the outlook of a whole church (Acts 13:1–3), to bringing about great miracles (e.g. Acts 28:1–9), to rescuing him miraculously from prison:

About midnight Paul and Silas were praying and singing hymns to God, and the other prisoners were listening to them. Suddenly there was such a violent earthquake that the foundations of the prison were shaken. At once all the prison doors flew open, and everybody's chains came loose. The jailer woke up, and when he saw the prison doors open, he drew his sword and was about to kill himself because he thought the prisoners had escaped. But Paul shouted, 'Don't harm yourself! We are all here!' The jailer called for lights, rushed in and fell trembling before Paul and Silas. He then brought them out and asked, 'Sirs, what must I do to be saved?'

(Acts 16:25–30)

God is still looking!

This brief overview of some key Bible figures should convince us that prayer changes things! But know this too: God is still looking for men and women who, like Moses, will pick up the staff of prayer, who will listen to him, and then come with bold prayers, expecting things to change as they do.

'I searched for someone to stand in the gap … '

(Ezekiel 22:30, NLT)

As God searched for those who would pray long ago, he still searches today.

Prayer changes people

But not only does prayer change *things*; prayer also changes *people*. In fact, it is often the change in people that is far more significant. When we feel our prayers haven't been answered, it is often because God is looking to bring about a change in *us* rather than in what we have been praying about.

Here are just a few examples of people who found that they changed as they prayed:

- ***Jacob*** – whose life was so changed as he wrestled with God that he was given a new name and left with a limp (Genesis 32:24–32)
- ***Hannah*** – whose deep sadness of spirit was changed as she persisted in prayer for a child (1 Samuel 1:6–8, 10–20, 26–28; 2:1)
- ***Job*** – whose self-righteousness (e.g. Job 33:8–10; 40:8) was knocked out of him through suffering until he understood his rightful position before God (Job 42:1–6)
- ***Jonah*** – whose attitude to sinners was changed to become more like God's own attitude (Jonah 4:1–11)
- ***Zechariah*** – whose unbelief was challenged by an angelic visitation and who had to bear his unbelief through dumbness until his barren wife bore him a child (Luke 1:5–20, 57–64)
- ***Stephen*** – whose attitude to his persecutors was changed as he prayed (Acts 7:59–60)
- ***Peter*** – whose attitude to the Gentiles, so long despised by him, changed as he encountered God in a vision (Acts 10:9–48)
- ***Paul*** – whose attitude to weakness changed when God didn't remove his 'thorn in the flesh' but gave his grace instead (2 Corinthians 12:7–10)

All of these bear witness to the fact that prayer changed, not just their circumstances, but *them*. Hearts were softened, preconceptions were challenged, attitudes were changed, and unbelief was dealt with. If you pray, be ready for God to change *you* too!

A FINAL PRAYER

Lord, what a change within us
one short hour
Spent in thy presence
will prevail to make!
What heavy burdens
from our bosoms take;
What parched grounds
refresh as with a shower.
We kneel – and all around us
seems to lower,
We rise – and all,
the distant and the near,
Stands forth in sunny outline
brave and clear;
We kneel: how weak! – we rise:
how full of power!
Why, therefore, should we do
ourselves this wrong,
Or others – that we are not
always strong?
That we are ever overborne
with care;
That we should ever weak or
heartless be,
Anxious or troubled,
while with us is prayer,
And joy, and strength, and
courage, are with thee?

Richard Chenevix Trench (1807–86), Professor of Divinity, King's College London, and Archbishop of Dublin

CONCLUSION

God wants to hear our requests and wants us to believe that things can change as we bring them to him.

He answered their prayers, because they trusted in him.

(1 Chronicles 5:20)

Relevance for today

Expect your prayers to be answered!

Do you *really* expect your prayers to be answered? Or has prayer become a religious ritual, a duty to be done? Remember: God has committed himself to answering our prayers when we call to him in faith.

'Call upon me in the day of trouble;
I will deliver you, and you will honour me.'

(Psalm 50:15)

Expect your situation to change!

There is little point coming to God with half-hearted prayers; God wants us to come to him confident that things can change.

Do not throw away your confidence; it will be richly rewarded. You need to persevere so that when you have done the will of God, you will receive what he has promised.

(Hebrews 10:35–36)

Expect your life to be changed!

If you pray about something, be ready for God to change *you*, not just your circumstances! His priority might be different from yours – so be ready for it!

Expect the biggest change of all!

The biggest change of all – the ultimate change – has yet to happen, when Jesus returns at the end of this age. The kingdom of God is already breaking into this world (e.g. Matthew 12:28; Mark 1:15; Luke 17:20–21); so the more we yield to this kingly rule, the more our lives change. But the change will not be fully completed until Jesus returns, just as he promised (e.g. Matthew 16:27; 24:36–44; John 14:3) and just as his followers taught (e.g. 1 Thessalonians 4:16; Hebrews 9:28; 2 Peter 3:8–13). In the light of this, we should surely pray for Jesus' return with the fulness of his kingdom, and for our doing all that we can (e.g. Matthew 24:14) to bring that day closer.

'Your kingdom come …'

(Matthew 6:10)

Come, O Lord!

(1 Corinthians 16:22)

He who testifies to these things says, 'Yes, I am coming soon.' Amen. Come, Lord Jesus.

(Revelation 22:20)

Index

Prayers by named individuals, etc., from Church history are included in *italics*.
References in this index refer to the book parts and then chapter numbers in which the word appears.